12MY'41P

SCIENCE AND CULTURE SERIES
JOSEPH HUSSLEIN, S.J., Ph.D., GENERAL EDITOR

RURAL ROADS TO SECURITY

J. Dobson

Ploven (*The Plowman*)

RURAL ROADS TO SECURITY

America's Third Struggle for Freedom

RT. REV. MSGR. LUIGI G. LIGUTTI, LL.D.

and

REV. JOHN C. RAWE, S.J., LL.M.

The Bruce Publishing Company, Milwaukee

Imprimi potest: P. A. BROOKS, S.J., Praepositus Provincialis, Prov. Missourianae, S.J.
Nihil obstat: H. B. RIES, Censor librorum
Imprimatur: ✠ SAMUEL A. STRITCH, Archiepiscopus Milwaukiensis
January 11, 1940

307.720973
L727r

Copyright, 1940
The Bruce Publishing Company
Printed in the U. S. A.

Dedicated to the Cause of

BETTER FIELDS,
BETTER HOMES,
BETTER COMMUNITIES,
BETTER HEARTS,
BETTER LIVES.

AGRICULTURE[1]

The husbandman that laboreth must be first partaker of the fruits.

— *St. Paul*

No other human occupation opens so wide a field for the profitable and agreeable combination of labor with cultivated thought as agriculture.

— *Abraham Lincoln*

With reference either to individual or national welfare agriculture is of primary importance.

— *George Washington*

---

[1] These quotations, carefully chosen and verified, have been chiseled in the entablature of the main façade of the new Administration Building of the Department of Agriculture in Washington, D. C.

PREFACE BY THE GENERAL EDITOR

STRAIGHTFORWARD, dynamic, and thoroughly documented, RURAL ROADS TO SECURITY is a book of interest and value to all. Its message goes forth alike to city resident and county dweller. For both it would procure a truer liberty and greater independence through a more effective, personal, and widely distributed ownership. That is the implication contained in its secondary title: "America's Third Struggle for Freedom."

In the first two struggles Washington and Lincoln stood out as the nation's leaders. But more difficult than these first contests, to make America the land of the free, is the third struggle, which must be fought without lethal weapons. It is the struggle most signally inaugurated, not for America alone but for all the world, by the *Rerum Novarum* of Leo XIII and no less gloriously reaffirmed in the *Quadragesimo Anno* of Pius XI. With these two names must now be associated that of Pope Pius XII, the champion of social justice and charity toward all no less than of a Christian Peace for all the world.

We have long allowed ourselves to be fascinated by the glitter of industrialized power, forgetful of its inherent weaknesses. Too much urbanized, too much mechanized, men know little about the great productive power that lies hidden in the land and in its organisms; in the things that live and grow and reproduce their kind; in the seeds that sprout; in the fruits that ripen; in the flocks and herds that help to feed and clothe mankind. America's agriculture has become biologically unsound. As the authors of this book scientifically express themselves, "we are merely soil chemists, not soil biologists; soil miners, not real husbandmen." And great, we all know, is the cost that America's manhood and womanhood are paying as the price of this neglect.

What consequently we must rediscover and dramatize for men anew is the romance of an, at least partially, independent life on one's own land, the romance of life as it can be lived at the fountain source of organic power, life on the soil. But closely linked with that ideal is the dream of the city dweller, the dream of the disinherited, that some time they too may achieve a greater liberation from an industrialism that has given us anew the Proletarian. "The immense number of propertyless wage-earners on the one hand, and the superabundant riches of the fortunate few on the other, is an unanswerable argument that the earthly goods, so abundantly produced in this our age, which is termed 'the age of industrialism,' are far from rightly distributed and equitably shared among the various classes of men" (*Quadragesimo Anno*).

Naturally, what most of all inspired the authors of this book was the purpose to arouse an intelligent interest in the land on the part of all classes, rural and urban. People actually living on the farm must still be taught to understand more perfectly the economic benefit of home productivity as contrasted with the destructive policy of purely commercialized farming. People in the mines and factories must be shown the possibilities of part-time farming where circumstances render that feasible. Homesteaders must be encouraged and aided in their laudable undertakings. And not least of all must city dwellers be given the vision of that far-reaching organic good which comes to every nation through rural culture, cooperation in rural communities, intelligent land programs, home production, home arts and crafts. It is the home, both urban and rural, which is at stake, and which the writers of this book would above all else seek to restore to the sublime ideal given it by Christianity.

Rural families and rural communities are living cells and members of the body politic. On their preservation and development depends the well-being of the entire state. Clergy, scientists, educators, publicists, and all citizens alike must give them intelligent support. For this it is necessary that all be themselves rightly informed, and hence the great need of this volume which represents the lifework of two men profoundly acquainted with this field and in practical touch with it. For the same reason it is important that this book be adopted as widely as possible, by way of text, in our schools, both urban and rural. Though definitely written for the general reader, it is nonetheless admirably adapted for classroom use and for study circles. We dare not raise up a generation ignorant of the land and unappreciative of it.

Preface by the General Editor

No one has more strongly expressed our indebtedness to the land than Pope Leo XIII. "Nature," he eloquently says, "owes to man a storehouse that shall never fail, the daily supply of his daily wants. And this he finds only in the inexhaustible fertility of the earth." Though divided among private owners — and the Pope's wish is that every laborer own the soil he tills — it nonetheless "ministers to the needs of all. For there is no one who does not live on what the land brings forth" (*Rerum Novarum*).

If we lose our grip on the soil; if we allow God's richly productive gift to be industrialized, commercialized, depleted by human greed, and ruined by stupid selfishness — then we ourselves shall be doomed to a just exhaustion and extinction. It is not ours to waste but to use for ourselves and our kind.

With incomparable force has this thought been driven home in the equally fine and powerful lines of Harry Kemp, too little known by those whom they most concern. Through the pulsing rhythm of the poet's words there thrills the whole history of the human race.

Hearken to the "Song of the Plow":

> It was I who built Chaldea and the Cities of the Plain;
> I was Greece and Rome and Carthage and the opulence of Spain.
> When their courtiers walked in scarlet and their queens wore chains of gold,
> And forgot 'twas I that made them, growing Godless folk and bold,
> I went over them in judgment, and again my cornfields stood
> Where empty courts bowed homage in obsequious multitude. . . .
>
> *For the nation that forgets me, in that hour her doom is sealed*
> *By a judgment as from Heaven that can never be repealed!*

JOSEPH HUSSLEIN, S.J., PH.D.
General Editor, Science and Culture Series

St. Louis University,
Epiphany, 1940

AUTHORS' PREFACE

OUR rural technique is not the technique which the husbandman practices. We are soil miners, soil mechanics, soil chemists. We are not soil biologists. We live by exploitation and extraction, not by husbandry. The roots of restraining grass and legumes and trees are loosened and removed in the mechanical production of cotton and wheat and corn. The rootless land drifts away by wind and water and the rootless people herd themselves by the millions in the industrial slums. Land drifts on the seasonal winds and with the floods. And the huge masses of directionless, rootless people drift in the ominous clouds of hate and false propaganda, insecurity and poverty. What could easily have endured as a nation of secure and free, landowning people, through an intelligent "agriculture" on our two billion acres, has become a nation of servile dependents on a mechanistic plutocracy, inefficient and exploitive. This book is written for the purpose of presenting some of the steps that must be taken to rebuild our land, our homes, our democracy, our culture, and our religion. We offer it also as a textbook in the field of rural sociology — a field as yet meagerly supplied.

We should like to express our gratitude for the unstinted assistance given us by Mr. James L. McShane, S.J., of St. Mary's College, Kansas; Mr. Eugene H. Murray, S.J., of St. Peter's College, New Jersey; Rev. Joseph C. Husslein, S.J., of St. Louis University; Rev. Francis J. O'Boyle, S.J., of St. Mary's College, Kansas; Rev. John Gorman and Sister Mary Consilio, R.S.M., of Granger, Iowa. We gratefully acknowledge the constant help which came to us through the scholarship and leadership of the Most Reverend Edwin O'Hara, D.D., and the Most Reverend Aloisius Muench, D.D.; Rev. James A. Byrnes, LL.D., editor of the *Catholic Rural Life Bulletin;* Very Rev. William T. Mulloy, former president of the National Catholic Rural Life Conference; and the Rev. Edgar Schmiedeler, O.S.B., author of many works in rural sociology, and

xii   Authors' Preface

national director of the Rural Life Bureau, National Catholic Welfare Conference, Washington, D. C.

Acknowledgments are gratefully made to publishers and editors for permission to use material published before and for permission to quote from their publications.

Many more acknowledgments should be made by the authors. We list the names of the following whose cooperation and contributions have been particularly helpful: Very Rev. Joseph Zuercher, S.J., president of The Creighton University; Rev. Gerald Fitz-Gibbon, S.J., and Rev. Thomas Bowdern, S.J., deans of The Creighton University; Dr. Stuart A. Mahuran, director of The Creighton University School of Journalism, and his class in editing; the members of the staff of the Queen's Work, especially Rev. Daniel A. Lord, S.J., Rev. George A. McDonald, S.J., and Miss Dorothy Willmann; the members of the Rural Life Department of St. Mary's College, St. Marys, Kansas, especially Rev. Edward Weisenberg, S.J., Rev. William J. Weis, S.J., and many of the seminarians; Sister Mary Stephen, S.S.N.D., Sister Mary Terese, and Sister Mary Francita of St. Louis; Rev. Joseph R. Moylan, S.J., Mr. John J. Walsh, S.J., and Rev. John J. Higgins, S.J., of St. Louis; Mr. John J. White, S.J., Edgar A. Miller and Anthony R. Inserra of Omaha, Nebraska; the editors of *Free America,* especially, Herbert Agar and Ralph Borsodi; and finally our students and associates in Granger and Omaha and The Creighton University.

                                                LUIGI G. LIGUTTI
                                                JOHN C. RAWE

The Creighton University,
Christmas Day, 1939

CONTENTS

Preface by the General Editor vii
Author's Preface xi

PART I: PROLETARIANISM: ABSENCE OF PRODUCTIVE FAMILY HOLDINGS

I   The Third Struggle for Liberty 3
II Centralization 15
III Proletarianism 28
IV The Urban Family in Mass Production 50
V   The Rural Family in Mass Production 73

PART II: MULTIPLICATION OF SMALL OWNERSHIPS IN LAND

VI   The Home on the Land 99
VII Some Problems in Modern Homesteading . . . 115
VIII Self-Sufficiency: After that, Production for Exchange 129
IX   Forward on the Land 138
X   Part-Time Farming: Soil and Industry . . . 149
XI   The Granger Homestead Project 171

PART III: LEADERSHIP IN BUILDING THE GOOD AMERICA

XII Intelligent Technology on the Land 189
XIII Agriculture and Biological Science 204

Contents

XIV	Training for Leadership on the Land	222
XV	Ideals and Education for Rural Boys and Girls	233
XVI	Cooperative Grouping on the Land	253
XVII	Advantages and Technique of Cooperatives	273
XVIII	Democracy Revived on Land and in City	293

APPENDICES:

1. America's First School of Living 313
2. Milling at Home 317
3. A New Design for Living 325
4. St. Teresa's Village 331
5. Factual Outline of the Granger Homesteads . . 332
6. Nova Scotia "Rochdale" Cooperatives 335
7. Farm Tenancy Report Made to the President . . 343
8. Extracts from Farm Tenancy Committee Report — Iowa 353

Selected Bibliography 361
Index 379

RURAL ROADS TO SECURITY

PART I

PROLETARIANISM

Absence of Productive Family Holdings

Chapter 1

THE THIRD STRUGGLE FOR LIBERTY

WHEN in 1775 British oppression threatened the human rights and happiness of Americans, the Minute Men united for the defense of liberty. That war gave us political independence. Ultimate independence, however, with liberty for all, Black and White, cost America another war. It then became a truly independent nation. Henceforth a future of freedom was to become the birthright of every American.

By a tragic paradox, at the very time when wars were being waged for political independence, there was injected into the veins of American industry a deadly virus which would tend more and more to paralyze the mind and spirit of American manhood. In a word, American life fell heir to the liberalistic system which Europe had fostered. When the renaissance individualism cast off moral restraint through the influence of the Reformation, the road was paved for a materialistic

OLD NORTH CHURCH

philosophy. Liberalism saw only good in the ambitions of men, demanded fullest liberty for the satisfaction of personal aggrandizement without hindrance of law, or organization, or any effort to safeguard one man against the greed of another. As the Rev. Joseph C. Husslein, S.J., points out in *The Christian Social Manifesto,* this liberalistic dream was taken seriously for more than a century and a half and it has not yet been dissipated.

The discoveries of science in the eighteenth and nineteenth centuries coincided with this liberalistic stream of philosophy, ever deepening and expanding the glittering sea of modern Capitalism. Heavy machinery, power, crowded factories, congested cities, large-scale production, greater and still greater profits and investments complemented each other, and accelerated the evolution of liberalistic industrialism. And so, with every new stage of the swirling cycle, liberty retreated farther from the wage earner, as economic necessity left him ever more helplessly at the mercy of the capital which he served.

The factory system, which today signifies concentrated mass production, took root in our country during the War of 1812. Its early growth was comparatively slow, for as late as 1850, the bulk of American goods was still produced in the household, the shop, or the small factory.

While the open frontier still continued in competition with the factory, the demand for labor was never filled. Gradually women and children were themselves drawn into the factory. Although hours were long for all alike, and although children were growing up illiterate and without the normal experiences of childhood, yet deluded Americans flocked to the factory as though it were the gate to prosperity.

The entrance of women into the industrial field tended to reduce the wages of men, since men were no longer the sole support of a family the idea of a family wage for the head of the family was slipping to that of a mere individual wage in competition with women and children. Still labor was not at once shackled by this condition. There was still a possibility of escape, and when escape is possible, liberty is not dead.

Harold Faulkner gives the alternative when he writes:

As long as public land could be had at nominal cost, "wage slavery, in the sense that there was no escape, did not exist. If times were hard and wages low, the worker could always go West.[1]

After 1850, transportation underwent marked improvements. Steam railroads increased 300 per cent between 1850 and 1860.

---

[1] Faulkner, Harold, *American Economic History*, 3rd Ed. (New York: Harper Bros., 1935), p. 553.

With steam transportation established, the factory system began that forward leap which continued, with but brief lulls during the great panics, through the remainder of the century.

This twofold development, growth of factories and improvement in transportation, was directly instrumental in changing from bad to worse the conditions of labor. Wages tended to become standardized at a minimum, since goods from one city were brought into competition with the same type of goods from another city. Price plus quality capture the market. By established custom the necessary curtailment was taken from wages. Transportation and growth of factories also made profitable the subdivision of labor, thereby creating vast numbers of detail jobs, simple enough to be classed with unskilled labor and each paid the correspondingly lower wage.

City Concentrations and Their Social Problems

The specialized capitalist, alert to the possibilities of saving by division of production, concentrated industry in fewer and larger plants. Labor, long below the ability of housing itself in health and decency, huddled more densely in the industrial tenements. This urbanization of population paralleled the concentration of industry and was, in greater part, due directly to it.

Labor declined rapidly, losing not only ownership of tools, productive property, and control of conditions of labor, but also home ownership as well. Company tenements, company stores, company commodities were being provided, but in a very inadequate manner, and under circumstances that left only a shadow of liberty or recognition of rights on the side of the working people.

Another factor that greatly stimulated urbanization of population was the rapid disappearance, since 1880, of desirable western land obtainable on easy terms. During the first half of the nineteenth century public land of rare quality was limitless and given on terms that were meant to be an invitation and reward for settlement. Little or no capital was required to secure and work a claim. The disappearance of such public land closed a safety valve of escape from the city and dammed the floods of immigrants in the already close confines of industrial cities.

Urbanization, so rapid and so concentrated, created a host of social and economic problems. Of these the most tragic to human freedom was the increasing depth of helpless surrender to which an ever greater and greater portion of the nation's citizens was reduced, succumbing to the unscrupulous and liberalistically sanctioned avarice of the "robber barons." Labor had become depersonalized as regards the relations of employer and employee. Corporate ownership and control lodged in the hands of a relatively few. These few, interested primarily in greater profits, better business, and more production, neither saw nor cared to see the laborers, nor still less the slums in which they existed. Public opinion protested, and government took action again and again, but the philosophy of wealth continued unconquered and almost unquestioned except in subconscious thought, and the conditions of labor, even though improved, lagged behind that of the favorites of fortune as far as ever.

Keeping pace with economic changes, the destructive influence of these new conditions on the home and family life now made themselves sadly felt. With the appearance of the factory system home occupations decreased quite generally. Competition with factory products forced members of the family to seek employment in the large-scale industries. Spacious homes were abandoned for dingy, unsanitary shacks near the noisy, smoking factory. The health and well-being of women were menaced. Low wages for men, brought lower by the competition of women in industry, left marriage to be deferred or renounced. After marriage both husband and wife were often compelled to continue in their former outside employment so that the family might be able to subsist. Ideals of family life were thus shattered by the absence of one or both parents. Children were left without care and childless homes became common. Self-interest was created by the separate purses of husband and wife. Divorce increased. Submarginal living was almost the rule for larger families. Commercialized amusements, the movie, dance halls, soft-drink parlors, saloons, and the automobile assisted in drawing people out of the home.

War, the War of 1812, gave roots to the factory system as already stated. Another armed conflict, the Civil War, immensely hastened the growth of the system by its army demands and high protective tariffs. Large-scale industry and a marked competitive *laissez-faire* policy date from this war. Finally, the World War surpassed all other periods of our history in the percentage of increase in capital, value of products, and also wages.

Depression and the Present Struggle

Materialistic philosophers taught that Liberalism, free and unrestrained, would bring the nation to the peak of prosperity. Capital falsely claimed that efficiency and security for any industry was attained by way of complete monopoly. Labor wondered wistfully, and submitted and hoped with infinite patience, but the peaks of prosperity seldom ever broke the level horizon of day-by-day toils.

Today, with consumption deadlocked for years and the unfulfilled desires of the masses soured to envy, distrust, and destructiveness, capital too has paused to calculate whether its excessively high profits were really so excessively profitable.

Have the unhampered ambitions of the fortunate brought about the highest common good? Americans form the wealthiest nation in the world. Our productive potentiality is, so to say, limitless. But consumption has collapsed, and gone on relief for artificial stimulation. Overproduction and starvation are puzzling neighbors. We think our money gods have tricked us. We are unhappy. We seem to have sold our birthright of freedom for a mess of pottage. Our tenants and sharecroppers are numbered in millions. Few slaves lived lives as wretched and insecure. A sharecropper "in the red" is bound to remain on his land, not as a serf with recognized rights, but as an exploited commodity. He is an American robbed of freedom.

The armies of America's third struggle for freedom are being mobilized. A struggle is under way, not against a foreign enemy, nor yet a mere strife of parties, but a struggle for freedom, for an individual freedom in accordance with the American ideal. It is the opening attack against a hard and selfish philosophy entrenched behind walls of gold that have thickened for over a hundred years. From time to time, much has been accomplished in exposing and tearing down this defense. But often, too, much was done in turn to pad the walls and mend again the breaches made in them.

There are more ways than one of storming these bastions. Loud-mouthed leaders raise their shout for Socialism, Communism, or Fascism. Give full control, they say, to the State or some dictator, and all will be corrected in a flash. Make everybody step in time. Only let an invincible, centralized, omnipresent organization be formed, with unquestioned authority to take, distribute, and rule, and all problems, social or economic, will be settled forever. So can proper provision be made for everyone!

Do these leaders forget they are speaking to Americans? Another mess of pottage, another, and still another, served by a paternalistic bureaucracy or a militaristic tyrant, will not content Americans. Our desperate proletariat is in a daze, where any change seemingly must be a change for the better. But even in them true Americanism will revive in a flash once their eyes are given half a chance to clear their vision.

We do not want to be "taken care of." We want our birthright back. Let those who despair use the methods of despair. We have our dream, our ideal. We dreamed of liberty, equality, precious freedom, our inalienable, God-given rights. We can give no more than a passing thought to anything less.

But, surely, all this is just another sour joke, they will tell us, that some day may come in handy to humor the crowd. An ideal! Americans with dreams? Observe those who pass, these dissatisfied, listless job holders with a haunting fear in their eyes lest the job that is theirs today will be no longer theirs when the sun rises tomorrow; migratory tenants always hoping for the better and getting the worse; dehumanized sharecroppers artificially always "in the red"; the army of unemployed frantically walking the streets till even the beautiful sunshine is cruel; spiritless men and women on relief, some wishing life could pass more quickly, others spinelessly content to remain as they are; old age filling in government blanks; youth staring into a blank future. Behold flourishing American cities grown tiresome, harsh, and cold; fertile American valleys commercialized, gullied, barren, and parched. This scene reminds us of the picture presented in the Seventh Prophecy for Holy Saturday:

In those days the hand of the Lord was upon me, and brought me forth in the spirit of the Lord; and set me down in the midst of a plain that was full of bones: and He led me about through them on every side. Now they were very many upon the face of the plain, and they were exceeding dry. And He said to me: Son of man, dost thou think these bones shall live? And I answered: O Lord God, Thou knowest. . . . Thus saith the Lord God to these bones: Behold, I will send spirit into you, and you shall live. . . . And the spirit came into them, and they lived; and they stood upon their feet, an exceeding great army. . . . And you shall know that I am the Lord, when I shall have opened your sepulchers, and shall have brought you out of your graves, O My people: and shall have put My spirit in you, and you shall live, and I shall make you rest upon your own land: saith the Lord Almighty.[2]

Mammoth-scale industry, commercialized farms, human lives ground by marvelous machines, efficiency substituted for liberty, money codes displacing justice, with God and His spirit forgotten — these, too, are lifeless bones, well shaped and bleached to a beautiful, gleaming white, yet mere bones. Bones that need not be destroyed, but rather let sinews and spirit be given them. We want to remain modern and also be human and live. We shall do this when we come once more to know that we are the Lord's, that He opens our sepulchers and brings us from from our graves, and puts His spirit into us, makes us live and brings us to rest upon our own land. If philosophy in the sixteenth and seventeenth centuries made mistakes, it can be set right in the twentieth, for the nineteenth already pointed out the error and the remedy. Rugged individualism must yield to love of fellow men. The striving to become rich, measuring success by fortunes, and seeing values in all things only by the dollars marked on the price tag, should give place to the joy of life. Human living must again be able to lift its thought above the passing things of earth to see the dignity and immortal destiny of man.

New Values — New Life

"We the people" are the power and authority that can make the change. Our first activity is to establish a new view of life. We

---
[2] Ezech. 37:1–14.

want truly to live. All our strivings should aim to win, not a fortune, but a greater fullness of life, for happiness, comfort, and security by honest, God-pleasing work. Next we need a plan to make this possible. From our side, it is only made possible by breaking down this iron-clad wage slavery. Pope Leo XIII, the workingman's truest friend, wished to see every laborer owner of some productive property.

Ownership of productive property in the industrial world is available to labor through coupon clipping. Though such ownership, when practical steps are taken to establish it, is good and commendable, it is not an ownership which gives effective control. A way to both ownership and control, for the many, in some productive property is the way *by land*.

Ownership of Homes with Small Acreages

The movement for ownership of homes on the land is eminently human and satisfying whether it is the relief garden planned toward ownership for the needy, the subsistence homestead or part-time farm for the industrial family, or the full-time diversified family-unit farm for the rural people.

Modern comfort and modern, small, human-scale machines in many forms of production without any loss of efficiency, point the way to restored freedom and security through the ownership of a few acres. A blend of the rural and urban modes of life, in both part-time and full-time farming, a mode of life which modern technocracy makes possible, is the one which can accomplish the aim expressed by Alexis Carrel: "Restore to man his intelligence, his moral sense, his virility, and lead him to the summit of his development."[3]

The major economic and social need in work for spiritual and cultural advancement and the preservation of liberty in American life is: *family-unit operation and fee-simple, family-basis ownership of land* based on religious principles and spiritually motivated. Landownership is a determining factor in human well-being. This is not a matter of selfish concern for rural life and rural people. It is a matter of great national importance. Perhaps the most tragic aspect of changing America is the general decline

---
[3] Carrel, Dr. Alexis, *Man, the Unknown* (Harper and Bros.), p. 296.

from landownership to mere factory work and tenancy. The number of landowners, tenants, and wage earners will in large measure determine whether the life of the nation is to be democratic or proletarian, and will ultimately decide the destiny of our civilization. Landownership goes hand in hand with a predisposition for education and the building of good communities and a democratic citizenship. The problem of this change from landownership to tenancy, the status of mere factory workers, demands the study and help of all those who are interested in the spiritual and democratic progress of America.

Extremes to Be Avoided

It is a wise policy, when discussing a complex problem, to avoid extremes. In the present instance, those who demand, for the good of society, a clean cleavage either in favor of agrarianism to the exclusion of industrialism, or industrialism to the exclusion of agrarianism, are extremists. Some zealots tell us to flee to the fields in order to avoid contamination of soul and body in the city, which is a blot on the face of the earth; others, equally foolish, extol commercialized, scientific progress and dream of the day when the countryside will be completely covered over with the sprawling works of big industry and big farming.

Both views are untenable. A nation cannot be prosperous, unless there is a proper balance between town and country, between the rural and urban way of life.

Why can't we develop a constructive economics and sociology? Why can't we restore some natural economic functions to the family, the natural economic unit? Why should all economic and social functions be swallowed up by corporations and states in a mad rush toward concentration and collectivism of one form or another? Why can't we plan and work for the proper preservation of many natural units in a food raising economy, a home-owning and home-building environment? We would soon discover that such work would result in the building of a new democratic nation at much less expense than it takes to give pensions and doles and maintain an artificial system that leaves human capabilities exposed to corruption and decay, and sets the mind in a groove of false thinking.

Some Family-Centered Production

The best way to restore the home is to provide for some family-centered production, family-centered activity where the child can soon become an economic asset instead of remaining an economic liability. That is why the food-producing homestead has economic, social, cultural, and ethical significance. That is why every housing program should be a homestead program. Nothing prevents the successful combination of industrial wage earning and part-time farming today save a certain spirit of narrow urban industrialism, an erroneous self-sufficiency, and a want of democratic vision. Many industrial workers would welcome the new type of living which homesteading embodies — a life which is neither strictly rural nor strictly urban, a life which is an intermediate type between the two, combining the benefits of both. These are some of the vital issues to be discussed in this volume.

St. Thomas Aquinas, the leader of Scholastic thinkers, gives us a very clear and helpful analysis of the problem of city life:

> Now since men must live in a group because they are not sufficient unto themselves to procure the necessities of life were they to remain solitary, it follows that a society will be more perfect the more it is sufficient unto itself to procure the necessities of life (Bk. I, c. 1).
>
> For an individual to lead a good life two things are required. The first and most important is to act in a virtuous manner, for virtue is that by which one lives well; the second, which is secondary and as it were instrumental, is a sufficiency of those bodily goods whose use is necessary for an act of virtue (Bk. I, c. 15).
>
> Now there are two ways in which an abundance of foodstuffs can be supplied to a city. The first is where the soil is so fertile that it nobly provides for all the necessities of human life. The second is by trade, through which the necessities of life are brought to the town from different places. But it is quite clear that the first means is better. For the higher a thing is the more self-sufficient it is; since whatever needs another's help is by that very fact proven inferior. But that city is more fully self-sufficient which the surrounding country supplies with all its vital needs, than is another which must obtain these supplies by trade. A city which has an abundance of food from its own territory is more dignified than one which is provisioned by merchants. It is safer, too, for the importing of supplies can easily be prevented

whether owing to the uncertain outcome of wars or to the many dangers of the road, and thus the city may be overcome through lack of food (Bk. II, c. 3).

Again, if the citizens themselves devote their lives to matters of trade, the way will be opened to many vices. For since the object of trading leads especially to making money, greed is awakened in the hearts of the citizens through the pursuit of trade. The result is that everything in the city will be offered for sale: confidence will be destroyed and the way opened to all kinds of trickery: each one will work only for his own profit, despising the public good: the cultivation of virtue will fail, since honor, virtue's reward, will be bestowed upon anybody. Thus in such a city civic life will necessarily be corrupted (Bk. II, c. 3).

Finally that state enjoys a greater measure of peace whose people are more sparsely assembled together and dwell in smaller proportion within the walls of the town. For when men are crowded together, it is an occasion of quarrels and all the elements for seditious plots are provided. Whence according to Aristotle, it is more profitable to have the people engaged outside the cities than for them to dwell continually within the walls (Bk. II, c. 3).

Consequently, the perfect city will make a moderate use of merchants (Bk. II, c. 3).[4]

---

[4] *The Governance of Rulers* (*De Regimine Principum*). Trans. by Gerald B. Phelan (New York: Sheed and Ward).

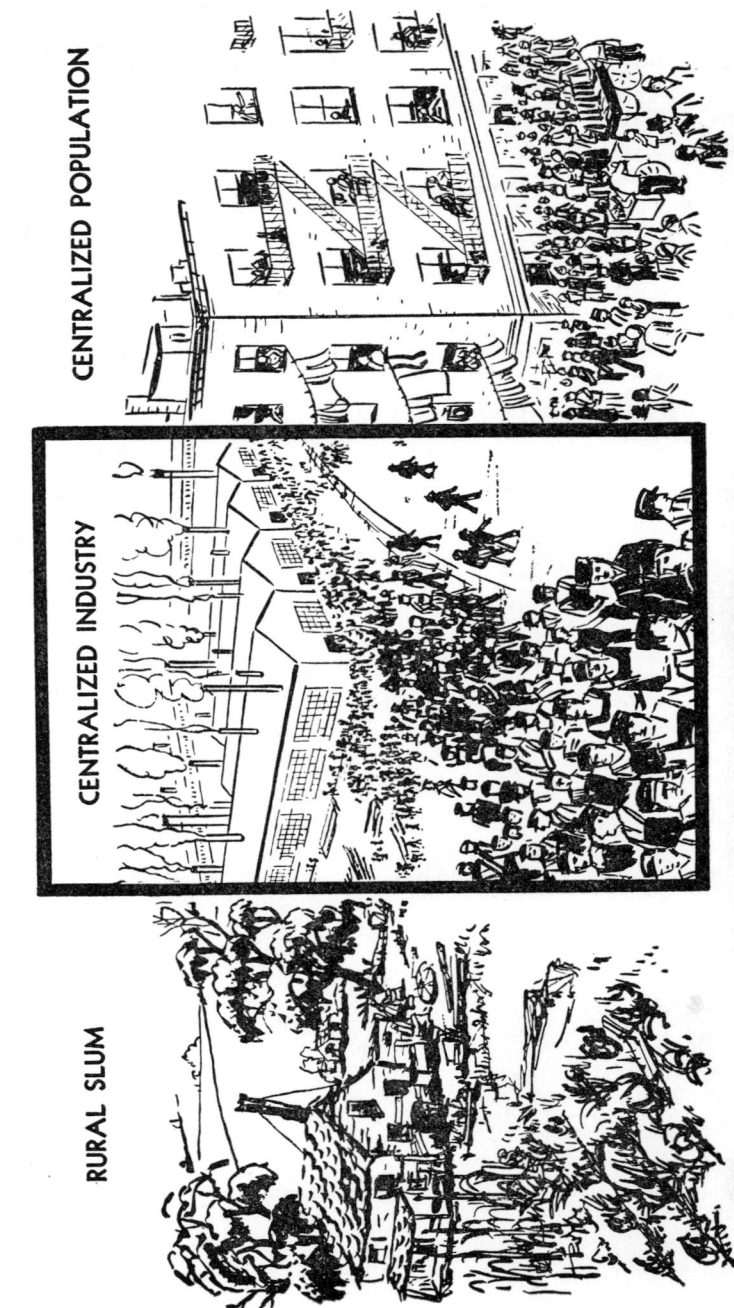

Chapter 2

CENTRALIZATION

WHAT does the future hold in store for the United States? As we survey the vast outlines of the nation looking beyond today's particular flood, drought, strike or election, we can trace two broad general tendencies, two main movements, two currents in American life. The one is a movement of population toward a few congested cities which are centers of finance-capitalism and mass-production factories. It is the movement of life from the farm to the city — change from the small proprietor to the feudalism of finance and industry. The other is a movement of population from the congested cities out to the surrounding countrysides. It is a movement to break up a number of the large inefficient corporations, to build small efficient units in localities where the goods are consumed. It is a return of life to its natural abode, the country, and a restoration of freedom through effective ownership.

The concentration of factories and mills in a few cities is the story of a hundred years. The industrial revolution grew up with the invention of the power loom to weave the cloth of England and the steam engine to furnish its power. The machines tended to get bigger, heavier, and more expensive. Big buildings had to be provided, and as time went on, staffs of office workers. Such a factory with power supplied by steam and coal had to be built in the city. Poor workers gathered round it. Farmers left farm homes and crowded into poverty-stricken dwellings around the factory where they hoped to get work. Slums were built up and unfortunately were perpetuated, even though electricity has for some time pointed the way to efficient decentralization of cities and industry.

Population Increase of Cities from 1790 to 1930

Population Groups	1790	1840	1880	1930
2,500 to 10,000	28	123	872	2,183
10,000 to 25,000	3	27	105	606
25,000 to 100,000	2	9	57	283
100,000 to 250,000		2	12	56
250,000 to 500,000		1	4	24
500,000 to 1,000,000			3	8
1,000,000 and over			1	5

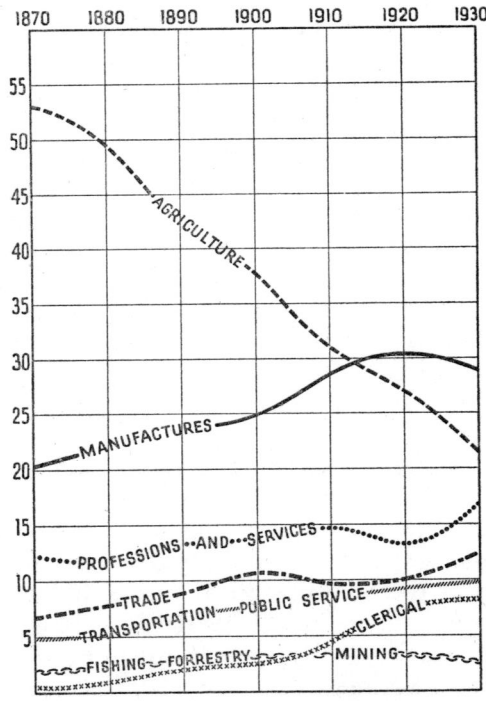

Abandonment of the Land Graphed from 1870 to 1930.*

Industrialism, steam and coal and their massive techniques, and the politically favored "corporate device," piled factory on factory

---

* These tables, based on data issued by the United States Census Bureau, show the vast changes in the occupational distribution of the population of this country since 1870. We have two billion acres of land, and yet, most of our people live in the highly congested areas of the cities.

and corporation on corporation. Such centralizing agencies put hordes of workers under the control of a few executives and jammed armies of men, women, and children into slums. Work was transferred from the manor and the cottage to the centralized plant where both work and ownership were dehumanized and depersonalized. New forms of "centralized control" emasculated ownership and maneuvered for a position where a few men could manipulate labor and capital, to reap profits in an economic action without the risks of any great ownership, and with the divorce of property rights from social duties.

"Collective" Property

To one who investigates the Minority Controls, the Management Controls, and the Legal Devices used today to place the direction of vast industrial empires in the hands of a few, it soon becomes evident that incorporated, industrial properties resemble "collective" property more than private property, and that what is left of private property in industry is scarcely more than an empty legal shell or fiction.

Dr. Richard B. Ransom indicates how corporations received the power to manipulate vast sums and monopolize industries:

By a legal fiction both State and Federal courts have assumed that the constitution guarantees to corporate entities every appropriate legal and property right in which it protects the private citizen. This is a richly fertile assumption. Under its stimulus corporations have not only flourished, and monopolized the most productive business fields within the States, but have made a veritable legal jungle of the no-man's-land that lies between States' rights and the entrenchments of the national authority. The extent of that territory has never been mapped or precisely defined, and practically its only explorers have been corporation lawyers and criminals seeking refuge. Neither of these is primarily concerned with the public interest.[1]

In calling for a reconstruction of the social order Pius XI found it necessary to deal with what may be called joint-stock "corporationism." In *Quadragesimo Anno,* Pius says that the "laws enacted for joint-stock companies with limited liabilities, have given occa-

---
[1] Agar and Tate, *Who Owns America,* contribution by R. B. Ransom (Houghton Mifflin Co., 1936), p. 68.

sion to abominable abuses." This modern economic "corporationism" results in the creation by the State of a vast number of pseudo-societies, based on legal privilege and organized solely for private profit. Unless these artificial entities, the joint-stock, private-profit corporations, are properly controlled, they engage in much antisocial manipulation. Their managements and stockholders often collectively accomplish by corporate acts and policies that which any decent personal morality in business would reject as unfair, unjust, or illegal. When these pseudo-societies become too numerous and too strong in every economic field, the organic character of the national economy is broken down. Everywhere the factors of production are divided into two widely separated artificial classes, the employer and the employee, the incorporated owners and the proletarians. The nominal, bare legal ownership by corporate title tends more and more to supersede the original, real, private, personal ownership and control of small holdings in productive property. The system of sound investment, based largely on private property in the real sense, tends to become, upon the multiplication of incorporated ownerships, a matter of universal and blind speculation. The middle classes were historically the personal owners of productive property — an ownership very different from the ownership of stocks and bonds, an ownership which once made the middle class the stable element in society. "Corporationism" has displaced the middle classes by a vast number who constitute the propertyless proletariat, helpless people who can get no stake in the country or in the city. Both the giant Wall Street with its incorporated concentrations and the government concentrations under commissars, which is Communism, move in parallel columns under similar management toward the common destructive objective, the Totalitarian State.

"Corporationism" and Economic Dictatorship

The two hundred giant corporations in America have less than three thousand separate individuals serving as directors. There are approximately five million to five and a half million separate individuals who are the investors and putative owners of these corporations. These stockholders hold their stock certificates in the expectation of profits without responsibilities of ownership, and for the most part they are ignorant and morally unconcerned about the methods in which their property is used and managed.

Toward the close of the Middle Ages the growing "absentee landlordism," with its delegated managements and the vast number of poor people working, on land that was not their own, brought death to the social and economic regime of that period. In this present period, the same, if not more serious deadening economic and social results are flowing from the absentee ownerships and the delegated managements of large corporations, with their vast hordes of exploited, propertyless proletarians.

In a syndicated editorial column Walter Lippmann gives a succinct analysis of the puzzling change that is gripping the world with regard to peoples and properties, rights and liberties:

We live in a time when great masses of civilized men have either voluntarily surrendered their liberties or at least have submitted without serious protest or resistance to the destruction of their personal liberties. It is important that we should understand the causes. This is not too difficult. For while a library of books might profitably be written on the subject, one fundamental aspect of the question at least is clear enough to any one who passes back and forth between the totalitarian and the free nations of Europe.

It is this: The peoples who have lost their civil rights had previously lost or had never obtained the means of economic independence for individuals, families and local communities. It is very clear, I think, that the masses who have fallen under the spell of demagogic dictators and their terroristic bands were recruited from individuals who had no property, no savings, and either no job at all or a job which they could not feel sure of holding. They were in the exact sense proletarians even if they happened to be earning fairly high salaries at the moment. For they had no reserves to fall back upon. They could not afford to lose their jobs. They could not afford, therefore, to speak their minds or to take risks, to be in any real sense of the word individual citizens. They had to be servile or they starved. Wherever a dictatorship has been set up in Europe, the mass of individuals had already become so insecure that they no longer dared to exercise the legal liberties that the demagog was attacking.

To have economic independence a man must be in a position to leave one job and go to another; he must have enough savings of some kind to exist for a considerable time without accepting the first job offered. Thus the peasant, for all his poverty and the exploitation which he suffers, is relative to his own needs still the freest man in central Europe. The fact that he can exist by his own labor on his own piece of land gives him an independence which every dictatorial regime, except the Russian perhaps, has been forced to respect.

But the industrial worker who has a choice between working in one factory and not working at all, the white collar intellectuals who compete savagely for the relatively few private positions and posts in the bureaucracy — these are the people who live too precariously to exercise their liberties or to defend them. They have no saving. They have only their labor to sell, and there are very few buyers of their labor. Therefore, they have only the choice of truckling to the powerful or of perishing heroically but miserably. Men like these, having none of the substance of liberty themselves, have scant respect for any law or any form of civil rights. . . .

The more I see of Europe the more deeply convinced do I become that the preservation of freedom in America, or anywhere else, depends upon maintaining and restoring for the great majority of individuals the economic means to remain independent individuals. The greatest evil of the modern world is the reduction of the people to a proletarian level by destroying their savings, by depriving them of private property, by making them the helpless employees of private monopoly or of government monopoly. At that point they are no longer citizens. They are a mob. For when the people lose this sense of their separate and individual security, they cease to be individuals. They are absorbed into a mass. Their liberties are already lost and they are a frightened crowd ready for a master.

Though the actual measures to be taken are debatable, the objectives for a free government are, I think clear. It should use its authority to enable the independent farmer, the small and moderate-sized enterprise, the small saver, to survive. It should use its authority to see that large enterprises are no larger than technology requires, depriving big business of corporate privileges and other forms of legal and economic advantage which make it bigger than on economic grounds it needs to be. A resolute democracy should favor the dispersion of industry rather than its concentration, and it should favor the rise in as many communities as possible of different kinds of enterprise rather than a high degree of specialization on some one product. For unless the means of independence are widely distributed among the people themselves, no real resistance is possible to the advance of tyranny."[2]

---

[2] Lippmann, Walter, New York *Herald Tribune*, July 15, 1936.

Concentrations in Business Enterprise

The depressions with their contractions of credit, foreclosures, liquidations, etc., hasten the process of concentration. Within the past ten years the loan corporations, financed by the United States Government alone, have come into possession of more than one fourth of the real-estate mortgages. The twenty largest life insurance companies hold 60 per cent of the remainder. Less than 5 per cent of all real-estate mortgages are held by private individuals. The national wealth tends to be massed in larger and larger aggregates of ownership, and these are held together under corporate business titles and perpetuated even though there is positive

Business Concentrations in Specific Industries, in the United States[3]

Industry	Number of Companies	Percentages of Nation's Business
Aluminum	1	100
Automobiles	3	86
Beef products	2	47
Bread and bakery products	3	20
Cans	3	90
Cement	5	40
Cigarettes	3	80
Bituminous coal	4	10
Copper	4	78
Corn binders	4	100
Corn planters	6	91
Flour	3	29
Glass (plate)	2	95
Glass (safety)	2	60
Iron ore	4	64
Lead	4	60
Oil wells	4	20
Steel	3	60.5
Whisky	4	58
Wood pulp	4	35
Zinc	4	46
Women's clothes	4	2

---

[3] Moody's Railroad, Public Utility and Industrial Manuals, Willard Thorp — Dun & Bradstreet; *The Modern Corporation and Private Property*, A. A. Berle, Jr., and Gardiner C. Means (Macmillan).

CONCENTRATIONS IN OWNERSHIP
Growth of the 200 Giant Corporations (Nonbanking)

	Combined Assets	
42 railroads	1909	$26.0 billion
52 public uitilities	1919	$43.7 billion
106 industrials	1929	$81.1 billion

economic and social disadvantage in the concentrated ownership. Many of the fields of American business are now entirely monopolized by corporations. Small independent enterprises are rapidly being forced into mergers or subjugated to the policies and economic pressure of the dominating corporation. The tables on pages 21, 22, and 23 show the degree of concentrations in ownership, in banking operations, and in pyramided, economic control.

In 1929 these two hundred companies controlled 49.2 per cent of all corporated wealth, while the remaining 50.8 per cent was owned by the 300,000 smaller companies. At the 1924–29 rate of growth it would take only thirty years for all industrial activity to be absorbed by the two hundred giants. Two tenths of 1 per cent of all industrial corporations hold 52 per cent of all corporate assets.

Concentrations in Banking Corporations

Bank Resources in the Nation, 1930	$72 billion
Bank Resources in 250 Largest Banks, 1930	$33.4 billion

One per cent of the banks directly controlled 46 per cent of the total national resources in banks. Twenty-four New York banks or less than one tenth of 1 per cent of the banks have combined resources of $10.8 billion, i.e., 15 per cent of total resources in banks. Their capitalization is nearly $700,000,000 — a sum large enough for the capitalization of 20,000 country banks situated in towns of 10,000 or less. In 1924 the one hundred largest banks had total deposits of $15,150,000,000. In 1930 the one hundred largest banks had total deposits of $22,158,000,000. One per cent of the banks control three fourths of the Nation's commercial deposits. Ninety-nine per cent of the banks control one fourth of the commercial deposits.[4]

---

[4] Craig B. Hazlewood, *American Bankers' Association Journal*, October, 1929; Committee on Banking and Currency, Seventy-first Congress, *Branch, Chain and Group Banking*, Vol. I, Part 1, pp. 3, 4; *American Banker*, 1931; New York *Times*, January 20, 1931.

Concentration in Economic Control[5]

1. Legal Device — blocks of nonvoting stocks pyramiding
    "Pyramiding" — control by a majority of stock in one corporation which in turn holds a majority in another, etc. An interest of one eighth or one sixteenth or less can become entrenched in control.
2. Minority Control — a group in a position to dominate through their stock.
3. Management Control — existing management appoints proxy committee and virtually dictates.

SUMMARY OF CONTROL IN SOME OF THE 200 LARGEST CORPORATIONS

42 Railroads:
    Minority Control...... 13
    Legal Device.......... 1
    Management Control.. 14
52 Public Utilities:
    Minority Control...... 17 — Thought to be so controlled — 5
    Legal Device.......... 10
    Management Control.. 5 — Thought to be so controlled — 5
106 Industrials:
    Minority Control...... 14 — Thought to be so controlled — 24
    Legal Device.......... 10
    Management Control.. 2 — Thought to be so controlled — 39

It is evident that business in the United States is marching on toward economic dictatorship, if it has not already become a dictator in many ways. The wealth of the nation is being concentrated rapidly in the hands of relatively few persons. When wealth is put into the form of corporation securities and the corporation itself tends to become more and more a veritable spider web for national and even international economic action, the control of property passes from the individuals who own, to the few directors. The directors are sometimes under the control of investment bankers. They are dependent upon them for entrance into the capital market. Interlocking directorates, banker-director relationships, and other legal devices place the banker in strategic positions. Directors of our modern corporations, investment bankers,

---

[5] *The Modern Corporation and Private Property,* Berle & Means; New York *Times, Wall Street Journal.*

and wealthy persons exercise a tremendous economic power. Of the three groups, wealthy persons are the least powerful, i.e., if they are merely the holders of large blocks of stocks. The investment bankers are more powerful than the corporation directors. However, the investment bankers are not in complete control, because they apparently do not act as a compact group. Indeed, it is known that they compete among themselves, but their cumulative power, though exercised in separate and conflicting groups, is enormous.

Inefficiencies and Giant Enterprises

Only those who refuse to look at the modern world realistically accept the assumption that all these concentrations lead to efficiency, security, or prosperity. It is becoming increasingly evident that the advantages that the giant enterprise has are more often the advantages conferred by grace of law and government than advantages of economic efficiency resulting from size. The success of a few large corporations is constantly before our minds and we soon forget the many cases of merger which fail to work. After ten years of operation 35 industrial mergers were studied by Arthur S. Dewing in 1919. He found that during this period the average earnings of 22 of them were less than the previous combined earnings of their merged units.

In March, 1938, *Fortune* magazine offered a sound critique of corporate bigness and gave expression to some philosophy of decentralization:

> ... It may be time to wonder whether profits and the national income would not be bigger if the corporate units of industry were not so big. ...
> This technique of bigness, involving the artificial control of prices and other basic factors, is a collectivist technique. And the operation of the collectivist technique has created for business a precarious situation. Business has carried collectivism so far in its private affairs that its affairs are no longer private, but, by the bigness of their impact, public. ...
> Thus collectivism in industry begets collectivism in Government. And if this is not collectivism as practiced in the so-called collectivist states, it is only a couple of theoretical steps removed from it. Carried

to its extreme it means the downfall of the economy upon which American Business has been reared; the perversion of the democratic order; the destruction of the right to risk-and-profit; and all too easily, the loss of those civil liberties that are at present based upon the principle of the limitation of governmental power. . . .

But if, finally, neither business nor government makes any moves whatever in the direction of breaking down industry into smaller, more compact, more mobile, and better earning units; if bigness is allowed to remain as the standard concept of economy: then the American business man, and the American politico, and in short all American citizens, must prepare themselves for a different order of things; an order in which the powers of government are not limited; in which the right to risk-and-profit is not clear; and in which the making, the selling, and even the buying of the products of the biggest show in history are all mysteriously directed from above.[6]

What Builds the Giant Corporation?

The usefulness and the efficiency of concentrated joint-stock companies or corporations operating on a national or international basis is highly questionable. Now and then a corporation becomes large because its large-scale operation is genuinely efficient. Most of them owe their gigantic size to *governmental privilege and skillful legal manipulations*. By the favor of the law, the business corporation is a permanent thing, except when an occasional corporation is limited in its life tenure by special legislative decree or charter limitation. The corporation can expand indefinitely; can get long-term or semipermanent control of credit; sell, divide, or concentrate aggregates of shares in its enterprise. With the prospect of incorporated continuity through many generations, corporate managements, and incorporated vendors of credit are encouraged to build up bonded indebtedness. The general trend leads to the burden of too much debt from generation to generation. Thus credit which would ordinarily be mobile and directed toward newly productive enterprises is absorbed. New bonds and stock certificates are often issued to cover the cost of new business and plant extensions. Payment of dividends is often unnaturally preserved and the stockholders are thus led into the

---
[6] *Fortune*, editorial, "Unmerging for Profit," March, 1938.

unsound expectation of permanently maintained high profits. Then, when it is suddenly realized that a large part of the pyramided corporate structure is insecure, the shock of loss is unduly magnified.

The corporation with its legal fiction of artificial personality sets its owners practically free of all personal responsibilities in the conduct of its affairs. The liability of organizers and owners is very limited according to charter or statute, and their general responsibility is highly impersonal. In practice the management is often entirely independent of the titular or actual ownership. These limitations in individual liabilities and responsibilities, make it impossible to repair the economic and social injuries which are inflicted on the investing and trading public. Armed with chartered privileges and statutory favors, the strong corporations become ruthless in their competition with private citizens. They frequently operate independently of the natural law. Small private enterprise fails, sometimes because it is inefficient but more often because it does not compete on a basis of equality with corporations. The natural person is limited by his expectation of life. At his death his enterprise is divided among his heirs and further diminished by inheritance taxes. The natural person is personally responsible for all his acts, and his entire estate is liable without limitation for the payment of debts. Creditors cannot be shut off from any part of the natural person's estate by reason of *"limited liability"* technicalities.

Results Under Giant "Corporationism"

When corporations become numerous, as in recent years, their privileged positions and complexities, their size and opportunities for expansion play an active part in the breakdown of small individual enterprises. Democratic foundations are disturbed. Individual and social securities are lost. Legal sanctions which may be quite adequate for the control of small enterprises and private persons in accordance with the requirements of the common good, are not adequate for incorporated monopolies and artificial legal persons.

The large corporation sometimes attains an apparent economy through volume of production and volume of sales. But there is always the tremendous and deadening overhead supervision plus the costs of distribution and advertising. The vast majority of the employees are usually on a low wage scale. When chain-store organizations are compared with groups of small independent grocers, the chain has the advantage in the purchase of quantity goods. The chain corporations set aside dividends more regularly than the independent grocers. The larger part of the saving in quantity purchases is appropriated as profits. The chains sell their goods at a higher average markup in prices than the independent groups. Yet, the independent grocers invariably pay a higher average wage.

There is no striking evidence that a growing monopoly makes for efficiency. Aluminum prices have held a ten-year fixed level. Four of these years were years of the greatest depression and price decline in history. The aluminum monopoly certainly had the opportunity to show its efficiency. There was on the contrary greater profit taking and uneconomic exploitation through patented processes. Farm-machinery monopolies went through the same period with the same profit taking, retaining their high price levels and high profits.

Chapter 3

PROLETARIANISM

THE real evils which men and society encounter when there is too much monopolization through corporations, too much urbanism, and too much commercialism, are not the losses sustained through the inefficiencies of new processes in the supply of necessities. The real evils are spiritual, social, and political losses. These grow with the gradual change of a democratic society into a proletarian society, the gradual change of the free man into one wholly dependent upon a wage, and often wholly dependent on governmental relief and charity. As this change continues the few privileged owners of productive property begin to live in dread of falling into the proletarian condition. And this catastrophe lies ahead for most of them.

Proletarians Lose Freedom and Ideals

The proletarians forget what it is to be free. In one country after another they accept a despot. This despot frequently speaks in terms of democracy to his new nation of slaves. The proletarians are slaves ready to accept another form of slavery, provided, of course, it be something new. They find but little difficulty in speaking of it under the name of Democracy.

The proletarian millions are a dangerous thing. Deprived of property, these men and women and children begin to regard work as an evil thing, a burden wrongfully imposed by another. They know that this work enriches someone else, not themselves. They cannot save anything and they would not acquire any independence if they did, because in a society which is generally speaking proletarian, the small owner is repeatedly ruined. Only the exceptional man can rise out of the proletariat into the privileged owning class, and when he does, it will often be at the expense of his fellow men.

The proletarian mind is not natural. It feels no incentive to save. In a proletarian society it is easy to sell worthless gadgets. The proletariat loses its sense of home, for it has no roots. It lives in a changing labor market. It drifts from place to place. It inherits nothing and it has no hope of handing on anything to its children. Save for the necessity of keeping alive, there is no incentive to work. Livelihood is doled out through the wage, relief, or charity. A low ideal becomes the highest; namely, get as much as possible for as little effort as possible. The privileged minority, the owners, set this example. Frequently their effort is slightly anything beyond the gambler's effort.

Proletarians Confuse Democracy and Tyranny

The proletarian mind finds no difficulty in the verbal profession of democracy. It openly acclaims leaders who glibly talk about the "new democracy" under the dictatorship of Fascism or the "new democracy" under the so-called Dictatorship of the Proletariat, which we know is the dictatorship *over* the Proletariat by the chief Communist Bureaucrat.

The confused minds of both the leaders and their followers are not able to see that the two concepts are contradictory. The ideologies of propertyless people and their leaders are often placed in juxtaposition with the words of the Constitution, and the philosophy of Washington, Jefferson, and Lincoln. This forced and illogical connection is errant falsehood. The democratic society of Washington, Jefferson, and Lincoln was inspired by the free mind of the free man. The proletarian mind, however, has well-nigh forgotten what it is to be free and it is incapable of democratic action. The mind that has no experience of anything but modern social injustice, oppression, and exploitation is filled with bitterness, hatred, and despair. It cannot grasp the strength and value of human bonds, of loyalty, affection, law, justice, liberty, and the rights and duties between those who are poorer and those who are wealthier.

Gardens and Farms and Homes Remove Proletarianism

This proletarian mind is found in every nation of the world today. It does not always appear in this bare, unyielding outline.

So long as the cities are not too large, so long as there are many families who own their own plot of land, so long as there are some independent craftsmen and businessmen who conduct small enterprises, the proletariat is in frequent contact with democratic modes of living. At this stage old loyalties, traditional ties, domestic and community solidarities will still tend to hold the two elements of society together. The proletarians too may still have the opportunity to possess themselves of a house and a garden. At least they share to some extent the mind of their neighbor who is a small-property owner and has a sense of being at home and taking an active part in the democratic responsibilities of his community. The proletarians at this stage are interspersed with the owners. Developments will not have reached the point where the cities are too large. The proletarians will not have been herded too closely together. All natural ties have not yet been broken and their individual lives do not yet take on the sharp angularity and sordidness of the average industrial working day and year. Warming rays of light still reach the proletariat as they stream from the richer life of the neighbors who own some property.

We do not have proletarianism in its extreme in America, but we do have entirely too much of it, and our concentrations and centralizations in social, economic, and political activity are unfortunately hastening its advance.

However, it is not too late to attempt the restoration of our world-famous democracy. That restoration will be measured in direct proportion to our sincerity and our success in the progressive abolition of proletarianism, which is the same thing as the multiplication of small ownership in productive property, the abolition of the proletarian mentality, and the restoration of the free mind. Private ownership is not fulfilled and proletarianism is not removed by the mere ownership of goods for consumption. Private ownership means primarily the title, possession, control, and personal management of productive property. It is precisely this distinction in the ownership of property that will "produce" and property to be "consumed" that makes or unmakes the proletariat.

Sufficiently Widespread Distribution of "Productive" Property

Editors of newspapers, politicians, magnates of industry, chamber-of-commerce speakers, economists, and commencement speakers are forever repeating the story of American wealth. They tell us that the United States with 7 per cent of the world's population and 6 per cent of the world's land area owns 45 per cent of the wealth of the world. These men continually repeat the statement that the distribution of our wealth is "reasonably equitable." For proof and illustration of this statement they repeatedly summarize the facts of distribution relative to consumable goods; namely, that there are in America 29,000,000 radios, 11,000,000 washing machines, 25,000,000 automobiles, 20,000,000 electric irons, 10,000,000 vacuum cleaners, and 9,000,000 million electric refrigerators. We do not deny this distribution of consumable goods. Statistics relative to consumable goods prove nothing. The statistics that we must study to determine the extent of property ownership are the statistics relative to *productive* property. What is the distribution relative to productive goods? What is the distribution of ownership in land, in buildings and equipment, in farms, factories, mines, in commercial enterprises, in machinery and appliances? Do those who always dwell on statistics relative to consumable goods want to forward the impression that the distribution of productive property is "reasonably equitable" too? Or are they obviously trying to evade this all-important point; namely, the facts about the distribution of land and homes, business and commercial enterprises, machinery and appliances used in production? Or do they want us to conclude that these things are reasonably distributed too? Their statistics are correct so far as they apply to consumable goods and gadgets, but if they make the conclusion of a reasonably equitable distribution of productive property from the statistics relative to the distribution of consumable goods, then, as Herbert Agar states, "the conclusion is an insult to the mind."

The statistics are doubtless correct, but the conclusion is an insult to the mind. Of course we have the lion's share of the world's wealth; that is what Providence did for us. But our special problem is the one

I described in the Prologue: the poverty of rich nations. Our problem, and the measure of our failure, is that being so rich we should have millions of destitute citizens. Forty-five per cent of the world's wealth — twenty-five million automobiles — the most prosperous middle class in the world's history — and God knows how many million workless, landless, undernourished people. We have not even taken the trouble to count them. Perhaps we are afraid that if we knew their numbers we could not dodge the question, "what has gone wrong?"[1]

Distribution of Productive Property

The statistics of productive property are an entirely different set of statistics, and tell an entirely different story. They are not the facts about the multiplicity of automobiles and radios, the multiplicity of bric-a-brac and the general use of similar accessories. The statistics relative to the distribution of productive properties tell the story of the rise of tenancy from 25 per cent to 50 per cent, the foreclosures of 600,000 farms within a few years, widespread tax liens on land, the heavy burden of mortgage debt. Likewise, the story relative to productive property is the story of gigantic mergers and extreme concentration of the ownership and control and management of industries into the hands of a relatively few corporations and the hands of relatively few stockholders. The story of the distribution of productive property is not a pleasant story. It is the story of the multiplication of the wage slaves, and the final appearance of millions who have become the paupers of the State. It is the story of the concentration of credit control, the continual removal of the small enterprise by the large corporation, and the growth of government holdings in properties that once belonged to individuals and small corporations.

Because the story relative to productive property is not a story of "a reasonably equitable distribution," we have an American proletariat numbering in the millions. Yes. This proletariat continues to exist. It drives an automobile; it listens to the radio; and it uses up its gadgets. It somehow eats and sleeps, but it has no plot of land, no tools, no small enterprises, no reasonable securities. This proletariat lives in the labor market — a market which is even more uncertain than the Stock Exchange. A description

---
[1] Agar, H., *Pursuit of Happiness* (Houghton Mifflin Co.), p. 357.

Proletarianism

of the commercialization of labor and its effects is seen in the following:

> One of the primary causes [of the Proletariat] is the commercialization of human labor power — the fact that labor has become a market commodity and that production, socially speaking, is nothing more than a money transaction between employer and employee. The effect of this commercialization is a lack of security, or assurance of a decent standard of living. . . . This may occur because of personal circumstances — sickness, accident, age, sex, race, disqualifications of one sort or another; it may be due to the lowering of the demand for a particular kind of labor; or it may be caused by those phenomena in the business cycle, crises and depressions, which occur in the very nature of modern economic life. . . . A second result of the commercialization of labor power is that labor and the employer-employee relationship are largely divested of their moral and personal quality. Both tend to lose the feature in their character that had so much to do in former days with the energy and the steadiness with which work was performed. In place of a moral willingness to work and a joy and pride in the work accomplished we now have the compulsion of economic pressure and shop discipline. . . . The raising of wages does assuredly take out of the industrial world a considerable part of the existing tensions, but not nine-tenths, as some writers would have us believe.[2]

Human Labor Marketed as Simply Another Commodity

When human labor is generally reduced to a commodity in the market, the social standing of the working classes begins to drop. Responsibility is concentrated with the aid of machines and corporations into the hands of a few. Most of the workers are reduced to the level of automatons. The wage is too meager and the work is too mean for the great majority to reach any important place, while achievement is under the false sign of the dollar. Financial success becomes the builder of an empty, artificial, social hierarchy.

Shop Discipline

Another primary cause for the existence and attitude of the proletariat is what Doctor Brief calls the "methodology of modern industry" with its relentless pursuit of profit, with maximum out-

---
[2] Briefs, Dr. Goetz, *The Proletariat* (McGraw-Hill Co.), pp. 33–35.

put for minimum outlay, continuous production, and all manner of segmentation of function and mass-production measures. Men are not desirable for employment after forty. Women and children are employed instead of men. Efficiency tests are given, etc. "The purely human, with its unpredictable possibilities, its curious vagaries, its moods and tempers, has no place in the gross materialism of factory organization." The modern shop is a military organization. Men and women must work under rigid limitations of time, space, and material. "This naturally leads to a minute division of responsibilities, and there is plenty of room for arbitrariness, for misunderstandings, for distrust, and for actual or supposed injustice."

Congested Areas

Another reason for the growth of proletarianism is the concentration of production centers in limited areas. With this come all of the evils attendant on highly undesirable, congested, living conditions. "Capital and labor find more and more occasions of friction — to say nothing of the mental tensions, the unwholesome restraints and deprivations which always exist where human beings are closely crowded together, out of contact with nature and away from their native sod."[3]

Dr. Alexis Carrel declares these conditions of the proletariat and proletarianism itself should be progressively abolished and he indicates the way:

> Gigantic factories, office buildings rising to the sky, inhuman cities, industrial morals, faith in mass-production, are not indispensable to civilization. Other modes of existence and thought are possible. Culture without comfort, beauty without luxury, machines without enslaving factories, science without the worship of matter, would restore to man his intelligence, his moral sense, his virility, and lead him to the summit of his development. . . . There have been, in the past, industrial organizations which enabled the workmen to own a house and land, to work at home when and as they willed, to use their intelligence, to manufacture entire objects, to have the joy of creation. At the present time this form of industry could be resumed. Electrical

---

[3] *Ibid.*, p. 41.

power and modern machinery make it possible for the light industries to free themselves from the curse of the factory. Could not the heavy industries also be decentralized? Or would it not be possible to use all the young men of the country in those factories for a short period, just as for military service? In this or another way the proletariat could be progressively abolished. Men would live in small communities instead of in immense droves. Each would preserve his human value within his group. Instead of being merely a piece of machinery, he would become a person. Today the position of the proletariat is as low as was that of the feudal serf. Like the serf, he has no hope of escaping from his bondage, no hope of being independent, of holding authority over others. The artisan, on the contrary, has the legitimate hope that some day he may become the head of the shop. Likewise the peasant owning his land, the fisherman owning his boat, although obliged to work hard, are, nevertheless, masters of themselves and of their time. Most industrial workers could enjoy similar independence and integrity. The white collar people lose their personality just as factory hands do. In fact, they become proletarians. It seems that modern business organization and mass-production are incompatible with the full development of the human self.[4]

The Proletariat a Slave of the System

It may be argued that any worker can always quit, and that therefore he is free. But is a worker actually free to quit when his livelihood and that of his family will end with his job? Can he quit and expect to be taken care of by charity or public relief? He cannot expect anything like a full subsistence from charity or relief. His family will suffer. This is a far greater grief to him than his own privations. His employer may hire him or fire him. His livelihood is in another man's hands; his fate rests with another man's will. The ordinary worker does not own any property which he could turn into enough money to live on. The propertyless worker is at the mercy of the employer's will.

Perhaps the worker could easily find some land where he could raise enough to satisfy his and his family's needs. Many obstacles block this. If the worker has no capital for such a self-reliant effort toward subsistence he is still helpless. There are difficulties about pulling up stakes to seek a livelihood in a new location. Ties of

---

[4] Carrel, Dr. Alexis, *Man, The Unknown* (Harper and Bros.), pp. 296 and 315.

friendship and blood relationship often make it hard to leave the old family circle. Associations formed over a period of years make strong bonds. Frequently a man has contracted debts with local businessmen. It is hard enough in this case to pay off his obligations; the old debts are an obstacle to his moving to a new place. Besides this, wherever he moves, moving will cost money. There will be new debts to pay.

When we glibly suggest that a man may go West to the harvest fields, or to some other big factory to get a new job, we forget that the expense may be more than the working family can risk. Work is promised in the harvest fields or in a factory. Yes, but who knows whether others will not snap up the opportunity before he himself arrives. Every year word comes from the West that hopeful young men seeking work in the harvest fields are being turned away disappointed. The worker, indeed, "seems" to be free; it "seems" possible for him to go to some new, less frequented spot, to take up a new line of work. But for pioneering he would need a little capital. Productive goods is one of the worker's greatest needs. If he had productive goods he would be on the road to freedom.

Besides capital the worker needs training in order to take up a new line of work. This is especially true if he tries to support himself on the soil. If he started with small capital, he would be in dire need of direction so as to avoid costly mistakes. At the present time there is no adequate provision for this training. Pioneering today is not quite so practicable a possibility as it was in the past century. Tax rates are much higher. The high taxes, county taxes and township taxes, State taxes and Federal taxes make it impossible for the untrained man to start on a shoestring and make ends meet.

Even at a time when there is a labor shortage the laborer has no assurance that the shortage will continue and that employment will continue. The typical employer on the other hand is assured of a livelihood even if he closes down his plant. He depends on still other property for his support. The employee, however, is at the mercy of another. When Henry Ford decides to lay off 150,000 men, he has only to make up his mind and the thing is done. The motive makes no difference. He may want to spite General

Motors, or show the Federal Government his power. In any case, the worker is simply dependent on the will of the boss.

If there is a labor shortage, the worker can find employment elsewhere. But suppose he has paid for a small home and has been living in it for a year or two. Often he cannot sell the property at a good price; he cannot afford to sell it at any great sacrifice. In order to realize on his investment, he must occupy the home himself. Once again his liberty is limited. He is not free to go out and get work somewhere else. Certainly if there is labor shortage in the future it will not necessarily mean a shortage of unskilled laborers. As machines are multiplied, they will replace men in many cases where work has been done by unskilled labor. This will make it all the more dangerous for the unskilled man to lose his job. The present substitution of strip mills for roller mills in the steel industry will ultimately mean that 85 per cent of the present steelworkers will have to find work elsewhere. The cotton picker, if expensively and massively built for the large commercial farm and not constructed inexpensively and along the lines of a human scale unit for small acreages, will in a few years render three million hand pickers jobless.

The Giant Factory Dictator is Supreme

The important thing to consider is that the owner of the means of production has the whip hand. If the owners decide to hire men, the workers have jobs, otherwise not. For the sake of argument we may admit that during a "boom," when there is a labor shortage, the worker can always move and find a job. Then, in the rare case of a labor shortage, the worker could move and pick up a new job at will.

The worker is not only dependent on the will of his employer, but there is also another element of insecurity in his hold on a weekly or monthly wage. The boss may not be efficient as the manager of a business. The two hundred giant corporations own more than half of the productive property. This staggering concentration of property gives the large corporations an advantage. The small enterprise is not certain of survival in the face of such concentration. Business failures for small enterprises is a source of insecurity for many workers. Hence, all-powerful concentration is not the only cause of failure. As already stated, the manager of the business may simply be incompetent or wasteful; he may not know how to manage; he may not know how to sell. As a result the worker will suffer in getting less than a comfortable, living wage; or in the loss of his job.

In ten years, over ten thousand banks went out of business. Once the depression set in, a tremendous number of firms were bound to go under. The various branches of business in this country are dependent on each other. If one branch suffers serious loss, the others lose too. This loss grows very quickly, like a snowball rolling down hill. Soon the whole country feels a severe decline in income, in employment. The propertyless worker finds himself in a position of utter dependence on the functioning of business machinery which is too delicate, because it is too highly concentrated. Too many external, arbitrary circumstances must be adjusted by a few men, or the worker must beg. If a single factor in the interlaced business mechanism fails, the worker's income falls below subsistence level, or falls farther below the subsistence level than it was before. Big business is governed by a few men. These men do not need to keep their plants in operation in order to live; the workers do. Workers may strike, but they cannot strike for long. They must live. Other men may be secured to take their places. With only one fifth of the workers organized, collective bargaining is not very effective. If labor were organized so that men could always have recourse to collective bargaining, they would, as a group, have tremendous power. The way to organization is a long and difficult one. And again, once in the union, the worker must surrender much of his freedom to the union. If union and corporation cannot agree, there must in the end be submission to government intervention. If capital and labor are deadlocked, a higher authority must be called in — either the local or national government. Again the wage earner becomes subject to the will of another. He is again dependent on the will of another for the chance to make a living.

Irresponsible Leaders in Unions

If big unions take over the work of collective bargaining, the worker often shifts his responsibility to the union's irresponsible leaders. Any complete unionization of workers which does not amount to a genuine partnership of capital and labor does not give us an occupational group. There must be a basis for cooperation between boss and worker. There is a basis of cooperation only when both employer and employee work for the good management of the industry, only when both shoulder the responsibility for that good management.

The Proletarian Low Ambition: Job and Pay Check

What has been the ambition of the employee in a giant corporation? Has he been interested in turning out a good product and in good management? The prevailing position of economic slavery puts the ambition of the worker too low. Working for a large corporation unfits the worker for taking part in management or taking the burden of management to heart. We all know that the chief concern of nearly all workers on a weekly wage is to keep their job, or get a slight advance in pay. The ambitions of workers are not connected with business realities; such as the production of goods of better quality, better management in the industry, more efficient and more abundant production at lower costs, and better service to the community, etc. Why do the workers throw off such responsibilities? They become irresponsible because the employer will not share responsibility with them. For the workers there is nothing but jobs and pay checks and layoffs. For the worker finally, the job and the pay check begins to mean "life, liberty, and the pursuit of happiness." He looks immediately to his job and not the company's product, as the thing on which his family depends. But the pay check and the job are not real things, not fundamental things. The job is an exceedingly insecure thing, an imitation of real employment. The dehumanized, impersonal, mechanized workman is not interested in the burden of responsibility. His whole tendency is to slough off such a burden, but the tendency is hardly conscious.

Slow Growth Disguises Hideousness of Proletarianism

If the wage system were suddenly placed on us while we were still peacefully occupied with our own tools, machines, and our own little farms, we would see the full effect of the system on the mind of the worker. Fortunately for our study, we have this scene practically enacted for us on the coast of South America. The Indians, native there, lived peacefully in a little village. Each family had what property it needed and for the most part supported itself. One day the world's great oil company arrived and built a pumping station. It hired Indians, paid them wages. The wages were not high by our standard, but to the natives the money represented untold wealth, especially since the industrialists brought to this quiet spot not only money but new things to buy. The Indian's appetite for money had been aroused. He developed a craving for this "token" wealth. His desire for spicy entertainment and gaudy baubles was inflamed. When his new source of income was threatened, he was ready to use any kind of violence to keep from losing his pay check. He had in a brief time become a wage slave. The oil company, of course, hired men as it needed them and dropped them as soon as the work was done. But the natives had been drawn into a state of mind where they demanded work and money. Grave trouble threatened if they did not get it. An official of the oil company sensed the danger and brought the facts to a prominent member of a religious order, the spiritual leader of the Indian colony. The official asked the priest to ask his Religious Order to set up a complete system of social service for the South American colony in order that the Indians might be pacified and kept under control. The priest turned a withering fire on the policies of the company and its willingness to have religion step in to palliate the evils which the company had worked on the appetites, ambitions, and outlook of the Indians. Before, the Indian had been interested in producing what the family could use and what the community could use. He had been engaged in genuine things. Now, however, his whole thought was to keep a job, to get money, and to buy accessories and novelties as well as necessities. His whole thought and desire was taken up with less essential things. Does this make a man more inclined to escape his own responsibilities? Does it make him less concerned about his fundamental duties as a father of a family, a producer for a family, and a leader for the community in social, economic, and religious matters? Obviously, it does. The effects, the results, are the same in any modern country.

Mental Effect of Economic Slavery: Fear

We defined economic slavery as dependence on the will of another who holds the whip handle, because he has complete control over the productive plant. The worker depends on the will of the entrepreneur. His tenure of employment is very uncertain. Curtailment of production does not necessarily conflict with the plans of the capitalist. He may prefer to keep high prices and cut production, or he may cut prices and sustain production. Curtailment of production and high prices puts certain firms at the mercy of the owners of other firms. This is often purposely done to force merger and bring pressure for concentration. It matters little what the motive may be, the practice is common, and the worker lives in continual fear of losing his job. Unless he has productive property or is the exceptional man who is indispensable to some employer, this fear undermines his independence of character.

By independence of character we mean self-reliance. We mean backbone. We mean the strength of will necessary to undertake responsibility rather than pass it on to another. We mean the courage to face a problem and take command, the courage to dominate a situation, to accept and carry duties assigned by nature and circumstances; duties of family life, duties of citizenship, duties in administering one's own property, duties of leadership in the social and economic betterment of one's own community. You will say that the necessity of doing one's duty is extremely general, that priests, preachers, educators, parents, and teachers have always labored at building up courage and strength of will. That is true but the circumstantial odds against achievement have never been as great as they are now. Economic slavery is the peculiar evil of our time which puts too many men and women in a position where they easily refuse to be responsible in the direction of affairs. When millions of people are managed in every detail of their work, they are soon in a position where they look for management in government, in play, in education, in social affairs, in all situations. This is the terrible surrender that economic slavery fosters. Courageous assumption of responsibilities, by the many, dies out. In its place comes subservience, dependence, a refusal to stand on one's own feet, a refusal to be self-reliant, a refusal of the drudgery, the anxieties, and the hazards of management, and consequently the tremendous loss of independence, security, freedom, and happiness. There is a general weakening of backbone and courage. And with this there springs up a general attachment to worthless gadgets.

Mass-production factories, owned and controlled by a few, introduce the "speed-up" system. From these factories "metal devices come forth, marvelously transformed, while men are abused, degraded, and corrupted." Adam Smith bubbled with enthusiasm when he found that the process of making straight pins had been divided into twenty-five operations, giving each worker a different mechanical motion. Smith did not see that this universal segmentation of labor would undermine character, leave deep dissatisfactions, wound self-respect, and dehumanize workers, tying them down to monotonous, mechanical repetitions.

Out of work, out of a job, propertyless, men become helpless and hopeless. And when men become helpless and hopeless they are all the more dependent on the job, or on the political boss and his dole. Boys who could support themselves on a little land go to the city and get a job in a factory. Because they are young and energetic they get jobs. They replace men of forty who are used up. Perhaps, they earn $150 a month for six months. When the job and the pay stops at the end of six months or a year, they putter about as well as possible until they can get a job again. They give up all thought and hope of independence. With some knowledge of agriculture and a little effort to obtain a home and a few acres they would have been capable of raising much food for themselves and their children. They would in fact have been capable of much more. They could have built up a new center of farm and cooperative life. They could have been leaders in the building of a relatively self-sufficient community. They could have made themselves and others partially independent of the big city factory.

The big corporations now possess all the approaches to domination. More and more men want the corporation to manage for them. The corporation therefore takes in more property, controls greater amounts of capital. As this centralization and collectivization proceeds, the worker has less and less chance of gaining any independence.

Economic Slavery

The bond of slavery in the mass-production wage system is by no means open and evident. The state of utter dependence is disguised by certain little concessions or apparent concessions to freedom. The first argument that opponents use to show that the worker is not an economic slave is that there are bosses and highly trained workers who are free and yet are wage earners. Officials of a company receive high salaries. They are not bound to do the bidding of a master, therefore, no special slavery seems to follow from the fact that a man is a wage earner. We readily grant that such wage earners are the exception. They are not always on the receiving end when orders are given. They do the hiring and firing. The fact that certain authority is delegated to them gives them more security. Consider the case of a valuable worker — the brilliant lawyer, retained with handsome fees. He has no great fear of insecurity as a wage slave. He is highly trained and his services are in demand. It matters little to him who employs him. The fact that he is a wage earner does not make him subject to economic slavery. This argument falls down because these particular pay rollers have special advantages the ordinary workers do not have. They are the exception. Economic slavery does not hold in their case. And yet, these high-salaried wage earners are often capable of showing a disgusting degree of subservience to their financial lord or political boss.

Another argument opponents use to show that the ordinary worker is free points to choice of occupation. Provided the worker has the necessary ambition, he may become a bricklayer, a plumber's helper, a plasterer, a mechanic, an electrician's helper, or a stage carpenter. All that the worker has to do, is to put in a little time making himself a little more expert in a commercial way. After that he is able to make a job secure. The answer is simply: the jobs are too few. Let us say, a union for stage electricians requires applicants to obtain certain training. Only a fortunate few are taken into the training school. Sons and nephews and favorites will be given the preference. In the building trades, how can the worker have the liberty of choosing to work at his trade, when building is not being done?

The clerk or factory "hand" has a family. He must support them and he must keep his job to do it. Is he a free man? He is bound to keep his job. He depends on the job for a living. He is not interested in the shaping of an independent career. He does not fit his work into the needs of his community. He throws off responsibility. His general attitude toward the control and direction of affairs is "Let George do it" — "Let somebody else run things" — "Someone else should take the responsibility, moral, economic, social, which makes up the burden of management" — "The world owes me a living" — "Society owes me a 'job.'"

This does not mean that the wage slave always expressly says, "Let someone else take the responsibilities. I throw the burden from my shoulders. I wash my hands of them." What really happens is that the ordinary job holder does not even think about the matter. He is not interested in the burden of any responsibility. His whole tendency is to slough off such a burden, but the tendency is not always conscious. If the industrial worker should put his feelings and his thoughts into words, he would refuse the burden of running, of managing a business or industry. But the matter simply doesn't enter his mind. Even if the industrialized worker bitterly criticizes the official management of affairs, even if he loudly proclaims how the government should be administered, he would shrink from the work itself. Proletarian talk is common. A greater freedom, and security and independence must exist before we can have the necessary occupational grouping and sharing of responsibility in industry. Any business depends not only on the character and skill of its officials, but also on the alertness and persistence of the workers in producing articles of superior quality and sharing a responsibility for efficient administration. Similar alertness and persistence are needed for the effective operation of democracy in government. These qualities spring from the character of independent, responsible people. Jobs and pay checks do not produce these qualities. People acquire these qualities through small holdings in productive property and some experience in effective ownership, management, and control.

Historical Growth of Proletarianism

As early as 1837 Simon de Sismondi in a publication — *Etude sur L'economie Politique* — warned Western civilization of the emergence of the proletariat and stated that unless social, economic, and political leaders, in fact all leaders, attacked this problem, society was face to face with a fundamental change that would ultimately spell its doom. He denied that there could be progress wherever there was an aristocracy of capital and a proletariat running into the millions. He used the word *proletaire* and described it in terms of the conditions which separated wage earning from property holding. One hundred years ago he saw pauperism developing in every country where mass production was growing. He spoke of many having no productive property, becoming aggregations of destitutes, exercising no foresight, displaying no thrift, and suffering acutely in crises which came with underconsumption. The *proletaire* was indentured, as it were, to capital, for it owned nothing. The competition among such workers operated to the advantage of capital, and on capital's part there was no portion of responsibility for the workers. The helplessness of the worker grew from generation to generation and where the proletarian lot seemed to be cast, there was no incentive to provide for the distant future. In a keen analysis, Simon de Sismondi saw, one hundred years ago, that there was already at that time in the history of urbanism, industrialism, and liberalism too wide a gulf between property and labor, between capital and the *proletaire*, that unorganized group of wretched human beings.

With a keen insight into industrial problems and what now seems to be an unwarranted faith in the State and the propertied classes as agents of reform, Sismondi called upon the State and the propertied classes to make a complete break with *laissez faire*, Calvinism, Economic Liberalism and, to a great extent, with mass-production technocracy. He recommended that industry be decentralized, that small factories be placed in rural areas as well as in towns, that a halt be called on large-scale production, and that employers accept responsibility for the personal welfare of their employees. Another French writer, Pecqueur, a contemporary of Sismondi, suggests in his *Nouvelle Théorie D'Economie*

Sociale et Politique, that the proletarians must expect their real liberation only from themselves, and that if they don't accomplish it, they will fall back into industrial and agricultural serfdom.

Productive Wealth Not Adequately Distributed

Productive wealth cannot make an important contribution to the welfare of a human society unless its ownership and control is somewhat equitably distributed. Do we have such distribution when it is actually true that "one third of our population is ill fed, ill housed and ill clothed"? We get a fair idea of the unequitable distribution of wealth in the United States from the figures drawn up by Senator La Follette. He says that if we take the figure one hundred as representing the total population and then take one hundred dollars as representing the total wealth, we have the following distribution or lack of equitable distribution: One individual would hold $59, a second individual would hold $9, then 22 individuals would each have $1.22, and the remaining 76 would each have less than 7 cents. The chart on page 47 indicates the distribution or rather the lack of distribution in incomes.

Subordination of All to Dollar Sign

Meanwhile the chartered companies manipulate their "gold-digging stocks," speculate greedily with their "big-machine" complex, and dehumanize large hordes of men, women, and children who work for them or wait for work, because they think that there is nothing to do but to be the willing slaves of a corporation. The entire nation is beset with a strange economy of disorder. Too many social thinkers and legislators try to clear the way for a greater and greater centralization of all incorporated enterprise, no matter how many human values must pay the forfeit. We are invited to surrender our liberties and pledge ourselves to the doctrine of larger dividends and bigger sales for the two hundred and more gigantic corporations who "humbly" serve us at a larger and larger profit to themselves. We are asked to overlook the fact that the sun rises and sets on a nation of bankrupt homes. We are asked to believe that if the corporations can make mergers, employ heavier machines instead of the nation's hungry workers, then

Proletarianism

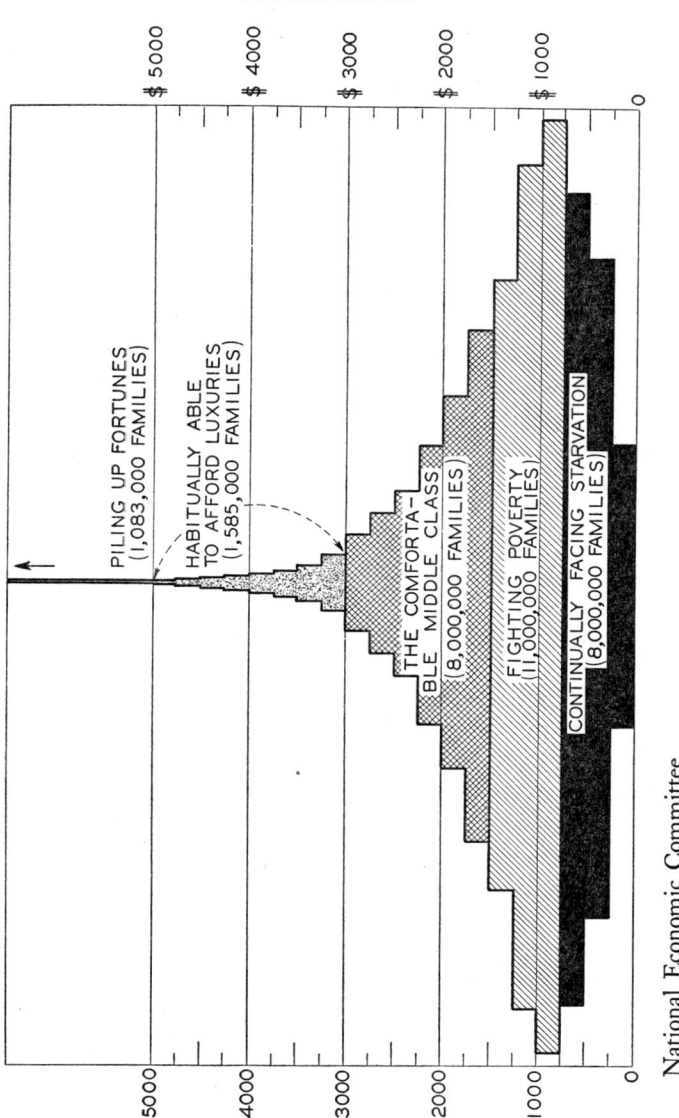

National Economic Committee

there is a greater dividend, then there is greater efficiency, and the ultimate good of mankind, the highest achievement of society, has been attained.

Will Other Standards Prevail?

How much longer will Americans have faith in such an empty philosophy of life and reap its barren fruits? Will we weigh human values in the light of a saner philosophy and a better civilization, or will we sink deeper and deeper into the treacherous mire of social and economic degradation under the false leadership of industrialists and bankers while they cling tenaciously to stock profit, usury, and monopoly? We, the people, are too often misled by the noisy promulgation of policies which are calculated to make all business bigger, all banks more independent and usurious, and all utility companies more monopolistic and avaricious. Industry and banking must be taught to talk in terms of the nation's welfare and help to carry their proportionate share of the social burden.

The leading corporations clamor on radio wave, magazine cover, and billboard: "We provide you with a new vitamin, we offer you a new cut in clothes, we equip you with a new model in everything each year, and offer you an installment plan which will rescue your purchasing power. We have harnessed science and nature. There is nothing left for you to do but breathe. We will supply leisure-time programs and educational frills. We will manage the government for you through our lobbies. It matters very little what views you have on any legislation. We will entrench our powerful, far-flung undertakings and supply you with every need."

Extreme Industrialism and Concentration March to Own Doom

We are somehow expected to have purchasing power, even though funds contract and banks offer credit only on a usurious basis. Even though there are fewer and fewer jobs, even though it seems to be cheaper to let crops rot in the fields, we are expected to relieve the incorporated magnates of their tariff-protected novelties. We are expected to become thoroughly indifferent about governmental responsibilities that we always thought somehow rested upon our shoulders as American citizens. Because of the fact that we still have our fundamental human nature, and that life always returns to a truer philosophy in which men assert their superiority to brute beasts, fight for their independence and their social, economic, and political liberties, it is not difficult to predict what history will record about such a period of extreme industrialism. History will one day present the truth about the greed, the economic and political trickery, which make joint-stock corporations thrive while families starve and great crowds of the nation's manhood wait in vain for a job.

Chapter 4

THE URBAN FAMILY IN MASS PRODUCTION

A FAMILY is defined as an enduring moral union of husband, wife, and children for a common good to be attained by their cooperative activity. A group of families united under an independent authority to effect the well-being of all constitutes a community.

Family, a Unit

Families, therefore, are the units which compose the State. The State is an outgrowth of the single family; a natural expansion because an increase in number of single families necessitates order and guidance. It exists to preserve the integrity and assure the well-being of its member families, not to supersede them. Destroy the individual family and ultimately you destroy the State. Likewise the religious, moral, economic, and social health of the State is conditioned by a like prior health in the family. This primary dependence of the State on the family may be likened to the dependence of a body on its cells. A body is made up of a multitude of cells in such a way that without them there would be no body. They are the manner in which the body exists, the units of its composition; and if the individual cells do not preserve themselves as cells, the body would cease to exist. So with the family. It is the unit of the composition of the State in such a way that without it the naturally perfect State would eventually disappear. Thus it has been decreed by the nature of things and inexorably follows from that nature.

Family, a Natural Unit

The term *natural* in reference to the origin of the family is explained in the following citation:

The Urban Family in Mass Production

The family is a natural society because it is necessary for the continuance of the race, and nature intends that the race should be continued. . . . The double tie of parent to parent and of parent to child originating in natural necessity is cemented by certain natural subjective impulses, such as the love of parent for parent, of parent for child, and of child for parent. And, therefore, the family is natural in the fullest measure, since the ties that bind the parts together are all from nature.[1]

People possess the gift of speech. They crave love, sympathy, understanding, and comradeship, and are eager to share their ideas with others. Isolation is not natural for them. Furthermore men and women differ in physical organism. In them has been implanted the mating instinct in order that a man and a woman form a union for the procreation of children for the perpetuation of the race. And since the child, the result of this union, is utterly dependent on the care of parents during infancy and formative years, the union must be permanent. A man is more virile physically to brave the exacting toil for daily bread, whereas the woman is blessed with a nature in keeping with her prerogative of childbearing and the management of the household. Her emotional, sympathetic, and domestic instincts are highly developed and flourish best in a sheltered atmosphere, free from the jarring aspects of the world of labor.

Family, a Living Unit

Activity is the sign of life. A stone is lifeless; unlike an animal it does not nourish itself, it does not grow, nor does it reproduce other stones. It has no activity. If a thing is living, it is active. The family is simple in structure but manifold in function and by its very nature active. Without activity it would deteriorate. Eva Ross calls the family "the mother cell of society." So to designate it, is to convey the idea that the family, as the organic unit of activity in the State, may analogously be compared to the cell, the organic unit of activity in the body. Activity in the body depends on the functioning of the cells. If the cells die, the body dies also. So, too, the activity of each member of the family, working with

---

[1] Cronin, Rev. Michael, *The Science of Ethics* (London: Gill and Son, Ltd.), Vol. II, p. 388.

the others for the good of all, achieves the end of preserving the family and the State. The more active a family is, the better it fulfills its nature and thrives; on the contrary, if it is not active, it dies. More important still, if the family is not active cooperatively, each member performing the duties assigned to it by reason, its well-being is imperiled. The activities of a family are many and varied.

Activities of the Family

Since the principal end of marriage is the procreation and education of children, it follows logically that procreation and education are the principal activities of parents. Children are the keystone of family life and an increase in their number is a blessing. Only when parents are unable to provide for the wants of children, or some other real impediment lies in the way of generation, may an objection be raised to additional children. But, as will be shown, it is natural and necessary that a family be in a position to satisfy the wants of offspring, and a well-ordered State will be characterized by offering a reasonably certain opportunity for parents to provide for children. Attainment of the happiness, welfare, and perfection of all its members through association and cooperation is the secondary activity of the family. Parents, active in providing for the religious, physical, educational, and social needs of offspring, are at the same time realizing the development and fruition of their own personalities. In a discussion of family activity, this principle is paramount: that family unity and development are best attained when the activities of its members are centered in concerns directly connected with the preservation and welfare of the family group.

Duties of the Family

Duties also may be classed as activities, of which the obligation to preserve existence is fundamental. For this purpose a family needs food, fuel, shelter, and clothing. Otherwise it would be impossible to keep alive. And since the animal, mineral, and vegetable kingdoms have no ascertainable purpose except to provide these necessaries, and since there is no other source from which they can be had, every family is entitled to use them to eke out a livelihood. It rests with the father to secure food and with the mother to prepare it for consumption. Until sustenance is assured, the members of a family cannot devote themselves to a second duty, that of ministering to their religious and social needs. Moreover, to fulfill the duty of self-preservation, certain other requirements are also essential; namely, the ownership of property, liberty, and responsibility.

The Ownership of Property

In his Encyclical, *On the Condition of the Working Classes,* Pope Leo XIII says that "every man has by nature the right to possess property as his own. This is one of the chief points of distinction between man and the animal creation. It is a most sacred law of nature that a father should provide food and all necessaries for those whom he has begotten. In no other way can a father effect this except by the ownership of lucrative property." The land, however, is the only self-subsistent unit. It yields the primary things — food, fuel, raw material for clothing, and lumber for a sheltered dwelling. Therefore a family should ordinarily own land as well as the tools to work it. As Eric Gill, in his book *Work and Property,* states, "only when men own the means of production is it possible fully to control the manipulation of natural materials." And when it is a question of securing the necessaries for existence, a family should fully control the means of production; otherwise self-preservation would be jeopardized, being dependent on factors external to it. This basic natural right to property secures the means of self-preservation.

Liberty

Ownership is an intrinsic guarantee of liberty. Within just limits a family must be free. If it does not own land, tools, and a home, it is under the domination of another; and to be under the domination of another in primary things is unnatural unless wages paid for hired-out labor are sufficient to enable a family to fulfill its functions. Freedom is essential to the economic life of a family. Take away freedom, the right of a family to engage in activities natural to it as an institution, and its very existence is insecure.

Responsibility

Responsibility flows from the nature of a human being. The philosophical definition of a man is that he is a rational animal. Like a brute beast he has a body, eats, sleeps, and dies; but what distinguishes him from a dog or a cow is his *reason*. Gifted with an intellect he perceives relationships between things and can convey ideas in language; he is pleased intellectually by the sight of a beautiful landscape in which symmetry and proportion are discernible; and most important for this discussion, he can form an *idea,* let us say, of a table in his mind, the spiritual part of him, and then proceed with the aid of tools and wood to express this idea in a material thing, a finished table as we see it. In other words he is responsible for the table. If it is made well, he is praised; if poorly, the blame rests squarely with him. A brute animal cannot form an idea of a table because the idea is spiritual whereas an animal is material and nothing else. Therefore, as often as a man makes a table, a chair, a barn, or anything else, he is acting in a way that proclaims him to be more than a brute animal. He is exercising that faculty which, because it distinguishes him from a beast, is more important than his body. As a maker of things, man functions spiritually and materially. Consequently, for the ordinary man to use things continually that have been made by a machine, or to work mechanically at a task that requires no exercise of his spiritual faculty, is to deaden that faculty and to make him less a man in the very thing which proclaims him to be a man and not a beast. This point looms large in a consideration of modern industrialism.

Modern Industrialism

Lest any misunderstanding arise over the question of terminology, let us define what we mean by the words *Modern Industrialism.* They are used to indicate that system now in vogue for the production and sale of material goods in which the means of production — capital and labor and land — are controlled by a few men who employ the masses at a wage, in which the large factory and the use of machines as distinguished from tools are dominant features, in which competition is rampant, in which high-pressure advertising is a weapon used to lure buyers, in which the profit motive is paramount, and in which the market is either flooded with goods regardless of demand or made scarce by monopolistic price fixing. The particular phase of Industrialism, thus defined, which is of interest here, is its effect on family life. Yet, when we prove that Industrialism militates against family life, the inference that it should be condemned does not follow, but rather there should be a correction of abuses in factories and the restoration of family activity whereby the family will not exist mainly for industry. To expose the pernicious effects of Modern Industrialism on family life, the relationship of each member to the industrial system will be considered. The father as a wage earner comes first; and four statements regarding him are to be examined. They are as follows:

1. The industrial worker too often is valued not as a person but as a thing, to be used or replaced at the whim of an employer.

2. The industrial worker too often does not receive sufficient wages, and therefore is not valued as the head of a family.

3. The industrial worker too often does not possess immovable property.

4. The industrial worker too often is mechanized — reduced to a subhuman condition because he is made an irresponsible workman.

1. *The industrial worker too often is valued not as a person but as a thing, to be used or replaced at the whim of an employer.*

To understand why this is so, one need only to take cognizance of the present plight of the industrial worker. More and more the machine is replacing human labor and the lines of the unemployed are lengthening. To confirm this point, several authorities will be cited.

While technological improvements in industry are steadily reducing the number of workers necessary to provide all the goods and service industry can market, the number of men and women who want work is steadily increasing.[2]

The labor-saving machine has done its work: it has "saved" labor

---

[2] Borsodi, Ralph, *This Ugly Civilization*, quoting William Green of American Federation of Labor (Harper and Bros., 1933), p. 30.

and dispossessed the laborer. In the United States alone, some twelve million potential workers are unemployed and are become a charge on the community.[3]

Consequently the owner of a business can replace a worker at a moment's notice and he is independent of his employees. An employee, whether a clerk in an office, a manual laborer, or the minder of a machine, who becomes dissatisfied with his lot, soon finds himself minus a job. His value as a person with rights is ignored by those whose norm of morality is expediency, and an expediency concerned with increasing the profits of the owner at the expense of the laborer. This temper of mind is exposed by Monsignor Haas writing:

> Prior to the National Recovery Act, as a nation we clung to the fiction that the wages and hours of each worker are purely private relations between the worker and the corporation, partnership, or individual employing him. We paid little heed to the social character of labor . . . our national policy was Individualism, Free Competition, Economic Liberalism, or Laissez Faire . . . the theory underlying this position was, as it is now, that employers, corporate or individual must be free to make profit, and must be left free. If they see chance for profits, they will operate, and even expand their plants, sell goods, and thereby keep workers employed. If they do not, they will curtail operations, or close down. Profit was the mainspring of the whole system, if system it could be called. That a country's economy should be operated to produce enough goods so that the entire population can live self-respecting lives and share the benefits of civilization was only a secondary consideration, if it was given any thought.[4]

In such a game of economic chess, the employee is only a pawn, not a person.

2. *The industrial worker too often does not receive sufficient wages in very many cases, and therefore is not valued as the head of a family.*

In his Encyclical, *Forty Years After,* Pius XI gives a complete treatise on the question of wages, from the standpoint of the employer, the employee, and the times. Regarding the employee, the subject of consideration here, Pope Pius said: "In the first

---

[3] Cram, Ralph, Adams, *The End of Democracy* (Boston: Marshall Co., 1937), p. 9.
[4] Haas, Msgr. Francis, *Wages and Hours of American Labor* (Paulist Press), p. 7.

The Urban Family in Mass Production 57

place the wage paid to a workingman must be sufficient for the support of himself and of his family." When we make a careful study of wages and the costs of essential necessities, we find that there are many laborers who do not receive a living wage. The elements of a decent livelihood are summarized as follows:

> Food, clothing and housing sufficient in quantity and quality to maintain the worker in normal health, in elementary comfort, and in an environment suitable to the protection of morality and religion; sufficient provision for the future to bring elementary contentment, and security against sickness, accident, and invalidity; and sufficient opportunities of recreation, social intercourse, education, and Church membership, to conserve health and strength, and to render possible in some degree the exercise of the higher faculties.[5]

Divorced from the land, and living in a complete industrial setting, the family becomes wholly dependent on the weekly wage.

3. *The industrial worker too often does not possess immovable property.*

An airplane view of an industrial city would support this contention. Long, interlocking rows of tenement houses, each harboring a colony of families for whom the payment of monthly rent is an important item in their budgets, would be glimpsed; also, near them, the two-family type of house, rented for the most part, not owned by the occupant.

Because factories employ a huge number of people at less than a living wage, it is necessary for workers to live close to the factory in order to eliminate the item of transportation; and since the weekly salary is needed for sustenance, the family of a laborer must seek living quarters proportionate to its income. Ownership of a home is too often out of the question. In commenting on the plight of the laborer William L. Chenery states:

> The possibility of being workless and without income hangs over the great majority of wage earners. The factory worker of today knows little else that he could turn to account. He must live by his trade or not at all. In order to obtain employment he must ordinarily reside in congested cities, where the possibility of subsidiary means of support

---
[5] Ryan, Msgr. J. A., *Distributive Justice* (Macmillan Company), p. 361.

are denied him. Usually he does not own the house or the tenement he lives in. He neither cultivates nor harvests vegetables and fruits which his family consumes. If he is able to eat eggs, or to drink milk, he obtains these articles from dealers who are themselves far removed from the scene of actual production. His clothes are bought, not made at home. The modern factory worker must retain his job if he wishes to continue to live, and yet knows that at recurrent intervals, regardless of zeal or fitness, many men and women will not be employed.[6]

A recent article in *Forum,* by Henry Goddard Leach, is illustrative of the fact that lower, nonfarming, income groups lack decent homes.

The National Housing Committee, of which the Editor of the *Forum* is a member, is a private organization with headquarters in Washington. Monsignor John A. Ryan is chairman. This committee recently issued a report on the housing shortage for non-farming families in the United States. For those who can afford to pay $30 a month or more, according to the report, there is no shortage of housing; this group is well supplied already with decent homes. For those who can afford to pay $10 to $20 a month in rent there appears to be a shortage of 1,405,779 units. This is 69 per cent of the total shortage. There are needed 146,409 units for those who can afford only $10 a month and 435,370 dwelling units for families who can pay $20 to $30 a month. In other words there is a latent market for 2,000,000 dwelling units outside the farming groups.[7]

It is a sad commentary on the condition of affairs today that, although real estate is at a low level due to the depression and the need of many owners to sell in order to get cash for other needs, buyers of individual homes now on the market are few and far between.

4. *The industrial worker too often is mechanized, reduced to a subhuman condition because he has been made an irresponsible workman.*

The following excerpts from three different writers present the issue clearly and succinctly:

We are witnessing nowadays not the control of machines by men, but the control of men by machines. . . . Every day fresh improve-

---

[6] Chenery, W. L., *Industry and Human Welfare* (New York: Macmillan Co.), p. 116.
[7] Leach, H. G., "A Housing Era," in *Forum,* Feb., 1938, p. 66.

ments are being made, more and more machines are becoming automatic, that is to say the human workman is becoming less and less necessary. More and more the human workman is becoming simply a minder or tender of machinery, and less and less is he responsible for the form and quality of what the machine turns out.[8]

Mechanical labor injures a man psychically and stunts his personality. Men who labor under such conditions cease to be normal; and ceasing to be normal they seek not culture in their leisure time but external distractions, for the pursuit of culture demands a measure of mental concentration and self-control of which they are incapable.[9]

If each new invention, if each new automatic machine, if each new factory means a degradation of a particular type of labor, then cumulative inventions, cumulative labor-saving machinery, cumulative industrialization, must involve a cumulative degradation of labor. With the perfection of factory production, the degradation would reach its apex. The work he did would express nothing of the worker's own capacities. The worker would become an automaton. He would have to compensate himself for his dehumanized labor by the increased joy which he would get out of the consumption of the things which greater production and lower prices would enable him to buy. Having been cheated out of all chance to get happiness out of his work, he would have to be satisfied with the happiness he could extract from an ever-increasing consumption of factory-made products.[10]

To stifle the potentialities of a worker gifted with a spiritual faculty that, if developed, would take pride in creative work and responsibility, is to blind oneself to the nature of a person — a sin too often committed by the custodians of the industrial system. The father of a family, blunted by monotonous work in a factory where the less intelligence he displays and the more he conforms to a clockwork performance of a mechanical task the better he is valued, is unable to fulfill the duty of guiding his children, to open their eyes to new wonders, or to enjoy playful leisure with them.

Mother and Children

The mother, lacking sufficient money for the management of the household, frequently resorts to sinful measures to prevent

---

[8] Gill, Eric, *Work and Property* (London: Hague and Gill, Ltd.), pp. 19, 20.
[9] Penty, Arthur, *Means and Ends* (London: Faber and Faber), pp. 99, 100.
[10] Borsodi, Ralph, *This Ugly Civilization* (Harper Bros., 1933), p. 145.

the arrival of additional children. Often too she is compelled to enter the business and industrial world in order to add her pittance to the weekly wage of the father, and thus the home is imperiled. Children lack her care and guidance if this happens. Besides, their failure to receive a wholesome home life is due to the poor environment of the home of an industrial worker. When a family is devoting all its time and interests to the problem of keeping the wolf from the door, the delights, normal to people, of cultural or recreational leisure, are unknown. Consequently, in a thousand ways, familiar to the social worker, the present setup of the industrial system is ruinous to family life.

Ours is a complex society in which reforms often counteract one another because of ignorance of fundamental issues. To overcome this shortsightedness, it is necessary to repeat again and again that the family is the natural, essential unit of all human society. Choke its activity and the social structure, whatever form it may have assumed, deteriorates. Yet this stunting of the growth of the family is an acknowledged feature of our urban life. Witness a recent commentary appearing in the *American Mercury* of March, 1938:

> Today the disadvantages of marriage are countless; the advantages chiefly a matter of illusion and outworn ideology. Marriage no longer necessarily implies a home. People live in apartments, with their possessions limited to an automobile, a radio, a few small pieces of furniture, some linens, silver, and glassware (chiefly wedding presents), and wearing apparel. Man no longer comes home to mow the lawn or to putter about the yard. He no longer sits up late at night devising a way to finance a new roof, buy tomato plants, and negotiate eyeglasses for Susy and a tonsillectomy for Bill. The landlord finances the roof, tomato plants won't grow in apartments, and most probably there is neither a Susy nor a Bill.[11]

This is indeed a setting wholly different from that of an English home of fifty years ago which, Douglas Jerrold, in his *Georgian Adventure,* says "bound its occupants to the past and gave them a sense of responsibility for its preservation in the future." Tradition is the leaven of society. A home that has witnessed the birth and death of generations of the same family

---

[11] "Why Get Married" in *American Mercury,* March, 1938, pp. 270, 271.

gives to each succeeding group ideals, a worth-while legacy from the past. Life is deeply significant when these ideals, cherished by ancestors, are imperishable, being deeply rooted in human nature. Incidentally, too, it was the members of such households who entered the political, professional, and literary worlds of their day and endeavored to impart to others the fruit of mature judgments. Such men and women did not miss the forest for the trees and they saw passing vogues for what they were, flotsam and jetsam on the surface of society. These men also were illustrative of the principle that "being" is more important than "change." And it is this valuable apothegm that has been nullified with the advent of the industrial city. The old homes personified familial solidarity; the new glorify familial divergence.

It would not be unkind to say that a city block has no soul. There is no common interest that could bind the many families living there into an organic whole. Industry, because of its concern with individuals, rather than with the family, has promoted the cleavage. According to H. Robbins, "it demands what biologists call 'segregation of unit characters.' That is, while the bulk of the industrial personnel, necessarily and under any conceivable political system, are deprived of integral responsibility, a minority have thrust upon them an undue strain of responsibility which is almost as fatal to human integrity as is the work of the 'single operation slave.'" Individualism in industry has been paralleled by individualism in the home. Nowadays occupational and social interests blaze a trail away from the hearth.

When the family ceases to be the natural, essential unit of economic life, it also ceases to be the natural unit of social life. Intellects, dulled and rendered stagnant by mechanical work in a factory, cannot be restored during the hours of leisure. Consequently, instead of creative enjoyment within the home being the nucleus of the social activity of a family, and because urban families in general are not bound together in a common, personal social life, a vast system of commercialized pleasure has been introduced. The family suffers. The home is now little more than an inn, a stopping-off place for eating and sleeping. It is foolhardy to talk of family loyalty or a wholesome gregariousness when old and young prance here and there, satisfied with ephemeral and synthetic pleasures. The poet's, "evening bringing all things home," has lost its connotation of twilight reuniting a scattered family. Today it refers rather to the witching hour, midnight, and the return of the nighttime revelers with one idea — to bed and quickly. In all this craze for pleasure seeking, passivity is dominant, creativeness conspicuous by its absence. Instead of manufacturing their own enjoyment, thus to stimulate the faculties given them by God, people allow others to attend to this phase of their lives until it has become a big business, the deleterious effects of which can be gauged by the admission of movie magnates who, when assailed for the intellectually inferior brand of pictures emanating from Hollywood, avowed that the average intelligence of Americans, to judge by the infallible box office, is slightly above that of a thirteen year old; in other words, moronic. Nevertheless no sensible person would want to banish all entertainment which is to be had outside the home. What must be decried, however, is the completeness with which passive enjoyment has won the day, and the disappearance of the home as a center for the unifying of life.

To a careful observer of an urban milieu, it is evident that the social structure today is composed of numerous quasi-societies whose reason for existence is the accumulation of profits protected by legal privileges. And by this encroachment on the economic and social activities of natural units, they have destroyed the organic character of life. These artificial class organizations are subversive of the two elements that guarantee security to the commonwealth; namely, the rural farm home and domestic solidarity in the city. This condition can be remedied only by a program that will adjust the relative economic equilibrium of local, natural units and provide those cultural and social elements essential for the reconstruction of the home. Units, natural and according to human scale, must be restored to vital function and vigorous, though perhaps limited, activity.

Seemingly paradoxical, it is nevertheless true that the good things in urban life will not be preserved unless supported by a sympathetic and practical attitude toward the land. When everything rural is scornfully dubbed "hayseed," the economic foundation of society is being undermined. That this is a destructive

The Urban Family in Mass Production 63

position is startlingly revealed in a comment of Stuart Chase in *Survey Graphic:*

> To give an overall picture, we are informed by the National Resources Committee that at least one half of the original fertility of the American continent has disappeared through water and wind erosion, and mining the soil for crops. . . . What are we, or our children, going to swap for automobiles, washing machines and electric ice boxes when we have nothing below our feet to offer in exchange. . . . It is an interesting question. It is interesting to know that already some ten million Americans have lost their resources base in land, water or mineral deposit and have nothing to exchange. So they go on relief.[12]

Likewise H. Robbins, Editor of *The Cross and the Plough,* organ of the Catholic Land Associations of England and Wales, observes that "of all forms of natural life, that of the farmer is the archtype. Next to it is that of the craftsman, who deals directly with realities. Whatever other forms of natural life there may be, these two are primary and secondary." The land existed before the advent of money. It endured throughout the changes in monetary systems, and will undoubtedly be with us even if money should cease to be the medium of exchange. Rightly, then, it is called the *"good"* earth. Directly it provides sustenance to the farmer, and indirectly to the dweller in cities who must depend on the activity of intermediaries in order to procure these necessaries, a fact which proves that in reality the distance between a penthouse and a farm is not as great as some New Yorkers imagine.

The important question of part-time farming for industrial families will be fully dealt with later on in this volume, particularly in Chapter 10, "Part-Time Farming: Soil and Industry." It is here, as we shall see, that the family is restored to its true function, making possible the building up of a true Christian Democracy, and so aiding the welfare of the community and the nation.

City Work and Play Do Not Unite the Family

The typical work of city wage earners does not bind them more closely to their own families. The farm family is an eco-

---
[12] Chase, Stuart, in *Survey Graphic,* Dec., 1937, p. 625.

nomic unit, but work in the office or factory takes a man away from his home. Not only is the father of a family taken outside the house circle by his work, but commonly sons, daughters, and even at times the mother, are drawn from the home to different places of employment. The work has nothing to do with the real family activities of the father, son or daughter; hence their work tends to draw them away from the home. The farm family is actually employed in building its home and supplying its need. City life is crowded; many children leave from their earliest years to find their fun away from home. We are all familiar with the idea that the city's bright lights and the distractions of its amusements tend to draw young people away from home. The city tends to draw the family apart, in that the members make contacts with different acquaintances who have different activities. We are all familiar with the picture. We know from experience the attractions of city amusements. We know that many of the entertainments, theatrical, musical, or even the simple business of keeping in motion, are vicious attractions. The distractions can come to replace home life so that in many cases children are not desired.

The Great Modern Evil

Artificial birth control is the insidious sin. It completes the breakdown of family life. Our falling birth rate is undoubtedly due largely to economic restrictions. The birth rate declines, of course, also among well-to-do families. Fashionable suburbs are occupied by the type that can best afford to raise children, and provide them with the education and background desirable. But fashionable suburbs do not harbor large families. The apartment and suburban rich are not even reproducing themselves. Many young married people feel they are too poor to rear children in the city. They fall into the evil practice of artificial birth prevention. On the other hand the small farm demands more helpers; it is the hope of our future generations.

Danger of Decline

Even in the world of economics, a falling birth rate is held to be a great evil. As a race we certainly do not care to pass out of existence. We do not wish to decline and disappear under the attack of some virile race of savages. But unless our families and our homes work for the strong and numerous youthful generation of tomorrow, this is not a remote conjecture. A steady decline in birth means, first of all, that we become a nation of old people. Since 1921 there have been 60,000 less babies born every year. The business of producing baby shoes is on the downward trend. The buying group in our nation dwindles. The demand for our industrial and agricultural products shrinks. There comes a smaller demand for housing, clothing, and even for what is called the luxuries of life. The attendance at football games will drop. Old folks do not go to these pageants of youth. Perhaps, the best business to enter will be the production of false teeth.

Cities: The Graveyards of the Family

The gradual disappearance of the normal family may be traced to the decline of births which follows immigration to the cities. Dr. O. E. Baker gives the record of this decline in population in the *Catholic Rural Life Objectives:*

> With urbanization the nation is becoming middle-aged, and the prospect is that old age will creep upon it prematurely — only twenty five to fifty years hence. During the next quarter of a century there should be the strength of middle age, and then, unless the birth rate rises, or there is heavy immigration from abroad, a decline will set in. No nation can suffer such a decrease — over twenty per cent — and not suffer the decline in strength that accompanies a rapid aging of the population.[13]

The population of the United States has become largely urban. For the purpose of comparative studies the rural population is taken to be that which lives in the open country plus the inhabitants of villages and towns under 2,500 in population. The urban population is taken to be that which lives in all cities, towns, or villages of more than 2,500 inhabitants. The movement toward the larger population units is very marked during the past sixty years. In 1880 the population was still 71 per cent rural

---

[13] Baker, Dr. O. E., "Population Trends" in *Catholic Rural Life Objectives,* Series I, 1936, p. 7.

and 29 per cent urban. In 1890 the rural percentage was 64. In 1930 the rural percentage of population had diminished to 43. In 1935 the percentage of American population *actually residing on farms* was placed at 25 per cent. Relative to employment statistics, in 1870, 51 per cent of the employed population worked in agriculture. In 1930 this employment percentage had decreased to 21 per cent. Interesting statistics are available for each state. In 1900, Iowa was 56 per cent rural; in 1910, 50 per cent rural; in 1920, 43 per cent rural; and in 1930, 41 per cent rural. And Iowa cities over 2,500 in population grew as follows: in 1910, 30 per cent; in 1920, 36 per cent; and in 1930, 39 per cent. In 1937, 16,000 young men and women left the farms of Iowa.

It is revealing to learn through the careful study of statistics on centralization made by Dr. Ralph L. Woods in his book, *America Reborn* (Longmans, 1939), that 20 per cent of our entire population resides in five metropolitan districts; that one seventh of 1 per cent of the nation's land area now contains 43.8 per cent of all the wage jobs; that two thirds of all the factory jobs are to be found in a few concentrated areas which constitute only 5 per cent of the total national land area. Recently a group of television engineers made a careful survey to determine where the television transmitters would have to be built in order to reach the greatest number of people. At present the range of the television transmitter is very limited, because television is broadcast on very short waves, which are effective only as far as the horizon. The transmission is effective only as far as one can see from the place where the transmitting antenna is situated. At this point there must be another transmission. The NBC's transmitter at the top of the Empire State Building has a range of about 45 miles. In their survey the television engineers found that, if 96 television transmission stations were strategically placed, television broadcasts would reach half the population of this country. In other words, half the population of this country lives and works in 96 highly concentrated urban areas.

An interesting study in connection with the urbanization and the cityward trends is the study of birth rates. In 1800 there were 976 children under five years of age for every thousand women of childbearing age (15–44), whereas in 1930 there were only 350

The Urban Family in Mass Production

children under five years of age for every one thousand women of childbearing age. The following chart shows how the birth rate has been decreasing in the United States for over a century.

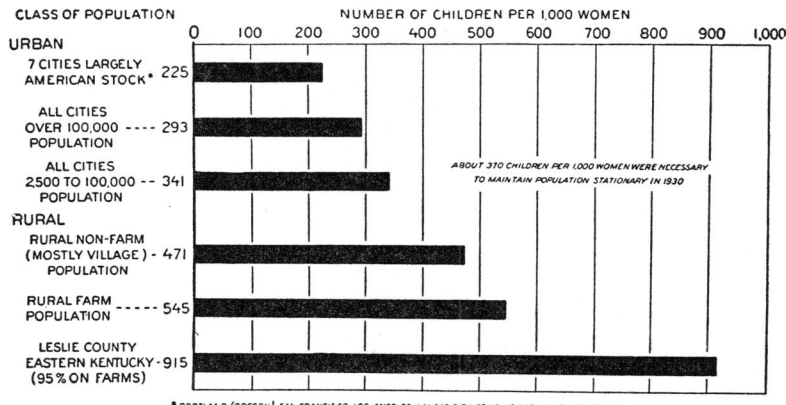

NUMBER OF CHILDREN UNDER 5 YEARS OF AGE PER 1,000 WOMEN 15 TO 44 YEARS OF AGE ON APRIL 1, 1930. URBAN COMPARED WITH RURAL POPULATION IN UNITED STATES

*PORTLAND (OREGON), SAN FRANCISCO, LOS ANGELES, KANSAS CITY, ST LOUIS, NASHVILLE, AND ATLANTA

The great decline shown at the end of the decades 1850, 1870, and 1890 is accounted for by an abnormal under-enumeration of young children, but for the rest the decline from 1920 to 1930 was over twice as rapid as in previous decades, while the drop from 1930 to 1934 equaled that of almost any previous decade.

The following chart gives the urban and rural distribution of the 407 children per one thousand women — the birth ratio which existed in 1930. About 360 children under five years of age per one thousand women, are required to maintain stationary population when the expectancy of life is 61 years, as it was in 1930. These figures indicate therefore a deficit of nearly 20 per cent in all cities over 100,000 population. The smaller cities had a deficit of about 6 per cent. The rural population had a birth surplus of about 40 per cent. This rural surplus often balances the urban deficits, but a national deficit, or decline from the number required for a national stationary population has manifested itself from time to time.

In 1910 the census of that year was made to serve as a basis

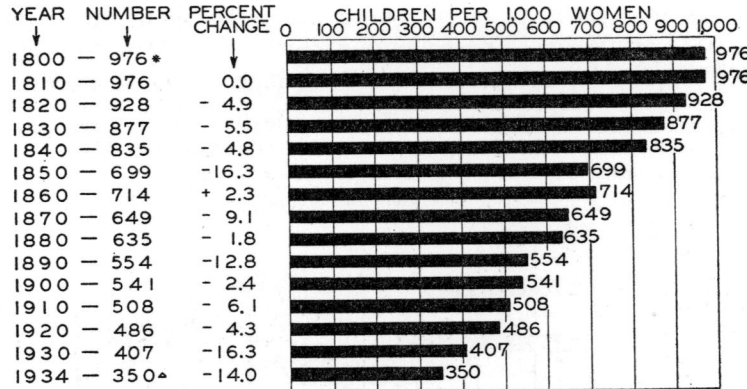

for the study of birth rates in a number of selected counties in accordance with the occupation of the husbands. The following chart indicates the degree of difference in the number of births.

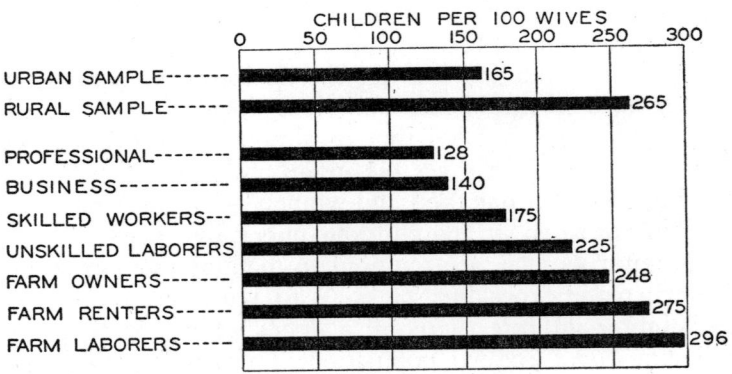

The following chart tells the story of how the nation is quickly growing old. In 1870 about 45 per cent of the population was between the ages of 20 and 60. In 1930, 52.6 of the population was between the ages of 20 and 60. From the trends that we have it is estimated that in 1980, 55 per cent of the population will be between the ages of 20 and 60.

The Urban Family in Mass Production 69

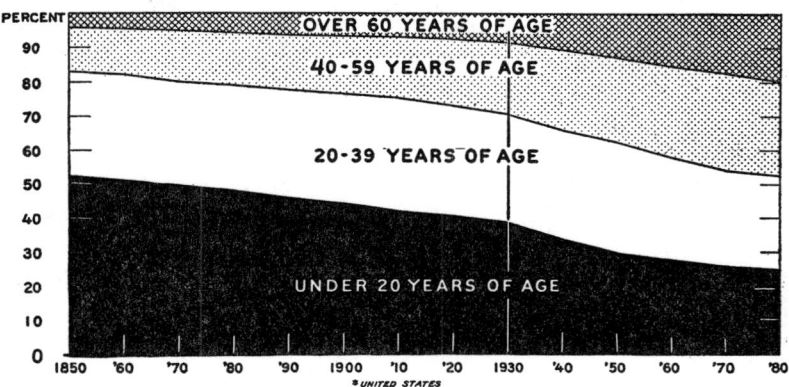

PROPORTION OF THE POPULATION IN VARIOUS AGE GROUPS, 1850-1930, AND THOMPSON'S AND WHELPTON'S "LOW" ESTIMATE, 1930-1980*

The charts and the figures of the Bureau of Agricultural Economics, prepared under the direction of Dr. O. E. Baker, tell the story of population declines which accompany our urbanization and the abandonment of the land. The New York *Times* in November, 1938, told the same story of how the family shrinks. It gave the method used by the administrators of relief to find the number of beneficiaries in the average family. They multiply the number of relief clients by 3.9. In other words the standard family according to relief statistics now consists of 3.9 persons. In 1910 the average family consisted of 4.5 persons, in 1920, 4.3 persons, in 1930, 4.1 persons, and in 1938 the average family consisted of 3.9 persons.

The rural and urban reproduction rates, according to present birth ratios, may be indicated as follows:

Descendants in 25-Year Periods

Cities: 10 Mothers	−7	−5	−3.5
Rural: 10 Mothers	−13	−17	−22

Nearly *four* children are required per childbearing mother in order to keep the population stationary. In this connection we must remember that only 55 per cent of the women reproduce the race. Fifteen per cent of the women die before they reach the age of 21, 15 per cent do not marry, and the other 15 per cent are sterile.

According to some estimates there are in the United States 21 million couples of childbearing age. Seven million of these couples of childbearing age have no children, five million of them have one child, four million have two children, and the remaining five million have three or more children.

Within recent years there has been a 31-per-cent drop in birth rate in South Carolina. In the years 1918 to 1921 and the years 1929 to 1931, Illinois, New York, New Jersey, Connecticut, California, Rhode Island, Oregon, Massachusetts, and Washington dropped below the number of four children per family — the number required for a stationary population.[14]

Graduates of Harvard in 1800 averaged eight children per family. Graduates of Harvard in 1930 average 0.5 children per family. The 633 graduates of Western Reserve University in 1915, who are now married, have 617 children in their families.

If these general American family statistics apply to Catholics, then we will have the following results. In 1939 there are approximately 20,000,000 Catholics. Sixteen million or 80 per cent are urban Catholics, and four million or 20 per cent are rural Catholics. When we apply the present urban and rural rates of increase over a period of one hundred years we get the following interesting results: If the rates apply and if urbanization and other trends continue, then in the year A.D. 2000 there would be in the United States five million urban Catholics and nine million rural Catholics.

For very many reasons it is time to study the family and the home and to work for their restoration. Should the nation have more or less people on the land? Undoubtedly there should be more people on the land engaged either in part-time or full-time farming; but there is no need for more farmers who will follow the destructive industrialized methods of commercial farmers. There is much room on the land for many people with the correct rural philosophy of life, much room for more real homes, more economic security, more children, more loyalty to the

---

[14] Insurance statistics and the Bureau of Agricultural Economics.

family and to national ideals. The land is the foundation of the family and the family is the foundation of the State. The small farm, the family farm, can be a veritable beehive of activities. Many hands are needed. None are unwelcome. Together the members of the family build their little world. The small farm is limited in earning power. Therefore, it is more dependent for self-support for its sustenance. Self-support means varied production and a variety of chores. Such a varied enterprise requires more members. At an early age children can help to lighten the labors and make contributions toward their livelihood without any injury, but with much profit toward their successful development. Work with the land brings them into close contact with fundamental realities — the growth of plant and grain, the work of soil and sun. The marvels of fertility surround country people. They behold the handiwork of God and the marvelous powers of nature working directly and visibly in growing things. In the city it is trade and commerce, money and machinery and monotonous work day after day.

Denmark, Sweden, Norway, Finland, Ireland, and to a great extent Switzerland, are countries of agriculture with family farms and small owners. Switzerland is largely agricultural; much of its advanced industry is still in the hands of small owners, craftsmen, watchmakers, and lacemakers. The people of these countries are God fearing; they raise their children in piety. Knowledge of God is the normal possession of rural parents and it is easily handed down to their children. One may say that this condition is easy to develop in a small nation. What is the answer? Suppose we transplanted two million New Yorkers to Finland to replace the population of that country, and organized them into city life, a replica of New York, based on mass production and centralized corporation control. Would we have a nation of God-fearing people, happy in their peaceful, useful, thrifty, economic organization, just as we had when the country was agricultural? It is rather obvious that the answer is, no!

In 1788 George Washington wrote to Thomas Jefferson as follows:

I perfectly agree with you that the introduction of anything which will divert our attention from agriculture must be extremely prejudicial, if not ruinous to us.

Benjamin Franklin held to the same view and he believed that as long as our interests were chiefly agricultural, our governments would remain virtuous, but that if we should ever get piled upon one another in large cities, as in Europe, then corruption would come. It is not pleasant to compare the reality in the United States today with the visions that the Founders had for it. When they looked at the fertile unravished West their thoughts were agricultural, not industrial, and they felt that Providence had designed this country for a new experiment where human life would be really free in a living democracy of homes and many small holdings. They thought that for most of the people there would be the peaceful setting of the farmer at his labor, removed from the hubbub of the industrial world with its tensions and rush and general commotion, its barrage of senseless advertising, its tabloids and indecent shows. Washington and Jefferson and Franklin thought that the generations in this great new country would always be sufficiently removed from the selfishness and greed which grows rampant when all is reduced to commerce and trade, when there is legalized robbery in high and complicated finance, and when there is concentrated factory industrialism. They thought that the greater part of the men and women of America would always be in the healthier atmosphere of the fields and their own farm homes and small communities. It would make them sad to learn how we have left the fields and piled ourselves up around the smokestacks of giant factories, and how squalor and sordidness and moral decay have entered into our lives.

We have two billion acres of land. We can decentralize our citizens. We are not forced to cram them into crowded districts. But somehow we have lost our land consciousness. When there is question of removing a slum, we build another slum on the very same spot. Our foolish cure for congested housing is to build a new congested house on the very spot of congestion, whether it be in New York, or Chicago, or St. Louis or any of the other smoke-defiled centers of proletarianism.

Chapter 5

THE RURAL FAMILY IN MASS PRODUCTION

Proletarianism in the Fields

INCORPORATED capital, with its profit-seeking, stockholding, and its mechanized, dehumanized proletariat, makes its bid today for the concentration of the last form of productive property which is operated in family units. It is setting up its "chain" farms, its "factory" farms, its wheat corporations, cattle corporations, fruit corporations, cotton corporations, sugar corporations, corn-hog corporations, etc. Under large-scale, commercialized, highly specialized cash-crop systems, the land becomes simply another factory for the exploitation of natural resources in the commercialized production of food and raw materials. Titles to land are concentrated in the hands of financial groups and with this concentration of ownership a new rural proletariat rises up on the land to take its place alongside the urban proletariat. Commercialism and its materialistic philosophy have led us to the point where we no longer appreciate the fact that agriculture and the land have an infinitely larger job in the life of any nation than the mere production of the nation's food supply and raw materials; namely, the building of better homes, better families, better hearts, better farms.

Commercialized farming on the family basis leads us into practically all the fallacies of corporation farming. When the family-farm owner and operator gambles in a special cash crop, and large-scale production, the result is that sooner or later banks, insurance companies, and other investment companies become the landowners. Then both companies and tenants rob the land of its substance, for the commercial investor will have nothing of diversified, subsistence farming; and the tenants, though they may prefer a less commercial land use, will nevertheless be compelled to follow the general profit-driving system. With the coming of farm service departments and company managers and agricultural charters, the landowning companies take over operations, and in consequence tenants become mere workers. They must abandon the land completely when massive machinery and cheaper labor is available.

Corporation Farming: A Public Menace

In 1932 the State of Kansas appealed to its Supreme Court for the abolition of a farm corporation — The Wheat Farming Corporation. This land company had obtained a Kansas Charter for agricultural purposes and at the time of the trial was cultivating 64,000 acres in a large-scale mass production, capitalistic fashion. In rendering its decision the court abolished the land company, revoked its charter, and firmly held that such agricultural companies constituted a public menace. Such corporate use of capital in land, the court continued, would destroy the distribution of land among many families, a distribution which had been achieved in some measure through state and national land policies of homesteading.

In this trial the supreme judicial tribunal of Kansas established a legal precedent of great, social, economic, and political significance, if only our leaders will have the wisdom and vision to follow its principles in other states. The decision affords the legal foundation for the preservation of farming as a worth-while, cultural occupation in which the owner of the land is himself the operator and in which there are many other important values beyond mere profit. The Court maintained that such an excellent social and economic institution as the distribution of land for many families was not to be put in jeopardy by grants of agricultural charters to privileged financial groups. It was the firm conviction of the judges that our past land policies were not merely temporary measures, to endure only until finance-capitalism should bring the corporation into agriculture; but that land policies were permanent measures, enacted to give this country a lasting social and economic foundation, permanent measures, promulgated and executed in order to give agriculture a rightful primacy in the lives of our people. In the opinion of the court the basic distribution of land and the family-owned and operated farm would not be permanent if agricultural companies and absentee landlords were favored.

And yet today, with commercialism to the right of us, commercialism to the left of us, commercialism above us, commercialism below us, and the worship of its sprawling gods around us — it will require more than one State Supreme Court decision to safeguard the future continuation of the good economics, the social values, the cultural advantages, and the security of our democratic principles through the preservation of a well-distributed freehold private ownership of farms by individuals operating with their families as the basic economic unit. The joint-stock companies or business corporations must not be allowed to displace them. The states which invented the sweeping charters for corporations in all enterprise have swept out whatever policies or limitations in corporate landownership that might have been established. Our people steeped in commercialism are now quite willing to see something else substituted for the family-owned and family-operated farm. The corporation, they predict, will mechanize the farm work and produce all crops with the extension of factory methods on the land. Those who can see no distinction between collectivism, concentration, commercialism on the one hand, and private ownership, private property, and private operation with the use of the family unit on the other, are already speaking of the vast, colossal farm corporation which will come to the fore to take its place with General Motors, American Telegraph, and Bethlehem Steel. Already they proudly boast of ten thousand agricultural companies and their income-tax reports. They favor an early use of the monopolizing, merging process, and they look for the day when *General Farms Incorporated* will send out its managers over its far-flung agricultural domain.

The Small-Family Farm

The homestead distribution of land, on the family-ownership and family-operation basis, was the system that we once used to build this free and democratic nation. This is the landownership structure that we must retain in order to preserve our freedom and democracy. But in the settlement of our pioneer families we often manifested woeful ignorance about soil and climatic conditions, encouraging many families to acquire the ownership of land that was submarginal — unable to sustain a family in comfort and with modern conveniences under any type of farm economy. In their efforts to remain on such land the farmers accepted a mortgage system devised by bankers who were attracted by high interest and inflated land values rather than by any concern about the welfare of farm families. In the more favored regions, excellent for the practice of an agrarian economy, where extreme droughts and submarginal acres did not run the farmers into debt, there commercialized, single-crop, factory-method, overmechanized farming with soil exploitation and land speculation brought an indebtedness. And after all these years foreclosures or transfer of deed to the mortgage holder seems to be about the only remedy, if it may be called a remedy, which is used. Some very weak efforts have been made to readjust debts and reduce interest rates, teach soil conservation and better methods of diversified farming with a supply of food for the farm home and a supply of feeds for livestock. In the meantime banks, land companies, insurance companies, and absentee landlords go busily on, gathering in the title deeds to farms.

The people on the land are moving down the agricultural ladder. Owners become tenants; tenants become sharecroppers; sharecroppers become workers. And the day of the land proletariat has arrived. The tables on the following pages indicate the growth of incorporated agriculture, some of the high tenancy rates, and the extent of commercialism on the land.

In 1926, the Bureau of Internal Revenue reported that nine thousand corporation farms had filed income-tax returns. The United States Chamber of Commerce made an analysis of 74 such farms in various sections of the country. The average acreage of each in this group was 11,797 acres, and the average capitalization was $553,743. In the group there was one general farm which contained 300,000 acres. One of the farms was a sugar plantation capitalized at $3,350,000. Another was a dairy farm with a gross income average of over $600,000 annually. In 1926 the gross in-

The Rural Family in Mass Production

come from the factory farms was $709,000,000. In this year this total was almost 6 per cent of the total gross income from American Agriculture.

Factory Farms[1]

Corporation	Acres	State
Miller and Lux, Inc.	400,000	California
Campbell Farming Corporation	95,000	Montana
Sibley Farms	12,000	Illinois
Miller Brothers	110,000	Oklahoma
Citizen's National Bank	10,000	Illinois
Albert M. Todd Farm	10,640	Michigan
San Jacinto Rice Co.	30,000	Texas

Within the past few years the Metropolitan Life Insurance Company has become the owner of a vast agricultural empire of 1,618,000 acres. This empire contains enough land to make a farm one mile in width extending from New York to Los Angeles. Since the depression years numerous nonfarm organizations find themselves in the possession of a chain of farms, numbering from ten to one hundred farms. Some banks and insurance companies hold many more. Individual farms in the hands of private individuals have also become much larger. In Musselshell County, Montana, in 1920, 1,604 farms had an average size of 623 acres. In this same county, in 1925, 650 farms had an average size of 758 acres. In Logan County, Kansas, in 1910, 809 farms averaged 562 acres, and in 1925, 582 farms averaged 911 acres.

In its work in 1937 the Iowa Tenancy Committee[2] found a decided relationship existing between the size of farms and the rate of tenancy. In a group of Iowa counties where 87 per cent of the farms were over one hundred acres, the tenancy rate was 60 per cent. In a second group of counties where 71 per cent of the farms were over one hundred acres, the tenancy rate was 51 per cent. And in a third group of counties, where 64 per cent of the farms were over one hundred acres, the tenancy rate was 38 per cent. The graph on page 79 shows the relationship of ownership and tenancy of smaller farms based upon three groups of counties.

---

[1] For a complete list of such farms see *Bulletin of United States Department of Agriculture* (BAE), "Large Scale and Corporation Farming" (Nov., 1929), Margaret T. Olcott.

[2] Cf. Appendix: "Farm Tenancy Committee Report — Iowa."

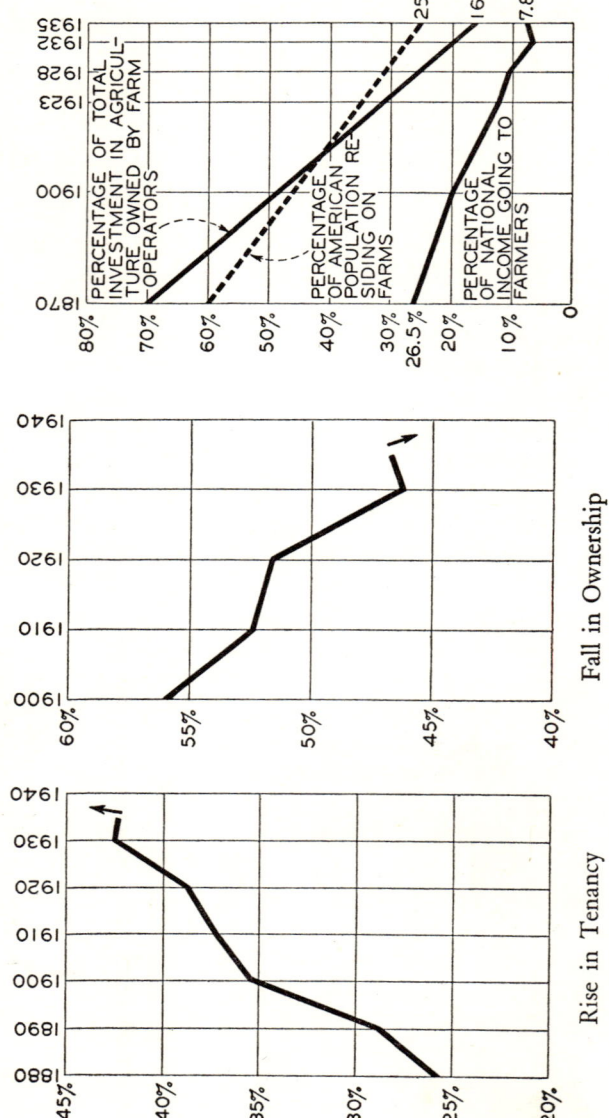

The Rural Family in Mass Production 79

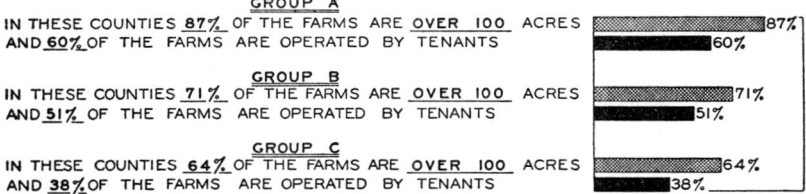

GROUP A
IN THESE COUNTIES 87% OF THE FARMS ARE OVER 100 ACRES
AND 60% OF THE FARMS ARE OPERATED BY TENANTS

GROUP B
IN THESE COUNTIES 71% OF THE FARMS ARE OVER 100 ACRES
AND 51% OF THE FARMS ARE OPERATED BY TENANTS

GROUP C
IN THESE COUNTIES 64% OF THE FARMS ARE OVER 100 ACRES
AND 38% OF THE FARMS ARE OPERATED BY TENANTS

The graphs on page 78 show the tragic picture of the ownership of American agriculture. The figures are based on the United States census.

This loss of ownership and rise in tenancy is repeated in each individual state with but slight variations. For example, in the State of Nebraska in 1910, 45 per cent of the farmers owned their farms, 17 per cent were part owners, and 38 per cent were tenants. In 1935, 50 per cent of the farmers of Nebraska were tenants, 32 per cent were part owners, and only 18 per cent had retained the ownership of their farms. The Department of Agriculture made a study of the equities in land in 1930. The table compiled from

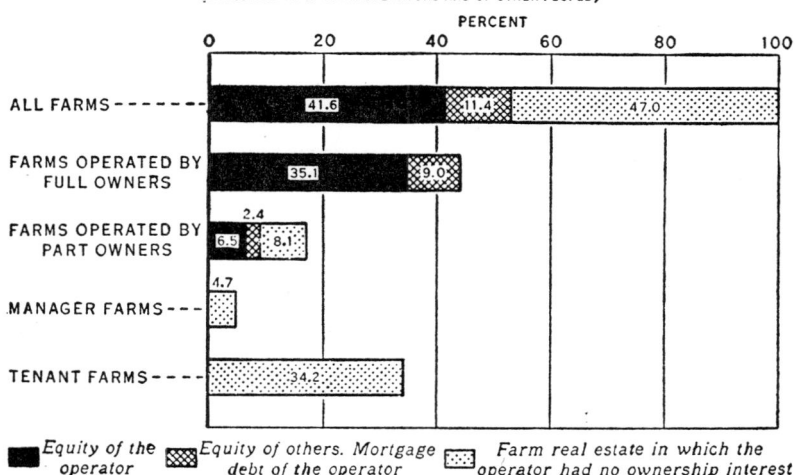

EQUITIES IN FARM REAL ESTATE, UNITED STATES, 1930
(INVESTMENTS OF FARM OPERATORS AND OF OTHER PEOPLE)

the figures available at that time showed that the land operator's equity was but a little more than 41 per cent of the total equities in land.

In its land studies in 1930 the Department of Agriculture found that the value of the farm dwelling was generally much greater where the land was owned by the operator. Under a system of tenancy such as prevails in the United States no one takes an interest in good housing on the land of the absentee landlord, neither the landlord nor the tenant. The following graph illustrates the value of farm dwellings in relation to tenure of land by the operator of the farm.

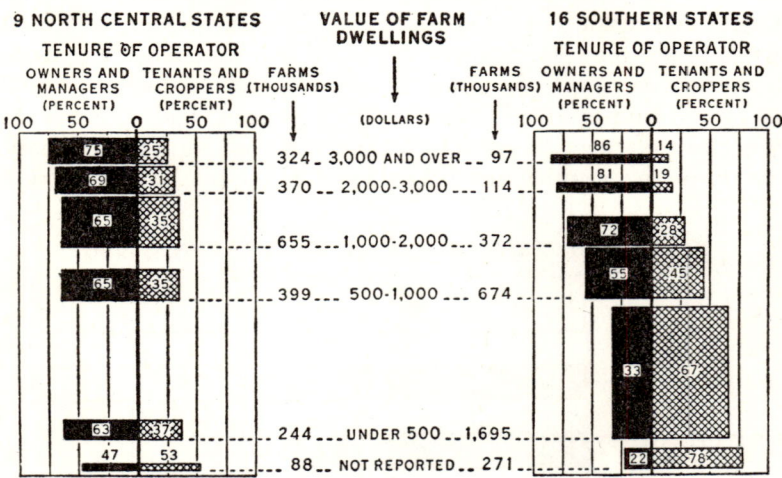

VALUE OF FARM DWELLING IN RELATION TO TENURE OF FARM OPERATOR
9 North Central Compared with 16 Southern States, 1930

The Department of Agriculture made a further study of 489 counties to find if any relationship existed between tenancy and the practice of a greater commercialism on the land, i.e., production for cash markets and securing necessities such as the food supply through the commercial economy rather than through the domestic economy or "production-on-the-land-for-family-use" and the farm production of feeds for livestock. This study of 489 counties revealed that there was a marked relationship between the rate of tenancy and the degree of commercialistic economy used

The beauty and security of farm life are suggested in this Dairy Farm in Lancaster County, Pa.

— Farm Security

The Rural Family in Mass Production 81

by the rural family. Self-sufficiency, or production for home use, [is m]uch less among tenant groups. It must be remembered that [polic]ies of absentee landlords whose outlook is commercial, [the polic]y of the migrant tenants whose outlook is exploitive, and [the] highly commercial nature of many rent contracts remove many opportunities for the practice of domestic economies in the case of tenant families. In counties where the tenancy rate was 49 per cent, the production for home use was less than 10 per cent; where the tenancy rate was 35 per cent, production for home use was from 10 to 15 per cent; in counties where the tenancy rate was 29 per cent, production for home use averaged from 15 to 20 per cent; and where the tenancy rate was 23 per cent, production for home use exceeded 20 per cent. Landowners tend to follow the more efficient economy of production for use on the homestead as can be judged by the following graph.

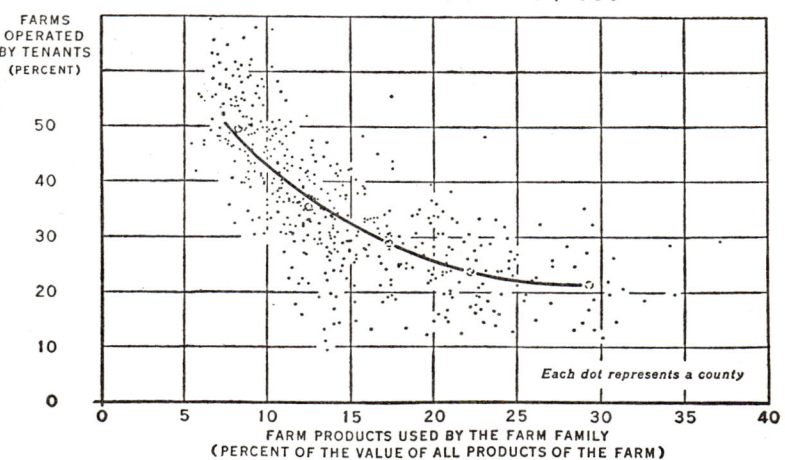

PERCENTAGE OF FARM PRODUCTS USED BY THE FARM FAMILY IN RELATION TO PERCENTAGE OF FARMS OPERATED BY TENANTS, NORTH CENTRAL STATES*, 1930

* THE 489 COUNTIES COMPRISE ALL COUNTIES OF OHIO, INDIANA, ILLINOIS, IOWA, AND ALL BUT THE SEVEN MORE IMPORTANT COTTON-PRODUCING COUNTIES OF MISSOURI

Within the past twenty years 600,000 farm owners lost their holdings in land. The loss of this family ownership in productive property is an economic disaster. In 1880, 75 per cent of the farms were owned by the families who operated them. Today more than

50 per cent of the farms are owned by absentee landlords. This alarming increase in farm tenancy and the problem of landownership are matters of vital, national concern. Some of the most significant contributions that pioneer farmers left as a heritage to American democracy are in danger of being lost.

Tenancy is a destructive force in society. The existence of almost three million tenant families on the land, the members of whose households constitute approximately thirteen million people, sets up a social problem of the first magnitude. The fact that the rate of tenancy has moved up from 25.6 per cent in 1880 to 42.1 per cent in 1935, and the fact that the number of farm-tenant families has almost trebled between 1880 and 1935 clearly indicates that this condition is being aggravated instead of being alleviated as time goes on. The problem of tenancy has long been a Southern problem, but it is rapidly becoming a Northern problem as well. The decline from farm ownership to tenancy is moving rapidly in all the states, and especially in the more highly developed agricultural states — in Iowa, Ohio, Illinois, Kansas, and Nebraska.

Percentage of Farms Operated by Tenants in Seven of the States[3]

	1930	1935
Kansas	42.0%	44.0%
Illinois	43.1%	44.5%
South Dakota	44.6%	48.6%
Nebraska	47.1%	49.3%
Iowa	47.3%	49.6%
Georgia		65.9%
Mississippi		69.8%

There has been a steady increase in farm tenancy from the year 1880. The rate of increase has varied from decade to decade, but throughout there has been a continual growth in number and percentage of tenants. The following numbers were added each decade in the fifty-year period:

From 1880 to 1890	270,392 new tenants
From 1890 to 1900	730,051 new tenants
From 1900 to 1910	329,712 new tenants
From 1910 to 1920	100,128 new tenants
From 1920 to 1930	209,561 new tenants

[3] Department of Agriculture.

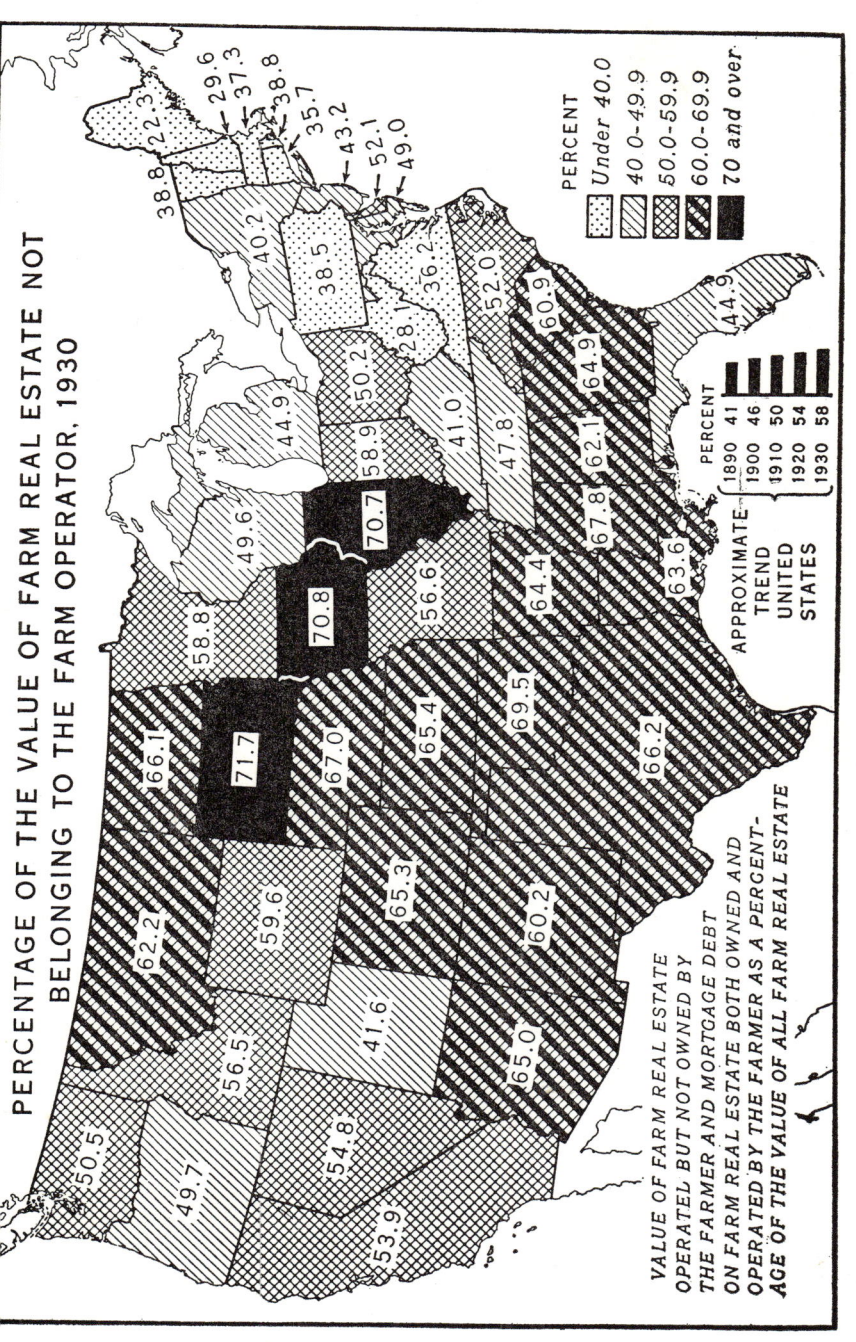

During the years 1930 to 1935 another 200,790 tenants were added to the total. This makes the total number of tenant families 2.8 times as large as in 1880, with a percentage increase from 25.6 per cent to 43 per cent in 1935.[4] The trend should have been toward ownership. In Denmark all tenancy has been removed except 6 per cent. This was accomplished through a wise land-tenure program and an effective use of cooperatives.

But in America we are approaching the strange condition of a democratic society composed of landless tenants. This condition is attested to in the following extract:

> Tenancy is a phase of social development, and the degree to which, either in city or country, families own their homes or rent them is a fairly good but rough measure of the extent and nature of democracy prevailing in any given State or nation. We had as well try to think of a democratic nation composed of men bound to the soil in servile fashion as of a democratic society constituted of landless tenants. A nation is aristocratic or plutocratic in which ownership of land or wealth is concentrated in the hands of relatively few. Where a strong trend exists in the direction of a nation of tenant farmers, we are obliged to think that agriculture is developing toward a condition in which the welfare of the masses of farmers is in jeopardy.[5]

Soil Erosion and Human Erosion

The economic aspect with its soil mining and soil robbery is only one part of the story of a land of landless tenants.[6] The social and spiritual loss is a loss of much greater significance. If the majority of farmers are tenants it is impossible to have a well-ordered community life. Tenants cannot and do not support the institutions of a community whether these be institutions of a social or religious nature. The distributed ownership of the land among tillers of the soil, the mode of settlement of families on the land, and the conditions which make it possible for tenants to rise to ownership are matters of great concern in democratic communities. Sound educational institutions and democratic citizenship go hand in hand with the ownership of farms in the various

---

[4] Cf. *Soils and Men,* Yearbook, 1938, Department of Agriculture. Cf. Also, Report of National Farm Tenancy Comm.
[5] Gillette, J. M., *Rural Sociology* (Macmillan Co., 1936), p. 505.
[6] Cf. Appendix: "Farm Tenancy Report Made to President."

communities by the families who operate them. The President's Farm Tenancy Committee took the problem of farm tenancy seriously. It recommended that a Farm Security Administration be created and that it deal primarily with the evils of tenancy. It points out that Federal and state legislation should aid tenants to become owners, help farm laborers to a better status, protect the debt-burdened farmers against the loss of their farms and conserve farm youth "whose future and insecurity is a threat to the integrity of rural life." The members of the committee were alive to the social and spiritual peril that is inherent in farm tenancy and they pointed out that rural decadence threatens the nation.

At its best, the tenant status is a normal rung on the ladder from farm labor toward farm ownership. Under proper rent contracts, the tenant status could serve as a useful apprenticeship during a period in which one might learn the successful methods of farming. Under properly planned rent contracts the tenant status, since it is a method of farm operation that requires a minimum outlay of capital, could serve for the accumulation of the partial purchase price of a farm. It is true that many farmers are tenants now because of commercialism, high land taxation, and severe foreclosure laws, and because of such conditions these land operators are probably also tenants by choice. They choose tenancy because they wish to follow the prevailing practice of mining out the greatest cash profits within the shortest possible time. There is no long-range planning. It is the general attitude in the city and on the farm to take the most profit today, and to forget about the depressions and the crop failures that will follow.

Tenancy could serve very well, when properly regulated, as a step toward ownership, as an apprenticeship or as a training ground for the acquisition of sound farming knowledge; but in commercial America these ends are not frequently found in the tenant status. As a rule, in all of the states, we have tenancy at its worst, because the rent contracts are short-term contracts; all improvements on a farm are made at the tenant's risk; and finally the absentee owners are primarily land speculators. With these circumstances and conditions present, tenancy forces family living standards below levels of decency, develops rural slums, breeds poverty, illiteracy, and disease. Competition among tenants and the commercial-minded landlords leave tenant familes to live in houses of poor construction, almost universally in need of repair, often without doors and windows, with leaky roofs, and sometimes even without floors. No one is interested in equipping these houses with running water, electricity, or bathrooms. No interest is taken in landscaping or in beautiful surroundings. The yard of the farm home is usually unsightly and devoid of beauty. The tenant family's food is simple, and often bought in the plantation store or in the chain store. It lacks variety and often lacks the essentials of good nutrition. There is no one who has not heard of Southern Pellagra induced by the starvation diet of cornmeal, molasses, and the rejected parts of the hog. Tenant farmers and their families in a great many cases wear clothing which is inadequate for the mere protection of the body. Thousands of families live under such conditions from year to year and incessantly move from farm to farm, from community to community. These migratory families constitute a disintegrating influence upon all social institutions. All forms and types of social participation — recreational, educational, religious — feel the effects of this insecurity and instability. Neighborhood relations are constantly disrupted. School attendance for the children of tenant parents is periodically interrupted. Systematic church attendance and participation in programs of leadership and effective action are impossible. The many benefits of community living and enterprizes undertaken for the common good are wanting to the transient families.

Land and Freedom — Productive Property and Freedom

If a study of the urban proletariat does not make it clear that men are not really free unless they possess completely — i.e., personally own and effectively control — some small holding in productive property, then a careful study of the rural proletariat should make it clear that there is an unmistakable relation between productive property (some land) and a man's freedom and security. The farmers will never achieve economic, social, and spiritual security through continued and rising tenancy. The owner-operated family farm is the only guarantee of the essential democratic liberties and securities.

The Renter a Transient

The agricultural renter is a transient, with no stake in a community, in a parish, in a school, in a cooperative, or in any other community institution. He has no stake in the land which he farms and therefore he neglects it. Statistics of the Department of Agriculture show that the cash renter has only 3.8 years as an average period of occupancy. For share croppers the period of occupancy is 2.8 years. For mortgaged owners, the period of occupancy is 9.2 years. This short tenure period has a destructive influence in many directions, and soon registers its evil results in soil, farm crops, farm livestock, school, church, and other neighborhood institutions. In Nebraska twenty thousand farm families move on the first of March each year. March first is moving day on the land in every state in the Union.

Again, under our system of farm tenancy, should the tenant improve the farm in any way, such as ditching, tilling, fertilizing the soil by outlay of manure or commercial fertilizer or by crop rotation, build fences or make other improvements, the tenant has no legal remedy to recover anything, in case of his removal from the farm. When tenants want specific provisions for reimbursement in the case of such improvements placed in the contracts, landlords look for other tenants.

There is too much ownership of farm land by large and small speculators. Many individuals and corporations buy and sell land today for the unearned increment. Their motive is always to make money by selling and by cash contracts, and cash-producing agriculture. It would be better to call this simply the hurried extraction of all fertility from the soil, a mining process from year to year and certainly not agriculture. There is only the predominant motive of exploitation of land and families and communities.

Whether agricultural lands are to be tilled by tenants or owners, is not a matter of secondary significance. This question is a matter of primary importance in any nation, but especially is it a question of the highest importance in a nation such as ours where we cling to the philosophy of our constitution and hope to build better and better from generation to generation, the democracy which it outlines. Democratic institutions, cultural attainments, cooperative efforts will flourish where the families own the land. When the families do not own the land, the livelihood of millions, the fertility of the soils and local community institutions and responsibilities are continually being broken up or they are at least weakened and undermined to such a degree that there is always insecurity where there should be security, there is always gambling and rugged individualism where there should be cooperation. These conditions will continue unless corrected or checked for we realize that:

> Tenancy like pauperism may become a state of mind. Whenever an individual is pauperized in mind he is practically hopeless. To be pauperized in mind is to be pauperized in soul, which indicates that the mainspring of life, the motivating power, is broken. There is evidence that a large portion of farm tenants in this country remain so for life. . . . The multitude of renters in the South, in the North and in the West have been molded into more or less apathetic acceptance of the status of tenancy by years of disappointment at not being able to scale the ladder of ownership.[7]

In the United States we have two billion acres of land — land which offers an excellent opportunity for the masses of men to acquire ownership and independence. And yet, tenancy with its moral, social, and economic consequences increases at an alarming rate. Under an exploitive land tenure, millions of once fruitful acres lose their fertility, and degrading standards of living are forced on a multitude of farm families. A stake in the land in earlier days gave the family an excellent anchorage, identified it with its rural community, gave it an abiding interest in its local, social institutions, tethered it to law and order, and gave it protection against the inroads of pernicious doctrine. Tides of increasing farm tenancy, however, have brought rural decadence. The wholesale dispossession of farm families is accompanied with the complete loss of the savings of a lifetime and the loss of hope for the future. In many places the tax loads on land are almost confiscatory, especially in certain drainage districts, and in many school districts, especially consolidated school districts. The land once having been lost to the owner is seldom regained.

---

[7] Gillette, J. M., *op. cit.*, p. 505.

No "White Spot" for Farmers

In the State of Nebraska, "The White Spot," we should expect to find the farmers owning their land and free from the burdens of heavy land taxes. When we investigate we find that the "White Spot" has no reference to Nebraska farmers. It refers to the absence of sales taxes and industrial taxes. The "spot" is "white" because these taxes are not levied on Nebraska industries. Nebraska is not an industrial state. If it intends to make a "White Spot," it should make a "White Spot" for its chief economic activity; namely, agriculture. But when we look at the land and its taxes in Nebraska we find that from 1910 to 1935, the farm real-estate values in relation to the total wealth of the state increased from 52 per cent to 54 per cent. During this same period the tax burden borne by agriculture in Nebraska increased from 54 per cent to approximately 70 per cent.

The following table summarizes the percentage of net income consumed by taxes on owner-operated farms in Nebraska, in the West North Central States, and in the United States as a whole.

Ratio of Land Taxes to Net Income on Owner-Operated Farms[8]

Year	Selected Counties in Nebraska	West North Central States	United States
1927	32.2	18.9	18.5
1928	24.2	17.1	18.1
1929	19.1	18.6	19.2
1930	31.2	100.0	75.4

In the years 1927, 1928, and 1929, the relative tax burden borne by owner-operators in Nebraska was somewhat greater than that borne by owner-operators of the West North Central States, and the owner-operators of the United States as a whole. In 1930, however, the burden on Nebraska owner-operators was considerably less than in the other groups. This is not enough though to extend the White Spot advertising to include farmers in Nebraska. It must be remembered that although the income from Nebraska farm property is at present less than 25 per cent of the total income

---
[8] Department of Agricultural Economics, University of Nebraska.

of the residents of Nebraska, almost 70 per cent of the total tax revenue of the state is secured by taxing farm property. In all of our states the tax burden on the land is too great to give any continued security to family landownership and operation. In every state the taxation system should be re-examined with the view of arriving at a more equitable distribution of the state tax burden according to the ability to pay. If the land must continue to pay the greater part of the rising state tax loads, then the states and absentee landlords will soon hold all the titles to farms, and as a consequence family farm ownership, approved throughout American history as a primary means of attaining security, for the family, the community, and finally the nation, will disappear.

Commercialism, inequitable tax burdens, wholesale foreclosures have very undesirable effects upon both land and living standards. Tenant families and rural laborers do not establish constructive contacts with the community: its churches, its schools, and its cooperative organizations. Farmhouses are not improved or repaired, buildings are allowed to deteriorate, crops are not properly rotated, the fields are allowed to erode, and the entire cycle of life on the land is caught in a downward spiral of decadence.

There is no correction for this except a development of a program for secure land tenure with family-unit ownership and operation. Secure tenure changes a man's attitude toward the land. The home is changed when eviction and foreclosure are not continually threatening. Where the prospect of occupancy is reasonably permanent the house will be repaired, improvements made, and trees planted. Intelligent methods of agriculture with a view to maintaining the fertility of the soil will be studied and followed. The tenure stability will increase the family's interest in community activities. Secure tenure removes the faint possibilities for speculative profits, but it increases the opportunities for steady income.

The only way that secure tenure may be had, is through the encouragement and protection of farm-home ownership, and improvements in landlord-tenant relationships. A well-co-ordinated use of both education and legislation will have to be made. Legislation without education and popular support is bound to fail.

The Rural Family in Mass Production

Education of the people in the values of secure land tenure is the most important line of action, but under present conditions education cannot bring about a substantial and lasting betterment in tenure conditions without the assistance of appropriate legislative action. There must be sane measures to prevent land speculation and the concentration of landholdings, especially in the hands of companies that hold titles *in perpetuum* and exist only for profit. In years of crop failure and depression there must be adequate legal protection for the owner-operator's equity in his farm. In most cases it is not the owner's personal disability or incompetence that causes defaults in payments. The farmer's inability to pay is very often the result of national policies which are unfair to agriculture, and to other conditions over which the farmer has no control. Statutory measures must be worked out in the states to give adequate protection to the encumbered landowner, whenever and wherever it is needed.

Tenancy Could Serve As a Step Toward Ownership

Tenancy is important as a step toward ownership. But even when it is used in this way the landlord-tenant relationship should not result in neglect of good techniques on the land. Intelligent agriculture requires that any tenant must be permitted to develop a genuine long-time interest in, and a reasonable security of tenure on a particular farm. Crop rotations with soil-building legumes usually run over four or more years. Frequently limestone must be applied before clover or alfalfa can be grown. Livestock investments must be made. Hay and adequate pastures must be provided for. In fact any intelligent farm program for soil conservation and successful farming must be planned ahead for four or five years. Such plans cannot be followed and will not be followed by the one-year renter or the two-year renter or even the three-year renter. Something should be done to guarantee reasonable security of tenure even under lease contracts. The annual transfer of farms to the highest bidder destroys land resources, the welfare of rural families and rural institutions, and finally the welfare of the entire nation. A simple statute protecting the tenant's equity in farm improvements would go far to help tenants take the initiative in improving the productivity of farms and in making farm homes better places in which to live. Tenants, under the protection of such a statute, would not be outbid by outside tenants. The landlords would not raise the rents because of such improvements, when a statute governing rent contracts wisely makes the landlords or the incoming tenants liable for compensation to the outgoing tenants for the unexhausted values of such improvements. In each state lease forms should be prepared which embody the principles of intelligent agriculture, long-range planning, and other helps for security of tenure on rented farms. These approved model lease forms should be made available in local courthouses, local banks, offices of farm organizations and real-estate offices, and their general use by landlords and tenants should be encouraged by every feasible means.

The Curse of Factory Farming

Tenancy and land speculation constitute a very serious economic menace and should be reduced to a minimum. But there is a more serious economic menace on the horizon which also involves the land, and follows when ownership and tenant systems break down; namely, corporation farming. Although this menace has not progressed very far, yet it is very serious because it is being promoted by the industrialized, urban-minded, mechanized, stock-gambling forces of this generation. The unsound, agricultural technique of corporation farming will ultimately bring this system to naught. But America, unless we do some thinking and take effective action, may try this unsound agriculture too, if for no other reason than that it makes so many promises under the aegis of our American economic idol, the corporation.

Corporation farming will in time destroy itself with its mechanical methods in a field essentially biological, but before this stupidity will reap its empty harvest, our American families will be finally and completely uprooted from the soil. All ownerships will pass to *United Farms Incorporated.* All rural skills, cultural patterns, traditions, communities will be obliterated. In many places, if not in all places, the present farm population will be replaced by people not now engaged in agriculture, for the inefficient land corporations will have great need of imported cheap labor. They will have to reduce the populations in their wheat, corn, cotton, livestock, and fruit factories—their vast soil-mining territories. Any rural homesteads remaining on soil acquired by them will have to be removed. Gigantic, collectivized mass shelters will have to be provided for the men and women and children who will come to the company camps. These laborers may be left to camp on the roadsides as we have witnessed in California and Missouri. Homesteads for these people will be unthinkable. The entire corporation process will make it clear that in its philosophy the giant factory farm is more important than the farmer whom it reduces to the status of the proletarian hired man. Tenancy does much harm to our rural population; but it remains for the land corporation to destroy the farm homes, reduce the farm families to serfs, and erase forever all the economic, social, and spiritual values in our traditionally free and independent, brave and democratic American rural life. This last octopus of Wall Street will drive the remaining families from the land and crush the enterprises upon which they have spent the best years of their life — the personally owned and controlled productive enterprises on which democracy is built. Senator Arthur Capper gives a correct report on corporation farming and its destructive implications when he says:

> Corporation farming is bad public policy. It is dangerous. . . . Every farmer and every business man in rural America and every worker in the big industrial centers should oppose it. I feel that we are justified by the facts as known and the possibilities of the future as indicated by those facts, in using every proper means to nip this corporate farming development before it gets firmly established.[9]

In the areas where farm corporations have picked up the title deeds to their 20,000- and 30,000-acre tracts, the experience of the man, the farm home, the farm family, the school, the church, the community has been a sad one. In these areas social and spiritual leaders have learned what to expect under a system of factory farming. These leaders know that their social, moral, and spiritual institutions are given but a small chance to establish themselves and can never hope to become vital factors in these rootless com-

---
[9] Dawber, M. A., quoted in *Rebuilding Rural America* (New York: Friendship Co., 1937), p. 38.

munities of landless people who are allowed to become even more transient than the harvest in their efforts to find work in the specialized farm factories.

Mark A. Dawber gives us a sound warning when he writes:

> The maintenance of the family the year-round is not the overhead of farming. It is the overhead of civilization. Replace individual farmers with floating hands employed for a few months in the year and you might just as well nail shut the doors of the churches and the institutions of learning. Individual farmers, not floating farm hands, rear children and give opportunities for scholastic education.[10]

A picture of what he calls "floating farm hands" is graphically given us in these verses. It will not readily be forgotten.

THE MOVERS

The East wind whips the skirts of the snow
with a passing shower,
and over Iowa on the first of March
wheels churn hub deep in the mud
or grit their teeth across the icy roads.

Home is only a shadow
flying down the wind in a
twisted swirl of snowflakes,
travelling down the road in an old lumber wagon
drawn by two shaggy horses
whose bones are too big for their flesh.

Even the wild goose
is not so homeless as these movers.
Peering ahead through the sliding curtain
of March rain they pass
with the furniture of home packed in a wagon.
Past corner, past grove, to the hilltop they go
until only chairlegs point from the skyline
like roots of trees torn from the earth.
And they are gone . . .

---

[10] *Ibid.*, p. 40.

The Rural Family in Mass Production

This, the parade of the landless, the tenants,
the dispossessed,
out of their Canaan they march
with Moses asleep in the Bible.

Who will call them back, who will ask:
are you the chosen people, do you inherit
only a backward glance and a cry and a heartbreak?
Are you the meek?
But the early twilight
drops like a shawl on their shoulders
and sullen water
slowly fills the wagon ruts and the hoof prints.
— James Hearst of Maplehearst, *Country Men*
(The Prairie Press)

PART II

MULTIPLICATION OF SMALL OWNERSHIPS IN LAND

Chapter 6

THE HOME ON THE LAND

Man not only should own the fruits of the earth, but also the very soil, inasmuch as from the produce of the earth, he has to lay up provision for the future. Man's needs do not die out, but recur; satisfied today, they demand new supplies tomorrow. Nature, therefore, owes to man a storehouse that shall never fail, the daily supply of his daily wants. And this he finds only in the inexhaustible fertility of the earth.... If working people can be encouraged to look forward to owning a few acres of land, the result will be that the gulf between vast wealth and deep poverty will be bridged over, and the two orders will be brought nearer together. Another consequence will be the greater abundance of the fruits of the earth. Men always work harder and more readily when they work on that which is their own, nay, they learn to love the very soil which yields in response to the labor of their hands, not only food to eat, but an abundance of the good things for themselves and those that are dear to them.

So in his *Rerum Novarum*[1] wrote Leo XIII. How have we heeded his words of golden wisdom?

Abandoned houses and impoverished fields mar the beauty of our rural landscapes. "Vast rural areas have the appearance of exploited colonies," was the description of our countryside given by Dr. O. E. Baker of the Bureau of Agricultural Economics. In an agricultural situation where one farmer in every two is a tenant, and where the other is an owner loaded with debt to the extent of one half of his investment and taxed far beyond his ability to pay, the farm home is no longer the place of beauty, the place of security, the place of freedom, or the place of independence that it was in the days of diversified agrarian life and culture.

---

[1] Latin words used by Leo in reference to ownership are: *dominatum,* full ownership, *adipiscendi* with *in suo.* This last phrase repeats the idea of complete ownership.

The Tenant "Shack"

Both tenant and mortgaged owner mine, exploit, and hunt for gold in commercial crops. Both work and sell for the cash that is needed to meet maturing obligations. The old homestead, once firmly established as the natural economic unit, where the family produced its own supplies of food and sometimes clothing; the old homestead around which technology could have built a grand modern life and culture; the old homestead, once a castle, a kingdom, and a secure dominion, is today scarcely more than another shack for the housing of an agricultural rent or wage slave. The farmhouse today bears great resemblance to the "company" shack, whether it stands on the farm of the land corporation or the farm of the absentee landlord. Those who occupy the farm home no longer advance slowly and securely in the ownership of property. They fall from owner to tenant, from tenant to sharecropper, from sharecropper to hired laborer. Already thousands of farm families move over the highways in trailers and old Ford automobiles to find new acres to rent, or to follow the seasonal harvesting of crops on mass-production, twenty-thousand-acre, incorporated farms, pitching their tents where the harvest is on, but where work will be available but for a few days.

Rootless Families

With the breakup of distributed landownership and the agrarian economy, the American family gives up its last distinctive economic function as a family unit. The American commercialized family may travel as a unit, sleep as a unit, consume goods as a unit, but it no longer produces wealth as a unit from its own productive property. Because the American family travels to find labor, having lost its own productive property as a basis for family economic enterprise, the life of the American family as a basic natural productive unit is well-nigh destroyed. Food, clothing, and shelter, the basic essentials for living and the sources from whence they come, are gathered up into the huge interlocking hands of incorporated commercial owners and distributors. With this continued centralization and industrialization of food, clothing, and shelter, the last vestiges of American freedom and security are wiped out. As far as the people are concerned, there is no land on which to build better homes and own them, there is no land for the production and consumption of food at home — the only efficient and conserving land economy. When absentee landlords, land corporations, and one-crop farmers shall have industrialized the fields, then there will be only wages for the many, wages both on the land and in the factory, while for the unemployed millions and their dependents, there will be relief extension whenever patronage requires it, rather than when, and as, hungry mouths may require it, and there will be odd gifts of food and clothing whenever charity takes the trouble to think of it.

What has become of this land of opportunity, democracy, freedom, security? What is happening to the billion acres of homestead land in this country? What is to be the destiny of this land where we built our homes for our children; this land that produced our food, fruits, vegetables, livestock and feeds for livestock, our lumber for homes and furniture? We are being reduced to slavish workers in the homes and fields that we once owned. Such a process of dispossession could not have the momentum that it has, had we not encouraged it in one way or another; had we not accepted a wage for ownership, a tenement shack for a home, a city street for a few acres of our own; had we not substituted the faint promise of a quick fortune in the wizardry of modern business for a permanent home and family on a few acres that give security; had we not become hunters and exploiters instead of remaining husbandmen, improving our homes and the culture of our families.

The Farm Not a Factory for Massive Machines

Wartime, high profits in corn and wheat and cotton made industrialists of our rural people. And as industrialism finally destroys the cities it creates, industrialism is now destroying agriculture. It is destroying our farm homes and their owners, our broad acres and their fertility.

The soil is not a machine for producing cotton, as the loom is a machine for weaving. Raw materials and typewriters and automobiles are not the same as animals and crops. Animals and crops are living things and they follow laws of nature that we must respect. We too are living things, spiritual as well as material living things, but rather than adjust ourselves to the laws of life in our material and spiritual being, we have in recent years spent most of our time in destructive efforts to reduce ourselves to machinery.

How anyone can speak of mass production as something which is inevitable, as something having its roots in the laws of nature, is hard to understand. Mass production is nothing more than a shortsighted, profit-driven, artificial work of incorporated device, centralized money, and heavy machinery. There is nothing natural in its development. It is chiefly the work of arbitrary power and conceded privilege. How can we dare to transfer this type of production to agriculture where above all the laws of nature must be respected?

A student of Rural Sociology once remarked: "Have diversified, family-basis agriculture in the South? Impossible! Why, God Himself wanted the South to be a cotton belt." Now, if God wants only the production of cotton in the South, then, why didn't He take measures to insure it? Then, why did He so carelessly construct the soils and climates and the laws of living things in such a way that practically all growing things flourish in the South, if they are given but half a chance? Then, why do the laws of crop rotation build up and conserve the soil in the South in the same way that crop rotation builds up and conserves the soils everywhere? Then, why does the continual production of the same crop, namely, cotton, impoverish the Southern soil in the same way that one repeated crop impoverishes any soil? No. It is clear from the facts of nature that God does not want the one-crop cotton South any more than He wanted slavery in the Southern States.

Industrialism is man-made and tramples upon God and His laws in its dealing with raw materials and men. Its engineers and financiers perhaps have the power to industrialize the farm and we as a nation have the economic ignorance not only to permit but to cooperate in the industrialization of agriculture. This final industrialization on the land will reduce a nation of free citizens to slaves, bring death to living things, barrenness to its soils, and the final reduction of its rich acres to deserts, gullies, rocks, and dust bowls.

The "Homestead" Way

Rich acres and productive plants and animals are safe only in the hands of the small owner, a man, a family man, who can respect and cooperate with the laws of nature, make provision for crop rotation, prevent erosion, and give paternal care to the plants and animals that feed and shelter him and his dear ones.

And strange as it may seem to the self-satisfied, capitalistic mind, blinded by profit and power, and the communistic mind, blinded by hatred and power, it is only in the hands of such small family-basis owners of productive property that democracy, culture, freedom, religion, and life itself are safe and secure. The man and his family, living on a few acres of their own land with a culture that is agrarian and a religion that is Christian, is the last bulwark against an extreme enslaving centralization and its final collapse into the hands of Red Commissars. The homestead and its family is the last bulwark in an urban civilization which is losing its property and freedom and failing to reproduce itself.

The men and women, who have gone commercial and admire themselves for it, while they cling to a pernicious ideology that considers life as a mere by-product of artificial economic process, must once again be taught that farming for home consumption is not only a worthy but an imperatively essential work for the majority of people in any nation. The men and women of the cities must be brought to change their sophisticated attitudes toward the man on the land.

However, the major attack is not to cry about false urban standards and attitudes, Communism, proletarianism, wage slavery, tenancy, etc. We need temporal and spiritual salvation for our people. Our time and best efforts must be directed in planting the seeds, nurturing the roots, and cultivating the elements of life which will reproduce a solid Christian order and culture. We must have a rising birth rate. We must have a new vitality in Christian home life and home culture. We must have a large increase of the primary natural groups of the family and the cooperative neighborhood. And we must make these groups more secure and independent through the development of a higher degree of self-sufficiency in food, clothing, shelter, etc. We shall accomplish all this in the most effective way if we rescue and perpetuate, renew and stimulate life and progress in the home on the land. In the past our populations came from the countryside and with them came our best moral and spiritual forces. Therefore among all social factors or social institutions, the home on the land must continue to be one of prime concern. Around the home on the land, our loyal American forces, whether they be educational, medical, social, political must throw their ramparts in order to protect its dignity, its health, its integrity, its ownership, its culture, its life, its liberty, its security, its independence. Our success in the philosophical, social, and political struggle that has overtaken us will be measured in terms of what we think and do about the home and the man on the land.

The Homestead: A Vital Economic Institution

One or two acres, or more, used for the home and the production of some food for family consumption, would go far to restore the proletarian clerk or industrial worker to a natural position as the father of a family with a measure of independence and security. A few acres where the family could live and grow a part of its food would do much to restore a correct philosophy of living and retain the family as a small but solid efficient unit of economy.

Soils and Men

Twenty-five million families, living in twenty-five million homes, on twenty-five million parcels of land! Some such distribution of land stood out as the greatest obstacle in the path of communistic tyranny, when the old Russian power had fallen. The Reds, therefore, reduced the 25,000,000 homes to 250,000 collective farms. The tyrants reasoned logically. With the family, the home, and other natural associations and institutions relegated to a position of unimportance, men could more readily be forced to accept a mechanistic life under political tyranny.

In this process the degradation of men is all too evident. In the unnatural structure of society where all are fitted by day and by  night to the big machine in mass production, men become the mere objects of technical process. They are forced to adapt their natures to the big mechanism. The engine and the motor are the important thing, not men. Mass production and its artificial institutions built around the machine are substituted for home life, family security, independence, liberty, and dignity. Men and their children are the raw materials of production in the same way that land and its products, its ores, its crops, are counted as so much raw material. "It does not matter how I use twenty-five million parcels of land, if that land is mine, is uninhabited and is free from the just claims of other people." Such is the argument of the commercial baron who invades the land. "I may reduce the parcels to one tract and put its cultivation into the hands of an irresponsible technology. My commercialization and my scientific technique need not make any modifications for the rabbits and the bears who may roam in the fields." However, if he should wish to preserve even these animals, he may have to take some precaution for their welfare. But if human beings are in the territory, he dare not make the mistake of judging that they are just so many animals. For theirs is the dignity and the right to rise up against him and claim the fields, even against any valid title that he may have, if his technical processes are destructive of their lives, their families, and their rights. When all these are involved, it is not enough for him to shout "scientific technique," "chance of greater output," "greater consumption," or any other terms in the ideology of a Marxist dictator or economic baron.

Since men are not mere animals, it does make a substantial difference whether the land is dotted with food-producing homesteads or with mass-produced State crops. Is it too much to ask scientific technique to accommodate itself to the larger requirements of human nature? In itself, however, it is not technology that is to blame. It is the lord of power and finance who retains and builds the big machine, long after the technologist has found a way to convert the large machine into a number of small ones operated by the efficient electric motor in the smaller factory and in the home.

One may ignore distribution of ownership and use his technical processes in any way he may wish as far as a mere animal, for example the cow, is concerned. She has no endowments of free will, personality, talent, no future life to prepare for. The cow should be equally contented on the food-producing homestead or the corporation farm, or the collective farm. But even in the case of the cow, it has been observed that she does not fare as well on the big commercial farm and therefore is not equally contented. But in the event that she is fed, it is not contrary to her nature to be on the collective farm. She has no rights which are violated.

It does not make much difference whether the cow eats from the private trough or the public trough. But eating from the public trough cannot be the chief business of the men who constitute civilized society. And even in the case of the cow, it makes some difference as far as men are concerned whether such animals eat from the public or private trough. If the cows eat from the public trough on the collective farm, then the men on that farm are Communists, slaves, so many more work animals. Whereas if the cows were eating from private troughs, these animals would constitute private property, private possessions of productive nature, prized animals standing between man and want, giving the owners their source of independence and security. Therefore, when Rural Life Conferences propose the family-centered program instead of the artificially erected program of the collective farm or the corporation farm with stocks and bonds in land, no American, not even the strictly urban-minded, can afford to be disinterested. What we do with the land, how we solve our tenancy problem, what we do about single cash-crop farming, will very soon affect both life in the city and country far more tangibly than it has already affected it.

Two Acres and a Cow

Recently an American Communist became the owner of a two-acre homestead and a cow. Soon it was the cow and her productivity, her contribution to economic security, that turned him and his family once more into the pursuit of democracy, once more into the pursuit of its own good and the good of the community. The ownership of the cow changed this man's philosophy. Sound thinking was restored. Where hard and straitened circumstances had before raised a difficulty about a just and loving God, land and cow—principally the cow—brought back a firm belief in God. God was after all just and loving, working for man's benefit through creatures. Here, through the cow, came a new security, a new promise, setting right a false philosophy more quickly and more conclusively than any raise in wages, or a new gadget or uncertain stock could have done. The raise in wages would have gone for higher cost of living, the gadget would have been used up, and the stock would only wait for a fall on the stock exchange. The owner of the cow was no longer a mere worker, a mere consumer, a mere individual in a mass-production unit, a mere cog in a cruel machine, a mere gambler on the labor and stock market: he was a free owner, an efficient dairyman for his family, a planner in a limited, but very natural, system of family economics, a master in a small but natural unit of production and consumption.

The privately owned, food-producing cow reformed the father and the family that had been all but ruined by inadequate wages, uncertain employment, and relief allotments.

The only way to restore the home is to provide for some family-centered production, family-centered activity, where the child can soon become an economic asset instead of remaining an economic liability. That is why the food-producing homestead has economic, social, cultural, and ethical significance. That is why every housing program should be a "productive home" program, the program of a modern home with acreage. Without this there can be no real "slum clearance." The old slum simply moves to a new area. The history of Federal Housing Projects shows clearly that they do not eliminate cave dwellings on concrete deserts. In most cases the funds used for these projects have in effect been subsidies to maintain congestion. And the housing that is provided is not low-cost housing. Low-cost housing was originally designed to supply adequate, modern, sanitary housing for families now living in slum areas. Instead it has provided modern luxuries for a middle-class group which is financially able to provide its own housing developments.

It is significant to note that a very small per cent of the apartments in the Housing Projects will accommodate large families.

An analysis of two completed projects, Harlem River Houses and Williamsburg Houses, both in New York City, reveals that only 4 per cent of the apartments will accommodate large families. A very large per cent of the apartments are built to accommodate childless or one-child families. One famous housing authority has called these houses "Birth-Control Houses."

The Urban Federal Housing Projects are anticipating a declining birth rate and the popularization of the theory of controlled family sizes. They are fostering the vicious practices which have already brought about the alarming decrease in our birth rate. Unfortunately, in 1939 the government adopted the plan of subsidizing such childless family apartments at the rate of $500,-000,000 for the next three years. Under the dramatic appeal of "Slum Clearance" practically every congested industrial community petitioned the United States Housing Authority for a share of the governmental housing bounty. The clamor at the door of the Federal Treasury for so-called "slum clearance" is surpassed only by the demands for WPA and PWA allotments.

It is rather late, but not too late, to ask ourselves some questions in reference to housing. Is there any real need for vast housing projects in the blighted urban areas? In these congested caves will rentals and prices ever come within the reach of our low-income families, the families who crowd the old slums? Are these houses built for the needs of normal-sized families? What real need is there for the retention of these slums as residential districts? Is there any real need to build new slums and attract new slum residents or even try to bring these new slum shelters within the reach of the old slum residents in order to have them stay where they are?

Homes built on top of one another in such blighted areas will never be productive homes, regardless of the number and variety of modern gadgets they may contain. Such homes whether of good or bad construction will always be nothing more or less than high-cost shelters. In them no provision can be made for any family-centered productivity. They are not homes for self-reliant American families. In them there is nothing that can safeguard the family's liberty and security, since they do not give any opportunity, even in a small degree, for any measure

The Home on the Land

of economic self-sufficiency through family enterprise and co-operation. Mere shelters can never be dignified homes in which one finds the intelligent cooperative labor of family members.

If there were adequate highway facilities in and out of our large cities, migration to productive homes on small acreages would quickly develop. An increasing number of workers have already solved their low-cost housing problem, by moving to a small plot in the country, where they are partially self-sustaining by raising their own vegetables, keeping a cow and some chickens. It has been the experience of these families that in the city they consumed their incomes, but on their country places, thanks to raising a considerable part of what they need, they are able to save something even in slack years and much more when times are good. They are attaining a security through part-time agriculture which is heartening, and they are near enough to the factory to drive to the city in a car or a bus in from thirty minutes to an hour.

After an extensive survey made in cooperation with forty-six state highway departments, Chief Thomas H. MacDonald of the United States Bureau of Public Roads concludes that in order to have the type of highway and parking facilities needed to meet the requirements of motorized communities, in order to develop the full use of the automobile, cities must be remade. Chief MacDonald insists that multi-lane highways, one hundred feet wide with adequate parking space alongside, must be cut through the built-up sections, preferably the blighted slum sections of the overcrowded cities, that the successful city of the future will plan and build its rights of ways vastly different from the rights of ways of the city of today, swamped in the "mud" of congestion. The surveys disclose the fact that many of our cities are almost as antiquated, trafficwise, as if they had medieval walls, moats, and drawbridges. Fast motor cars crawl through city streets at a mule's pace, just as they once had to crawl through rural mud. There is so much motor crawling that the sheer cost in terms of time wasted waiting in traffic jams or crawling through is a cost that is mathematically terrifying. The old routes, the horseback trails, and the cowpaths that became city streets are not much wider now than they ever were.

No city can be said to be equipped for the motor age unless its busy areas can be approached on rights of way several hundred feet wide with adequate parking space alongside. The cities which will take an active organized part in the development of productive homes on small acreages, and provide multi-lane highways for buses and motor cars, will stabilize their land values and production areas, double the use of the automobile and scatter the benefits of prosperity to the hundreds of industries, businesses, and individuals that share in the benefits of widespread automobile use. Highway and motor-car facts and figures which indicate the development that the prosperous, decentralized city of the future must take can be blocked for a time, but these coming changes which concern business prosperity, employment, social convenience, pleasant, secure living in productive homes cannot be permanently stopped.

Organic Units in Society

As an effective counteragent against the destructive forces in modern society, the Agrarian Rural Life Conferences recommend not a revolt against all mass production, but the widespread use of the food-producing homestead. Through this homestead many of the fruits of family life can be saved, many religious ideals can be pursued, real democracy can be lived, true liberty enjoyed, happiness and contentment rediscovered. All these advantages lay the foundation for a better social and economic order, even in the presence of much mass production. In such land tenure the essential organic unit — the family — can be saved. In such an environment the families in the new communities will group themselves naturally in mutual endeavors and cooperative activities. The new community organizations will be able to keep the natural, social, and economic pattern of small local democratic groups working toward a greater self-sufficiency, with common bonds of mental, emotional, social, and cultural interests.

In local groups with respect to local problems, the people can function democratically, intelligently, with initiative and self-reliance. We have indeed much organization in America today, but it is not the localized, functional, organic type. It is set up and fostered in artificial ways by expensive advertising, by high-pres-

— Farm Security Administration

(Above) The home of a subsistence farmer in Roanoke Farms, North Carolina. (Below) A happy group of farm children at Decatur Homesteads, Decatur, Indiana.

—Farm Security Administration

Typical homes of farm folks in the Penderlea Homestead Project, North Carolina.

The Home on the Land

sure publicity, by empty promises. The unwieldy centralized unit operating on a national scale, serving some highly specialized purpose, with management and problems far removed from the people, cannot serve them in an organic, democratic way.

Natural Groups Must Be Restored

The food-producing homestead, in the not-too-rural and the not-too-urban setting, will make a considerable contribution to domestic solidarity and family integration. Work on the homestead lends itself to the cooperation of a number of persons in a family enterprise. Individualism is absorbed and merged in the promotion of family welfare. Permanence of residence, by lessening mobility and transiency among the inhabitants of an area, will pave the way for cultural stability, the formation of cooperative economic enterprises, and the final organic integration and stabilization of local group life. Families will bind themselves together in living natural units when there is identity of attitudes, identity of objectives, of ambition and ideals. Such identity for natural groups can scarcely be found on any modern city block. Here the individual, detached from his family and his community, is lost in the big mass.

The family and the local community group, the food-producing homestead, and the community cooperative are then the natural institutions which point the way toward social *revitalization*. It is a fundamental principle of sound social democratic philosophy that the State and other large organizations, such as the American corporations, must not arrogate to themselves functions which can be performed efficiently by smaller and lower bodies. The "smaller and lower bodies" must re-establish their life and their autonomy in many ways, in many things. To this new life, new association, Pius XI refers in *Quadragesimo Anno* when he speaks of the "Reform of the Social Order."

But even if the philosophic basis of such a plan be admitted, the objection will be raised: "It cannot be done in the present economic state of things." Then we say, what good is our social philosophy if it bogs down in economic determinism? The day has arrived for us to show a good measure of economic self-determination. Otherwise our teaching on free will, vitalism, norm of morality, etc., has been outlawed by the economic mechanists as far as any social order is concerned.

We are a nation of poor people. But the land is rich. Could we take possession of it through the homestead, buying it and paying for it? Yes, if long-term loans were granted to qualified families for thirty years or more at 3 per cent interest. These loans should come, not from the government, but from private individuals and from the local banks.

Ralph Adams Cram, in a speech delivered before the National Catholic Rural Life Conference at the fifteenth annual convention, suggested a plan for the rich.

If, instead of giving or bequeathing generous sums for the founding of business schools, technological institutes and college chairs of journalism, scenario writing or eurythmic dancing, or still further enriching art museums which already have trouble in expending their funds except for the purchase of doubtful "old masters" or even more doubtful examples of "modernist" and "surrealist art," they would build, equip and populate self-contained agrarian-industrial communities of human scale, they would make the most important contribution possible to the solution of most of our current social and economic problems.[2]

A new type of school should be founded — an Agrarian, Homestead School where in short courses community leaders could be trained in the following subjects:

1. Religious motivation for this new living.
2. Problems of ownership, liberty, democracy.
3. Local natural social grouping for economic needs (cooperatives).
4. Local natural social grouping for problems of health, education, recreation, etc.
5. Scientific techniques in soils, crops, and animals adapted to the family farm.
6. Scientific techniques in engineering, electricity, and in machines adapted to the family farm.

---

[2] Cram, R. A., *Catholic Rural Life Objectives*, 1938, p. 35.

Chapter 7

SOME PROBLEMS IN MODERN HOMESTEADING

THE idea, that the multiplication of homesteads can rebuild security, independence, and freedom in the modern world, is growing among all classes of people. It is the idea that Leo XIII had when he spoke of working people and the ownership of a few acres, of farmers and their ownership of the land. Within the past decade this idea of a greater distribution of landownership on a family basis has made a remarkably sound and steady progress among the American people, in both urban and rural districts.

The Original American Plan

Homesteading may be said, in a certain sense, to be the American spirit. For did not homesteading in the old sense of staking land on the frontier play the major part in our national development? True, there were gold rushes, oil booms, and mass-production techniques, but it was chiefly the golden grains, the growing herds of livestock, and the annual supply of ample food crops that provided us with a good living, with security, with freedom, with long periods of stable economic progress. With a notable return of agrarian thinking and planning within recent years, it begins to look as if America may be able to recapture the spirit of homesteading — not the rugged homesteading on a remote frontier, but the modern, local homesteading which will take our large, wasteful, inefficient, single-crop, commercial tracts of land and break them up into efficient, modern, diversified family farms and homes — homes on the land for full-time family farming and part-time family farming. In this modern homesteading there will be full-time family farming on small farms ranging from 40 to 200 acres in a system of land utilization which is biodynamic, that is, with a variety of food crops and livestock on every farm. In this modern homesteading there is also a place for part-time family farming on smaller farms, ranging from five to ten acres, providing some ownership and security and subsistence for many low-income industrial families.

The Return to the "Homestead" Way

Here and there throughout the country small urban groups and individual families are already turning to the land in order to grow and store a year-round food supply for the family. Many full-time farmers are giving up their former single-crop gambling, soil mining, and land exploitation to take up the more scientific, biodynamic system of land husbandry in which they use a natural cycle of crops and livestock, with many food crops for family consumption and feed crops for the livestock. In this method of land settlement and utilization the biodynamic farmers discover that there is no loss of efficiency or technology, but rather a gain in both. These farmers are discovering that electricity with its efficient operation of many family-unit machines makes food processing for family consumption not only a highly profitable work but also a pleasant task. In their modern family system these farmers find that their small unit of home production and consumption is far more efficient and economical than any large-scale enterprise of food processing and distribution. These farmers have discovered that it is right to have a cash crop, but that it is all wrong for them to have to pay out the money they get for it, for something they can grow with much profit for themselves. These farmers have discovered that with too much of the cash crops; namely, corn, wheat, cotton, etc., the soil gets sick, the weeds get bad, bugs and pests and diseases eat and destroy the crop, and dust storms and droughts grow in intensity, bringing destruction to both land and crop. These farmers know now that if they would stick to one crop long enough, it would put them out of home and business, as it has already done in the case of many of their fellow farmers.

Farmers who own their land can readily, with some headwork and planning and family teamwork, return to a modern system of homesteading. With the cooperation of all our people our fields everywhere could be turned back into the most efficient, the most effective system of husbandry — the small, highly diversified, biodynamic, family-unit farm. But tenants cannot become homesteaders in this sense. Neither can the sharecropper, nor the hired rural worker, unless perhaps absentee landlords may come to see that gardens, orchards, woodlots, pastures, livestock, and regular rotation of crops are sorely needed to restore the fertility of the vast acres ruined by their current type of commercial rent contracts.

To sum it up, then, the absentee landlord is not a homesteader. The farm tenant is not a homesteader. The sharecropper is not a homesteader. The rural hired man is not a homesteader. For the only man who can be a homesteader in any true sense of the word is one who owns sufficient land to give adequate economic activity that requires headwork, handwork, and teamwork in the production of food for the family in a simple but scientific way, and the processing of food for the family along simple but technological lines, scientific care of many animals and many crops, careful selections of the best cash crops for the particular climates and the particular local markets, and finally for a few distant markets. In addition to all this a good homesteader and the members of his family will try to develop various skills in crafts and creative artistic work for home needs and home beautification. They will learn and take an active part in the occupational grouping of their fellow farmers, for economic, social, and spiritual advancement through cooperative community efforts.

The definition of a homesteader just outlined applies of course to the full-time farmer. The same definition holds in very large measure for the part-time farmer, the subsistence homesteader, with this exception, that in the case of the subsistence homesteader, the family economic unit on the land does not have adequate or full-time employment on the land, and hence certain members of the family seek some employment in some other economic activity — one or other of the industries — but the natural family unit even here continues to keep one foot on the soil and considers that way of living most important.

High Intelligence Required in Homesteading

When we come to define modern homesteading in these terms, we see at once why people, who understand us, no longer characterize a homestead farmer as a stupid and ignorant person, nor do they refer to his work on the homestead as slavish and undignified work. School authorities throughout the country are beginning to see that homestead farming is a dignified occupation, that homestead farming requires good judgment, a fairly wide knowledge, good innate abilities, and a broad education. They are beginning to see that such a well-regulated farm is one of the best institutions on earth, economically, socially, politically, and spiritually. Homestead farming and local community occupational organization and leadership are being proposed here and there to the high-school and college graduate as an opportunity for a substantial and dignified life through which the graduate will be likely to make a valuable contribution to American civilization, culture, and religion — a contribution that can be equal in importance to that made by any person of highest urban occupation and distinction. Some educators are beginning to tell their graduates that they can take up homestead farming with the same, if not greater, sense of dignity than that which accompanies much commercial work; that in homestead farming there need be no retreat from the demands of civilization or the giving up of ambitions for a life of high cultural and intellectual achievement.

Already a few high schools and colleges are tackling the problem of curricular adjustment in cultural and technical subjects to give adequate training for a cultural and successful life on the land. Adequate training in modern homesteading — a training for a worthy career in rural life — is certainly entitled to its proper place in any rural elementary or secondary school and in colleges that are not strictly urban or commercial. Even the commercial college should see to it that its graduates form the proper mental attitudes toward rural life.

In this work of opening up opportunities on the land for rural and even some urban youth, we must be careful to make the training one which outlines and develops the homestead way

Some Problems in Modern Homesteading

of farming. Why do we insist on this? For the reason that the terms *homestead* and *homestead farming* are not clearly understood. The confusion results from the fact that there are so many other current varieties of inefficient, destructive farming in the ascendancy, and there are so many economic determinists among the masses, that it is often taken for granted that we, who speak of homestead farming, are not speaking of a system of farming for America, but that we are speaking of a system of farming that can only be launched on some remote frontier, such as Alaska. Great numbers of people take it for granted that there is no way to refashion or to replace the commercial, tenant, sharecropper, and absentee-landlord varieties of farming. Since tenancy and absentee landlordism prevail in America, they argue, there is no room for homesteading. Beginning students in rural sociology have expressed the opinion again and again that homesteading is only for such a place as Alaska. It is difficult sometimes to make them see that homesteading is the farm system which can be introduced and ought to be introduced on the acres and acres of land in all the states of the Union, whether in New England, or the South, or the Middle West, or the Northwest or the Southwest.

Again, among urban and commercial people there is much contempt and ridicule of farmwork and farm people. Recently on the campus of a Catholic college, situated in a definitely rural district, the students were giving an original play offered by a student's dramatic club. The lines of the play gave frequent reference in a sophisticated way to glorified city life, enough to give the students who were recently from the country a decided inferiority complex. To exemplify, one of the actors asked the question — "What is a homestead?" Others on the stage took up the question repeating it — "A homestead, a homestead? What did you say — a homestead? Well now, let us see what could that be?" Finally with an air of superiority one of the puzzled actors exclaimed — "Oh! Yes — a homestead — why that was something the 'hicks' used to have before we moved into apartments and got rid of corn silk and hayseed."

And so, even at the risk of repetition, we must again and again explain what we mean by the term *homestead,* and make it stand out as a necessary foundational institution for many families in a free and democratic country — an institution that saves the home, human values, human culture, and even the human race itself — an institution so essential to our country's well-being that positive steps must be taken to prevent its continual replacement by flats and hotels, dormitories and restaurants, apartments and professionalized housekeeping.

To repeat, then, a homestead in our rural program for America today is not a log cabin and a few acres in Alaska. It is not a cabin in a summer-resort area, or a country club with a golf course. A homestead is not a rural birthplace of some sentimental bank president or corporation executive of New York, Chicago, or St. Louis, who retains the bare legal ownership of the old country place and keeps it up as a sort of museum, employing a caretaker. A homestead is not a farm operated by a tenant, a sharecropper, or a hired man. It is not a single-crop, mass-production farm. It is not a place where the farmer slashes in and plows up the whole landscape in order to put in one or two big crops. A homestead is not 160 acres somewhere in a semiarid region where a family is left to starve to death. A homestead is not primarily a place of business, neither is it a slum in any sense of the word, even though the house may temporarily resemble a tenement shack.

It is easier, perhaps, to set forth what we do not mean by the term *homestead* than it is to set forth adequately what the term implies. This fundamental institution — the homestead — as other fundamental things is difficult to define in terms that are clearly understood by the mechanized, proletarian mind. There must be a house and land, and this house and land must be owned by the family that occupies it, and the land must be used in a modern scientific way for the production of much food for the family, and only when this has been done is it used as a further source of income — a cash income. The members of the homestead family will make an effort to advance in the knowledge of home arts and crafts. They will strive to play a leading part in the building of an agricultural occupational group to work for community progress in cooperative economic enterprise, in education, in health, in recreation, in culture, in religion.

Homestead: Definition

We may put down the essential points in our definition, then, in this way: "A homestead is a home on a small holding of land, in any modern country, where a family, preserving the natural bonds of integration and unity, lives and works; cares for the home gardens and orchards, cows, pigs, and chickens; cultivates and raises a variety of food for its own table, engaging in some carefully selected cash-crop enterprise only when a considerable supply of year-round home-grown food for the family and for the livestock has been provided for." From this definition we see that homesteads are the solid, natural institutions which Denmark set up and multiplied and protected during the years that we were tearing them down with the destructive forces of commercialization, debt foreclosure, and high taxation.

Land Taxation Must Be Reduced

Before rural life and homesteads can come into a place of great prominence in our national life, we shall have to do much to combat the spirit of commercialism, the problem of debt and its rigorous terms, and the problem of taxes. Land has always been taxed as if all of it were devoted to commercial enterprise. Until recently, taxing bodies have made no distinction between land for the home and land for business. That is one reason why our American homes on the land have come to engage in more and more commercialism until we have in many areas complete gambling in one crop and the buying of all family needs. But today many legislatures have come to realize that the home in the homestead comes before any business activity, and they are trying to exempt the home in the homestead from taxation. More or less in accordance with the explanation of homestead farming given above, twenty-three state legislatures have seriously considered homestead exemption laws. Ten states, within recent years, have passed definite homestead laws by constitutional amendment and statutory laws. Legislators, too, have their difficulties in defining what is meant by the terms *homestead* and *homestead farming,* and hence the laws differ considerably in the amount of acreage and the amount of exemption. But none of these laws are intended as relief or a bestowal of charity on pauperized farmers.

Tax-Exempt Status for the "Homestead"

These homestead tax-exemption laws recognize that homestead farming is not simply a career, devoted to ordinary self-seeking business, but that it is first of all a way of life, a dignified, secure, independent way of life, contributing notably to the integrity of the essential natural units; namely, families, out of whose integrity the state itself draws its vitality and strength.

It is a sound national social policy to mark off the homes in their best environments as institutions of special social and spiritual values. It is a sound national policy to release the homes from the burdens of taxation, placing these burdens upon strictly business activities whether on the land or in the cities, upon commercial properties and incomes. And we who generally speak of the homestead in connection with rural life find no fault with the tax-exemption laws which extend the meaning of the term *homestead* to include an "urban homestead," the home and the lots owned and occupied by an urban family, provided the home and the lots are used directly for family living and are not used for commercial purposes. Homes owned and occupied by the family, whether in urban or rural districts should be set free from taxation, with an exemption that is large enough to cover the value of a good substantial home and the amount of land that can be used directly for family living. Such an exemption protects the home and sets it free to accomplish its high objectives of producing a cultured and responsible citizenry. We have long ago exempted gifts for education and gifts for the Church for such purposes.

Continued Land-Taxation Places an Unjust Burden on the Land

Land-taxation units and land taxation were mapped out in this country when our people were predominately agricultural and when land represented 75 per cent of the income-producing property. This tax policy has not been changed very radically, although at the present time, even with all our commercial farming, farms represent only 10 per cent of the income-producing property. Much of the great expense of public schools remains saddled upon the farms. The 23 per cent of the nation's adults who live on the farms rear and educate 37 per cent of the children of the nation. These farm parents pay the bills for the costly, yet, inadequate and inefficient "little red schoolhouses," and in some areas they help pay the bills for consolidated schools in the larger villages — schools which are too remote for their children. For their tax money country people should be given an adequate school in each township. And these schools should emphasize training in farm problems and farm living. School authorities have given the country taxpayers not only inefficient and costly school units, but also a curriculum that is more urban than rural, more commercial than agrarian, and a staff of teachers who for the most part preach the philosophy of commercialism and city life. Costliness and inefficiency characterize practically all of the outmoded rural governmental agencies and services. It is a matter of simple justice, as well as social and economic wisdom, that there should be a drastic reform in the century-old structures of local government and its old system of taxation.

Land-Tax Delinquencies

During the years the burden of taxes has been only a little less serious in its consequences to the farmer than the burden of debt and its rigorous terms. Land taxes are not computed on the basis of ability to pay. Although the land may be worth only twenty dollars per acre, and although its owner has only enough acres upon which to make a fair living, yet the taxing bodies will place an annual tax of one dollar or two dollars or in some places even three and four dollars on each acre. In many places the landowner every ten or fifteen years pays into the state and local governmental agencies in the form of taxes the full value of his farm. Although land taxes have been reduced somewhat since 1929, nevertheless, they stand today at an increase of 100 per cent over the land taxes of 1914. Taxes never drop back to where farm income and values do. Taxes take an ever larger portion of the declining farm income. Eventually farmers become delinquent in their payments and default. In the whole country in the ten years — 1926 to 1935 inclusive — 8 per cent of the farms were sold for taxes. In the Old South the proportion of the tax sales was about 12 per cent. In the Middle Atlantic States, 13 per cent of the farms were sold for taxes. As with foreclosures, the greatest trouble occurred in the areas devoted to a single crop.

To put the case more graphically, in the average for the whole country during the ten years — 1926–35 — seventy-nine in every one thousand farms were sold for taxes. In some sections the situation was much more grievous than in others. In one Middle Atlantic county in one month — November, 1932 — 665 pieces of property, mostly farms, were sold for taxes. In one Western community the seriousness of the situation is shown by the percentage of the land already sold for taxes and the growing percentage of delinquency. In this community, in 1931, 1 per cent of the farms were sold for taxes and 34 per cent were delinquent. In 1932, 16 per cent of the farms were sold for taxes and 72 per cent were delinquent. In 1933, 24 per cent of the farms were sold for taxes and 60 per cent were delinquent.[1] To repeat this in a graphic way, the following has been the condition of farms in this Western community:

1931 .... 1% sold for taxes — 34% delinquent
1932 .... 16% sold for taxes — 72% delinquent
1933 .... 24% sold for taxes — 60% delinquent

Under taxes, such as prevail in this community, it takes only three years to destroy practically all landownership, make

---

[1] Senator John S. Callan, of the Nebraska Legislature, pointedly said: "I believe the majority of farmers, small owners, and businessmen are worse off financially than they have ever been, but still we are taxing them to the very limit." He makes the following comparison between the farmer's and the salaried man's income and taxes:

Farmer No. 1.	Net income	......	$ 85.50 — Taxes	$141.50
Farmer No. 2.	Net income	......	$ 635.00 — Taxes	$155.00
Farmer No. 3.	Net income	......	$ 518.00 — Taxes	$ 96.20
Salaried Man No. 1.	Income	....	$1,800.00 — Taxes	$ 9.47
Salaried Man No. 2.	Income	....	$1,500.00 — Taxes	$ 7.98
Salaried Man No. 3.	Income	....	$1,500.00 — Taxes	$ 2.70

People are not paying the taxes, he concludes, because the ones who are to pay them do not have the money or the income to be able to pay them.

absentee landlordism complete, drive out the old population or permit them to remain in the reduced role of tenants to pay high commercial rents.

If we add the foreclosure for debt to the sales for taxes, we find that in the ten-year period of 1926 to 1935 no less than 298 farms in every 1,000 were foreclosed or sold for taxes. On the average, for every community this would mean that about one third of the families lost their farms because of debt or taxes. Some regions were harder hit than others: one half of South Dakota's farms, two fifths of Iowa's, and well over one third of Minnesota's and Montana's farms changed hands because of debt or tax. In the West North Central States in this ten-year period 339 farms per 1,000 were taken for debt and 59 for taxes. In the East South Central States, 185 farms per 1,000 were taken for debt and 119 for taxes.

To put these facts in a more striking way, in order that we may grasp the stark reality, let us apply the percentages to the approximately three million farm owners on the land today. We said that during the ten-year period of 1926 to 1935 approximately one third of the farm owners of that period lost their farms because of debt or taxes. In another period, such as that, this would mean that among the farm owners of today 1,000,000 farms would change hands, in each year during such a decade, 100,000 farms would change hands, and in each day 274 farms would change hands. And the hands that take possession are the profit-seeking, commercial hands of distant banks and corporations.

This is land speculation and exploitation with a vengeance — a strictly money and tax deal which shows no regard for stable ownership and family security on the land, no recognition of the social and economic and political fact that in farming the home element and not the business element should be given first consideration. The fact that we tolerated all this and still do, is proof sufficient that we have lost the significance of the institution of the home and homesteading. We have succumbed to the subversive, commercial philosophy contained in the slogans: "Farming is nothing more than a business," "business is business," and "taxes are taxes." With such slogans in the air we fail to think. We put secondary things, such as business and taxes, first and we put first things, such as home, family security, and independence, last. In fact, we seem to care little whether they come in at all.

Giant Plows Destroy Homes

We are surrendering our rich acres — the land upon which we should establish our homes and upon which we should raise the food to feed our children in a way of living in which family security, freedom, and independence can send their roots down into the good soil from generation to generation. We are opening up the broad fields to the money lords and their giant tractors so that they may slash and plow for dividends or rent, while we go off to join the dispossessed proletariat to live in company houses, flats, apartments, and hotels in the hope that we shall find ourselves as a cog in the large-scale, machine world. Proletarian, machine-minded as we are, we think that the noisy, mass-production plows of the new agricultural barons will produce more food, more efficiently. We forget that such specialized agriculture builds up an insoluble problem of distribution. We forget that food is multiplied, not by the size of machinery or the calculations of deterministic economists, but by the laws of biology, the laws of Divine Providence, and we forget that besides being inefficient and destructive in food production these giant plows, plow up our best social institutions — the free, secure, and independent homes.

The undemocratic, inefficient, destructive trend toward the complete substitution of commercial farming for homestead farming gets its impetus from the prevailing commercialism which, in its materialistic madness, tries to prove that bigness is efficiency in every field of activity. In agriculture such economic insanity will sooner or later have to reckon with the higher laws of living things. But this strong commercialistic trend on the land may go much farther than it has already, unless we can set forth in unmistakable terms the enormous values of homestead farming. We must train and educate many for a homestead life on the land, a life of security, freedom, and independence — a life of many cultural and spiritual advantages. But it is not enough to set forth the outstanding wisdom of homestead farming. We must remove the practical difficulties under the present money-mad economic system and its prevailing proletarian mentality. What do we gain in the way of concrete achievement by shouting about the fine principles of homesteading and its integrated family life when approximately 300 homesteads are taken away each day for debt and taxation? In working in conjunction with our fellow citizens and our state leaders for land and tax revision, we must not be misled by critics who will try to make us believe that homestead exemption is not practical or fair or that it will injure the schools or make it impossible to have adequate government functions. Where there is inefficiency in government, the homestead tax-exemption law, with its consequent restriction of revenue, acts as an automatic device to prevent waste and force the adoption of important and highly desirable reforms in local government organization and the use of more modern and efficient administrative practices.

Again tax exemption for homesteads does not destroy all revenue in real estate, especially today when there are but few homesteads on the land. In most states, even with an exemption of $5,000 for the homestead (house and land), the amount of the tax received from real estate would be reduced only about 25 per cent. In Oklahoma, where the exemption is placed at $1,000 and was applied last year to 106,968 homes in the cities and to 65,319 homes in the country, the resulting reduction of revenue from real estate was only 9 per cent. The objection is raised that this percentage will grow as ownership increases. Our answer to this objection is that while ownership increases there will be ample time to work out ways and means for adequate and equitable replacement taxes. Wherever the decrease in revenue must be replaced, the burden should not fall automatically on other commercialized real estate. Today property is held in many intangible, invisible forms. Tax evasion in such property is a matter of common knowledge. The Oklahoma Tax Commission makes the report that there is probably enough intangible property in Oklahoma alone that, if taxed as the law contemplates, would offset the loss resulting from homestead tax exemption. We must discover ways and means to make stocks, bonds, securities, savings accounts, and other invisible forms of wealth bear their share of the tax burden.

Replacements and Adjustments in Revenues

Again if tax replacement is essential, provisions might be made for a sales tax on luxuries, but not on food and clothing, seeds and machines for the home. Exemption of Federal and state employees from income taxes ought to be removed, and in general the burden of taxes should be placed more and more on incomes — personal incomes and the incomes of corporations.

Our homestead tax-exemption philosophy is not, as some industrialists and their henchmen of the press and politics argue, an attempt to blacken the "white spots," but it is an honest attempt to place the tax burden more nearly where there is ability to pay. We are interested in "white spots" for homes and homesteads, rather than in "white spots" for trusts, monopolies, utilities, financial barons, and other big-business groups. And we take this stand, not because of prejudice, but because in business, big or little, in commercial investments and activities, whether in industry or on the commercial farm, there is the ability to pay. This ability to pay from year to year may be small or it may be great, and we simply warn the tax collectors and governmental officials to calculate their expenditures and fix their tax bills accordingly. We and our governments perform a greater social service in working out sound measures that will enable the people to own their homes and keep them, than we do when we set up agencies of public relief after their homes have been lost.

Chapter 8

SELF-SUFFICIENCY: AFTER THAT, PRODUCTION FOR EXCHANGE

THIS is a true human-interest story. A family lives in the outskirts of one of our Iowa cities on a five-acre plot of land. Some months ago, a welfare worker from the County Relief Office called at the home. She made all sorts of gentle suggestions and hints as to the need of relief, and finally when they were not taken up, she blurted right out: "Is it true that you are not eating enough?" There was a broad smile upon the handsome countenance of the intelligent mother of seven children. She conducted the welfare worker through the basement, cave, and whole house, then to the few unpretentious buildings on the grounds. There were potatoes and vegetables of all sorts, fruit and jelly glasses aplenty — all properly kept. A most generous supply of meats was stored in various ways. A calf had been butchered; there were pork, lard, sausages, bacon, and ham. There were two contented cows in the small pasture; fifty chickens in the coop. Flowers graced the windows, and shrubberies and trees told the story of summer blooms. A free American family lived in that home!

Delivery Wagons and Necessities of Life

You may ask: What prompted the welfare worker to make the investigation? Just this: The neighbors had reported that the delivery boy had not stopped at the home for weeks, and they were worried over the actual existence of the family in question. Kindly and thoughtful neighbors indeed! But isn't that type of conclusion a sad commentary on a terrible condition existing in the State of Iowa? There it is, with the earth's best soil, and yet it seems to be taken for granted that the delivery wagon must furnish its people with the necessaries of life. No family in Iowa ate any better or healthier food than the family about whom the neighbors worried. That family, upon being asked: "Did the depression affect you very much?" answered: "Hardly at all." "Did the drought affect you?" — "Yes, some, but on a small acreage you can sprinkle or carry water if necessary." This home had modern conveniences: electricity and good plumbing.

> Happy the man whose love and care
> A few paternal acres bound,
> Happy to breathe his native air,
> On his own ground.

The intelligent farmer will first of all raise what he can for the year-round needs of his family, and then corn and hogs, or wheat or cotton, or anything else for exchange.

Recall the history of the West. First came the Yankee, the Pennsylvanian, the Kentuckian, the Ohioan. In their footsteps followed the German, the Dane, the Swede, and the Irish. They came to the West to establish a home, to make a living for their families — and they did. The land, the atmosphere were most favorable. There was no better spot on God's green earth. They purchased the land. They planned their work and the use of their products. Wheat for the mill and bread, hogs for lard and bacon and meat; cows for milk, butter, and cheese; the calf and beef and sheep were butchered when needed. There were potatoes and vegetables. There were the orchards, the bees, the chickens, the ducks, the geese, and the turkeys. Corn and hay to feed the animals fertilized the land. Every Western farmer produced a surplus that he exchanged with his neighbor or traded at the store for clothing and other material that he could not produce himself. Whatever cash he received was used to pay for his land and for taxes, and he always had a nest egg for a rainy day. He had little cash, but he had independence. He paid his bills, he built and maintained churches. The community in which he lived prospered. The whole nation was better because of his prosperity.

Then what happened? The Western farmer began to commercialize his farming. He wanted more cash. He raised more corn, more oats, lots of hogs and cattle. He sold them and bought the necessities of life. He sold the wheat and bought flour that had

Self-Sufficiency and Production for Exchange

been emasculated and treated with chlorine gas to make it white. He thus cheated himself and his family. He raised the beef and hogs, and he bought steak and pork and bacon. He donated a penny here and a penny there all along the line. He paid for tin cans and labels; he paid for salesmen and advertising, and in return he secured an inferior product. He bought apples from Oregon and allowed his orchard to decay. He thought he was smart, but the city slicker patted him on the back, handed him a brand new dollar bill, and took two out of his pocket. He felt so good over it. He had become a part of the great cycle of American commerce. He was making lots of money, so he thought, but he spent more than he was making. He did not pay his grocer or the doctor, and incidentally he did not support the Church. So tenancy rose to dizzy heights in the agricultural states.

The new commercial farmer (and there are millions of them — many of them commercial because they are renters, and many of them farm owners who are commercial because they will not stop to figure the costs of their farming operations) set up the world's most destructive and inefficient farming system.

The new system does show a saving in labor costs, but the costs of all other things used in commercialized farming far exceeds any saving there has been in labor used in production. What has been saved in the way of man labor on the mechanized, commercial farms may be estimated from the following table:

United States	1878–1882	1896–1902	1928–1932
Wheat (100 bu.)	17 man hours	12 man hours	7 man hours
Corn (100 bu.)	46 man hours	38 man hours	26 man hours
Cotton (500 lb.)	119 man hours	113 man hours	85 man hours

In some technological statistics it is estimated that there has been a saving of 20 per cent in labor costs. In other words 20 per cent of labor formerly required is no longer required. This does not mean any saving in the total farming operation unless there is a saving in machinery and other costs involved in commercial operations. When we examine some of these costs, we obtain the figures found in the tabulation at the top of page 132.[1]

---

[1] *Technological Trends,* June, 1937, "The National Income and Its Purchasing Power," National Bureau of Economic Research.

	1909	1928
Tools and Implements	$ 177,000,000	$ 487,000,000
Fertilizers (artificial)	115,000,000	206,000,000
Feeds (bought from processors)	307,000,000	615,000,000
Taxes	74,000,000	171,000,000
Twine	17,000,000	29,000,000
Autos	24,000,000	403,000,000
Harness	58,000,000	37,000,000
Totals	$1,147,000,000	$2,572,000,000

In the few things listed above we have an increase of farm production costs of 52 per cent plus. A saving in harness is indicated but this soon vanishes when we begin to count the machinery that takes the agricultural jobs away from "old Dobbin." The tractors and their fuels are not cheap and never will be cheap on the farms. Tractors and fuels must be bought and the prices are not parity prices. In 1928 the farmers bought 171,469 tractors, and in 1936 the farmers bought 221,246 tractors. This is no small item in the costs of modern farming. Many farmers, who have discovered that besides being too expensive the tractor does not fit into the biological integration of farm activity, have returned to use of nature's horsepower. If they use the tractor at all, they use it very sparingly, and only for work that cannot be done without it.

Farm tractors alone accounted for 42.0 per cent of the farm-equipment sales of 1936 and 1937. During the three-year period, 1935 to 1937, farm-machinery manufacturers sold for use in the United States 565,792 tractors. In 1937 alone, the estimated farm costs for tractors purchased was $214,192,212. The rate and magnitude of tractor mechanization is very great.[2]

In 1938 there were 1,527,989 tractors in operation on American farms. Any saving that may be achieved in the removal of man labor is completely eliminated when we add up the tractor costs and debts to the total farming operation.[3]

Advocates of commercial farming will, after looking at these increased costs, hasten to say that yields have been increased, and hence the commercial farm proves its efficiency on the basis of increased yields. There has been more plowing and more specializa-

---

[2] Source — U. S. Department of Commerce, Bureau of the Census. *The Manufacture and Sale of Farm Equipment and Related Products*, 1937, p. 5.

[3] *Farm Implement News*, April 7, 1938.

tion in certain crops and therefore problematical surpluses in these crops, but the efficiency of any yield must be judged on the basis of yield per acre. What are the facts? In yields per acre commercial types of farming have made no advance. Land is mined out in the single-crop system and heavy expenditures are required to keep yields per acre from falling lower and lower.

Yields per Acre of Farms in United States

	1878–1882	1898–1902	1928–1932
Wheat	13.2 bu.	13.9 bu.	14.4 bu.
Corn	25.6 bu.	25.9 bu.	25.0 bu.
Cotton	196.0 lb.	198.0 lb.	181.0 lb.

The following tables indicate that our mass-production agriculture makes a very unfavorable showing when it is compared with the agriculture that is carried on in other countries on small farms and family units on soil that has been producing for centuries.

Comparative Production Statistics Indicating America's Inefficiencies in Mass-Production Agriculture[4]

Corn — 1937–38		Corn (within U. S.) — 1923–32	
United States	28.2 bu. per acre	New Hampshire	41.9 bu. per acre
Italy	37. bu. per acre	Rhode Island	40.1 bu. per acre
Austria	44. bu. per acre	Connecticut	39.4 bu. per acre
Hungary	35.9 bu. per acre	Maine	38.0 bu. per acre
Egypt	39.9 bu. per acre	Illinois	36.0 bu. per acre
Czechoslovakia	29.7 bu. per acre	Iowa	37.8 bu. per acre
		Indiana	34.6 bu. per acre
		Ohio	36.6 bu. per acre

From these state yields, it is clear that the best production does not take place in the so-called mechanized, commercialized, specialized "corn belt." Notice further these figures:

	Wheat — 1925–37	Rye — 1925–37	Oats — 1925–37
United States	13.5 bu. per acre	12. bu.	30. bu.
Denmark	42.0 bu. per acre	28. bu.	79. bu.
Italy	22.9 bu. per acre	23. bu.	39.8 bu.
Finland	25.9 bu. per acre	24.9 bu.	43. bu.
Hungary	20.4 bu. per acre	18.6 bu.	37.5 bu.
Netherlands	44.5 bu. per acre	35.6 bu.	82.2 bu.
Scotland	44.4 bu. per acre		57.6 bu.
Egypt	29.5 bu. per acre		

[4] *Agricultural Statistics,* 1938.

Again, it is evident that the soils that have been producing for centuries in a system of small farms and family units of operation give the more abundant return. The same story is told us in the results obtained in other farm products:

Potatoes — 1923-32		*Potatoes (within U. S.)*	
United States	114. bu. per acre	Maine	252 bu. per acre
England	248.1 bu. per acre	Minnesota	93 bu. per acre
Norway	263.3 bu. per acre	North Dakota	76 bu. per acre
Denmark	209.5 bu. per acre	South Dakota	77 bu. per acre
Netherlands	273.4 bu. per acre	Iowa	90 bu. per acre
Belgium	305.4 bu. per acre		

Barley — 1925-30		*Sugar Beets — 1925-30*	
United States	23.3 bu. per acre	United States	10.9 short tons
England	38.5 bu. per acre	Sweden	12.5 short tons
Scotland	41.9 bu. per acre	Denmark	13.1 short tons
Ireland	47.7 bu. per acre	Netherlands	14.8 short tons
Denmark	50.3 bu. per acre	Italy	11.4 short tons
Netherlands	56.2 bu. per acre	Switzerland	12.8 short tons
Egypt	36.1 bu. per acre		
Japan	37.2 bu. per acre		

Thus we see that the small-size, diversified, family farm leads in practically everything, even on the soils that have produced for centuries.

In order to defeat commerce at its own game the farmer raised more corn, more oats, more wheat, and the more he raised of these surplus commodities, the more money it cost him to buy fruit and vegetables and meat for his own table. Then he complained about the chain store or the corner grocer, or he blamed it all on the taxes. He bought or rented more land to raise more corn, more wheat, more oats; he went into debt to buy machinery and still more land, and he naturally had to raise more to pay off his obligations. In the meantime, he worked and slaved to raise a bigger crop, only to get less and to pay more in purchasing what he could have raised himself.

The result of this "pressure" farming for crops which will bring greater returns on the market is the defeat of its own purpose. The buying and selling on the floor of the Board of Trade in Chicago fluctuates according to the supply. A too plentiful supply causes the price to fall. Hence, those who have raised a crop for the commercial market may lose because of a poor price. In the end more of these crops must be raised to be able to purchase necessities, with the result that the market is overflooded and rampant speculation causes the farmer to lose on what he believed would be a "big-price" crop. A farmer possessing God's most fertile land, and having the ability to raise any and all of the necessities for life, becomes the dupe of a system of commercial exploitation and big-business gambling.

When Farmers Own Their Land It Is Not Peasantry

Now what is objectionable about these two aims? Is this to be called "peasantry"? Do the objectors want more industrial slaves in the cities? Do they want the farmers to think of everybody's welfare first and think of their own family last? Agrarianism is not peasantry. It is liberty; it is independence.

Agrarianism aims at increased efficiency. The mere displacing of man power is not efficiency unless thereby human values have been increased. Agrarianism wants to use all modern means at hand. It aims at an increase of cultural values by better family life, more ownership of productive property, by better and real living. It maintains that in spite of the vaunted progress of our nation, there has been a retrogression. It claims that, having been blessed with God's choicest gifts, there should be no need of concentration of wealth, no need of poverty, or of suffering in our country.

Consumption of Food

The statement, so often heard, that the American standard of living is higher than elsewhere is not supported by facts. A comparative report in the *Consumers' Guide,* August 23, 1937 — an official publication of the United States Department of Agriculture — illustrating "how consumption of certain foods by wage earners in Detroit compares with consumption by workers in other countries," does not indicate a high American standard.

The Detroit workers do excel in consumption of eggs and fresh fruit as compared with the countries studied. Yet they would not excel even in that if compared with Italy, Spain, or France where fresh fruits are available. Official figures prove that the Detroit "standard of living" is not as high as that of the average shown by five other European countries with which it is compared. Queer, but true! And Detroit is certainly an American industrial city.

Flour Equivalent

Detroit	100
Sweden	91
Germany	94
Belgium	150
Norway	102
Poland	162

Average

Detroit	100
Other countries	119.4

Meat and Fish

Detroit	100
Sweden	112
Germany	92
Belgium	105
Norway	151
Poland	89

Average

Detroit	100
Other countries	109.4

Margarine and Butter

Detroit	100
Sweden	115
Germany	108
Belgium	140
Norway	132
Poland	28

Average

Detroit	100
Other countries	119

Potatoes

Detroit	100
Sweden	130
Germany	184
Belgium	272
Norway	106
Poland	242

Average

Detroit	100
Other countries	186.4

Milk and Cheese

Detroit	100
Sweden	159
Germany	103
Belgium	105
Norway	141
Poland	54

Average

Detroit	100
Other countries	113.2

What is the agrarian solution? Is it to let the government buy up big farms, divide them up, and give easy credit to all the families who want to go on the land? No, absolutely and unqualifiedly, no! The government may and should help, but we need a reasonable philosophy of life and action on the part of the many to change a nation. Let us make progress. If there is something wrong with our right hand, let us not apply remedies to the left foot. If the road we have taken has dispossessed the majority, if our standards of living have been lowered, let us arise from our self-complacent lethargy, let us analyze the causes, let us be truthful with ourselves, let us admit our fault, let us improve and not persist in our error. Properly using their intelligence farmers must make it a point to raise a living first, and then plan a commercial crop.

Agrarianism is Progress

Agrarian distributists want progress, charging that the advocates of commercialized agriculture preach a doctrine that leads to slavery, to peonage, to pauperism; that the practice of extreme commercialized agriculture has forced the demand for a paternalistic government. If commercialized farming, to the exclusion of the first and main purposes of farming; namely, a home and living, has actually any value, why do we need so many artificial props for the farmers who engage in it? Evidently there has been a retrogression in the pursuit of liberty, independence, and the better living. We need more farm homemakers on the land. Then only shall we enjoy the blessings of God's choicest gift to mankind, the country, our home! We need a practice of self-sufficiency and only after that has been secured are we to think of production for exchange — cash, corn or cotton or wheat, or what else we please.

Chapter 9

FORWARD ON THE LAND

PRIOR to 1934, while stationed at a parish in Toronto, the problems of unemployment and relief had become very well known to Rev. Francis J. McGoey. Here in one small section of Toronto were over 150 families of one religious denomination on the relief rolls. Several things were all too apparent. The impossibility of obtaining employment was undermining the morale of the fathers of these unfortunate families. Despair was coming to be the predominant note, bitterness and unhappiness were settling down over their homes. Men of ability, willing and earnest, were denied the right of earning their own living, of participating in the joys common to their communities, by a set of circumstances beyond their own control. The stability they needed was only to be secured by placing themselves on the mercy of the State.

Father McGoey's Plan

Certainly something had to be done before it was too late. Surely there was some way of restoring to them the rights of men. After careful study and consultation a plan was evolved which might solve their difficulty. This plan, Father McGoey felt, would be the foundation of a definite and lasting answer for men of all creeds to the charge that unemployment and relief must be considered a permanent fixture in Canada's problems. The idea was not something new but at least it was a practical move at a time when theories and cure-alls were being recklessly tossed about on every side. Here was the birth of *"Catholic Action in Rural Districts."*

The first step contemplated in the founding of this rural community was realized when a kind friend loaned ten acres of land at King, Ontario. Supplemented by donations of $200 each by five well-wishers to build five very modest houses, a start was made. Upon completion of these houses five families, totaling 38 human beings, were moved in and started to work.

Supplied with a plot of land, the necessary implements, and sufficient seed, these men, with no previous farm experience, but strong in willingness and desire to regain an independent living, were placed under the supervision of an experienced farmer who appreciated and understood their problem. Each family was provided with two acres of land and 50 chickens, two cows serving the entire infant community. The city of Toronto contributed relief food vouchers for the first four months of the experiment. Once the migration was completed, 16 by 30-ft. frame dwellings were constructed by the men at approximate cost of two hundred dollars each. The total cost of establishing the five families, complete with cottages, fowl, seed, and implements, was about $2,500.

Throughout the warm summer months the men and women, and even the children, worked long hard hours for their new homes. And when the harvest season arrived, every cellar was filled with a variety of vegetables, enough to supply each family throughout the long winter. But more than that, there were 970 bags of surplus vegetables, which were taken to Toronto and sold for $1 a bag, thus providing each family with nearly $200 of much-needed cash. The following spring saw the original families established in permanent homes, and for each family ten acres of land, a horse, a cow, and a flock of chickens. Fifteen more families were selected from the relief and welfare rolls, always with the assistance of the parish priest, and moved into the original cottages and new ones which it was now necessary to build.

The permanent houses built by the now seasoned settlers were frame structures two stories high, resting on a stone foundation about 25 ft. wide by 27 ft. long, and costing in the neighborhood of $500 each. Last spring this second group of 15 families, having proved their earnestness and capabilities, were graduated to permanent homes of their own, and 20 other families left Toronto to take their place.

Cooperation

Because each man in the community pursues his own trade, on a cooperative basis, all the work is expertly done. A community store was established, and the labor rendered by the carpenter, mason, and tinsmith on the homes of the settlers was credited to their individual accounts — credits against which they may make purchases of equal value in food, clothing, or other commodities.

Education

Two school teachers reside in the little community to care for the education of the 78 scholars. Once each week a physician visits King City, and twice a year the dentist calls. The families requiring the services of these doctors pay their own individual bills.

Liturgy

A frame church 50 by 25 ft., seating 125 people, was among the first buildings to be erected in King City. There Father McGoey daily celebrates Mass and conducts evening prayer.

Today there are 19 families dwelling on 10-acre tracts of land and 21 additional families are serving their preliminary year of training. In all, 240 men, women, and children, forgetting selfish interests, are living together happily, and are working out a better system of economy. They are no longer dependent on relief for existence. With despair, bitterness, and distrust far behind them they have regained what men must have; namely, economic freedom and independence.

In addition to the regular curriculum in the school, the children are taught how man must live with thought for his fellow men, how individuals must work with a common aim, and not at someone else's expense.

The winter is not passed in comparative idleness, for it is the season in which the trades flourish. A weaver is now engaged in making household linens and imparting the knowledge and skill of a disappearing art to the younger generation. Then, of course, there is the community store. The women, too, have taken up their share of the work. Fruit and vegetables must be canned and stored away. Those who had never knitted before have now been taught and they are able to make socks, scarfs, and sweaters, efficiently and well.

A Community Built on Sound Principles

A community has been established which, if one can judge by the amazingly increased health of the children, the contentment of the mothers and the fathers, and the disappearance of fear and dread for the future, certainly more than adequately justifies one's fondest dreams.

The Families Enjoy New Life

The families of this community tell what the plan has done to give them a fresh start in life.

Family No. 1

We were, my wife and I, brought up to city standards of living. We had been used to a better than average working man's income. We had a nice home, well furnished, and the usual small car. Then I lost my job. In our mad scramble to keep our heads above water, car, insurance, and saleable furniture went for a song. Even the baby's carriage was sold. At this point we might quote the old melodrama, "Then came the dawn." We met Father McGoey and he accepted us as one of the families for his community at King.

After almost two years in the Mt. St. Francis Community we are convinced, my wife and I, that Divine Providence smiled on us the day I lost my job. We now find that, in our palmiest days in the city the feeling of security and true happiness did not exist. It was at best a hand to mouth existence in which we paid in cash, when we had it, for any pleasures we received and resolutely chased future possibilities from our minds. We know of course, that a good living and secure old age is there for some, but for thousands of others it will never be, no matter how hard they work and slave. Here we have our land on which we live and work as a family unit. We can make our living by growing it on soil that is ours and experience the joy of accomplishment. Instead of being the cogs in the wheel of an industrial machine, we can now be personalities planning and doing many things we thought we couldn't do or did not have the opportunity to do.

We live a healthy life here in God's sunshine and fresh air. We can take a more leisurely pace now and therefore jumpy nerves, nervous headaches, nervous indigestion, are absent. Our children can run and play and have plenty of room in which to grow. We are not driven frantic keeping our children off the street. Our children are a help to us here. We can give them little chores to do, thereby teaching them responsibility and to be useful citizens. Our children are learning at a very early age many things about plant and animal life which city children must learn in school, and in most cases do not learn at all.

With regard to our own education, we have community study groups in religion and sociology. The groups are numbered a dozen and more people to a group. These study clubs teach us to think and to express ourselves on government and economic questions pertaining to Canada.

Our amusements are spontaneous, carefree, partaken with our neighbors, whom we know intimately. We have a weekly dance and euchre to which young and old go and enjoy themselves. We have modern and old-fashioned dances and the young people are as eager for the old-fashioned square dances as are the older people. It does our hearts good to see father and mother, son and daughter, laughing and dancing and having a great time together, without I might add, the necessity of liquid stimulant. Here one is not put on the shelf when the first grey hair appears, not even when the whole is silvery white. Checker tournaments, boxing bouts and dramatics are among our public entertainments, none of which require an admission fee.

It might be said that we dislike city life, judging from the foregoing criticisms. That is not so, however. We have merely tried to convey to others who might be interested, the benefits that we, a city family, have found in Father McGoey's land settlement scheme. It seems to us that we can more clearly portray the benefits we have derived from our rural life by comparing them with our former life in the city. Is it not significant, that of the 44 or so families that have been settled here in the three years, only three have chosen to return to the city?

The family is more closely drawn together in working the soil and the fruits of one's labor more abundantly returned. In our community, our co-operative efforts, we shall be as it were, a family of families working together for our mutual benefit.

Family No. 2

Back in the winters of 1934 and 1935 there were difficult times. And the joy of raising a family meant debts which must be cared for in a reasonable manner. I myself during this time was not in a position to discharge these debts, and with such circumstances there necessarily

Forward on the Land

follows either a collapse in morals, or a turning to new fields of endeavor.

It was a kind Providence that vouchsafed the latter for me. In the early spring of 1935, I moved, under the direction of the Director of Rural Catholic Action, Reverend Father McGoey, back to the land.

In this new life we have moved steadily forward. My whole family is happy and contented. We are imbued with the spirit of building, whether it be a shelf for the pantry, or a pantry for the house.

In many respects thus far we have made our way, and are confident for the future.

I whole heartedly believe in the "Back to the Land Movement" and am convinced, if it is carried on in the true encyclical spirit, of its ultimate triumph, and with its triumph the emancipation of my fellowmen caught in the wages of world depression.

Family No. 3

It is like a dream to have your own 10 acres, to see vegetables and fruit growing in your own garden, and to see your children growing healthy in the open spaces. No longer that daily fear of losing your job, no lack of food for those dear to you, no insecurity as to the future. What a change. Oh, that thousands of others could experience what we are enjoying!

Family No. 4

The community is like one large family. The children play as one community. They are always learning to do something useful, the girls to prepare a meal, to bake and cook; the boys to gather the wood, look after the garden. There is no drudgery in this work, there is variety. Community singing, community dancing, study clubs, everything to enable us to enjoy life in a real way.

During the week nights we have our entertainments, clubs for religious and social study, boxing and wrestling. Sometimes a picture show. Every Friday night a dance, checker tournaments and amateur shows, things that many of us never enjoyed in the city during the dreary days of the depression.

Family No. 5

I was out of work, sick and disheartened. Being 54 years old and with so many young men unemployed, what chance was there for me? This community gave me hope, something to look forward to. We like it here. We are all improved in health, able to look the world in the eye instead of that awful feeling that nobody wants you.

On the relief rolls today are many ready and eager to work and become independent members of society. This willingness and eagerness is lost when the spirit is broken, and the spirit is broken when no respite is in sight. Those of us who are more fortunate must realize that these are our fellow men who are worthy of help and encouragement. They would do credit to any wisely conceived and carefully considered scheme. It is our belief that community projects such as the one we are describing offer a permanent and fundamental solution to combat the loss of morale and the despair into which many of our families have been plunged. It is the salvation of them and of you, for the change in thinking, the pride of achievement offers security to society at large.

Hundreds of Families Await a Start

There are on file hundreds of applications from families wishing to join the community. The following letters speak for themselves:

Dear Father:

As we are almost driven to despair, we are appealing to you for a home. We are behind five months with our rent and in danger of getting notice to vacate any time.

My husband is an engineer, works in the summer time. When times were good he made good wages, but these last few years seasons have been short and the cut in wages has made it impossible to get along.

We were wondering if you could take us out there. As the greater part of my life was spent on a farm, I feel I would be happy in your community and would be able to teach my five boys to work, and I am able to work myself, and am quite willing to put up with any inconveniences.

Dear Father:

I heard you are doing a great many things for many people, I wonder if you would be kind enough to help my family. I have five children and we live on relief. I am very heartbroken, because I'm not used to it, and that's why I want to try to go some place where I can make my own living.

I got a house, but I am three years behind in taxes, and I can't tell you what a terrible condition I am in. The man who has a mortgage on my house wants to foreclose, and that means I'll be put out on the street. I hope before that happens God will open some other door to me and my family. That's why I have come to you.

—Harold M. Lambert

A small home acreage affords the opportunity for raising a considerable variety of vegetables and small fruits.

A complete rural church plant is that of St. John's Parish at Carrolton, Illinois. From left to right the buildings are the Sisters' Convent, the High and Grade School, the Church, and the Rectory.

Dear Father McGoey:

I wrote you some time ago in January regarding a placement on that settlement of yours. I am very sorry I did not write in March as you requested me to do, but we moved from ——— Avenue, and on the 7th of March I had a baby boy, and I guess my letter went astray, as I got no answer, and just about that time we moved again. The conditions of the times is certainly not any better here in Toronto, as the relief hardly lasts us three days. I can faithfully say that for three days we don't know what to eat, and it is certainly hard to see little children crying for something to eat.

We can't even hardly get any clothes for the children or ourselves, as we haven't had any new ones for five months. I would be very thankful to you if you would please be able to give us a chance up there with you, as we would certainly work hard and get a home together. My husband and I would be satisfied with anything as long as we had a little home that we know we wouldn't be put out in a month or less. So will you please be so kind as to try your best, Father, and let us know if there is any chance at all for us. Please let us know as soon as possible, Father, and may God bless you and reward you in your wonderful work you are doing.

Prominent People Endorse the Work

I am glad to commend the self-sacrifice and devotedness of Rev. Francis McGoey in his work of trying to rehabilitate Catholic people on the land. It is a difficult, though meritorious work and is worthy of any help or encouragement that can be given to it. I gladly bless this endeavor and those who help to make it a success. — *Most Rev. James C. McGuigan, Archbishop of Toronto.*

The work of this young priest is nothing less than sensational. All honour to him, may his work prosper more and more, that men and women may increasingly turn away from the mental anxiety and spiritual mortification that is too frequently their lot in the city, to the more enduring satisfactions and the pride of accomplishment which has already given meaning and purpose to the lives of those who by their labors have made Father McGoey's scheme the success it is. — *His Honor Dr. Herbert A. Bruce.*

I greatly admire the enterprise now being tried out in King Township so successfully by Father McGoey. I think his work is admirable and worthy of wide emulation. — *Rev. W. E. Wilson, King Street United Church, Toronto.*

The point that struck me most when I took charge of the people at St. Francis Community was that on consulting me, they seemed to feel something was seriously wrong with them physically. Nearly every child was supposed to have his tonsils out, a typical hospital out-patient's viewpoint. As you know, a mind unoccupied is a mind distressed. After getting interested in building a new home for themselves, the change in these people's outlook has been almost miraculous. While we have been fortunate in the absence of epidemics, yet the following facts taken over a two and one-half year period from 250 people who were all on relief are to me, significant. I feel these facts could not be possible if they had remained in the city.

(1) Only one death in the Community to date and that was a lady up in years and a very advanced heart case before coming to the Community.

(2) Only one appendix operation — complete recovery.

(3) No tonsils removed in two and a half years and no rheumatism or complications such as patients are supposed to develop. Diet and fresh air seemed to cause some very large tonsils to disappear.

(4) Birth rate has been high.

(5) Very few house calls are necessary. Most patients are able to attend the weekly clinic.

(6) Every child receives toxoid. To date we had no diphtheria, scarlet fever, typhoid. The nurse watches colds very closely and influenza has been less than expected.

(7) The health of the school children is above the average, and days missed from school from sickness are lower than Town schools.

(8) Above all, I feel the most important is the great, almost unbelievable improvement in the mental attitude of these people. They are happy, and happy people are a healthier people. I feel Father McGoey is doing a splendid work and I would like to see it tried out on a national scale. — *Dr. C. J. Devans, Aurora, Ont.*

Extension of Father McGoey's plan on a large scale, backed by the Provincial Government, would probably go a long way toward solving the unemployment situation. It has turned out wonderfully well, and up to the present has been a huge success. — *G. Harrison Smith, President, Imperial Oil Co., Ltd.*

We might continue with still other testimonies. Thus we are told that official investigations were made by the experts of both the Ontario Minister of Public Welfare and of the Federal

Minister of Labor, both giving their "unqualified approval." But here, in fine, is Father McGoey's own answer to any criticism that might be brought against this undertaking. He says:

If a lack of security in industrial life is progress, then we can be accused of retrogression. If poor health and late marriages, due to economic conditions which make impossible the reproduction of the human race, is progress; if education preparing for professions that are already overcrowded and for white collar jobs that do not exist is progress, then we must plead guilty of retrogression. But if the steady improvement of health by living in a natural way is progress, then we are making progress in our community. It is interesting to note our birth rate of 46 per thousand, as compared with 16 per thousand in the city of Toronto. If giving men, women and children an opportunity to use their brains in the development of art, music, work, entertainment, and play, as against the artificial city life, is part of progress, then we have it. Land ownership and agrarianism gives the poor something better than a choice between finance-capitalism, and communism.

In support of the statement that homesteading is the rational choice between finance-capitalism, and communism, the Rev. Vincent McNabb, O.P., thus delightfully writes in defense of it:

The socio-economic answer to that statement is the thing for which the land movement stands, the idea of essential poverty necessary for the full development of family life. On the land only can you get the three things that are the staples of all stable communities — poverty, chastity and obedience: poverty with property, chastity with the family, obedience with authority. That is the reason why, as long as I live, I shall be a staunch friend of the land movement.

Colonization Practical in Middle Western and Southern States

Social leaders should become actively engaged in the work of colonizing on the land carefully selected families whose love of the land and aptitude for farm life have been ascertained by preliminary investigations or trials. Individuals and groups who have money to invest can do no better social work than to assist families in acquiring small family farms through long-term, low-interest loans. This colonization should be worked in the better soils and better climates of our Southern and Middle

Western states. Modern progress is not incompatible with plain, inexpensive living in homes of simple and even somewhat primitive construction which the homesteaders can build for themselves, or at least can afford to pay for within a reasonable time.[1] Elaborate theories that rural colony projects must provide all the modern comforts from the very start are absurd and are responsible for more than one expensive failure in the field of rehabilitation. Improved living standards that involve increased expenditures should be the outcome, first, of improved income; and secondly, of improved mental attitudes toward environment. Only such adults as agree to cooperate in an educational program that is religious, inspirational, and practical should be accepted. The educational program should adequately deal with diversified farming and the use of cooperatives, home arts, in a word, chiefly such things as are adapted to the particular needs of the rural group and their environment. Adult education, properly conducted, can do wonders to improve the condition of any group and such a program should be carried out today in every rural parish. Improved living standards, united planning and efforts, less dependence on government, cooperative action in buying and selling, and the improvement of local credit facilities should be the outcome of the educational program. The government should encourage and protect rural colony projects. It should not formulate all plans and dictate all terms. All colony groups should have a large measure of local autonomy.

---

[1] Cf. Appendix: "St. Teresa's Village."

Chapter 10

PART-TIME FARMING: SOIL AND INDUSTRY

THE agrarians deplore the results of industrialism, of finance, capitalism, and they regret in a special way the unbalanced population of today and the economic insecurity. They point out, the real, harmful results of urbanization, concentration of wealth; they seek to make people know that what is heralded as a blessing and could be a blessing and a help to humanity has been turned into a curse and a handicap. They, therefore, urge in season and out of season that for the betterment of our nation it will be necessary to have more families on the land. They also state most emphatically that farmers who are on the land should make farming a way of living first and not a commercial enterprise. The belief that individual security is first to be achieved marks the homestead movement.

The ideal agrarian state would consist of a predominantly agricultural population and in general of decentralized industries with small efficient factories driven by electricity. The agrarians believe in the private ownership of productive property in land and industry and commerce. They believe that economic independence is the essential foundation stone for political freedom and for a stable nation. They contend that, for a higher degree of national culture and for real development of native abilities, widespread ownership of productive property is most desirable. We are face to face with the present arrangement, an evil one, bringing forth evil fruit — lack of ownership, wage slavery, and commercialized agriculture. What then might be done to create a new order, to establish a new way of living, to embrace a better and safer philosophy of life? First of all, let us be convinced that the aim or the end toward which we should strive is right. Let us know why — let us be firmly established in our philosophy. Then let us have the courage of our convictions. Where there is a will, there is a way. Halfhearted interest, laziness, selfishness, will never achieve results. Then let us take steps in the right direction, small and perhaps insignificant, but every move in the right direction is a move toward the goal.

Standing on Two Feet: Soil and Industry

We have in the United States, an army of workers who are part-time workers. Technological improvements and seasonal demands are the chief reasons. Even though the hourly wages might be very high the yearly wage is in many instances below that which a family needs for an adequate living. The part-time employment creates enforced leisure and we need not fool ourselves into believing that the majority of humans can use prolonged and enforced leisure in a profitable way. Hence there is a proper place for Subsistence Homesteads as a partial solution. Briefly it consists of this:

Move the families of part-time industrialists from the crowded city slums or mining camps, to decent homes in the open country. Surround these homes with small acreages. Make it possible for these families to purchase the homesteads by long-term amortization and low interest rates and preferential taxation. Thus we would peg these industrialists on the land—as owners first of all, and that is essential. Leisure time would mean an opportunity to dedicate oneself to the soil, to raise foodstuff, to care for animals that would produce more and better food for the family. This arrangement would enable a family to stand on both feet—one foot in industry, the other on the soil. An industrial or commercial upheaval, so possible and so frequent, causes the industrial or commercial groups to become unbalanced because the proletarian family is standing on but one foot—the job in industry. A foot in the industry and a foot on the soil has social as well as economical advantages, since industry and soil are most intimately related. It was not difficult to see the possibilities and feasibility of such a movement in 1932. And so by legislation of Congress the Subsistence Homesteads came into existence. Regardless of newspaper or magazine articles, of speeches in the

Senate or political harangues, the Subsistence Homesteads idea has never been discredited, because it is fundamentally sound and feasible.

What is needed for the success of homesteads:
1. *People of the right kind.*
2. *Land, homes, and proper credit.*
3. *Leaders.*

If the right kind of families are not available or present on a homestead, it is in vain that any efforts are expended. Qualifications must be carefully studied. Applications must be investigated, and checked up by references. First of all, the family should need a homestead. That means it should need better housing, more wholesome surroundings and greater economic, social, and religious opportunities. To have a desire for the open country, for a new home, or just for a change is not sufficient. These desires wear out with time and difficulties. *The family should be a real unit.* It should have solidarity of purpose. If husband and wife do not agree, if children try to run the home, if there is a continued struggle within the home itself, no matter how hard individual members work, the family will never get ahead. Failure stalks in its path and the members of the family should look within themselves for the cause of failure and not attribute it to outside causes. The desire to get something for nothing, to live off the government, to "get by," will not and cannot be the spirit of a successful homesteader family. An appreciation, not in words only but in actual deed, of the opportunities must be present. The home itself, with whatever conveniences it has, must be kept up, and there must be a continued improvement and constant care given to it. That does not mean new or expensive furniture, but rather cleanliness, tidiness, taste, ambition to make it better, pride in its appearance, realization that the mother can train the children by example more than in any other way.

There should exist a thorough knowledge of the value of God's earth, of the soil attached to the homestead. It is really amazing how quickly human beings get away from love, appreciation, and knowledge of the value of soil. An old Irish hymn of thanksgiving expresses it thus:

> Thanks be to God for the light and the darkness;
> Thanks be to God for the hail and the snow;
> Thanks be to God for shower and sunshine;
> Thanks be to God for all things that grow;
> Thanks be to God for the lightning and tempest;
> Thanks be to God when the harvest is plenty;
> Thanks be to God when the barn is low.

In our commercialized world, it is not a hymn of thanksgiving to God but to the machine, the railroad, the board of trade, and the middle man. Milk is connected with a bottle and not a peaceful, kindly cow. Vegetables appear on market stalls, fruits come wrapped in tissue paper, flour in sacks, potatoes in chips, and carrots are diced.

If the mind of the homesteader is thoroughly imbued with the false advantages of commercialism, if he is completely fooled by the clever propaganda that made possible his own poverty and misery, and if he wants more of it, then no one can help him. But if he can see how a piece of God's earth can produce for him what he and his family need, if he can realize that independence can really be achieved by controlling his food production, this man will make a success of the homestead. If he thinks that it is better and cheaper to buy what is necessary for his needs, he will never succeed. On a homestead of less than 10 acres or so it is almost impossible at the beginning to expect to derive a complete living from it. There must be a supplementary income from an industry or other source, and it should be sufficient to make the payments on the home and to pay for such goods and services as one must buy even in an efficient, modern, home economy. The family must know how to plan, or must learn to do it. One of the girls in the Assumption High School, Granger, Iowa, stated in a brief essay:

> In this class we also learn the use of money and what is necessary for our use. We learn that we are never poor when we are able to manage our homes, raise and can our own fruits and vegetables, plan proper meals, and make our own clothes, launder them properly, and repair and remodel them. We may not have riches, but we have many comforts if we just learn how.

A spirit of willing cooperation should also exist. A selfish homesteader, even though he may believe himself a success, will eventually be a failure and will help others to fail. We do not believe in collectivism, or even in a thoroughgoing cooperative commonwealth, but we consider willingness to help, Christian charity, and the golden rule as essentials for individual success or for the community advancement. The above are essentials. The people must regard themselves as the main spokes in the wheel of success or failure. Is it not ridiculous that we, as free human beings, should blame someone else for our failure? Or that we should expect success to be thrown into our lap by a benevolent government or a Santa Claus? Success must be personal. If it is not personal, it is not success. Likewise, complete and lasting failure is always personal. We are simply deceiving ourselves, if we blame it on someone else.

It is evident that in the second place a homestead program needs *land suitable for cultivation,* credit at low interest and for long terms, and finally the building of good homes. The homes should be well planned and comfortable. They must not be too pretentious or too far out of line with the economic and social standing of the families. If possible at all, the homes should be modern, supplied with plumbing and electricity. The financial question must be faced and worked out in accordance with the family's ability to pay. Too big a debt burden will kill all possibilities of success. Long amortization, very low interest rates, and preferential taxation are most essential. Nonsensical and impractical schemes of housing or land operation for homesteaders come to no good end, either for the social planners in the community or for the families on the land. Homesteads should, of course, be exempted from taxation. But if the community has not the social and political wisdom to understand the objectives and the social advantages of such exemptions, then the only just way of taxing is proportionate taxation in accordance with the means and the income of the family on the land.

We should not any longer stultify ourselves with the cheap and easy commercial slogans, such as, "Equal rates of interest for all," "A homestead is nothing more than a 'business,'" "Equal taxation for all," "The same foreclosure procedure, and the same bankruptcy for all." Such slogans are never completely followed out in practice, and they are perhaps followed, least of all, by those who keep them forever on their tongues. Nevertheless, by such slogans, many people are led to think of men as being "identical" rather than merely as equal. "Identity" and equality are not the same. Modern society suppresses individual differences, crowds all men into a few classes, and offers the few classes standardized work. We should strive to bring about equality of men and stop trying to make them "identical." The Founding Fathers rightly grounded our liberty and equality in God when they declared:

> We hold these truths to be self-evident: that all men are created equal; that they are endowed by their Creator with certain inalienable rights; that among these are life, liberty, and the pursuit of happiness.

As long as men admit a God who has given them their rights, they have a basic guarantee of freedom and equality. Obviously, this does not make them "identical," nor does it mean that society should strive to make men "identical." The recognition of the equality of men is not inconsistent with a recognition of the dissimilarity of men.

Thirdly, it is clear that community programs for homesteading require *unselfish leaders*. We have criticized the government for the money we say it wasted on foolish projects. But what are we actually doing to enable the one third of our population to solve the problem of undernourishment, poor housing, and rags? Are we doing anything to help the poor help themselves? Is it possible for us to *lead* in making for less poverty and suffering in this country? We may give to the Red Cross, build libraries, museums, stadia, but what have we done toward the cause of educating the poor to improve their conditions? Can we develop cooperation in our communities? lead others? teach others? When do we actually help a poor family in need? We help them best when we teach them proper planning and make them conscious of a sense of values, when we help them to develop those very qualities which make for success. If we have no time to be leaders, then why not give our *means* toward the cause of educating the poor to help themselves? Why not make it possible for the ones who do it, to extend their activities and reach out for greater accomplishment? We have heard of unsuccessful Subsistence Homesteads. Who has not? In most cases the people were of the right type, the places were fine, but local leaders were not ready and willing to lead. Too often they were interested in selling land or material to the government, or in "high pressuring" homesteaders into foolish purchases on time payments. It is part of the battle to warn poor people against unscrupulous leeches who are looking out only for selfish interest.

Government Survey of Part-Time Farming in the Southeast

Although the government survey of part-time farming in the Southeast was limited by the fact that the families investigated were carrying on a haphazard, disorganized type of industrial and agricultural life, nevertheless, it revealed that this dual existence can be productive of economic and social benefits for individual families. How much more, therefore, could be expected of a local, organized program, as well as of a broader one that included regional communities of part-time farmers? If regarded from the point of view of the people, part-time farming means a movement away from the city to the country, or to near-by acres. From the point of view of industry, it involves a transference of factories to the country in order to bring work to the country people. That, by such a concession, industries could intend the exploitation of the farmers, is a possibility; but in spite of the danger, part-time farming should be encouraged. Certainly, the possibility of exploitation is heightened when the farmers are unorganized; whereas, if organized, the community could present a strong front to the overtures of industry.

That everyone who owns a farm does not rely on the income derived from crops and dairy products for the entire support of his family is a well-known fact. Many farmers supplement their earnings by intermittent work in mining, fishing, lumbering, or some other form of remunerative activity available in the general locality of their farms. In recent years, however, better transportation facilities have brought the farmer into closer communication with life in the city.

With the coming of the automobile and improved roads, the rural dweller was placed within reach of industrial employment in the city and the urban industrial worker was placed within reach of land on a scale that had not existed since the rise of the factory system. City-weary people with city jobs could and did move to the country for esthetic reasons, for the creative pleasure of growing things, for space for their children, and for the economy and freedom of country life. The farmer went to the nearby village, town, or city for a cash wage that would help to stabilize income.[1]

It was natural for farmers to obtain periodic employment in industrial plants, the accessibility of their farms permitting. And the general definition of part-time farming formulated by the United States Department of Commerce takes into consideration this dual character:

> A mode of living whereby a family resides on a farm but receives income, in a more substantial degree, from nonfarm sources; briefly it usually connotes a combination of industry and agriculture.

Prevalency of Part-Time Farming

According to governmental figures, the number of part-time farmers in the United States on January 1, 1935, was 2,077,474, representing 30.5 per cent of the 6,812,350 total number of farm operators at that date. In both 1934 and 1929 approximately three out of every ten farm operators had a side or main occupation in addition to managing their own farm operations.

The number of days in which the farm operators worked away from the farm has also been tabulated for the year 1934 by the Department of Commerce:

Farm Operators Reporting Days Worked Off the Farm

Total Number	2,077,474
Per Cent of All Farms	30.5
1 to 24 days	595,472
25 to 49 days	360,628
50 to 74 days	235,277
75 to 99 days	125,325
100 to 149 days	188,815

---

[1] "Part-Time Farming in the Southeast" in *Works Progress Administration Survey*, Research Monograph No. 9, p. 16.

150 to 199 days 159,336
200 to 249 days 115,667
250 and over 296,954

In order to divide part-time farming into proper geographical sectors, another chart was made, listing the per cent of owners operating thus in contrast to the total number of farms in the same locality.

Part-Time Farming (Percentages)

New England......................... 40.9
Middle Atlantic 31.8
East North Central................... 28.8
West North Central.................. 28.4
South Atlantic 31.8
East South Central................... 25.9
West South Central.................. 26.3
Mountain 42.3
Pacific 37.1

Rapidity of transportation has likewise effected the partial decentralization of industry. This movement is conducive to part-time farming, for it enables the factory employee to strike root in an industrial plant. It is indicative of decentralization that Sears Roebuck and Co. had been purchasing its saleable merchandise from manufacturers located in large cities even though the bulk of their selling was done to farmers. The executives of this company now report a radical change. Decentralized industries in the smaller districts and towns of the nation are producing goods desired by Sears Roebuck, and orders are being placed there accordingly. Eighty per cent of all the purchases of the company at present come from towns with less than 40,000 population. Sears Roebuck and Co. give a simple explanation for the change.

As electric power is now available in little cities, manufacturing is on the move, abandoning the crowded cities for smaller towns, where costs are lower. And business is following them out of the big cities.

Recently, too, Mr. W. A. Julian, one of the largest manufacturers of shoes has become an ardent booster of decentralization and the union of industry and agriculture. This conversion was the result of an experience connected with his work that brought him in contact with a small factory from which he procured a special type of shoe. The plant is situated in the country and functions periodically when there is a demand for these shoes. As soon as orders flow into the office, the officials of the little factory send out a petition to the neighboring farmers who come to the town, perform the skilled work necessary for the production of the shoes, and return again to the land, richer on account of the opportunity to augment their income. Mr. Julian said:

> What converted me to the idea of decentralizing was the standard of living of the people who worked in that factory, in comparison with the standard of living, of the workers in our plants at Holyoke, Mass. Despite efforts made to keep them working the year round, they live so much more poorly than those in Ohio who earn less, that I became convinced that the wisest thing we could do in this country was to shift manufacturing from the city to the country, and let the two activities of industry and agriculture supplement each other and furnish people with the security of which they have been deprived by the present separation of the two.

Garden Plots and Industrial Workers

The recent business depression and subsequent unemployment turned the eyes of sufferers toward Washington in the hope that the government would evolve a general policy and undertake practical measures for the restoration of the economic order on a sound basis whereby the opportunity of attaining to a reasonable degree of security would be assured to everyone eager to work. In many instances, suggestions were forthcoming and, where feasible, were included by the government in its program. Among the latter was a suggestion from numerous quarters that an investigation of part-time farming in conjunction with industry be instituted, and its practicality be made known to the country at large. Acting on this proposal the Division of Social Research of the Works Progress Administration began a thorough study of the phenomenon in its present guise, encompassing the families actually engaged in an attempted fusion of agriculture and industry. The survey was limited to three states, Alabama,

Part-Time Farming

Georgia, and South Carolina. Nevertheless the conclusions would be valid for other regions where industry and farming are extant as separate enterprises.

The various proposals, pertaining to part-time farming, offered by interested individuals to the government for analysis, fall under three main headings:

1. Provision of garden plots for industrial workers in order that produce from these plots may supplement their income from industrial employment and aid in tiding them over seasons of unemployment.

2. Establishment of new communities of families, each family to be provided with a small acreage on which to raise a considerable portion of its food, with the expectation that industries will locate in such communities and provide supplementary cash income.

3. Settlement of families on small farms near communities in which industrial establishments already exist, where they may produce a considerable portion of their food and may also obtain some employment in the industries.

With these proposals in mind the researchers began the task of examining the existing modes of part-time farming in order to render a decision for or against its suitability as a permanent venture. It was necessary for them to compare the average income of a nonfarming, industrial worker with that of a part-time farmer who receives a wage for industrial employment, to contrast the living conditions of the two groups, to find out if the farm is neglected during the time spent by the farmer in industry, to decide whether industry suffers on account of such an alliance, and finally to determine whether partial self-subsistence is obtainable by part-time farming at a saving impossible for the nonfarming worker.

A paragraph, in the letter of transmittal to the Administration in Washington, sets forth the conclusions logical to the survey.

The report emphasizes the fact that while part-time farming has proved beneficial to families engaged in it, such farming activity can be expanded only where industry has sufficiently recovered from the depression to offer satisfactory wages and hours to its workers, or where future prospects for an industry's development are promising.

It is unlikely that industries will resume the long hours of predepression days. Workers today are in the process of adjusting their habits to the additional leisure that shorter hours have given them, and the encouragement of part-time farming activities at this time, under proper safeguards, will help to absorb this margin of leisure time and will increase income.

For those living within reasonable proximity to factories and shops, and already employed at wages sufficient to support their families, part-time farming is recommended. It was pointed out in the report, however, that it would be doubtful wisdom to build new communities in isolated places with the expectation that a speedy rehabilitation of industrial workers would be accomplished, because part-time farming alone is by definition not sufficient for the support of families engaged in it. Yet small loans were given to present part-time farmers desirous of increasing their farming activities, and to nonfarming industrial workers with regular employment who wish to begin farming and who appear to have the qualifications necessary to make a success of the undertaking. The survey also stated that part-time farmers grow food products for their own consumption and effect a large monetary saving in grocery bills.

When the momentous question of direct participation by the government in the furtherance of a part-time farming program was discussed by the experts, several predisposing factors were listed. There is an increasing interest in part-time farming on the part of industrial workers wishing to experience liberation from the shackles of a confined life in the city; shorter hours of work prevail in industry; and the reliance of people on the government in many ways would guarantee cooperation with such a program. The Farm Credit Administration and the Federal Housing Commission could provide credit to individual part-time farmers, while advice, experience, the grant of loans to finance the purchase of land or equipment would be taken care of by the Resettlement Administration. It is worthy of note here that the Granger Homestead Development in Iowa could not have become a reality without government aid on account of the impoverished condition of those who were capable of making a success of part-time farming, and the fact that special circumstances

Part-Time Farming

militated against the private collection or borrowing of the money necessary to inaugurate the project. Nevertheless, the dangers accompanying the introduction of the government into too much direct activity are many.

Of special import are the particulars that formed the basis of the general conclusions submitted by the Division of Social Research.

Size of Household on Part-Time Farms

Size of Household	Part-Time Farm		Industrial Nonfarming	
	No.	Per Cent	No.	Per Cent
Total	1,113	100	1,334	100
1 person	6	1	4	—
2 persons	101	9	235	18
3 persons	161	14	328	25
4 persons	203	18	273	20
5 persons	213	19	192	14
6 persons	157	14	137	10
7 persons	105	9	79	6
8 persons	66	6	41	3
9 persons	37	3	25	2
10 persons	32	3	11	1
11 or more	32	3	9	1

Nearly a fourth of the part-time farming households consisted of seven or more persons, while only one eighth of the non-farming industrial households consisted of seven or more persons. Part-time farming was found to be advantageous to large families —an implication that has much significance for the statisticians who envisage the not-far-distant day when the population of the country, according to present birth versus death rates, will begin to decline rapidly.

Income from Work in Industry

In 1934, the average income of part-time farm households from nonfarm sources was $712; the average income of strictly industrial households, $751. Looking backward to the "prosperity era," the part-time farm average for industrial work in 1929 was $944; strictly industrial households, $1,108. In two diverse periods, therefore, the relation between the two remained a constant.

Nearly every phase of industrial work is listed, with iron and steel, cotton mills, knitting mills, and agricultural work away from individual farms the predominant fountains of revenue. The highest quota of part-time workers is found in the category of semiskilled occupations, 321 out of the total number of 1,113.

That a man's status as a part-time farmer did not affect his opportunity for regularity of employment is suggested by the fact that the commercial part-time farmers averaged almost as many days employment as did the noncommercial farmers, though the former lived farther from their jobs and spent much more time working on their farms. Only 19 per cent of the part-time farmers and 27 per cent of the nonfarmers had 250 or more days' work in industry, while 57 per cent of the part-time farmers and 53 per cent of the nonfarmers had less than 200 days' employment.

Contribution of Farm Enterprise to Family Income

If part-time farmers grow crops and offer dairy products for sale, they are classified as commercial; if they restrict farming activities to crops intended mainly for home use, they are styled noncommercial. Now and then this latter group does sell a portion of crops and dairy products, but since there is no concentrated effort along these lines, the profit is negligible, and the value of noncommercial farming can only be estimated economically in terms of a lightened food budget which will vary from family to family, depending on acreage and the size of the household, and ranges from $40 to $400. The commercial part-time farmers in 1934, realized a net income on the sale of agricultural products variously estimated at $165 in some localities and $343 in others.

Only when less than $50 worth of farm products were sold by part-time farmers did cash expenses exceed receipts, exclusive of taxes and, if the land was not owned, rent. The average cost of implements and machinery used by commercial part-time farmers was surprisingly low — $35. Contrary to a general preconceived opinion, work on part-time farms did not incapacitate the workers and prevent them from doing justice to industrial employment. Moreover, no one complained that it was not possible to harmonize part-time farming and industry, especially since the advent of a forty-hour industrial week.

Home Ownership

It is noteworthy that nearly all of the part-time farmers who were home owners were able to retain their status during a period of depression when so many owners were losing their homes, and that a few part-time farmers were able to raise their status.

Home Owners	No.	Per Cent
Part-Time Farmers	368	33
Nonfarming Industrial	175	13

Of the 368 part-time farmers owning their homes, 47.3 per cent were debt-free, and of the 745 who were tenants, 77.9 were likewise unburdened.

Living and Social Conditions

Another finding of the survey was the lower cost of living of part-time farmers in the suburbs and open country compared to that of nonfarming industrial workers in towns. Lower rents, too, are to be added to the advantage of the part-time farmer. There is, however, a sharp contrast between the types in the possession of conveniences. Although automobiles, radios, and telephones were evenly distributed for both, only two fifths of the part-time farms had running water. In health and education the honors remained even, but a greater percentage of farmers took active part in organized social and community life — a fact not to be attributed to comparative isolation because:

Young people's organizations, for example, were available to 83 per cent of the part-time families and to 88 per cent of the nonfarming industrial families. Yet, there were 40 per cent of the part-time farm and only 24 per cent of the nonfarm families who had one or more members participating in such organizations. Fraternal orders were available to 74 per cent of the nonfarming industrial workers but to only 59 per cent of the part-time farmers. Yet, 25 per cent of the part-time households in comparison with 14 per cent of the nonfarming industrial households had participating members. The same situation was true of other organizations.[2]

---

[2] "Part-Time Farming in the Southeast" in *Works Progress Administration Survey*, Research Monograph No. 9, p. 67.

After a painstaking study of the report, one is forced to conclude that nothing prevents the successful combination of industrial wage earning and part-time farming today save a certain spirit of narrow urban industrialism, an erroneous self-sufficiency and a want of democratic vision. It would hardly be a weaving together of fanciful thoughts if, after a demonstration of the feasibility of part-time farming from its actual and successful practice here and there by individuals in an unorganized fashion, it should be asserted that, with a more extensive, national program of part-time farming sponsored by private initiative, the social and economic problems of the family would be partly resolved and a saner order compatible with the nature of human beings appear.

An Objection Answered

Typical of the objections voiced against part-time farming for low-income, industrial families is the following:

There is an economic side, too, of the modern movement countryward with which I am not entirely in agreement. It is summed up in what is called subsistence homesteading, a plan for settling people on the land, where they are to produce as many of the necessities of life as possible, and supplement this with a cash income from part-time employment. Back of the idea is the instinct of men to scurry to the land in hard times. When everything crumbles about our heads, we turn to the earth like scared children to a mother.

All very well; there is reason in this, and work for men to do where otherwise they would have no work, and hope where there was only hopelessness, and perhaps food for empty bellies. But if the earth can be a good mother, she can also be a hard and indifferent one. And I think there is a great danger that subsistence homesteading, on a large scale at least, would be merely turning back to the peasant way of life. I confess I do not see how it could well be otherwise for men of small means. In spite of government aids and modern science and all the rest of it, a small patch of land yields only so much, only a meager part of the necessities of comfortable living; and natural forces wipe out even that little intermittently. The peasants of Europe, of India, of China are inured to this way of life; they have not known anything else for centuries. There are, in fact, many virtues in peasantry, and these fill the minds of the advocates of subsistence homesteading. I would rather be a peasant in the country than a pariah of the industrial system; but it is a sorry business to be forced to either.³

On the other hand, when Gilbert Keith Chesterton cast into book form his reflections on America, he gave proof of phenomenal perspicacity. Observing that business and the modern industrial city were sacrosanct to Americans, he said:

> In America there is something that might almost be called the sanctity of labor; but it is subject to the profound law that when anything less than the highest becomes a sanctity, it tends also to become a superstition. When the candlestick maker does not blow out his brains upon the flute, there is always a danger that he may blow them out somewhere else, owing to depressing conditions in the candlestick market.⁴

And Mr. Hambidge offers incense to something less than the highest—the superiority, gratuitously asserted, of urban civilization over rural. He would have people remember the fate of Lot's wife who, looking backward, was turned into a pillar of salt; and those, toying with the idea of a movement landward, if persistent, will share the same fate. Yet he forgets that salt serves another purpose; it flavors the meat. Without a peasantry, our cities would be rotting carcasses. Peasants are the salt that gives them flavor. Nevertheless, to Hambidge, industrialism is preferable to part-time farming, even though conveniences are present to modern homesteaders. Here values are again being measured by the yardstick of material gain; and this, according to Chesterton, is a superstition. Superstitious people are blind to everything but the disproportionate object of their imaginings. It is adoration stripped of intelligence. To regard the lot of a part-time farmer as that of a peasant and therefore inferior; to think of the land as a last resort for weaklings unable to assert themselves successfully in a competitive world; to look upon it as a Mother Hubbard's cupboard, not bare, but filled with food for the hungry and downtrodden, is to distort deliberately the nature of the reality. Do engineers regard the girders of a suspension bridge as inconsequential, of less importance than the graceful span

---

³ Hambidge, G., *The Enchanted Acre* (New York: McGraw-Hill, 1935), pp. 24, 25.
⁴ Chesterton, G. K., *What I Saw in America* (New York: Dodd, Mead & Co., 1923), p. 106.

visible to the far-off eye? Does the captain of a ship speak disparagingly of the engine room below the artificially decorated salons? Does, anyone, to put it in a homely way, scorn the mouth that feeds him? And yet, scientific advancement, colorful and capable of producing new wonders, has blinded the superficial who, carried away emotionally by the gifts of progress, have missed the content for the form. Agriculture, concerned with the basic requirement for life, is more essential than industry. In the last analysis, the factory could be sacrificed, but not the land. Therefore to offer an apology for the existence of part-time farming, or to think it impractical and retrogressive in an urbanized society, is palpably false. There is needed today a union of both. The new homestead projects will be modern in the sense that ordinary material comforts, regarded as unattainable luxuries heretofore by the "Bible Belt" and unknown to the peasant civilizations of India and China, will be included. In every Granger homestead[5] there is heating, electricity, telephone service if desired, running water and bath.

What if the land, as Mr. Hambidge claims, yields only a meager part of the necessities of comfortable living — a misleading statement because a family is satisfied primarily by food and secondarily by fine appointments — the wages for regular work in the factory are supplemented by revenue, whether in the form of a saving on the food bill or profits from the sale of surplus farm products. No advocate of part-time farming expects that full self-subsistence will be obtained from working the land. The wages paid for industrial work represent the necessary difference and constitute the larger portion of the total income. But if employment in factories be scarce, there is always the possibility of the restoration of the crafts. The homesteaders could learn, and indeed on the Granger project are learning, to fashion usables by hand. Cooperatives, local not national, are the other half of a resettlement project because canning, preserving, and the like can be done economically and efficiently when there is a corporate union of the homesteaders.

It is not true, as the objection states, that natural agents of

---

[5] Cf. Appendix, "Factual Outline of Granger Homesteads"; also Chapter 11, "The Granger Homestead Project."

destruction undo the work of the farmer. Although a severe drought that would ruin a farming region is a possibility, still in most instances the farmer himself is blameworthy. If he refuses to protect trees, conserve moisture, allow part of his land to lie fallow, and if he produces one crop consistently, of course, dust storms, pest, and other plagues will play havoc with his farm. It is the wiser policy to vary crops and thus to stand an even chance of weathering a drought. In this, from experience, the part-time farmer has fared better than his commercial confrere on the land.

Perhaps the best answer to the objection is that given by Pope Leo XIII when he said:

Man's needs do not die out, but recur; satisfied today, they demand new supplies tomorrow. Nature, therefore, owes to man a storehouse that shall never fail, the daily supply of his daily wants. And this he finds only in the inexhaustible fertility of the earth.[6]

Method of Instituting a Part-Time Farming Resettlement

If a number of families, fifty let us say, wish to unite in a part-time farming project, the approach to its realization is twofold, financial and educational. Both are essential and when fused harmoniously, the chances for a successful outcome of the experiment are enhanced. Money must be procured in the form of long-term loans at low interest; long term because the homesteaders, usually of the low-income group, should not be burdened with the obligation of meeting large payments monthly; small but regular payments are more satisfactory; low interest because it is not a get-rich-quick scheme; it is one in which the whole community will benefit, and therefore it is no more than right that the creditors should be content with a moderate return on their money. Possible sources for such loans are private organizations whose members are responsible citizens, local banks, absentee landlords, and men of wealth, men who are not money mad but interested in rebuilding society in a solid way. A relatively self-sufficient community with a steady income for every family is the only firm support for any private wealth.

---

[6] *Catholic Mind* (America Press), April 8, 1931, p. 149.

We may thus parallel the financial arrangement in an educational program intended to cover these necessary subjects:
1. Religious motivation (doctrine and action).
2. Property, ownership, security, liberty (doctrine and action).
3. Social grouping for some economic needs (local cooperatives) (doctrine and practice).
4. Social grouping for health, recreational, educational needs (doctrine and practice).
5. Scientific technique for family farm in soil, crops, animals (doctrine and practice).
6. Scientific technique in small, family type of machinery, electricity, food processing, and building (doctrine and practice).

In the rural high schools the morning classes should be devoted to cultural subjects, and be common to both boys and girls. In the afternoon, however, the boys should go to a farm shop or a carpenter shop or soil laboratory to receive technical training in repairwork, building, and farming, whereas the girls in the afternoon should take courses in practical domestic science and all the problems of homemaking. This union of the cultural and the practical is the best possible mode of procedure in view of the nature of the part-time farming project. Not only are low-income groups given an excellent opportunity for cultural development but also, by the inclusion of *crafts* and *domestic science*, the bread-and-butter aspect of life, formerly to them all-engrossing and dubious, is made rational and certain. Thus the boy and girl are saved from two extremes: the boy from considering life as one long battle with grinding poverty, or its opposite, a parasitic attitude without obligations and devoid of worth-while accomplishment; the girl from a vision of married life that sees malnutrition, disease, and squalor, or its opposite, an unreal, silken, exotic, workless, childless existence — an existence often purveyed by the movies. A blend of the cultural and the practical is the antidote, because it is true to reality, to the nature of human beings, and therefore, to the family.

Garden Programs for Subsistence

In many counties, county agents and home demonstration agents are on hand who can readily help families map out garden plans. Local charts showing possible crop cycles in the particular areas and charts showing scientific diet standards are available. The family can easily map out an outline for a garden that will supply a complete "long-season" supply of fresh vegetables and fruits, with enough to store or can for the winter months. When we know where the family diet is shy, and the amount and quality of land available for the garden, it is an easy matter, with expert help, to decide on a garden program that will most nearly meet the family needs in terms of vitamins and nutrition.

When the family knows how much of each product is needed, and the amount that is to be planted, the next job is to space food supplies so that they are available the year round. The Department of Agriculture has prepared a further chart to guide families in outlining their own "seasonal distribution of fresh and stored farm-produced goods." With his chart, one can tell at a glance how many months of the year vegetables will be available in the garden, how many plantings should be made of different varieties, how many months the families may expect storage vegetables to keep, and what vegetables have to be canned in order to insure a year-round supply. Simple in their outlines, such plans have behind them sound scientific research based on experiments undertaken by the State Agricultural Colleges. They are correct farm plans hinged to a family diet plan. With sound schedules that carry through from soil to supper, families who are willing to undertake a program of "garden crops" have the chance to build the foundations both of good health and economic independence.

"Garden crops" have been one of the major successes in all farm rehabilitation work. A survey of 250,000 families who had subsistence gardens in 1937 showed that they processed a total of 65,000,000 quarts of fruit and vegetables alone, as against some 25,000,000 quarts before they undertook a home-management plan. The number of quarts canned per person increased from 21 to 53. These figures do not tell the supply of fresh fruits and vegetables taken from the garden or stored for winter use. Final figures for last year (1938) are still being computed, but already they show very large increases over the 1937 record.

Reports of farm and home advisers in the field are dramatic barometers of the program's success:

As a result of concerted efforts to produce and conserve foods of good nutritional value, rehabilitation families are enjoying improved health.

Some of the families exchange produce to enable them to better balance their food supply.

The whole family *cooperates* in raising a garden.

The grocery bill of the T—— family for one typical month, ran about $7 and $1.50 of this was for ice. This family is indeed making the farm feed the family.

The food supply of the H—— family was very inadequate in 1936, but they were supplied with a pressure cooker and sufficient jars to can eighty quarts per person this year.

When the O—— family came to our attention in the Spring of 1935 their net worth was $150. Now wealth has greatly improved and a more nutritious diet is being followed. A song or a jest can now be heard where before only growls or complaints could be heard. Mrs. O—— said "I wouldn't take $100 for my pressure cooker and what it has contributed to my family and do without it." And Mr. O—— said: "My health is better. I do not know what my family and I would have done had the government not helped us when we were most in need. It is quite a satisfaction to know this winter we have a cellar to go to, filled with a variety of food. We no longer need to ask for a grant."

Chapter 11

THE GRANGER HOMESTEAD PROJECT[1]

HERE and there individuals have demonstrated to their own satisfaction the value, socially and economically, of part-time farming. It is evident that this type of economy could be expected to guarantee to a group of families, united in a part-time project, the same fruits and even greater fruits in the form of a wholesome community life. Part-time farming can be the keystone for the building of substantial communities. By nature families are impelled to join forces in order to promote the common good. The Granger Homestead Settlement in Granger, Iowa, is offered as proof that part-time farming is an effective instrument in the rehabilitation of families and communities where they are innocent victims of a wrongheaded economic policy.

The Old Slum

Picture for yourself a series of mining camps in which families live devoid of the necessities to satisfy elementary personal and social needs. The camps are company owned and the workers are completely at the mercy of the industrialists in control of the bituminous-coal output. There are ill-kept houses and yards, dilapidated sheds of every description, dirt and grime, impassable streets and unsanitary, unhealthy living conditions abound. There are filthy pool rooms, overcrowded four-room dwellings. Immorality, truancy, delinquency, and low standards of living prevail. The coal miners and their families present serious economic and social problems due to low and insufficient incomes, a low standard of living, poor housing conditions, lack of means of transportation, the absence of religious, recreational, and educational facilities, and the bad traditions of the mining camps.

---

[1] A community of families engaged in part-time farming.

The average wage of a mine worker in Iowa for the year 1935 was $890.35, or approximately $75 a month. Many Granger families were compelled to apply for a place on the government relief rolls. Nevertheless, the amount thus gained, while it was a help, could not remedy the evils inherent in such an atmosphere. The roots went far deeper. Besides, work at the mines was uncertain and seasonal unemployment the rule. Something drastic had to be done. The Federal Subsistence Homesteads Corporation had been formed by the U. S. Department of the Interior in accordance with Section 208 of the National Recovery Act which read:

> To provide for aiding the redistribution of the overbalance of population in industrial centers $25,000,000 is hereby made available to the President, to be used by him through such agencies as he may establish and under such regulations as he may make, for making loans for and otherwise aiding in the purchase of subsistence homesteads. The moneys collected as repayment of said loans shall constitute a revolving fund to be administered as directed by the President for the purpose of this Section.

The New Community

It was now possible to utilize this agency in an attempt to convert a section of Granger into a subsistence homestead community. The Granger Plan proposed to settle 50 families on five-acre plots of good Iowa land, away from mining camps, near churches and schools, yet not too far from the mines where they work. Options had been obtained on 250 acres of fertile land which could be purchased for $125 an acre. The prospective homesteaders would be selected only after they had filed a formal application and after a careful investigation had been made. The homesteaders would be required to have permanent employment, at least on a part-time basis, so as to insure a regular, though limited, cash income with which to make monthly payments. In addition, they would be required to give evidence of those qualities that tend toward success: industry, sobriety, honesty, responsibility, and thrift. A maximum of five acres would be sold to each homesteader upon which would be constructed a home and necessary outbuildings. Each homestead, including land and buildings, was intended to be sold at a cost of not more than $2,000.

At first the government decided to limit itself to supervision and guidance in any homestead project, preferring to have responsibility and initiative shouldered by interested groups. A loan would be granted if a corporation, composed of trustworthy and prominent citizens in touch with the local situation in question, produced part of the necessary capital. The loan would be made to the corporation, not to the subjects of rehabilitation, and the corporation would be a semiprivate profit-making organization with obligations to the Federal Government regarding administrative policy and loan transactions. Another stipulation insisted that the homesteaders be in a position to pay $10 a month on a loan and to amortize over a period of twenty years. The loan desired and approved for Granger amounted to $125,000. Just prior to actual work on the project, however, the government reversed its stand and decreed that each project would be in complete, exclusive charge of Federal agents; this ruling to include the Granger settlement.

It is fitting here to consider the implications of exclusive government control of a homestead project. While it is true that, in individual cases, this method may prove advantageous to everyone concerned, still many dangers lurk in the general policy. Indeed it is a familiar and well-tested axiom that a government governs best which governs least. It is the duty of the State to provide sufficient means to its citizens in order that they, by diligent application, may secure for themselves temporal prosperity. Since families precede the State, they are the fundamental units of action, and only when the activities of individual families interfere with the common good should the State determine the limits of action. A wholesome society will be characterized by the responsible activity of local groups, each within its proper sphere and intent on promoting the welfare of all. Pius XI voiced this thought succinctly in his Encyclical *Quadragesimo Anno*:

> Just as it is wrong to withdraw from the individual and commit to the community at large what private enterprise and industry can accomplish, so too it is an injustice, a grave evil and a disturbance of right order for a larger and higher organization to arrogate to itself

functions which can be performed efficiently by smaller and lower bodies. This is a fundamental principle of social philosophy, unshaken and unchangeable, and it retains its full truth today. Of its very nature the true aim of all social activity should be to help individual members of the social body, but never to destroy or absorb them.[2]

In the past few years the Federal Government has been introduced into private affairs to an extent heretofore unknown. The drift is in the direction of bureaucratic control. Wherever possible, this tendency ought to be curbed if the democratic ideal is to persevere in America. Under the general policy of complete, exclusive government control of resettlement projects, the homesteaders would be subjected to dictation from Washington. This seems to be unwarranted if a local corporation of responsible citizens could produce the amount required by the government before a loan would be forthcoming and would pledge itself to guarantee to the government the monthly payments from the individual homesteaders who would not be selected for rehabilitation unless sufficiently possessed of the qualities of honesty, industry, and sobriety to warrant the risk.

An Economic, Social, and Spiritual Advance

Under government supervision, the construction of the fifty Granger homesteads was begun in the spring of 1935, and completed in October. They were ready for occupancy in December of the same year. The prospective homesteaders, all of the low-income group and selected after careful winnowing, were given a choice of the size of homestead desired.

Houses	No. of Rooms	Cost per House
5	4	$1,590
33	5	$1,660
12	6	$1,950

Included in the cost of each homestead was a barn or a combination garage and poultry house, according to individual wish; 12 chose barns and 38 the garage-poultry houses. Telephone service, if desired, landscaping, modern plumbing, electricity, heating — all were features of the Granger homesteads. Compared to the old environment, the new setting was salutary. In three

---

[2] *Quadragesimo Anno*, National Catholic Welfare Conference Edition, 1931, p. 26.

years the project had taken on the appearance of a beautiful real-estate development. The houses located at irregular distances, the various types of houses, their orientation, the different kinds of colors used in the finishing and trimming presented already a very pretty picture. From a barren field of oats stubble, a dream had finally come to be a reality. You see fertile gardens, attractive shade trees, colorful flowers, and all may have, as Virgil states in his first Eclogue:

> Ripe apples, mealy chestnuts, and a wealth of pressed cheeses.

Granger homesteaders, have fruits, vegetables, peanuts, popcorn, pigs, chickens, geese, sheep, rabbits, goats, cows, etc.

Socially, the gains in Granger are exceptional. From single families, there arose a community united in aim, and sharing a common cause. Healthful living, sanitation, fresh food, religious and social and recreational activities, educational programs with courses in arts and crafts, the feeling of independence created by the possession of homes, all these are not to be measured in terms of money alone. To have raised the families from abject poverty to a position of reasonable security, is to have revivified the human spirit.

The 224 acres purchased were nominal properties of two farmers who also owned additional acreage. The mortgages were so heavy that the insurance companies were ready to take them over and thus almost 600 acres of land would have become the possession of two corporate interests with tenant farmers and absentee landlords, a curse to Iowa and to the nation.

The government paid $125 per acre, a very acceptable but not exorbitant price. The insurance companies received their pound of flesh, and the two farm homes were saved to the original owners and fifty more home owners live and prosper on these "paternal acres." The government will get all of its money back and 3 per cent interest. The nation will have better families, better children, better citizens.

New Activities: New Securities

During their three years of existence the Granger homesteads have been an interesting laboratory of sociology and economics.

They have been in existence long enough to give us a glimpse of what can be done with people sunk deep in poverty and hopelessness, people actually at the bottom of things with reference to standards of living, environment, and the like. The basic problem was worked out by wedding their new homes to a few acres of productive soil. In this arrangement of home and acreage, the productive labors and the intelligence of the people themselves could be counted on in building the new substantial community. The Agricultural College at Ames, Iowa, took a great interest in this work of remaking men and women and rehabilitating families. The extension department of this college was always ready to give substantial aid in an educational way. Speakers from the college came to Granger to give the homesteaders, for the most part beginners in agriculture, interesting lectures on such topics as vegetable crops, small fruits, cooperatives, landscaping, bee culture, etc. For the women there were lectures on vegetables and vitamins, canning, home economics, home budgeting, and all the arts of the household.

How quickly the homesteaders mastered the work of increasing the productivity of their homes and acreages can be learned from a study of the comparative figures for the production of the homesteads in 1936, 1937, and 1938. The first year will always be the difficult year in such a project as this. Besides having the ordinary difficulties of getting started in this new way of life, the Granger homesteaders had for their first summer on the land, a summer of extended drouth. Nevertheless, in this first year the families succeeded in producing a very considerable amount of food. In the second year, 1937, the housewives had stored away more than 15,000 quarts of canned vegetables and fruits, and 330 glasses of jelly. More than 500 bushels of potatoes, 975 bushels of cabbage, squash, and other vegetables, 8 bushels of peanuts, and 68 bushels of popcorn had been stored away for the winter months.

These figures already indicate in the second year of homesteading that three acres have a very decided relationship with family security. The land is producing the primary needs for the family and domestic economy has developed intelligently and efficiently.

Air view of Granger Homesteads.

A Granger home.

The Granger Homesteads are grouped so that neighborliness is fostered.

A boy apiarist of the Granger Homestead at work.

New designs in work.

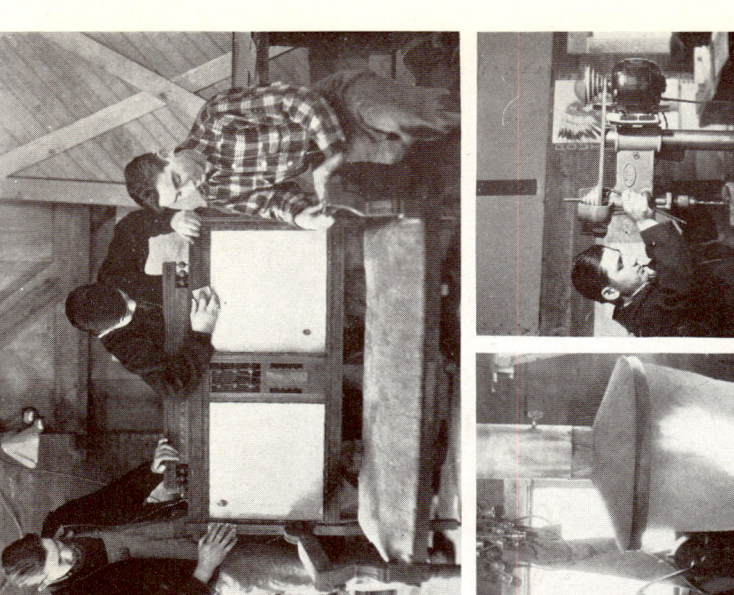
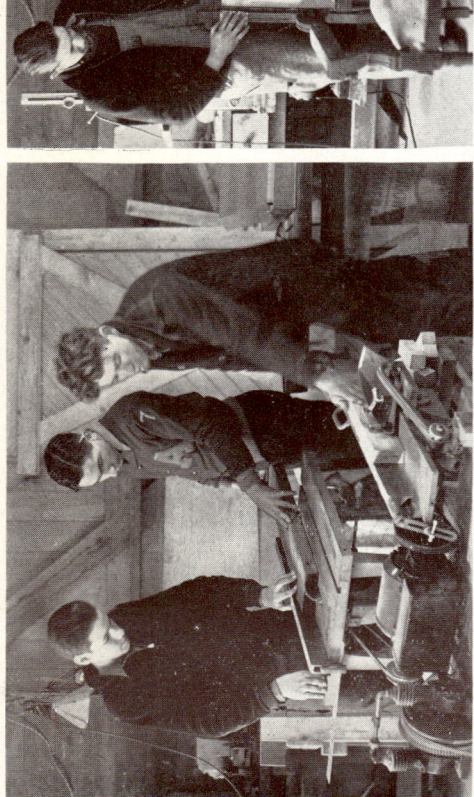

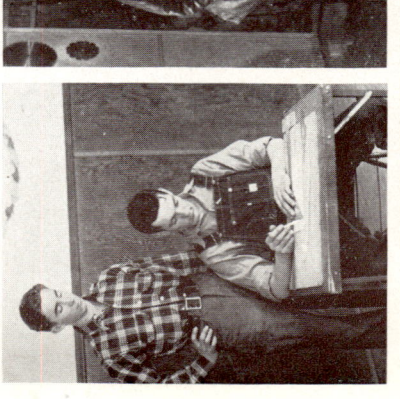

The shopwork at Assumption High School, Granger, Iowa, includes such practical activities as (top left) construction of wood farm utilities, (top right) furniture repair, (bottom left) mechanical drawing, (bottom

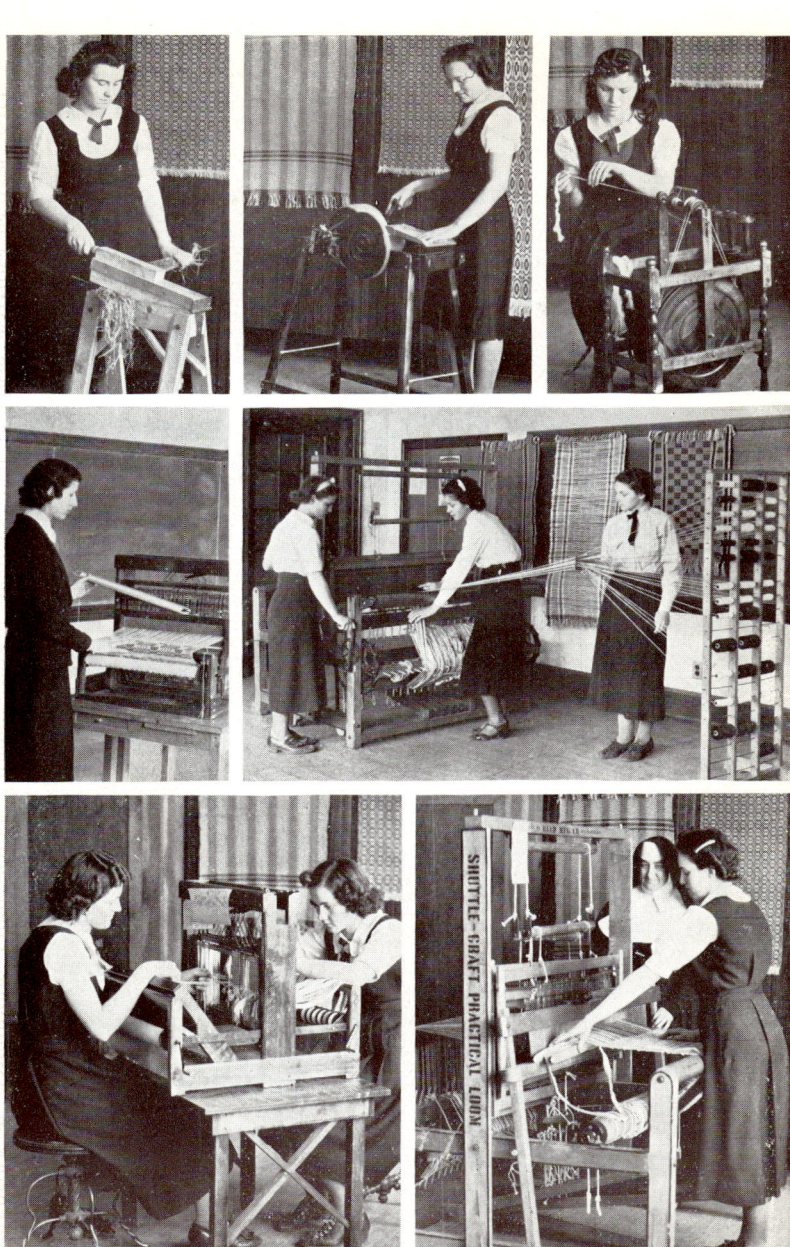

Processes in weaving done by girls of Assumption High School, Granger, Iowa.

The Assumption High and Grade School at Granger, Iowa, is housed in a modern one-story building planned and equipped to best serve the instructional program in a rural situation. The building serves as a social center for adult and youth groups.

The boys with their teacher, Father Gorman, and the shop they built from two old mining-camp houses.

Methods of needlecraft used by girls of Assumption High School.

Girls of Assumption High School doing (from left to right) Needle Point — Needlecraft Rug — Knitting Rake — Waffle Weaving — Hooking.

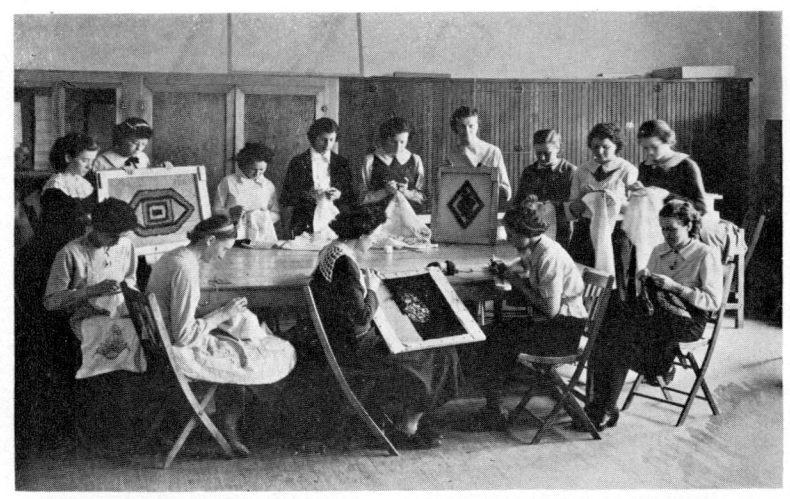

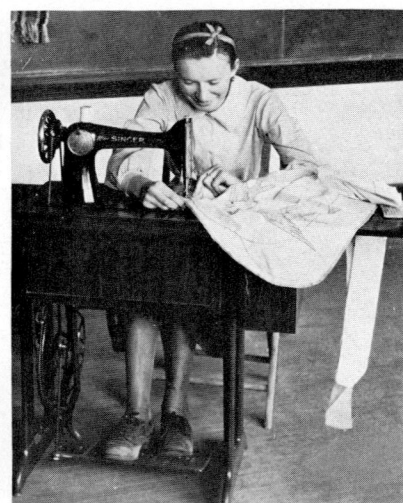

Various types of work with textiles done by the girls of Assumption High School.

The Granger Homestead Project

Amounts of Food Stored — October, 1937

Canned vegetables and fruits	15,325 qts.
Glasses of jelly	330 glasses
Potatoes	556 bu.
Other vegetables	102 bu.
Cabbage, squash, etc.	975 bu.
Peanuts	8 bu.
Popcorn	68 bu.

Livestock on Hand — October, 1937

Cows and calves	28
Pigs	79
Chickens	1,570
Geese	9
Sheep	42
Goats	4
Rabbits	65

Cash Received from Surpluses, 1937

Vegetables and fruits	$707.00
Grain, hay, etc. (incomplete)	79.00
Hogs, calves, chickens, eggs, cream, etc.	150.00
	$936.00

We must bear in mind that the people in the Granger project are part-time farmers. They are first of all employed in the coal mines of Iowa for approximately 150 or 200 days per year. In 1936 the wage earners of the fifty families received an estimated industrial income of $54,554. New Deal pump-priming activities do not seem to have stimulated production of coal in Iowa, and hence in 1937, this annual industrial income for the families fell to $53,009, and in 1938 the estimated wage income fell to a new low of $49,311. Ordinarily this falling curve in the wages of coal mining in Iowa would, in the case of the industrialized family, mean a drop in purchasing power or a fall in standards of living. However, in the case of the Granger part-time farmers, it did not give us these results. These people occupied their own productive homesteads. The land and its productivity would keep up their purchasing power, and through intelligent utilization of their land these families could continue to raise their standards of living and accomplish all this as independent and free men and women.

The facts which prove the statements made are graphically portrayed in the two following charts:

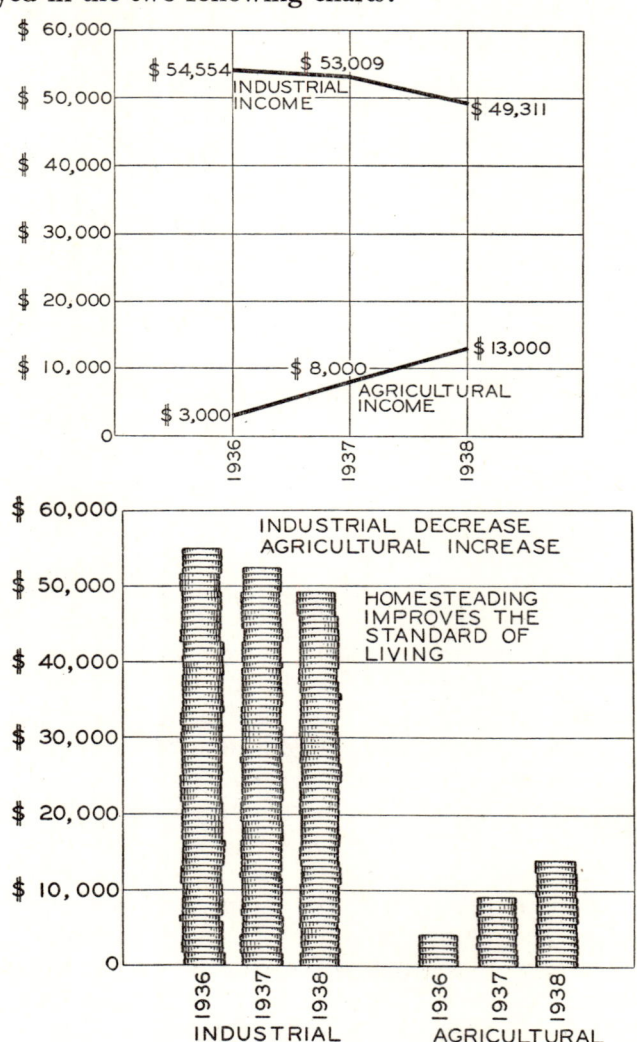

The Land Raises the Purchasing Power

The income from the land in 1938 easily makes up for the industrial loss in wages for that year, a loss of $5,243, and gives the fifty families an increase of purchasing power of $7,757. This income of $13,000 from the land in one year also represents the ability of industrial people to gain a knowledge of intensive and diversified agriculture. It was their own self-reliance, initiative, and intelligence which enabled these homesteaders to raise the homestead production from $3,000 to $8,000 and then to $13,000. The figures are much more significant than they appear to be, since we must remember that farm products reached new lows in 1938, as compared to the few previous years. And these new low market prices were used in setting up the productive tables for 1938. We can obtain a good idea of the productive, diversified agriculture in which the miners engage from the following tables for 1938.

Estimated Value of Vegetables Produced on the Homesteads — 1938

Item	Quarts	Price	Estimated Value
Tomatoes	7,350	.20	$1,470.00
Carrots	316	.15	47.40
Beans	1,414	.15	212.10
Corn	986	.20	197.20
Peas	392	.20	78.40
Pickles	1,009	.40	403.60
Peppers	299	.15	44.65
Raspberries	193	.30	57.90
Strawberries	283	.30	84.90
Suckatash	105	.15	15.75
Relish	447	.30	134.10
Soup Mixture	332	.10	33.20
Spinach	330	.10	33.00
Kraut	500	.15	75.00
Jam	1,045	.40	418.00
Catsup	114	.20	22.80
Sweet Potatoes	60	.15	9.00
			$3,337.00

In addition to the above products which represent the canned goods, the following vegetables were stored on the homesteads during 1938:

Item	Unit	Estimated Value
Potatoes	285 bu.	$270.75
Turnips	6 bu.	6.00
Carrots	52 bu.	52.00
Sweet Potatoes	25 bu.	27.00
Onions	11 bu.	15.40
Beets	7 bu.	7.00
Peppers	2 bu.	2.00
Popcorn	15 bu.	11.50
Peanuts	10 bu.	30.00
Cabbage	47 heads	4.70
Celery	100 stalks	8.00
		$434.35

The grain production was estimated at the new low prices for corn, alfalfa, and soybeans in 1938.

Item	Unit	Price	Estimated Value
Corn	1,430 bu.	$ 0.35	$ 500.50
Soybeans	56 tons	7.00	392.00
Alfalfa	90 tons	13.00	540.00
Grass	23 tons		138.00
Oats	180 bu.		27.00
			$1,597.50

The livestock and chickens maintained on the homesteads are continually making their contribution to family food supplies. The following table gives the estimated value of the livestock on the homesteads in November, 1938:

Item	Unit	Estimated Value
Cattle	30	$1,800.00
Pigs	186	2,500.00
Sheep	6	36.00
Chickens	1,456	728.00
		$5,064.00

In Granger, men once disheartened and crushed have taken a new lease on life. They are experiencing the thrill of happiness that comes from the security of an existence rooted in the soil. They are leading better lives, fuller lives, happier lives, and all because they are "out on the farm." On their fathers' farms? No. These people were not led "back to the land." Their movement is a forward movement. No hovels for homes in Granger today! Each homesteader has a neat, modern house, electrically lighted, furnace heated, with running water, indoor bathroom facilities, and with rising income the opportunity to make other acquisitions. Of course, these homes did not spring up with anything of the miraculous about them. They required time and labor and much of both. But the time being assured, the labor was done in great part by the homesteaders. With a spirit of comradeship, able leadership, and good will, the miracle would be that the houses did not literally "spring up."

Intelligent Land Utilization

The land surrounding each farmhouse is laid out in lawn and trees. The remaining land is used for garden plots, orchard, and pasture. The gardens produce all the vegetables needed for family consumption during the summer and winter months. Anything over and above family needs is for the market. But there is absolutely no destructive, commercial farming. Each homesteader maintains a few chickens to produce eggs for home consumption. In the spring the flock increases and the families frequently use chicken for their meat supply in summer and autumn. In addition to the chickens, nearly all the families have a cow and a few pigs.

Children Are Economic Assets

The work on the homesteads is done by the members of the families. The growing boys and girls make substantial contributions to family needs. They are out on the land where — to repeat once more — children are assets to the families, not liabilities. Clothing and other articles which the homesteads do not produce are purchased with the income from the sale of a few surplus farm products and the money received for part-time industrial employment. The community has set up cooperatives to keep money and goods within their own locality. Last year one of the Granger cooperatives declared a 67-cent patronage dividend on every dollar of purchase. Such dividends will go far to improve the purchasing power of the homesteaders.

On the Land — Not on the Streets

Granger achievement, Granger security, Granger independence, Granger farm modernity, Granger technique in blending advantages of city and country through a sound philosophy of economic and social planning, stands as an object lesson for other hard-pressed families and groups and social leaders. But we have become so money minded within the past few decades that most of us cannot reason this way until we strike "rock bottom" and realize that our money mindedness is only "mindedness." The strange thing about the whole affair is, that many people have to be driven into narrow straits before they come to appreciate a very normal situation — that life on the land is in every respect a more natural thing than sitting in a stuffy office tapping a typewriter, standing eight hours a day and saying stupid things over a ten-cent-store counter, repeating some monotonous motion in a factory, or walking the streets in search of a job.

The big difficulty in getting people to take, with alacrity, to the idea of rehabilitation on the land lies in the fact that they have a false notion of what the agrarian movement aims to do. They have some preconceived idea that they are expected to take themselves away from a remotely possible, future good, in a commercial, postdepression life, and to locate themselves back on the farms of their grandfathers, thereby depriving themselves of all conveniences. Yet tragically funny it is that many of the very same people who believe this have themselves none of the conveniences they dream of as their own. They seem to find satisfaction in the thought, however, that rubbing elbows with their neighbor who, although poor, has a car, a frigidaire, and a radio, they themselves are just a wee bit nearer to having these things than they would be if they lived out on their own homesteads, with food growing to the right of them and food growing to the left of them. It is not easy to understand why this idea should be prevalent in the minds of so many people. But it is there, nevertheless. Shall we call it hope? Psychologists would call it empathy — that same feeling which gives us a thrill when we see a kite flying gracefully up against the blue — the feeling that comes because of the unconscious identification of ourselves with the object which excites our admiration. Now possibly, and a little more than likely, these same people are, *in prospect,* driving in imagination a car like Mr. Nabor's, listening to big-league games over a similar radio, and cooling their water with ice cubes. By a nearness, in space, to conveniences, they are *empathizing* with a situation which, in time, may be as far removed from their lives as the nearest star is from their bedroom window.

The New Farm Is Not the "Old" Farm[3]

Most emphatically, we are not advocating a return to the old type of farm. If we were we could understand the feeling of aversion with which a rural program would be greeted. Many of us have come from the old farm or have been to that old farm on a short visit. We can still remember — and with a feeling which even now, years after, amounts almost to repugnance — the old water buckets with their family dipper; the dim, smoky oil lamps with their encircling halo of nasty little bugs: the dread that always came with the darkness, the feeling of utter isolation, the almost palpable stillness. And then, the long rides at night, in the old buggy, often in pouring rains, through roads which were difficult enough to travel in the dry and daylight, down to the town to meet a relative or a friend, with nothing to light our way but a tiny carbide light which, of course, could have been a flashlight even in those days. With such a background of experiences and others even less appealing, farm life would hold little to attract. But this is the farm of yesterday, and as far as any successful landward movement is concerned that farm has gone out with yesterday.

The homestead-to-be is a modern, almost-more-than reasonably convenient farm, located somewhere out beyond the city smokestacks, an only too fair substitute for the rooms in the flat or tenement which many of us are wont to call "home." Can you

---
[3] Cf. *Rural Electrification on the March,* Rural Electrification Administration, Washington, D. C.

imagine Payne visualizing a dark, musty, hot, brick flat, wedged so uncomfortably between two similar buildings as not to be able even to cast its own shadow, when he broke out into that theme of universal delight: "Home, Sweet Home"? Don't you rather feel that the picture in the poet's mind was that of a little cottage, with the woodbine clustering about the door? There is something appealing about the little home which is wedded to the soil; just as though it grew up from the warm earth together with the very ivy that clings to it, and as though it understood and cherished the kinship which existed between them.

Much of this may sound idealistic and poetic. But isn't there any poetry in life? Go to your window, alone, very early some clear, cool morning in spring, just before the sun rises even if it is rising from behind chimneys instead of hills and trees; look at the pink and blue of the sky; listen to the birds. They will probably be sparrows, but note with what a joy and assurance they chirp away. See if the morning star is shining. Let your spirit free itself for a brief moment from the shackles of artificiality and convention and drink in the beauty of the dawn. Sing — if you dare. Poetry? Yes; but in the city there's a premium on it. You will have to pay for being your natural self those two seconds of the day; for, from across the hall you will hear somebody talking to God (and it won't be a morning prayer, either) about the way some singing fool woke him five minutes before the usual time. Our sense of true values is piteously warped. We grow eloquent over a game of golf or over the color of a new spring hat and the possibilities of matching our fingernail polish to its particular tint, and at the same time we are blind to the wonderful realities of beauty that surround our daily lives.

But, granted that all this is fanciful, that we are putting the wagon in front of the horse, reaping the fruits of security and contentment before we have sown the seed, nevertheless, the plan rests on a purely sane and realistic basis. It is not a nebulous something which may accidentally take shape in some hazy future. True, it will not mature in one generation. It is too vast and too substantial to grow up overnight. But grow it will, if there is to be any material or spiritual salvation for our America.

We have come to a time when sterile discussions on social problems are being ruled out in favor of concerted action. You can't talk citizenship and patriotism, social justice and charity to men on relief. What they want and need is good food in a sufficient quantity. To have these means having a little plot of earth somewhere out on the land with vegetables, a few chickens, a few pigs, and a cow. Direction of the people to the land; keeping the people on the land; encouraging the people to hold to the land, to work with the land, to love the land is practical as well as poetical. There is both poetry and sound economics in such a community as Granger.

PART III

LEADERSHIP IN BUILDING THE GOOD AMERICA

Chapter 12

INTELLIGENT TECHNOLOGY ON THE LAND

The land! That is where our roots are. There is the basis of our physical life. The farther we get away from the land, the greater our insecurity. From the land comes everything that supports life, everything we use for the service of physical life. The land has not collapsed or shrunk in either extent or productivity. It is there waiting to honor all the labor we are willing to invest in it, and able to tide us across any local dislocation of economic conditions. No unemployment insurance can be compared to an alliance between man and a plot of land. — *Henry Ford.*

It is a serious mistake to think of the building of agricultural communities, if we neglect at the same time to develop a sound land technology. For people on the land there should always be adequate direction in biodynamics and biological techniques, for agriculture is a biological science. If there is no such training available, the families on the land will drift in the prevailing current of commercialism with its bigger units, its preoccupation with mechanics and physics and commercial chemical developments which have no interrelation with vital processes.

Adam Smith expressed the maxim that the prudent master of a family will never make at home what it will cost him more to make than to buy. The maxim is true enough. But we did not have the right to assume that, therefore, fewer and fewer things should be made in the home for the needs of the family; that there was nothing that would cost less to make at home; that it will always be cheaper to buy family needs; that the giant factory is the final development in supreme efficiency; that the giant farm producing corn and wheat for the market is better than the homestead with vegetables, fruits, and livestock. These conclusions are mere assumptions. Even in these days of advanced factory techniques and extreme centralizations, the efficiency of the modern production of many things in the home unit for home use is easily demonstrated.

Domestic Economy

In their economic research studies at the School of Living, Suffern, New York, Dr. Ralph Borsodi and his colleagues prove that the modern home can contribute productively and creatively to family prosperity and well-being in many ways. The facts revealed in their comparative study of home and factory productions are available in the Homestead Bulletins published by the School of Living.

The experiments in comparative economy made by the School of Living have been carefully carried out in actual homes over a period of years. The complete data and research shows that in the average home by means of domestic production, life can be made "creative, productive, independent, satisfying to the spirit, and creditable to the nation." The homestead studies show conclusively that production by the family unit for family use is the best economy in such varied activities as baking at home, milling at home, gardening, canning and preserving, the home dairy, berry and fruit growing, home laundering, sewing, weaving, knitting, spinning yarn, home building, woodworking, poultry keeping, etc.[1] Modern home equipment is used in their home activities. Electricity plays an important part. And it is presupposed that with such modern homes there will be small acreages of productive land, and that cooperation in family groups will be practiced.

The Suffern list of efficient domestic activities clearly indicates the many things in which the modern home can still prove its superiority in the economics of production and consumption. In such homes the machinery is not gigantic or massive. Horsepower is not concentrated. There is no great speed or noise or rapid flow of articles. Power, speed, energy concentration, and size are lacking in modern machines for the home. But what

---

[1] Homestead Bulletins on these and similar subjects have been issued by the School of Living, Suffern, New York.
Cf. Appendix: (1) "America's First School of Living"; (2) "A New Design for Living."

are the criteria for an intelligent technology? What are to be the principal gauges to calculate the rate of progress we are making in technical matters?

Narrow Technology

In one of several studies in the techniques of decentralization, it is pointed out that we have to be intelligent, reflective, human, broad, and truly progressive in our judgments of what constitutes "high" technology.

Pre-occupation with the mechanical departments of applied science produces a spotty and irregular development of technical knowledge and skills amongst our population. On the one hand we have extraordinary ability and training concentrated in the designing, production and management personnels of our plants and factories; on the other hand we have an increasing number of skill-less (or single-skilled) workers, whose principal role is to serve as consumers of the vast bulk of goods produced by the automatic machines. The monumental ingenuity of the tin-can factory is countered by the imbecility of the can-opener and the delicatessen meal; the vulcanic audacity of the oil refinery is countered by the inanity of the filling station; the balanced perfection of the assembly line is countered by the vapidity of the salesroom. A technology which yields such discrepancies is a high technology only in limited zones.[2]

The psychology of the factory dominates society, government, rural and urban communities, the city and the farm. Efforts are repeatedly made to bring land and its production under factory processes. We depreciate the arts and crafts and the vitalistic biological sciences. All these are not mechanistic enough for proletarian mentalities. They do not measure progress in terms of horsepower and bulk of manufactured goods or bulk of surplus crops. Arts and crafts and vitalistic biological processes are too small and individual for those who genuflect before the altar of mere bigness. Too many conceive the commonwealth as one big factory run by a few economic planners and mechanics.

In this conception of "mechanical utopia" the eighteen-story town will be "better" than the three-story town, the three-story town will be "better" than the one-story farm. If making everything bigger makes everything better, if centralized enterprises

---

[2] Dresser, Peter Van, "The Human Side of Technics" in *Free America*, Dec., 1938.

and centralized institutions furnish a more genuine economy than the home and the small community, then we should fall in line with industrialists, finance-capitalists, New Dealers, Socialists, technocrats, Communists and Fascists in their subsidies for bigger governments, bigger cities, bigger industries. But giant farms, giant utilities, giant governments, and giant factories have had the opportunity to prove their superior economy. Social, economic, and political units all over the world — owned and controlled by individuals, families, and neighborhood groups — have sacrificed their existence within the past century and especially within recent years in order that a few big industrial units or one big government unit should presumably be able to reach a scale large enough to make them efficient. With the surrender of local and home production, were sacrificed ownership of productive property, independence, liberty, individual skills and craftsmanship in order that industrialism, urbanism, and nationalism might freely move on toward centralization, massive mechanization, and congestion in their solution of the all-important economic problem. The time has come now for us to ask ourselves what measure of prosperity and security, centralized industries and centralized cities give to the real world peopled with such human beings as exist in it. For after all, the central problem is that of prosperity and security for individuals, for members of families, and for members of communities. Recurring depressions, and especially the more recent and tragic depressions, can hardly be placed at the doors of family production for home use and small local enterprise. These depressions must be placed where they belong, at the doors of centralized factory production for exchange. An indictment of inefficiency must be drawn up against bigness. An indictment must be drawn up against all of us because of our one-sided interest in the physical and mechanical sciences, and our neglect of biological science and the social sciences.

Inefficiencies in Mass-Production Technique

Notwithstanding unlimited promotion of commercial machinery and the factory, the industrial process is backward and uneconomic with regard to the bulk of the wants of the average family. Costs of sorting, delivery, packaging, distribution, national advertising, hidden taxes, and similar items give domestic economy the advantage over commercial economy in many things. Although household machinery with its new electrical apparatus, is prepared to give an economy which far surpasses the economy of commercial machinery, most modern families continue to live out of the factory by the factory, with the factory and for the factory. The industrial and collectivist propaganda, both commercial and political, continues to bewilder American families. The average rural family and the average urban family continues its costly, unprofitable, insecure existence on cash jobs and cash crops, without realizing that there are at least a billion acres in America for home building and home production. This would still leave approximately another billion acres for forests, for grazing, for game preserves, and for parks. Somehow we do not seem to realize that much of the good land is attractively situated near the congested metropolises, within easy commuting distance for urban employees, giving them the opportunity to take up the cheaper modernized rural way of living and production, as well as to rear the families whose every member can here be helpful.

A very simple little study in figures, if we will only take the time to go into them, will show us at once the fallacies with reference to efficiency which are involved in high-powered commercial farming and proletarian urban living, with their cash-consumer, tidbit purchase plans.

Costs of Puffed Wheat

We can buy eight ounces of puffed wheat wrapped in cellophane at a price of 13 cents. For the eight ounces of wheat to be changed into puffed wheat the farmer is paid 0.4 of a cent when the price of wheat is 50 cents per bushel. The consumer hands the other 12.6 cents, out of the 13-cent purchase price of puffed wheat, to the processors, distributors, tax collectors, etc. The farmer who buys his puffed wheat must raise 15 pounds of wheat in order to buy 8 ounces of puffed wheat. Some adjustments in these figures have to be made from time to time when markets fluctuate, but the wide difference between what the farmer gets for his products and what the consumer pays for the processed product generally continues in the same proportion as in the above figures. Generally the markets fluctuate even more seriously against the farmer. Are the food monopolies really efficient when they must take so much from the consumer for their built-up services? Is the farmer following a good economy when he raises 15 pounds of wheat in order to buy back 8 ounces? Would not home processing of foods, home milling, and community milling be better economics?

Costs of Bread

When we buy a loaf of bread, cut and wrapped in cellophane for 10 cents, we are buying 12 ounces of wheaten flour. Twelve ounces of wheat will produce twelve ounces of pure wheat flour. For the 12 ounces of wheat to be used in milling and baking a loaf of bread, the farmer is paid 0.8 of a cent when the price of wheat is 50 cents per bushel. The consumer hands the other 9.2 cents, out of the 10-cent purchase price for a loaf of bread, to the processors, distributors, tax collectors, etc. A very small portion of the 9.2 cents goes for lard, butter, milk, yeast, etc. The farmer who buys his bread, cut and wrapped in cellophane, must raise at least 10 pounds of wheat in order to buy a 10-cent loaf of bread. There are 80 loaves of bread in a bushel of wheat, but if the farmer sells a bushel of wheat at 50 cents per bushel, he can buy back only 5 loaves of bread out of the 80. The average acre of wheat in the United States produces 14 bushels. That means 1,120 loaves of bread! But if the farmer sells his wheat at 50 cents per bushel, out of the 1,120 loaves of bread produced from the 14 bushels on the average acre, the farmer can buy back only 70 loaves. In the mass-production "shuffle," the farmer takes a loss of 1,050 loaves. Even when wheat sells at a dollar, the farmer who buys his bread in the system of mass-production exchange is many loaves behind in the deal. The farmer who buys flour and bakes at home must still sell 48 ounces of wheat in order to buy back 12 ounces of flour. One can readily see why the School of Living emphasizes the efficiency of home milling and baking.

No Parity in Prices

From the above figures it is clear that the ratio of prices received on the farm to the prices paid by farmers, i.e., the price spreads between producer and consumer are very great, in particular products even much greater than official index numbers indicate. The following are the index numbers compiled by the Bureau of Agricultural Economics. The figures indicate the absence of parity in prices received by farmers and prices paid by farmers in the purchase of goods. The ratio of prices received to prices paid in a just exchange of agricultural and industrial goods or the buying power of farm products should stand at 100, but since 1921 this ratio has always been much lower. The ratio went as low as 61 in 1932, returned to 88 in 1937, but during the greater part of the year, 1938, the ratio stood at 77, 74, 75, and 78. The following is the table provided in *The Agricultural Situation,* issued by the Bureau of Agricultural Economics:

Year and Month	Prices Received	Prices Paid	Buying Power of Farm Products
1921	125	152	82
1922	132	149	89
1923	142	152	93
1924	143	152	94
1925	156	157	99
1926	145	155	94
1927	139	153	91
1928	149	155	96
1929	146	153	95
1930	126	146	87
1931	87	124	70
1932	65	107	61
1933	70	109	64
1934	90	123	73
1935	108	125	86
1936	114	124	92
1937	121	130	93
1937–September	118	130	91
1937–October	112	128	88
1937–November	107	127	84
1937–December	104	126	83
1938–January	102	126	81
1938–February	97	126	77
1938–March	96	125	77
1938–April	94	125	75
1938–May	92	125	75

Year and Month	Prices Received	Prices Paid	Buying Power of Farm Products
1938–June	92	124	74
1938–July	95	123	77
1938–August	92	122	75
1938–September	95	121	78
1938–October	95	121	78

In the mass-production "shuffle" the cards always come out against the farmer. From the following table it is clear that the price spreads also work to the disadvantage of the consumer in the city. Are these price spreads due to inefficiencies in the big food industries or are they due to the taking of huge dividends?

Farm to Retail (Producer to Consumer) Price Spreads for 58 Foods Purchased by an Average Workingman's Family[3]

Years	Farm Value	Retail Prices
1913	134	252
1923	173	384
1933	92	264
1935	138	331
1936	152	342
1937	160	353

There is an ever-increasing distance between producer and consumer, to the disadvantage of both. The following shows that during the period of increased costs we have had decreased consumption.

Per-Capita Consumption of Foods in the United States

Kinds of Food	Consumption — 1889	Consumption — 1932
Wheat Flour	223.9	162.2
Cornmeal	117.0	21.3
Dressed Meats	142.0	133.2
Butter	19.5	17.7
Eggs	1.35	2.03
Apples	105.9	67.5
Irish Potatoes	176.4	50.2
Sugar	52.0	98.0
Peanuts	4.88	5.68
Gum	88.0	89.0

[3] This and the two following tables are taken from "Domestic Commerce Series," No. 38, and from "Supplement to Series," No. 38, Report No. 9091, United States Department of Commerce.

Intelligent Technology on the Land

There has likewise been a drop in the consumption of asparagus, cabbage, tomatoes, cucumbers, lima beans, peas, sweet potatoes, pumpkin, squash, fresh fish and frozen fish.

Additional Per-Capita Consumption Statistics

Product	Ten Years — 1900–10	Years — 1926–35	Per Cent of Decrease
Wheat	6.2 bu.	5.5 bu.	11.3 less
Corn	30.2 bu.	19.5 bu.	35.4 less
Cattle	737 head per 1,000 persons	519 head per 1,000 persons	29.6 less
Hogs	634 head per 1,000 persons	455 head per 1,000 persons	28.2 less

No doubt the reductions in food consumption have a very definite relationship to the increased costs of foods. The increased costs of foods must be attributed to the factory methods of production, processing, and distribution. Foods are priced much higher now than they were in the times when domestic food economy prevailed. People with a greatly diminished purchasing power cannot keep up the same standard of nutrition under factory food prices.

Losses in Nutritional Values

A question of extreme importance here is the one of the nutritional value of quality of food products. From the investigations of experts the nutritional value of mass-production food products seems to be very low. Dr. Greene, chemist of Notre Dame University, states in his book, *The Chemistry of Health* (p. 34), that "any worms in white flour starve to death shortly after emerging from the egg from a lack of the elements essential to life," and that practically all the prepared breakfast foods are "subverted chemically for business reasons."[4]

Doctor Alexis Carrel points out in *Man, the Unknown,* that not only has commercial chemistry destroyed nutrition through factory processes, but that the very biological processes in plant and animal growth have been disturbed, so that when the exhausted elements of the soil (elements biologically balanced)

---

[4] Appendix: Homestead Bulletins, publications of the School of Living, Suffern, New York.

are replaced by the commercial chemistry of artificial fertilizing, there is a change in the nutritive value of cereal grains and vegetables. Dr. Carrel thinks that when hens are compelled to join the ranks of mass producers by artificial diet and mode of living, the quality of their eggs is modified; that when cows are confined to the stable the year round and fed on manufactured provender, their production may have the familiar appearance of milk, but lacks nutritive value.

The Raising of Vegetables

It is time that economic and sociological leadership explode the many myths about mass production, especially in foods. A good myth to begin with is the vegetable myth. Today the average farmer will tell you that he cannot afford to put aside much land for a home supply of vegetables. For the loud and empty commercial propaganda has taught him that it is cheaper to buy vegetables in bunches or in cans at the chain store. What are the facts? Again we have to study comparative figures. For a family of five, a year's supply of vegetables in an adequate diet will come to an approximate cost of $260. How does the commercial farmer go about getting this supply of vegetables? He will concentrate on a cash crop. If he is in the "corn belt," his crop will be corn. That is probably all the agriculture he knows. Commercial farmers soon forget how to cultivate other crops and do not show much ambition to learn the processes of intelligent agriculture. The commercial farmer who needs $260 worth of vegetables for a family of five will set to work in the production of 50 acres of corn. If there is any life left in his soil, he may produce 40 bushels per acre. He is also probably gambling on two weeks of rainy weather in July. He will work in his cornfield, 520 hours in the production of 2,000 bushels of corn. This 2,000 bushels of corn will bring a cash return of $1,000, if corn sells at 50 cents per bushel. The cash-corn farmer will then figure his costs. His production costs will be $20 per acre if he counts his labor at a value of 50 cents per hour. When all is added up and subtracted, the corn farmer will find that his only return is 50 cents per hour for labor. In 520 hours the average time expended in the growing of 2,000 bushels of corn, this amounts to $260. The production of 50 acres of corn enables him to buy the supply of vegetables at $260.[5]

Now let us compare vegetable statistics published by the Iowa Subsistence Garden Record. These figures are averages for the summer of 1938. On a plot of land 50 by 100 feet with $1.25 worth of seeds, with 50 hours for field work and 25 hours for canning and storage, $312 worth of vegetables are produced. Study the figures and judge which of the two obtains his vegetables in the best way. Which of the two is the most efficient, the man who raises corn in order to buy vegetables or the man who raises his own vegetables? Five hundred and twenty hours of labor in a cornfield as compared with 75 hours of labor in a garden, with a profit of $52 going to the man in the garden! An intelligent study of statistics would lead most of our farmers in the wheat belts, corn belts, and cotton belts, to take a much greater interest in their home gardens and make them quite willing to put forth much greater effort there. The Iowa figures should also encourage many city families to try to locate a garden for their family supply of vegetables.

Questions to Be Investigated

Instead of applauding every substitution of industrial economy for the domestic economy, the reduction of homes to flats and tenements, dormitories and restaurants; instead of encouraging the abandonment of farms for city life; instead of surrendering local control for a centralized control in economics and government, we should seriously propose the following questions and study them carefully. Is there not a better program for producing a desirable society than that which centralizes every aspect of life under the domination of remote economic planners and public officials? Did an efficient industrialism build the big cities or were they built with the ruthless exploitations of men and land and natural resources? When semi-deserts remain and the wealth of small communities and small enterprises has been extracted, can industrialism, urbanism, and finance-capitalism carry on? Will the huge factories compensate for the loss of

---

[5] For these various costs, cf.: *Agricultural Statistics for 1938*, Department of Agriculture.

ownership of productive property by the many, and will the resulting proletarian masses be secure in the basic needs of clothing, food, and shelter? What efficiency is gained by increasing the physical and commercial distance between the production point and the consumption point of goods? What efficiency is gained in compensation for the vanishing freedoms of the individuals, families, and small communities? What foundation is there if any for the self-satisfied belief that our standards of living are so superior? When the facts of efficiency so often favor production at the home for home use, why should centralization be considered to be an inevitable doom?

Results of Some Useful Research and Study

The School of Living under the leadership of Dr. Ralph Borsodi has been investigating these problems in actual homes — the problems of centralized versus decentralized production and their effects on social institutions, such as families and communities.

Scientific data and research, covering a long period of years, form the basis for the conclusions that two thirds of the products which the average family consumes can be more economically produced on a small scale at home or in local neighborhoods, provided modern methods and modern machinery are applied to small-scale production; that it is possible to cook and bake at home more economically than to secure food processed in centralized canneries, centralized mills, and centralized packing plants; that it is possible to sew and weave at home, produce better cloth and more artistic garments with less labor than is involved in trying to earn the money with which to buy factory-made products; that it is much more economical to house people in individually owned homes in the country, than to house them in large apartment houses in the cities. It is less costly, and much less wasteful to install electric pumps for running water and septic tanks for sewage disposal in each household, than to furnish these services by the best and largest centralized system developed up to the present time.[6]

---

[6] Cf. Homestead Bulletins, School of Living.

As an observation upon such investigating, Dr. Borsodi says:

> The simple truth of the matter is that the products and services in which centralized production is genuinely economical are much fewer in number than is generally supposed. It may be conceded that the only way to produce electric light bulbs inexpensively is in a large factory (though the most economical size of the factory may not be as large as is generally supposed). But because it is practicable to produce electric light bulbs in factories it does not follow that flour can be ground from wheat more economically in a large centralized mill, than it can be ground in the individual home. . . . Already we see in the perfection of the domestic refrigerator, what may happen to centralized industry. So great are the natural advantages of small-scale production — the elimination of all distribution costs — that the ice industry has not only ceased to grow but may ultimately follow the conestoga-wagon industry into oblivion. The automobile, which furnishes individual transportation, is threatening to destroy the system of mass-transportation which railroads represent. Unless power of the government is used even more than it is being used today to tax automobiles and gasoline, this decentralized form of transportation which we call the automobile has so many inherent advantages over the railroad that the railroad will slowly follow the canal into the museum of historical curiosities.[7]

Family machines, built on the scale of the many small modern machines of the domestic type that inventors could produce if they would keep the family and not the factory in mind, machines built to a human and family scale for family use in the supply of family needs, are far more efficient than the machines of "bulk" and "horsepower."

Bulk and horsepower may be able to produce an ocean of plenty, but that ocean will bring on an appalling disaster. That is unavoidable if by levies, tributes, profits, costs of inefficiencies, and all other demands made on them, millions of families are continually marooned on the bleak, bare, eroded island of social and economic wants and spiritual decay.

Engineers for Home Economy

Engineers can make their contribution to the solution of social

---
[7] Borsodi, Dr., "Decentralization" in *Free America*, Feb., 1938.

problems if they will keep the home in mind as an efficient economic unit. Again we quote Dr. Borsodi:

> The development of the steam engine before the hydro-electric generator furnished factories with power at a time when it was denied to home-producers; spinning and weaving were transferred from the manor and the cottage, to the great centralized mill, not because mass-production was necessarily more economical, but mainly because in the beginning of the industrial revolution, the only way in which power could be utilized was by moving the machine to a place where steam boilers and steam engines were available.
>
> But the coming of electricity transforms the situation. Electric power can be decentralized. The electric motor can be utilized not only in the custom shop and small factory; it can be used in the home itself. Even the generation of electricity itself can be decentralized. Giant power plants are wasteful. Small power plants are actually the most economical. The time may come when we will develop hundreds of small hydro-electric generating plants, instead of concentrating water power at one point and having to build costly distribution systems to absorb the savings which large generating plants seem to effect.[8]

Decentralization and Liberty

We need only make the wise choice between centralization of population and decentralization of population. Simply because the city can produce a shallow glamor, it does not follow that centralization of population is better for human beings. There are and have been both centralized and decentralized governments. It does not follow that centralized governments are better for human beings. Greater liberties have been enjoyed under decentralized governments. There are and have been centralized and decentralized economic systems. It does not follow that the centralized, mass-production system is more efficient in everything. There have been little machines and big machines, factory machines and home machines. There is no reason for assuming that all home machines should be replaced by factory machines and factory economy. The factory replaced the home not on grounds of economic efficiency, but rather because it has long been the beneficiary of political, economic, social, and technical

---
[8] *Ibid.*

favors. Technical processes and machines have been invented and designed by engineers and inventors with their minds subservient to the one-sided advance of the large-scale producer. Engineers and inventors could show more intelligence and a higher technology if they planned and built more machines for the primary social unit, the family, an economic unit which has natural advantages in many fields of production.

Architects and the Productive Home

Not only engineers, but also architects are beginning to see that the technology of the big machine is not mature, not integrated, not interrelated, not adjusted to the social and biological factors which condition the lives of human beings. Two famous architects, Baker Brownell and Frank Lloyd Wright, develop the thesis that urbanism is the curse of our modern world.

The stainless tower (skyscrapers) . . . a monument to extreme concentration of power, population, wealth, deadly facilities, that mark the new era. It is tense and shining, but the instability of a people that knows no rest shows there. On streets laid out for a three-story town, an eighteen-story town must operate with a corresponding increase in velocity and interference. On human beings built for a slower pace of spasmodic action and repose the city lays a driving pressure and urgency. It seeks experiments and expedients in the emergency. It fails in sincere courage and vision. The natural integrity of life is broken down into intense activities, each in its special compartment having little or nothing of the whole.[9]

---

[9] Brownell, Baker, and Frank Lloyd Wright, *Architecture and Modern Life* (Harper Bros., 1937), p. 3 f.

Chapter 13

AGRICULTURE AND BIOLOGICAL SCIENCE

IF THE centralist technology has so many limitations and is so poorly co-ordinated in the strictly material or mercantile fields of processing, manufacturing, distributing, and retailing, then, the advisability of its complete transfer and its nonsynthetic technique to the field of agriculture, a field replete with life processes, a field rich with new relationships between man and soil and animals, may be questioned very seriously. If the transferred, mechanical technique is not in accord with the more complicated life processes and operated with complete disregard of them, disaster will not be long postponed. Growing things have an adamant way of following their own laws.

Neglect of the Productive Home

With minds unable to grasp the incompatibilities of their projects, the mass-production engineers, chemists, and mechanics are trying to contract a marriage between soil and machinery. Nothing would please them better than to be able to set up the unstable household of Soil and Big Machine on the domain of United Farms Incorporated. All other households would then be reduced to suitcases, trailers, tents, and boxcars. Transfer the big-machine technology, and our little modern minds, unable to integrate and interrelate, trample out the life technologies of good livestock breeding and expert livestock feeding, the technology of scientific plant cultivation, and the technology of good seed selection, the technology of man and culture and agriculture.

Agriculture Is Not Mechanics

Animals, plants, living organisms in the soil, soil bacteria, all require biological technologies. If vital processes are not respected,

Agriculture and Biological Science

death and deserts will swallow up homes and families and communities.

In a discussion of the productivity of soil P. G. Holden makes the following statements in regard to the soil:

> The soil is a sacred thing. Out of it comes that which sustains life and supplies the commerce of the world. . . . To leave the farm more productive, than you found it, is a blessing to humanity. To leave it less productive is little less than a crime, and especially against your children who must farm this soil after you are gone. We are learning that it is just as necessary to feed our crops as it is to feed our livestock and ourselves. . . . There is no more important question facing America today than that of making and keeping our soil productive. . . . A desert has no industries, no homes, no life. . . . Plant food — fertility — making and keeping the soil productive, is the foundation for successful agriculture, for national prosperity. . . . The most important thing in the world is that which makes it possible for a human being to live — that is, *Food,* something to eat.[1]

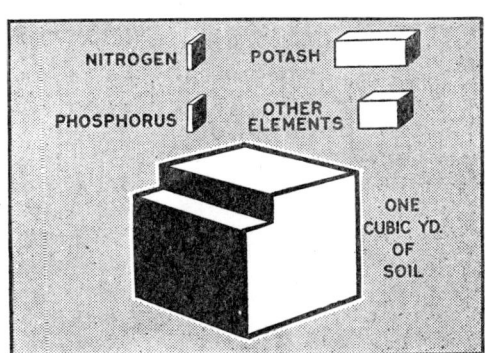

A block of fertile soil and the comparatively small portions of it which are plant food.

No matter how rich the original soil is, the "technology" of a miner and a robber can destroy it. Only the intelligent husbandman, using a biological technology, can preserve it. Soil contains small portions of plant foods. Each harvested crop removes some

---

[1] Holden, P. G., *Make the Soil Productive,* pamphlet published by International Harvester Co., p. 63.

of the plant foods from the soil. And if there is no replacement these plant-food elements of the soil can soon be exhausted. In a bulletin on *Soil Fertility Losses,* the Agricultural Experiment Station of Missouri State University shows that the nitrogen and humus content of our soils has fallen about 35 per cent. Many soil specialists agree that a third of the cultivated area of the United States is on the way to becoming useless.

Estimated Pounds of Plant Food per Acre in the Top Six Inches of Soil When First Plowed[2]

Hill Clay Soils:

Nitrogen	1,500 to 2,000 lb.
Phosphoric Acid	1,000 to 2,000 lb.
Potash	38,000 to 46,000 lb.
Lime	None to 25,000 lb.

Black Rich Soils:

Nitrogen	5,000 to 9,000 lb.
Phosphoric Acid	3,000 to 4,500 lb.
Potash	36,000 to 46,000 lb.
Lime	None to 50,000 lb.

Comparatively small portions of the soil constitute plant foods; namely, humus, nitrogen, phosphoric acid, potash, lime, iron, etc., but these small portions in their proper balance are very important.

Some soils had more, others much less than is shown here. The figures above are approximate only and are shown to bring out the fact that the original stock of plant food in the soil is limited.

Estimated Pounds of Plant Food per Acre That May Become Available Through Moisture, Decay, Decomposition, Action of Soil Bacteria, Earthworms, Good Cultivation, etc.[3]

Hill Clay Soils:

Nitrogen	30 to 50 lb.
Phosphoric Acid	10 to 20 lb.
Potash	80 to 120 lb.

Black Rich Soils:

Nitrogen	100 to 175 lb.
Phosphoric Acid	30 to 45 lb.
Potash	80 to 120 lb.

---

[2] Hayne, R. A., *Make the Soil Productive,* International Harvester Co.
[3] *Ibid.*

We cannot tell definitely how much plant food in a given soil will become available for a crop during a growing season. When a yield of corn is 25 bushels per acre, the crop takes about 30 pounds of nitrogen, 15 pounds of phosphoric acid, and 20 pounds of potash from the soil.

Removal of Soil Plant Foods on Commercial Farms

With continued commercial cropping the soil plant foods are shipped away to the elevators, mills, packers, and food companies. On the specialized farms nothing is returned to the soil. Wheat and corn and hay are hauled away to market year after year and with these crops goes a large portion of the nitrogen, phosphoric acid, potash, and lime which was originally in the soil. Any observant reader or student can see that the technology employed on a commercial mechanized one-crop farm is a technology with a destructive, breaking-down cycle. It may be "high" technology in a coal mine, but it is not intelligent technology when one is working with soil.

Removal of Soil Plant Foods on Livestock Farms

Even on livestock farms, every animal takes away plant food in its bones and flesh and blood. But animals take out of the feed only about one fifth of the plant food, leaving the rest on the farm in the form of manure. Eighty per cent of the plant food in crops is returned to the soil when fed to livestock. When five tons of alfalfa are hauled off to market, 255 pounds of nitrogen, 55 pounds of phosphoric acid, 200 pounds of potash, and 400 pounds of lime are taken from the farm. When five tons of alfalfa are fed to livestock on the farm and then marketed "on the hoof," only 51 pounds of nitrogen, 11 pounds of phosphoric acid, 40 pounds of potash, and 80 pounds of lime are taken from the farm. Approximately the same proportion is true for all other crops which may be used as feed for livestock. Selling butterfat and feeding the skim milk to young livestock removes much less plant food from the farm than selling whole milk. Most of the plant food is in the skim milk. One can easily see from the figures how readily the store of plant food on a farm is depleted when everything is hauled away to market and no feeding of livestock is included in the farming operation.

Results of Soil Mining

The livestock farmer, too, if he uses the soil-mining, soil-robbing technology will find in a few years (although not nearly as quickly as the one-crop farmer) that his crops are starving for the want of sufficient plant foods on which to live and flourish.

When the crop does not mature quickly and evenly, and when the seed kernels are light and deformed, the plants are not getting enough phosphoric acid from the soil. When the straw or stalk is weak and limber, then the crop is not getting enough potash from the soil. When the plants are small, the leaves narrow and too light in color, then the nitrogen supply in the soil is exhausted.

After years of robbing and mistreatment, the humus, the best source of plant food, is completely destroyed. The soil becomes sour and hard to cultivate. It packs and bakes easily and will hold no moisture for plants to use during dry periods. When it rains on soil without humus the water does not run into the soil, but it runs away with what is left of the soil in the floods pouring into the sea.

Humus and Its Part in Water Conservation

Humus acts as a sponge in the soil. Soil full of humus will absorb seven times as much water as hard, lifeless soil from which all plant foods and soil bacteria have been removed. That is one reason why crops burn up in dry weather on old, worn-out soils. It takes one barrel of water to produce one stalk and ear of corn. When we realize that it takes approximately 300 pounds of water to produce one pound of dry matter in the growing plants, then, we can see the value of the presence of much humus to act as a sponge for water storage.

Moisture and Its Conservation

In moisture-storage and moisture-conservation experiments conducted in 1938 by the Nebraska Agricultural Experiment Station at Lincoln in cooperation with the research division of the Soil Conservation Service under the direction of F. L. Duley and J. C. Russel, the rate of runoff on bare soils and the rate of moisture evaporation in the surface foot of bare soils were found to be the biggest moisture "thieves." On seven plots of ground, some covered, some uncovered, some plowed, some unplowed, and some basin listed, moisture-conservation tests were made from April 23 to September 8, 1938. The complete results are published in the *American Journal of Agronomy,* 1939.

During the test period 17.9 inches of rain fell, certainly an adequate rainfall to produce a good yield of corn in eastern Nebraska. Moisture losses, through runoff and evaporation, enhanced by the prevailing agricultural practices, led to the production of a very unsatisfactory corn crop during the year.

Results of the Moisture-Conservation Tests

Plot	Moisture Stored and Retained	Total Rainfall During Period
PLOT No. 1 Covered with straw, disked	6.9 inches or 38.7%	17.9 inches
PLOT No. 2 Disked, no straw (uncovered)	3.5 inches or 19.5%	17.9 inches
PLOT No. 3 Covered with straw, cultivated with a wide-type duckfoot machine working under the straw to kill weeds; no disking; no plowing	9.7 inches or 54.3%	17.9 inches
PLOT No. 4 Covered with straw and the straw plowed under ("Summer Fallow")	6.1 inches or 34.2%	17.9 inches
PLOT No. 5 Plowed (no straw) similar to ground plowed when stubble has been burned	3.7 inches or 20.7%	17.9 inches
PLOT No. 6 Covered with decayed straw and plowed (all straw plowed under)	3.1 inches or 17.4%	17.9 inches
PLOT No. 7 Basin listed. No runoff	4.9 inches or 27.4%	17.9 inches

These experiments show marked differences in moisture storage and retention. In the seven different methods of soil treatment, from the standpoint of moisture storage and retention some methods were more than twice as effective as others. A major part in water conservation is the job of keeping the water in the soil once it has entered. Surface evaporation will take all of the moisture out of the top six inches and most of it out of the top foot when the surface is uncovered and exposed.

None of the water ran off of plot No. 7, for it never overflowed the basins. Yet only 4.9 inches of the total rainfall remained in the ground in this plot at the end of the test period. Where did the other thirteen inches of rainfall go? It evaporated. The ridges and the furrows forming the basins actually doubled the exposed soil surface. Basin listing or any "dust mulch" system, with the soil loose and uncovered, cannot be called a moisture-conserving method of agriculture.

The old moisture theory assumed that moisture moved up from the subsoils to the surface and that if there were a fine film of dust at the surface, the moisture could not escape. The fact is that below the surface foot, the moisture neither moves up or down, but stays there until it is taken out by deep plant roots. In the surface foot of soil the moisture evaporates quickly through the "dust mulch" even though it has not been blown away. Furthermore when rain begins to fall on bare soil it will at first go in rapidly. Soon the rate of intake begins to decrease and the rate of runoff quickly increases taking much good soil with it. On a bare dusty surface the grinding, churning action of the rain, quickly forms a compact, almost watertight surface film, and no matter how long or how hard the rain falls, water cannot get into the soil any faster than it can penetrate this thin, watertight surface covering formed of dust particles and water. Duley and Russel found that something on the surface of the ground, i.e., straw, grass, decayed matter with water-holding capacity, a cover crop, anything that will break the churning action of the rain and prevent the watertight film from forming, will reduce the runoff. Once the water is stored in the ground this same covering prevents loss of moisture by evaporation. Duley and Russel applied a sprinkler to straw-covered ground for several hours and found that it would still take water at the rate of three-fourths inch per hour. When they applied the sprinkler to bare ground, after several hours, this ground would take only one-fourth inch of water per hour.

No matter how much plant food the soil contains, plants cannot use it without water. This water is taken from the soil by the fine roots of the plants and it is given off through the leaves. This water must be in the form of soil moisture retained in the humus. Wet, soggy land with pools of water will not produce. Water dissolves plant foods from the soil and carries it to the plant cells.

Soil, water, air, and plant constitute a vast, intricate processing enterprise. The raw materials are humus, water, potash, nitrogen, phosphorus, lime, etc. The living beings employed in the process are the soil bacteria, earthworms, etc. There are more of these working in one square yard of good soil than there are human beings employed in the factories of a state as large as Indiana.

About 95 per cent of the plant, tops and roots included, is carbon, oxygen, and water. Carbon and oxygen are taken from the air through the leaves. The other 5 per cent of the plant is nitrogen, phosphoric acid, potash, lime, etc., minerals taken from the soil. Plants get these ingredients and the water that carries them only through the roots. It is this 5 per cent which is all important. The yield of a crop depends on the plant foods and the soil moisture in the soil. What is in the soil is always the farmer's problem. The air will take care of itself. There is no air depletion or "erosion" in the country. Air depletion or "erosion" takes place only in the canyons which are lined with smokestacks.

Water — the Transportation System for Plant Foods

In this building process of plants with air and water and soil and plant foods, the water constitutes the great transportation system. The heat of the sun's rays lifts the water into the air, invisible and light, but it is there. Winds meet the floating vapors. From the colder regions the winds move in on the water-laden atmosphere, and the result is an *Asperges* from on high, the soft pitter-patter of spring and autumn rains, or the drenching rain in the summer with its theatrical display of thunder and lightning. If there is humus in the soil and the rain can really enter it, instead of running away with it, the newly fallen moisture soon applies itself to its planned work. It mixes with the minerals. The sun shines and the water is on the move again with its train of food elements which it lifts up with it as it comes up through the wheat and cornstalk, through grass blade, tree, or flower. It delivers its food parcels at the cell doors of the plant, the flower and the fruit, supplying the food, the medicine, the flavor, and the delicate tint, and when this has been done the water is set free again to be lifted up on invisible wings, and ultimately repeat its delivery service up through the soil — a task which water can perform only when there is humus to act as a sponge.

Integration and Correlation on the Farm

On a farm there is an entire train of correlated and interrelated life processes — all technologies which must be taken into account in any system of intelligent technology on the land. The mining technology, the soil-robbing technology, the machine technology which applies itself simply to efficient plowing and efficient removal of crops, each of these soon proves itself, even on the richest soils, to be a stupid, breakdown technology.

Many thousands of farm youth come into the cities. They come in much greater numbers than the urban traffic can bear. There in the cities these young people cause economic and sociological breakdowns through urban unemployment problems. Out in the fields the tractors have replaced the farm youth. It is not simply a question of the horses being out of a job. Considered as an isolated object, a power machine for pulling and hauling, or as a finished product in relation to its designer, its manufacturer, or its salesman, the tractor probably involves a "higher" technology than a team of horses. But if one considers this tractor in its relation to the farmer himself, in its relation to the farm as an integrated whole, and in relation to the wholesome organization of the national economy, agricultural and urban, it is clear that nothing has been given consideration except the mechanical side. In the production and use of the farm tractor no consideration is given to biological and sociological relationships. As a farm asset, the horse is much better integrated into the complete farm and community picture. The horse is a self-sufficing power unit. It is fed chiefly on the products of the farm it helps to operate. On the other hand, the farm tractor and its fuel can be obtained only by exchanging the products of the farm for those of other economic groups, an exchange in which there is no parity for the farmer.

The diversified, horsepowered farm, as a well-managed, well-planned unit, is technically better integrated, technically better advanced than the tractor-powered farm. When there is too great a preoccupation with tractors and similar machinery, the farming process, a process which is necessarily biological, is reduced to mere machinery and soil mining. The entire community suffers from such a technological mistake.

Peter Van Dresser indicates the agricultural fallacies that a narrow machine technology falls into:

> To understand how this may come about, let us visualize two contrasting farms. One is a diversified, dairy, poultry, and cereal farm such as might be owned by an intelligent man in certain sections of New York State. . . . There is no tractor in the barn. In its place the farmer has two, or several good draught horses. These horses are the product of a very old and highly developed technology — the technology of livestock breeding. The farmer himself is something of an expert in this science. He has assisted in the process of selective breeding which has produced these animals; he has supervised their foaling and knows how to treat their sicknesses and maintain them at peak efficiency. He produces their "fuel" himself and utilizes their waste products in maintaining the fertility of his soil.
>
> Contrast this picture to the role of the tractor . . . on many farms, such as those in the wheat and corn belts of our midwest, it is true that the possession of the machine enables the farmer who owns it to plow many more acres a day. But he obtains this mechanical advantage at a considerable cost. His relation to his machine is that of a mere auxiliary and operator. . . . He is helpless in the event of a breakdown and must call on outside assistance. He has no control over the production of the fuel it consumes. He is deprived of the valuable waste product, manure (the technology of which is also an old and well-developed one), and must purchase chemical fertilizer in its place, which unbalances the soil-hygiene of his land. He uses his increased mechanical power to cultivate wider and deeper than he should, in order to pay for his tractor and its fuel, which further endangers his soil. He forgets the science and art of livestock breeding, feeding, and handling and becomes by so much the poorer, more specialized and routinized.[4]

---
[4] Dresser, Peter Van, "The Human Side of Technics" in *Free America*, Dec., 1938, p. 15.

Driving a tractor, reaping a decreasing harvest and hauling it out to market, may be a "high" commercial technology so far as it goes, but this cannot be called scientific agriculture. In its narrow stupidity it ignores too many factors related to soil and its productivity. It ignores too many important biological factors and their interaction in making a farm an efficient economic unit.

Results of a One-Crop and Tractor Process

When no legumes are sown and no manure and compost — controlled decay of organic matter — are provided for, the process simply becomes one of plowing year after year, removing what plant foods there are in the soil, until the humus is worked out and the soil becomes bare and hard, ready to be carried off to the sea by wind and rain. The United States Department of Agriculture estimates that soil washing and soil blowing costs the farmers of the United States about $100,000,000 every year.

In a speech to Congress in June, 1938, President Franklin D. Roosevelt said:

Nature has given recurrent and poignant warnings through duststorms, floods, and droughts, that we must act while there is yet time, if we would preserve for ourselves and for our posterity the natural sources of a virile national life. . . . Floods, droughts, and dust-storms are in a very real sense manifestations of Nature's refusal to tolerate continued abuse of her bounties.

Soil Erosion in the United States[5]

Sheet Erosion —	Area affected	855,260,347 acres
	"gone"	192,000,000 acres
	"going"	663,000,000 acres
Gullying —	Area affected	864,818,281 acres
	"gone"	4,000,000 acres
	"rapidly going"	337,000,000 acres
	"beginning to go"	523,000,000 acres
Wind Erosion —	Area affected	332,181,740 acres
	"gone"	9,000,000 acres
	"going"	80,000,000 acres
	"beginning to go"	223,000,000 acres

---

[5] United States Department of Agriculture; "Farm Problems Visualized," *The National Forum*; *When the Crop Lands Go*, Stuart Chase; *Rich Land, Poor Land*, Stuart Chase.

Causes and Results of Erosion

Sheet Erosion — almost invisible, but the most destructive form of erosion

Causes:
1. Removal of natural cover
2. Constant plowing
3. Tilling steep slopes
4. Too many soil-depleting crops

Results:
1. Loss of actual soil
2. Smaller crop yield
3. Decreased land value
4. Losses by floods and sand deposits

Gullying — advanced form of sheet erosion

Causes:
1. The causes are the same as the causes of sheet erosion allowed to go unchecked

Results:
1. Carries away fertile soil
2. Interferes with operation of machinery
3. Undermines buildings, roadways, etc.
4. Fills streams, lakes, canals, etc.
5. Covers bottom lands with soil deposits

Wind Erosion

Causes:
1. Lack of rain
2. Denuding plains of natural grass by overgrazing and cultivation, which reduce the level of the water table

Results:
1. Removes valuable top soil thus taking away fertility
2. Destroys crops
3. Covers land with sand deposits
4. Destroys buildings, fences, etc.

Under present "low" technologies of agricultural mining, we lose by the three processes of erosion over three billion tons of good soil every year. From the great plains on a single day, in the summer of 1936, three million tons of rich top soil were lifted and blown as far as the Atlantic, two thousand miles away. Fifty-nine per cent of our countryside is affected by erosion. With this destruction 126,000,000,000 pounds of plant food are lost each year, a loss of $200,000,000 annually. If the present rate of riotous cultivation, and therefore loss by erosion, continues for the next fifty years, there will be a cumulative loss of thirty billion dollars.

Soil Problems and Social Problems

With such depletion of soils and pauperization of farmers, social problems become serious. Intelligent technology on the land calls for a good deal more than any technology of commerce or chemistry or mechanics can offer. The centralized factory technology, if it desires to make any contributions to the farm had better build its machines to the size fitted for the family unit, because only on a family farm can the century-old, biological technologies be respected and efficiently carried out. Only the man on a few acres can know his soil, grow his crops in proper rotation, feed as many of them as he can to livestock, and return the manure in its best condition to the soil. Only on a small farm is it possible to protect manure (which is worth $2.55 per ton if it were bought in the form of plant food in commercial fertilizers) against heating, leaching, and blowing away. Only a family-size farm can make provision for the growing of the legumes which do best and fit into a well-studied crop rotation. Only the family can make a common-sense use of land and work with the dictates of nature.

Depleted Acres Must Be Restored by Biological Techniques

But even though the intelligent family farmers strive to master conservation and biological technologies in their proper relationships, they must at present resort to the growing of a much larger amount of legumes than would ordinarily be necessary and lime must be bought to restore depleted acres, because of the fact that on so many farms the plant-food supplies have been depleted by "the-farm-is-a-factory" technology.

Lime may be needed in many places in the beginning, but after that legumes and livestock can rebuild our farms. Legumes and livestock will rebuild the land biologically, and the restoration will be much more efficient and biologically and scientifically correct than the purveyors of the by-products of commercial chemistry can do it.

Vast New Supplies of Nitrogen from the Air

Legumes take two thirds of their large stores of nitrogen from the air through nodules on the roots. These plants have vast root systems. They form sods and when in addition to the roots and the sods we plow under a green legume crop now and then, we can return a vast new supply of nitrogen to the soil, a supply taken from the air at no cost, and made with biological accuracy, an ingredient of the soil. The successful farmer will always be a biologist using the technology of biodynamics.

Biodynamic Farming: A Soil Biology

Within recent years the Agricultural Research Laboratories at Dornach, Switzerland, have perfected a soil technique to which they give the title, *biodynamic*. At Dornach, agricultural experts, who are soil biologists, not merely soil chemists, are developing the traditional farming wisdom of centuries into a well-integrated, scientific technique. These scientists see the cultivated field as a living organism, a living entity in the totality of its processes. Their method aims to make a farm live and produce as a self-contained organism, and not as the average farmer thinks of it today, as a series of unrelated processes. Their concern is primarily with the health of the land. Their soil-building program concerns itself chiefly with the organic ingredient of the soil — the humus — the basic reservoir of soil fertility. Fermentation of organic substances is important in the restoration of humus. In order to get a quick and good fermentation of layers of manure, thin layers of earth, leaves, trash hay, straw, weeds, bones, garbage, in fact any organic refuse, special methods of controlled fermentation for better humus formation have been developed. The right kind of fermentation is induced in the shaded barnyard compost heaps through certain plant preparations — medicinal herbs in proper mixture — camomile, valerian, dandelion, horsetail, nettle, etc. Before small amounts of these plant preparations are inserted into the carefully piled up manure heaps, the plant preparations are themselves put through a fermentation process. They are first buried at specific depths in the earth with some organic refuse where the whole is transformed into humus-like masses. When inserted into the manure heaps, these preparations speed up the rotting process. The result is a blackish-brown mass, rich humus material.

In a book which relates the achievements in the Dornach Agricultural Research Laboratories, Dr. Ehrenfried Pfeiffer states:

Researches have shown that during the rotting process, the bacterial content of such a manure pile is ten times that of one not so treated. Particularly noticeable is the presence of a great number of earthworms. Such piles are constantly filling up with earthworms which, after their humus forming activity is completed, die and provide an additional fertilizing substance through the decomposition of their own bodies.[6]

The Earthworm and the Farm

On the *biodynamic* farm, the earthworm is recognized as a welcome visitor. In fact he is rightfully recognized as the chief humus maker, the irreplaceable agent in agriculture. On the biodynamic farm, efforts are made to prepare a good soil home for him, because the earthworm is a connoisseur of the better soils. He disappears from the soils that are choked by soil chemists, and soils that are completely mined out by commercial farmers. Besides being the ideal humus maker, the earthworm works up the soil into a crumbly structure, helps in soil aeration and drainage, and makes it a tolerable medium for organic life. The earthworm eats earth and prepares it for planting. The excrement of the earthworm provides the perfect soil.

Dr. H. Powell Spring of the University of Vermont states:

> The weight of earthworms per acre of good soil equals that of a good-sized cow.... In healthy soil this subterranean "cow" is constantly at work. In a single year this "cow" handles enough earth per acre to fill three freight cars (European size).[7]

Charles Darwin observed the work of the earthworm and devoted an entire book to this lowly creature. Darwin observed the earthworm at work, transporting into deeper strata gravel and bits of sand that obstruct plant growth, depositing upon the surface the "predigested" humus which plants require. Upon a site observed by Darwin during a period of ten years earthworms heaped up 2.2 inches of topsoil. One of Darwin's co-workers, Dr. King, conducted an experiment in which he estimated that the earthworms were bringing to the surface 14.58 tons of earth per acre.

In 1890 another earthworm investigator, Dr. Wollny, conducted

---

[6] Pfeiffer, Dr. E., *Bio-Dynamic Farming and Gardening* (New York: Anthroposophic Press, 1938), p. 46.

[7] Spring, Dr. H. P., "Our Friend: the Earthworm" in *Free America*, Dec., 1938.

experiments in which he compared plants grown in earth containing earthworms and plants grown in earth without them. The earthworms succeeded in getting a 35 per cent to 49 per cent increase in cereals and other grains, a 59 per cent increase in case of oilseeds, and considerable increases in the yields of potatoes and beets. The very volume of the humus was increased by the presence of the worms by 27.5 per cent. The holes and the passageways and the loosening of the earth — the work of the worms — greatly enhanced the ability of the soil to absorb decaying matter for the next crop. The earth was found to be more fluffy and a better absorbing medium for water and air. An eight-day trial revealed 8.04 volumes of nitrogen per one thousand volumes of air in soil containing worms. In soil without worms the volume of nitrogen per one thousand volumes of air was only 3.08. When one considers the importance of the nitrogen content of the soil, this contribution of the worms is no small item.

Our habits of thinking, which may be adequate in the cities of machinery and manufacture, break down when they face the many organic factors which we call life. Whether we like it or not, nature makes the rules for the vital processes. Nature will not permit her rules for vital processes to be replaced by the rules of commercial mechanization. An effort must be made to understand nature and follow its rules in its far-flung integration and interrelation of minute biological processes, if the game of life is to go on.

Soil Biology — Not Chemistry and Mechanics

We till our soils with mechanized greed, we destroy the biologically formed and balanced layers of humus, and still expect to get the same results with artificial, costly, and unbalanced mineral fertilizers. With a threefold increase of artificial fertilizers we are not increasing our average yields per acre. And a number of very destructive plant diseases have developed. The industrial chemicals sold to remove the superfluous wastes of chemical production give the soil a "commercial" shock, bombard the living organisms which vitalize the thin layer of topsoil, and finally force the earthworm to abandon his work. The men at Dornach know that commercial farming has ruined American soil, and they maintain that chemicals only aggravate the sickness of our soils. They say that we are merely soil chemists, not soil biologists; soil miners, not real husbandmen. They are amused at our childish commercial faith which makes us feel that anything that we can pay money for and take home in a bag or in a truck is better than the many things that we might have free at hand, things that can be put to work merely by a little intelligent labor. They warn us that our potassium and ammonium nitrates and the tons and tons of sulphates and the poisonous sprays with arsenic and lead compounds are undermining the health of our soil, stamping out the living soil organisms, doping the soil with injurious, alien matter, and therefore making American agriculture biologically unsound. They caution with reason that it takes more brains to manage a farm than it does to run a factory; that the technology of a farm is more complicated than the technology of a factory; that the so-called "high" mechanical technology of the factory has very limited applications when there is question of intelligent land use; that on the land there are many technologies which good mechanics completely overlook — to mention only one, the soil technology of our friend, the earthworm.

Soil Biology — Practiced Only in the Family Unit

It is quite evident that the complete technology, the complete series of highly interrelated agricultural processes will never be followed by specialized farm corporations and their farm laborers. Absentee landlords and migrating tenants, too, work for immediate cash. Their interest does not reach very far beyond the current monetary opportunity for gain. Only the family unit intelligently trained and owning its own land can give a nation the many fruits to be derived from an intelligent technology on the land.

Biodynamic Farming — Intelligent Land Technology

Chauncey Stillman, editor of the magazine *Free America,* and one of the few *biodynamic* farmers of America, made a tour of certain *biodynamic* farms in the Rhine Valley cantons of Switzerland. In Europe there are about two thousand farm units large and small run on this method. These farms stood out as green oases amid dried-up farms, and while the growing grains on neighboring farms were falling and lay completely flattened in places by windstorms, because of a lack of vital substances in the weak stems and stalks, on the *biodynamic* farms the strong, healthy grains stood proudly upright. In an article, "Challenge to Famine," the author gives us the earnest reflections which this visual proof of intelligent technology on the land brought to his mind:

> I thought of how this method [the biodynamic method] is putting whole cantons on a sound and permanent basis. Some farming villages are as much as eighty per cent *biodynamic*. The most conservative of men is the European farmer, and scores of them are quietly adopting biodynamic methods every year. The poorest Swiss farm has a higher life expectancy than the richest American farm, thanks to the health of its neighboring land and the methods of its owner. . . . A bitter contrast rises to mind. Here is a craggy little country whose meanest slope responds to intelligent care. Back home one third of the world's richest cropland has been turned to waste within two generations. The Dust Bowl widens out as we frantically plan more schemes to stop it, such as the production of phosphates on a gigantic scale. And all our schemes are futile because as a nation we have not learned the true nature of the soil, nor man's relation to it. Will a few biodynamic farms stand forth, in another century, as green oases in the Great American Desert? Before famine wins, will their slow influence spread from single farms and valleys and forests, widening out over verdant regions beyond the horizon?[8]

---

[8] Stillman, C., "Challenge to Famine" in *Free America,* Oct., 1938.

Chapter 14

TRAINING FOR LEADERSHIP ON THE LAND

The greatest fine art of the future will be the making of a comfortable living from a small piece of land. — *Abraham Lincoln.*

Interest and Participation

Words are not strong enough to express the absolute apathy of Americans in the much mooted questions of sociology and economics, problems of prime significance which will have tremendous influence upon the lives of all of us, and of our children. Some months ago the *Queen's Work* conducted a contest in Social Action. With a membership of over half a million subscribers, this publication should have succeeded in obtaining enough participants for a noteworthy contest. What was the response? Only seventeen young men and women entered the contest. A federation of Christian churches attempted a similar contest. And again the results were the same. Young America is not awake to its problems. It is simply astounding how little we know of social problems, social justice, and the really serious questions of our times. Pius XI was calling for valiant soldiers in the cause of justice and charity when he wrote:

Constituted Pastor and Protector of these innumerable sheep by the Prince of Pastors who redeemed them by His Blood, We can scarcely restrain Our tears when We reflect upon the dangers which threaten them. Our Pastoral Office, moreover, reminds us to search constantly, with paternal solicitude, for means of coming to their assistance, appealing to the unwearying zeal of others who are bound to this cause by justice and charity. . . . And, in truth, the world has nowadays sore need of valiant soldiers of Christ, who strain every thew and sinew to preserve the human family from the dire havoc which would befall it were the teachings of the Gospel to be flouted, and a social order permitted to prevail, which spurns no less the laws of nature than those of God.[1]

The United States is far behind Nova Scotia, Ireland, Belgium, France, Switzerland, Portugal, and other European countries in producing leaders imbued with the spirit of the great Social Encyclicals.

Leaders and Leadership

Leadership must be assumed. It must be taken upon oneself through personal initiative. There is no forcing or compelling in a matter of this sort. It is a question of being motivated by a glorious ideal. The leader must have a vision broad enough to take in the future, a vision that recognizes the possibilities of a course of action. Leadership is effective when there is enthusiasm and tenacity of purpose in throwing oneself wholeheartedly into an accomplishment determined upon, cost what it may. If there ever was a period that may be singled out for its feverish activities, it is the present era. We see athletes outdoing themselves in performing feats of physical prowess, establishing new world records only to be bettered by the next competitor. Urged by the thrill of conquest and the goad of ambition, flyers master the air with huge man-made machines. They travel faster than man ever dreamed was possible. Others risk life and fortune to discover unexplored regions of land and water. Do we, followers of Christ, keep pace for Christianity and the Kingdom of God in achieving economic, social, and spiritual goals?

A leader must have personality and enthusiasm in order that he may win the heart and respect of his followers. He must embrace his cause wholeheartedly and be spurred on by high ideals of justice to his fellow men. Finally, he must possess the virtues of courage, unselfishness, and a willingness to work to a high degree. Without special knowledge and training, one is hopelessly lost in the morass of conflicting social reforms and panaceas for economic ills.

---

[1] *Quadragesimo Anno,* National Catholic Welfare Conference Edition, pp. 40, 41, 47.

Proper Choice of Plans and Organization

To obtain the leaders we sorely need, we must develop effective plans to train the youth in many forms of leadership. The activities embraced in our training programs must build up domestic, spiritual, and community solidarity. One club for John, another for Sue, one club for mother and another for father, are too often special interest groupings which ignore family interests, parish interests, or community interests. The innate tendencies to selfishness have been nursed all too successfully to vigorous growth under present-day conditions through social and economic specializations that bear in themselves the seeds of the dissolution of family, community, and nation.

Society Must Be an Organism

The concept of the *organic* in society must return as the basis of thought and action. Youth programs must contain activities that will conserve and rebuild home life; its interests, its surroundings, its culture. They must contain activities which will bring the Christian homes together in the larger life of the parish and community. The leadership must be built around the primary units — family, parish, community — and activity in the wider units must be such as will strengthen the work of the smaller unit, the family. Parents and children must not only conserve the wellsprings and sources of physical life and sustenance, but also develop *mutual* regards and services for their higher spiritual and religious selves. These results can best be achieved, if youth leaders think in terms of *family* activities, *parish* activities, and *community* activities. Youth programs should not be mere temporary movements. They should contain plans extending from youth through maturity, invigorating the life of home, parish, and community.

Bearing the burden of toil together, interpreting the problems and meaning of life together, exchanging goods and services, playing and recreating together, will give the foundation and the background of experience necessary in order that human nature may comprehend and appreciate the demand for social virtues — social justice and social charity.

The recruiting of leaders in each parish and the organization and development of training courses are the first requirements for successful programs. The priest in the pulpit can help immensely for he, as no one else, can elicit the support of members of the parish and enthuse possible leaders by setting forth, in an appealing way, the dangers that beset present-day society. The new leaders should familiarize themselves with programs that are the outcome of the tried experience of leaders elsewhere, e.g.:

1. The Programs of Rural Youth Sodalities (fashioned to meet the interests and needs of rural groups).
2. The Programs of Parish Sodalities (adapted to rural needs).
3. Rural Life Sundays and Conferences.
4. Rural Discussion Groups.
5. Little Country Theater.
6. Homemakers' Clubs.
7. 4-H Clubs.
8. Future Farmers' Clubs.

For such activities manuals or bulletins may be obtained, giving up-to-date information and sound directions, compiled by experienced leaders. All these activities when inspired, guided, and strengthened by the teachings of the gospel and the grace of God will build up good morals and result in wholesome, integral social living in the home, in the parish, in the community. For country people, however, these activities should have distinct adaptations for rural interests, rural ideals, and rural progress. Thus the parish sodality program is ideal from the spiritual point of view, but it should embrace in its activities in rural communities many of the farm plans, farm projects, and farm programs developed in 4-H Club planning.

Rural leaders and teachers in rural schools owe it to the preservation of society to interest themselves in the social and economic problems of rural life; such as, farm tenancy, rural slums, cooperatives, rural child welfare, population trends, rural vocational guidance, rural homemaking crafts, legislation in the interest of farmers, projects of county, state, and national conservation and planning boards, farm-labor unions and parties, rural electrification, the project of the ever normal granary, the relation of human-scale technocracy to rural social and economic problems, etc.

Leadership must apply itself to the issues that are *living*. In all phases of human needs the leadership must be in the *lead* and participate actively and constructively in present issues, giving spiritual motivation, giving direction according to solid principles, and warning against destructive trends, tendencies, or developments. If the young are guided in their initial steps, they will help plan in the field which is opened to them and they should be encouraged to accept this responsibility.

Such leadership is exemplified in the activities of:
1. Cooperative Parish Activities Service, Effingham, Illinois.
2. St. Francis Xavier University, Antigonish, Nova Scotia.
3. "Farm Folk Forums" of Northern Europe. (These are discussion groups in which competent sympathetic leaders relate the content of religion, its truths and practices to specific farm interests and problems. All economic and social problems have religious implications and the leaders must help the people to discern the religious truths and principles involved.)

The responsibility for the unsolved rural problems of today must be laid at the door of the schools, and the types of education provided by the administrators and directors of rural education in the past. The rural population has all too long been dependent on teachers without any sympathy or understanding of rural problems, often giving the rural child an inferiority complex in regard to his origin, his culture, manners, customs, present lot in life, and outlook for the future. The rural school should aim first to train the young in better rural leadership and in the special technique of cooperative rural organization. Content and methods in rural teaching should in the case of most rural children prepare them for rural living on family farms. Some rural children with definite aptitudes for the professions and the ministry should be given the full classical training, or perhaps some commercial training. There should be no great emphasis on commercial, urban curriculums in rural schools.

If rural-parish foundations have been saved, during the depression and migration to the cities, it is due to the fact that the parish schools have in such parishes made invaluable contribution through agricultural subjects and the teaching of handcrafts, in what makes for contented and successful living on the farm.

This influence on the part of the schools should be more sensed; their curriculums, methods, and teachers should be selected with a view to increasing such influences, to the end that the rural parish and the rural school may radiate a satisfied, progressive, complete, and secure rural life.

Teachers preparing for rural schools should take courses in rural sociology and rural economics. Such teachers should become conversant with the following publications:

1. U. S. Bulletins, Department of Agriculture.
2. Bulletins, surveys, agricultural colleges.
3. The *Queen's Work,* "Rural Life Study Club Outlines."
4. The *Catholic Rural Life Bulletin, Catholic Rural Life Objectives* (Publications of National Catholic Rural Life Conference, 240 Summit Ave., St. Paul, Minn.).
5. Pamphlets, Rural Life Bureau, N.C.W.C.
6. Publications of Francis Xavier University, Nova Scotia.
7. Monthly magazine of Southern Agrarians: *Free America* (Address: 112 East 19th Street, New York City).
8. *Land of the Free,* Herbert Agar (Houghton Mifflin).
9. *Pursuit of Happiness,* Herbert Agar (Houghton Mifflin).
10. *A Better Rural Life,* Rev. Edgar Schmiedeler, O.S.B. (Wagner).

In too many instances the rural population is following the guidance of those who are not in the least concerned about their spiritual welfare. The rural pastor should be able to acquaint his people with the best literature on rural problems, the literature that contains the agrarian philosophy of rural living, the literature in which they can find help for the solution of many of their problems, through enlightenment as to the processes to be used in bettering the methods in diversified farming, and through enlightenment on the technique of cooperative, functional, community organization. It is the priest who can help rural parents build a rural community center to prevent the pernicious work of commercialized amusements in roadhouses at the crossroads or in near-by cities.

Only in bending down into the more immediate life interests can pastors draw the people, and especially the young, to the best practices, purposes, and ends of life. The young will become more loyal and devoted to their priests in the activities of sodalities, Holy Name, and other societies, when they see that the priests have an intelligent, sympathetic interest in the everyday struggles for a more satisfying and indeed a better farm life.

4-H: Head — Heart — Hands — Health

The 4-H is an organization of sons and daughters of farmers. It stresses the development of the four H's; namely, Head, Heart, Hands, and Health through farm clubwork. The 4-H movement dates back to the so-called pig club for boys, founded in Louisiana in 1910. Soon after, the idea was taken up by the Land-Grant Colleges and the United States Department of Agriculture. With official direction of county agricultural agents and the unofficial aid of public-spirited citizens, it extended to all parts of the country. Today 4-H clubwork is a regular and important educational project of the cooperative Extension Service, established in 1914 by Act of Congress and approved by all the states of the Union.

The insignia or "earmarks" of the 4-H clubwork are emblem, pledge, motto, and colors. The National Club emblem is the four-leaf clover with an *H* on each leaflet. The National Club pledge is:

I pledge my *head* to clearer thinking, my *heart* to greater loyalty, my *hands* to larger service, and my *health* to better living, for my club, my community, and my country.

The National Club Motto is: "To make the best better." The National Club Colors are green and white. Green is nature's most common color and is an emblem of springtime, life, and youth. White symbolizes purity and high ideals.

Boys' and girls' 4-H clubwork is a specialized educational enterprise for rural youth. It not only helps the rural boys and girls develop desirable ideals and standards for farming, homemaking, community life, and citizenship, and gives them a sense of responsibility for their attainment, but it provides rural boys and girls an opportunity to "learn by doing" through conducting certain farm or home enterprises and demonstrating to others what they have learned. It trains rural boys and girls in cooperative action to the end that they may increase their accomplishments and, through associated efforts, better assist in solving rural problems.

Training for Leadership on the Land

A standard 4-H club has at least five members, from 10 to 21 years of age, who are working upon the same club project. A local club leader is in charge from the time the club is organized until the final annual reports are made. The club has a regular set of officers, elected from its own membership. There is a definite program of work with the officers in charge, working under the guidance of the local club leader. An exhibit of club projects is held some time during the year, preferably at the local or county achievement program. Principles of correct judging of livestock, handcraft work, etc., are taught in order that the members may learn to judge their club products. At least one public demonstration of this is given. An achievement club program, or "roundup," is held during the year. The purpose of a 4-H is to improve the homemaking, agricultural, educational, cultural, and social advantages of the boys and girls of the community. These purposes are accomplished by carrying out the standard club requirements.

Each year a new project, or a continuation of the foregoing project, is carried on. The 4-H Club projects are: animal husbandry, dairy husbandry, home economics, agricultural economics, forestry, horticulture, poultry husbandry, and soil conservation. Pig raising, canning, and homemaking are not hobbies for these boys and girls. They are a serious preparation for their role as citizens.

Each state sponsors its own program for a 4-H Club activity. Clubwork is conducted by the College of Agriculture and the United States Department of Agriculture in cooperation with organized counties, local communities, and schools of the state. The county extension agents and home demonstration agents are in charge of the work in their respective counties. No rural community goes farther or faster than its own local people and leaders carry it.

A local leader should be selected for each 4-H Club in the community, or the leader suggested by the club members should be approved. These leaders usually are former club members, successful farmers, farm and village women, and teachers who have identified themselves in their work with the same farm and home problems on which their club projects are based.

The officers of each club are elected from its own membership.

These officers are: president, vice-president, secretary, song leader, and reporter. They serve throughout the club year, provided they attend the club meetings regularly and discharge the duties of their office.

A "health and sanitation" club was organized by a certain rural group and proved very successful. The object of the 4-H Health and Sanitation Project was to promote health. This was done by the daily practice of health habits by each member, by teaching the relation of sanitary surroundings to health, and by developing through the club activities a sense of responsibility for community health conditions. In this project each club member was required:

1. To know the health rules.
2. To practice the health habits.
3. To learn the fundamentals of sanitation relating to water supply, proper location of wells, disposal of waste, use of septic tanks, fly control, ventilation, the home production of clean milk, and vermin control.
4. To make and install in the home a window ventilator or wind deflector and to take deep breathing exercises out of doors.
5. To make and install a flytrap.
6. To score the home water supply.

The members kept records of their practice of health habits, of sanitary equipment made or provided; of the sanitary improvements introduced in the home, school, or community; of the meetings, demonstrations, and exhibits held. All these things were duly recorded in a record book provided by the Extension Service of the College of Agriculture. The expense to each member in such health projects is very small, as most of the material needed can usually be found in the home. Each club is also asked to have an outside interest such as, courtesy, good grooming, folk games, wild-life conservation, wild-flower conservation. Wild life cannot be covered fully when correlated with other subjects, but a start can be made.

Demonstration is the objective method used in teaching and learning in every standard 4-H Club project. In a demonstration the equipment consists of the actual materials required to do a job on the farm, in the home, school, or community. First the leader gives individual-method demonstrations on the practical problems under consideration at the regular meetings. Then the members redemonstrate the process before the club group. The leaders and members at the same time give an explanation of the processes being demonstrated and of the results obtained. The demonstrations in this particular project were, the repairing of screens, the making of flytraps, window deflectors, and window ventilators.

Parliamentary procedure is always followed when conducting a meeting. The club president is in charge. The meeting is called to order by the president, who leads the members in repeating the national 4-H pledge. During roll call by the secretary, the members respond by giving a health rule, or a progress report on their project. The secretary reads the minutes of the last meeting, which if approved by the club, are adopted as the official club record. A new committee may be appointed, or suggestions may be given for the benefit of the club. There are short talks on topics studied for that particular meeting and club songs with the song leader in charge. Discussion and demonstration with the local club leader in charge are followed by group discussion of the subject. The local leader assigns work for the next meeting. The game committee leads the members in playing games.

An achievement program is held at the close of the work for the club year. At this program all club members have an exhibit. Two members are selected by vote for the club demonstration team which represents the club and community on the county achievement day.

The 4-H Club movement has a healthful and wholesome influence on the young people in the rural districts. It develops their personality. They acquire a certain poise and self-confidence. They develop a sense of comradeship and cooperation, and learn early to exercise good judgment in making life decisions. It also teaches them a love for ownership, and makes them real leaders. Since the 4-H movement is a character-building program, it must have some kind of philosophy of life. It must have spiritual motivation. The 4-H program is excellent for rural sodalities. A rural sodality in 4-H work will succeed in building up a better evaluation of country life, a respect for the land, and a correct understanding and appreciation of the family, the parish, and the community.

After attending a 4-H meeting, the Reverend James A. Byrnes, editor of the *Catholic Rural Life Bulletin,* wrote:

> I had seen a meeting in which young people really became alive and interested about important things, a meeting carrying a personal enthusiasm. . . . I must give more thought to 4-H. If it can combine so flexibly the recreational and the educational, the social and the cultural, then methinks it cries out to the country pastor for the spiritual element, which alone remains to perfect it.[2]

---

[2] Byrnes, Rev. J. A., "I Am a Country Pastor" in *Catholic Rural Life Bulletin,* Feb., 1939.

Chapter 15

IDEALS AND EDUCATION FOR RURAL BOYS AND GIRLS

IT IS good to dream dreams. It is almost wholesome to see visions. To boys and girls of the countryside, to young men and women on the farms we address this question: What are your dreams for the future? What are your ideals? Calmly and sensibly, let us analyze the principles that should guide our dreams. First of all: Do have dreams about your future. That means think about the future. Do not drift along, but reflect, consider, plan, and seek to accomplish. Dreams that run riot can never be fulfilled and leave us forever dissatisfied. Let the dreams of your future be sensible. Let them be realizable. There is no use dreaming of a perpetual-motion machine or of a train to the moon. There are thousands of Napoleons and Caesars in the wards of insane hospitals. There is no use dreaming to be that for which you are unfitted. You will never be an acrobat, or the man on the flying trapeze if you weigh 400 pounds. If you are short and pudgy you might attain to membership in a German band, but it takes a tall and comely young man to wear a striped uniform in front of a movie. Physical fitness is important but character and mental fitness are even more essential. Who can advise you of your fitness? Your parents, your teachers, your friends. Do not follow the advice of a salesman who tells you that he can see it in your eyes that you will make a radio engineer or a Diesel-engine specialist. Do not "hitchhike" to Hollywood because you were elected queen of the basketball tournament.

Even though you may be fitted, there is another important question to be answered: Can I achieve my dream? Have I a chance? Is it within my grasp? Not as a result of miracles or pure luck, but as a possible result of ordinary development in an ordinary way. Too many high-school graduates dream of college and even register in the freshman class, but are doomed to failure from the start. By all means go to college if you can see your way through in any reasonable way, but weigh carefully all the hazards, the difficulties, and the possible drawbacks. If you feel you can take them, then go on, otherwise save packing your "Rah! Rah! pants!"

Good Sense — Good Judgment

Overambition is just as harmful as not enough ambition. Good sense, good judgment, are essential in discovering your possibilities of achievement. Fitness and possibility of achievement are not the only measures of our dreams. A most important item to consider is this. What measure of usefulness to myself, to my future family, and to society does my dream promise me? This necessitates a pretty well-formed philosophy of life, a fairly good elementary understanding of life's purposes, of society's needs, of family ideals, of the individual's proper aims in life. Parents, educators, religious leaders must present these in proper perspective to the young. It is a difficult task indeed but a necessary one. The majority of failures in life may be traced back to the initial failure of improper judgment, of false ambition, of undertakings where the philosophy was not basically sound. Insight and desire in vocations must be sensible.

A Sensible Ideal

A sensible ideal, and an ideal which can become a reality, is to be a farmer if you are a rural boy, and to be a farm-home mother if you are a rural girl. This was the dream of your forefathers as they moved westward to the land; it was the dream of the village dwellers in Europe as they crossed the Atlantic to their new home in this land of the free — a home on the land. For physical well-being, there is no work like the work on a farm. The sunshine and the air, the bronzed countenance of the boy, the rosy cheeks of the country maiden! Compare that physical existence with the stuffy, sunless apartment dwelling, with the chemical smells of a shop. Compare the song of the birds soaring

Ideals and Education for Rural Boys and Girls 235

overhead with the shrill noise of trolleys and trucks, with rumble of subways, with jangling of bells. For sheer physical comfort and peace choose a home on the land. How can a girl prepare herself for motherhood, her highest ideal, midst the nerve-racking artificial life of a city, standing on her feet all day, and then snatching a restless sleep from a bed pulled out of a wall?

Are you a boy, and do you like a machine? Do you want the city where man-made machines make a machine out of a man? Have you ever thought that in a factory or a machine shop a man becomes simply another lever, another punching arm? Repeated, monotonous motion is the slavish work of men on the belt lines. Is there nothing for men on the land? Yes, tractors and combines, but when they are built for mass production they destroy men and land. Cannot men rise above machinery and understand the powers of nature—the strength of a kernel of corn and the tiny flower seed? The farmer plants it and plans its proper place on his farm and around his home. Gentle mother earth nurses it in her bosom, the sun warms it, the rain moistens it and it bursts forth. Two tiny leaves break through the ground. Man, the human, rejoices in seeing his work begin to show results. It grows. The farmer cares for it, cooperates with God in the ever-new process of creation. The farmer is a co-worker with God. He is a scientist; he is a planner; he is a free man. His work is not "punch, punch, punch" till his eyes grow dim, till his very soul is deadened.

Are country girls envious of their city sisters, of the girls in the office and the factory, the sales girls, the waitresses? Where will the girl accomplish most for herself, for the future family, for society? She will achieve the higher destiny in a happy home in the country as the mother of happy children. On Sunday afternoons rural girls board the trains to go back to the cities for another week of commercialized work. Wealth? Perhaps. They make it for others. For every dollar they get, there are heartaches and failures, and the pennies received are not saved. They are used for food and room and fine clothes; turned back to the greedy ones who allow their dollars and pennies to be handled for a few moments; when work is invested in a country home and land, there may not be so many flighty greenbacks floating here and there, but the interest comes back to a family over a period of years and the capital is always there. Work in a home, rather than in office or factory, returns social and cultural values that are not to be measured in dollars and cents.

Rural Parents Advise Too Frequently in Terms of Commercialism

But Dad and Mother say: "There is not enough work for all our boys and girls on our one hundred or two hundred acres." No work? What do they mean? If they had a family of twenty there would be enough work on a forty-acre farm. Parents don't see the work that might be accomplished by their children. They think in terms of corn, oats, tractors, combines, marketing products, buying family needs. Parents have forgotten the proper use of their land and the welfare of their children for the sake of a cash-crop farming system that leads to bankruptcy. Rural parents should plan their farming with the welfare of the children uppermost in their minds. The human family values received from such farm practice will be immeasurable and the dollars and cents will go much farther than they do in a bankrupt system of commercialized farming. The first step in the ladder of success will never be the running board of a rattletrap car. There must be saving, a willingness to learn, a use of one's God-given intelligence. Know the soil, care for the stock, plan for proper cropping and marketing. Don't simply do what others do unless you know they are right. Learn to fit your farm to the needs of your family.

False Measures of Success and True Standards

The dance halls and saloons do not train for success on the farm or elsewhere. Activity in 4-H work, in church work, in social and educational work, leads to success and fun too. Cash income should never be the first and last aim in one's life. Even on a very low income, life may be lived and enjoyed to the fullest. High degrees of culture, intellectual achievement and perfection do not depend on riches. Standards of spending and standards of false thinking are not standards of living. If there are to be any future homes, girls must learn to sew, learn all the fancywork they can; learn to weave, learn to cook, to plan meals, to can vegetables and fruits and meats. There should be a crafts department and an economics department in every home. Members of the family must learn to know what they can do in the home and be given the opportunity to do it. Every farm home can and should give profitable employment to every boy and girl in that home. But the "Joneses" don't run their home that way and of course we must follow them. Only a little reflection will bring us to see that of all the families upon whose example the American people might pattern themselves the "Joneses" are the least admirable. The family which produces for its own consumption and serves its own needs as far as it can on a modern, organized, laborsaving basis approaches the only proper ideal for American families — the ideal of the spiritual liberty and the economic self-sufficiency of the family. Work in the home is just as truly productive as work outside the home. When too many people spend their time outside the home earning cash, then much cash has to be spent to secure the things and the work that should have been done in the home.

Education for the Restoration of the Productive Home

If the work in the home is no longer creative, productive, independent, satisfying, and creditable, it is because we have not been educated to do it, because we have been lured away by false visions of wealth, prosperity, bright lights, and ruined lives. Human beings produce wealth. Why not produce it and keep it as we produce it? Who has made possible the amassing of great fortunes, the concentration of wealth? No one but the producers of wealth. We have allowed others to plan for us, we have been too lazy to think for ourselves. We have said: "Give me a wage and relieve me of responsibility and I shall be happy." Then greed came along and enslaved us. Keep your freedom. Stay on the land, plan for yourselves — not for opulent, material riches, but for a home rich in happiness, rich in satisfactions, rich in those elements that build up men and women into independent citizens, men and women who are stable and reliable, the necessary elements of a free democratic nation.

Educating for a Home on the Land

There must be more families on the land, and the families on the land must think to make farming a way of living first of all. That does not mean that we advocate a check on inventions or technological progress, rather we advocate a most complete application of all modern means to the end that farming will be both economically and socially attractive to the family. We contend that under the guise of progress we have debased agriculture both economically and socially. Witness: the lost ownership, the lower living standards, the stranded youth, the lost men and women in the cities.

The world was created for men, women, and children. They should be the first concern of society. The educational program in a country should furnish the ideals for young and old. If industrialism, urbanization, and commercialism in farming are to be our goals, then let us train young and old to that end. Let us then build up a system of education that will throw more people into the cities, to fill the slums, to be wage slaves, to be propertyless proletarians, to clog the relief roles, or become sharecroppers for corporations on the land. But if our ideals are to be for a free people, for an independent nation, for fully developed individuals, for faithful members of families, for useful citizens in society, or humans destined for immortality; then let us educate young and old to those goals and let us guide them toward and along the path that leads to those ideals.

Individual happiness (not based on selfishness), family loyalty, free citizenry! These are three ideals worth achieving. "A Home on the Land" with its various possibilities and even limitations comes closer to making them attainable than any other type of human family existence. *Individual happiness* presupposes liberty, independence, self-determination. It is achieved when the whole of oneself is able to exercise both the physical and mental gifts which a bountiful God has bestowed upon us. The independence of a farmer, in planning and working, his manifold interest from marketing to entomology, from grafting trees to trade agreements, from genetics to harvesting, from winter work in his farm shop to the glorious outdoors of the springtime plowing, all offer to him a chance for the exercise of both physical and mental gifts that make for individual happiness. It is not the narrow, self-styled happiness of greed. It is like the happiness of a bird's song denoting joy and making others joyful. *Family loyalty* in its fullness is easier and is attainable where the family is an economic as well as a social unit. The home on the land, where father, mother, and children each contribute a share to the maintenance of the home, where planning is done on a family basis, where outside influence play but a small part; there is to be found the ideal habitat of the family. What is a *free citizenry?* Where does a free man live? A man is not free if his existence and well-being depends upon a wage or salary no matter how high it may temporarily be. A man is not a free citizen if he possesses no productive property. The height of human freedom is achieved by the man on the land, who owns it, who controls his own food production, his own credit and his sale or exchange of goods. There goes a free citizen: the farmer who owns his farm and makes of farming, first and foremost, a mode of living. If we believe in the above ideals, they must be taught to the young and old. And the young, especially, must be prepared to conduct their children to the land.

Urbanism and Commercialism Are Destructive

The majority of farmers in the quest of prosperity lost not only independence and never achieved prosperity but lost even their children in the vortex of the cities. Bigger farms, less human labor have demanded an economic and human toll. The commercial phrase so often repeated: "You can't make anything on a farm," has driven many a youngster to the slavery of the city. There is no more independent existence, no greater freedom attainable under our present economic system than to have a home on the land!

The school is another important factor in the education of children. And the school should educate its children so as to direct them to such goals as are both attainable and desirable to them. Have we in the country districts failed? We fear we have. We fill our pupils with urban ideals, we commercialize their outlook, we sing the praises of industrialism, we picture the bright lights of the city canyons as more attractive than the humble home by the side of the road. We prepare our girls for offices, factories, and stores, in place of preparing them for the queenship of the home. Does it mean happiness for them? Does humanity gain?

In this problem of an educational system which tends toward the dollar sign, the archbishops and bishops of Canada give us a guiding hand in their Joint Pastoral Letter on *The Rural Problem in Relation to the Social Doctrine of the Church,* issued in 1937. They say:

Esteem for farming and its social prestige will depend greatly, in fact, upon the character which is maintained and developed through the education of our country boys and girls, and by practical rural training. Parents, in this regard, have no minor part to take. First, they must create a moral atmosphere in the home. They must explain to their children that luxury and the desire to be considered as wealthy have often impoverished and ruined the farmer; that virtue and knowledge ought to be more appreciated than gaudy clothes and jewels; that the qualities of the heart and the endowments of the mind far surpass those of the body; finally, that, according to the old adage, a good name is better than riches.

Instead of disparaging in the presence of their children, what we shall term the agricultural vocation, to which Providence has called them, on the contrary, let parents teach young children to cherish this vocation, to prepare for it, and to continue faithful to it by labor, thrift, and the spirit of sacrifice inspired by Christian piety.

Let them not wait to prepare their sons to settle on the farm until the latter are twenty or thirty years of age. As soon as their children frequent school, parents should begin to instruct and interest them in this matter, training them particularly to be thrifty, and to accumulate a reserve fund. They should gradually collect for their daughters house linen, furniture and other objects, and early acquire for their sons a piece of land, or at least a few animals and divers farming implements. All this will be a living lesson as well as an encouragement. The instinct of personal ownership is natural in man; to develop and support it, in moderation, is the best incentive to labor. Nothing is more apt to render him satisfied with his condition than the enjoyment of resources, through which he may assert his personality.

Should parents think themselves obliged to allow their boys and girls to accept salaried tasks . . . they should guard them against the dangers of losing their agricultural vocation, by impressing upon them the fact that in a farmer's life, such tasks must only be incidental and temporary. . . . Furthermore, how many of those girls who leave their villages to be employed in cities, often far away, are forever lost to rural life, sometimes in a most deplorable manner! . . .

Concerning the school, it is perhaps not untimely to remind parents that it is obligatory for them to see that the children prepare assiduously both their oral and written assignments. Hence, among other things, when opportunity offers, girls should be given the advantage of attending a boarding school for a few years, in order that upon their return home, they may diffuse, in all simplicity, the knowledge they have acquired and the good manners they have learned, and thus become helpful assistants to their fathers and mothers in the intellectual development and education of their younger brothers and sisters. . . . Each home could thus become at night and on Sundays a school of its own. It is often objected that convents and academies, even those established in the villages, uproot from the soil the children who come from country homes. Let us hope that the charge is unfounded. At any rate, everywhere a reaction is being felt which will soon avert this evil, if evil there be. More than ever, country day-schools and boarding schools must develop a rural attitude, and increase their lessons in domestic and culinary arts. In this respect, let all concerned be cautioned against the marked tendency to emphasize the fine arts and fancy work. The curriculum should include cooking, knitting, sewing, spinning, weaving, and the making of garments adapted to country needs and to our climate. Already along these lines, fruitful results have been achieved. May they everywhere increase in number and quality! They will considerably reduce the family budget, and strikingly improve health, morality, household welfare and happiness.

It goes without saying that such a rural atmosphere in the school requires the contribution of all factors. Textbooks . . . teachers, school inspectors and commissioners, public authorities, religious Orders and the Clergy, should all magnify the really national importance and the advantages of a rural life.

And to make these advantages more attractive, nothing forbids them from being associated with appealing charm. A spacious house, well lighted, furnished with simplicity, good taste and order, provided with all the ordinary conveniences of modern life, surrounded by gardens and shade-trees, and in which pure air and light circulate, where peace and joy reign, generally costs less money than care. A table garnished with fruit from the orchard, with vegetables from the garden, or with the produce of the farmyard and the fields, well prepared and well served, provides more savoury and appetizing meals than the best grand hotel can offer.

It will also be necessary to make our country people feel that there is more real and enthralling beauty in nature itself than in its representation on the screen. Some people hold that there are too few amusements in the country. We are inclined to think that our farmers will have all the enjoyment they require when they learn how to appreciate their environment and condition.

It has been truthfully said that had parents known how to retain many a young boy and girl in the family circle, they would never have thought of leaving it. They have left it because of the attractions and comfort offered by villages and towns, in striking contrast with what they experienced at home. A little paint or white-wash on the farm-house and barns, a pleasant lawn and flowers around the house, a nicely shaded grove, and some cozy spot for relaxation, would speak louder than words. . . .

Rural education is a complex problem which must be seriously examined. Would it be advisable or necessary to have two programs? Some are inclined to think so. This would necessitate a double scheme of primary education, one for the cities and one for the country; a dual series of normal schools, the one industrial, the other agricultural; two kinds of convents, and academies, and so on. We deem it unnecessary to go so far or to act too quickly, as unfortunate reactions might ensue.

But, without neglecting catechism, spelling, arithmetic and history, a certain atmosphere should prevail in our rural schools to imbue children with a deep sense of pride in their estate, and the privileges it holds in store for them. Dictations, compositions, object lessons, even the explanation of the catechism, should tend no less to this end than the technical teaching of agriculture.

But the rules pertaining to agriculture may often be explained perfunctorily or in a disdainful and indifferent manner, thus turning out arrogant youths rather than true lovers of the soil, that *Great Friend*. On the contrary, the rural school should be less artificial and less bookish; it should throw open its windows to the surrounding fields and trees to teach our youth the beauty and grandeur of their mission, instead of turning them into little more than grocery clerks. We rejoice that textbooks have already been published, and that others are in preparation, which will prove instrumental in bringing about practical results of this character.

Ideals and Education for Rural Boys and Girls 243

Moreover, we are aware that the attention of the educational world is focused upon this problem of rural education. Suggestive programs have recently been proposed. Concerning the teaching of agriculture proper, apart from the superior agricultural schools, affiliated to one or other of our universities, whose enterprise promises great and necessarily bold undertakings, a plan has been outlined, with a definite program of studies, which has already been carried out here and there, and which aims at increasing the number of intermediate farming schools, in which our country boys will learn more precisely and intensively the science of their natural calling. For our girls, courses in domestic science and culinary art are increasing along similar lines. We commend our Governments for their excellent attitude in this respect. . . .

Will not even the heads of families themselves have to change their language and attitude, and begin to regard with esteem what they used to call a dejected profession, when they realize that the difficulties they had to face, may be overcome by a new technique and further knowledge? Will they not think of stimulating the interest of their growing sons in the farm by entrusting, for example, each boy with the care of a small plot of land, with the raising of some kind of produce the value of which would be turned over to the boy's personal account in some savings-bank? This would be a reward for endeavor and initiative, and develop the habit of thrift and self-reliance. . . .

A young men's agricultural association, better known in this country as the J.A.C. (*Jeunesse Agricole Chrétienne*), has been organized, and will, in time, spread the desire for technical rural knowledge and further its acquisition. The priest will permeate it with the Christian spirit, the agronomist will provide practical lessons in farming. If the least results obtained were only the assiduous reading of periodicals dealing with agriculture, the venture would be well worth while; but we are convinced that considerable profit and enjoyment will also result. Upon leaving their different schools, our young people, better equipped, ought to be able to diffuse knowledge about them. Their elders will be inclined, we hope, to listen and to help, rather than rebuke them. We know that in some places the pupils of certain agricultural schools gather the farmers periodically for the purpose of spreading the information they have acquired; that free and friendly debates ensue, where the experience of some corrects what is too theoretical in the knowledge of others. As a result improvement in the local farming methods has followed, and eventually, these parish assemblies, presided over by an intelligent and devoted village pastor, truly concerned with the welfare of his parishioners, will become a blessing to all. . . .

The teaching of agriculture, reduced to its fundamental and essential ideas, imparted in a suitable manner by experiments and direct observation, can be thoroughly carried out in all our rural schools; and, in this way, far from hindering the study of other subjects, it will be a great help to the children's education in general and to the development of their intellect in particular. The rural school will have specifically fulfilled its mission, if it knows how to inspire the children who frequent it with the love for agricultural labor, and with the desire to apply themselves intelligently to it, that is to say, with the help of sufficient knowledge and of modern farming devices. Let us even hope that the idea, at least, of cooperation and professional union will be instilled in the minds of the pupils, concurrently with the teaching of ethics, mathematics, patriotism, and civics. . . . It rests with our normal schools, now that all future teachers have to attend them, to impart the indispensable knowledge of the elements of agriculture. . . . Moreover tentative plans for the training of rural teachers are being made and tested. . . .

A Curriculum for Rural High Schools

The purpose of an education is to develop the spiritual, mental, and physical faculties of a child. In other words to teach him how to live properly the life he is to live. In our present educational system, some very faulty philosophy of life is taught. The first, and perhaps the most damaging, is that manual labor is degrading and disgraceful. Such expressions as, "go to school so you won't have to work," is heard in many classrooms, and tends to develop in the child the idea that work is only for those of low mentality. From this we get a group of educated and "uneducated" misfits in the world. Again, money is held up to the child as the goal of life. We honor those of great wealth rather than those having achieved great things in this world. Because of this many boys and girls leave honest labor and try their hand at some quick money-making scheme. Change of textbooks will not be a remedy. Only the words and actions of the teachers can change this. Another fallacy, namely, that farm life is slavery and full of drudgery, and on a level far below that of urban life, can be remedied both by the change of instruction and by a change of curriculum.

Ideals and Education for Rural Boys and Girls

Life in the urban centers is quite different from life in the rural centers, both as to employment and living. In the country, man is usually working by himself and for himself. He is the boss, manager, and supervisor of his farm. His income depends upon his ingenuity, labor, and skill, all cooperating with God's resources. The man in the city is usually working with others and for others. His success as well as his income depends upon his satisfying his employer. The difference is even more apparent in the living provisions for the two places. In the rural district most of the food for the family should be raised on the land, hence, one of the big problems is what to raise, and then how to preserve it after it is raised. The city dweller, however, is bound to buy all he needs. A farmer should raise most of what he consumes, hence, need of careful planning for the future. On the other hand the city man must depend upon wise buying for success.

A Rural Curriculum for the Rural School

If the life is different in the country from that in the city, and the purpose of education is to develop the child for its future life, then we must have a different curriculum for the rural school than we have for the city school. Up to the present time we have been priding ourselves in the rural schools that we teach the same things here that are taught in the urban centers, without asking ourselves if this should be done. The solution of the problem is a rather difficult one, but it is not insoluble. If we change our curriculum to fit the need to the rural district, we are not going to fit for the life they will lead all such students as plan to devote themselves to teaching, or other professions, especially to a religious vocation. Those who will enter the professions certainly have the right to receive an adequate training beginning with their rural-high-school curriculum. The classical course and perhaps certain commercial courses must be retained for some. On the other hand those going to high school and knowing that they are not going into any of these professions (either because of love of the land, lack of funds, or the absence of any desire for these professions) certainly have a right to a high-school course that will do more than equip them for a college education which they know they will never be able to receive.

With this as a background we can see the need of different curriculums for the rural and urban high school. Realizing that life in the urban center is different from that in the rural center, and that education is to teach one to live the life he is to live, we see the reason for the curriculum we propose for the rural high school.

The Rural Curriculum for Life on the Land

In the first two years of high-school work, the students would take the usual course now offered in most of our high schools; such as Religion, English, Latin, history, algebra for the first year, and general science for the second year. This we believe necessary that the child may have a good course in fundamentals. All students in the third and fourth years, should take their courses together in the forenoon. They should take such subjects as Religion, English, and history or civics. Once or twice a week instructions should be given on cooperatives, credit, buying or selling, and also a course in bookkeeping, not the usual course, but one dealing with incomes and expenditures of a rural home. Few families know how much their food, clothes, and recreation cost them. Fewer still know the value of their garden, poultry, cows or canning, to them in a year's time.

Special Courses for the Few Who Will Go to the City

In the afternoon, those intending to go on through college for any reason, and those intending to spend their lives in the urban district should take the usual classical courses during their last two years in high school. Since in most rural communities only a few should take this course, they will receive almost private tutoring.

The Farm-Shop Training

Boys and girls, not intending to go on through college, should be given special courses in farm-shop and general and applied agriculture. In these courses the principle, that one learns by doing, should be carefully carried out. The shop course has for its chief aim to teach the boy how to do his own repairing around the house and farm. This includes the repair of buildings, plumbing, machinery, and the sharpening of tools, as well as the welding and tempering of steel, electric wiring, and simple repairs of motors. Instruction should also be given in painting, both outside work and interior work. Along with this should go refinishing of furniture. Once the boy knows how to repair machines, he will know what causes them to get out of working condition, and be able to operate them better. In later life most of this repairing can be done in the winter months, and thus save a large repair bill every summer and spring. Mechanical drawing should be given to enable the boy to read blueprints, and draw the plans for the smaller buildings on the farm. Along with this should go the teaching of how to figure lumber bills for a building. Repair and upholstering of furniture is also very important. In regard to metalwork we may say that soldering, forging, and tempering of steel will about complete the course.

Then, too, electric switches in and about the house, the farm shop, and barn, locks, and such things always need fixing. In addition the efforts of the boys may be practically applied to building hog houses, brooder houses, and hayracks at cost of materials. They will thus be learning useful skills for their future life. At the same time they will be rendering a useful service to the community.

In teaching agriculture we should be careful only to supplement the knowledge the boy has of agriculture. There is no way of killing a class any quicker than to try to teach the boy something he already knows. The primary aim should be to teach him how to raise vegetables, fruits, and poultry needed for the house. He can learn more about feeding cattle, raising corn and, in short, commercial farming from those experienced in that line. His greatest sin is apt to be that he will think only of raising for sale and not for consumption. Instruction on pomology and forestry is sadly needed. Teaching on the raising of trees from seedlings and grafting, both whip and bud, is alike interesting and profitable. Spraying and pruning of both fruit trees and grape vines is also very necessary. On the other hand, teaching agriculture from books is very unsatisfactory, because suitable textbooks do not exist. Perhaps the best plan at this time is extensive use of pamphlets issued by the state colleges and the

United States Department of Agriculture. The school should also carry on extensive project work, have a tree nursery, and a vegetable garden.

Rural Homemaking Courses for Girls

The girls not intending to go to college should take the homemaking courses. These should have a twofold purpose: first, to teach the girls how to conduct a home in the country as it should be conducted, and secondly, to cultivate in them an appreciation of the arts and crafts, so that later they may be able to employ their leisure time usefully. The two main divisions in the course are, clothing and foods.

In the clothing sections the girls should be taught how to determine and select the various materials for garments, as also to recognize the advantages or disadvantages of the different cloths. They should be taught how to sew both by hand and on machine, stressing the need of making their own clothes. After this they should be taught to make other things for the home, which might be both necessary and also beautify the home. The various types of so-called fancywork should be learned by them. The weaving field opens up many opportunities, both for pleasure and profit. With a small number of looms one can give a good course in weaving, and with this once learned, the girls can make a nice income in their home. There is always a big demand for woven goods. The boys can easily make the looms in the farm shop.

Farm-Shop and Homemaking Courses Successfully Conducted

The Assumption High School of Granger, Iowa, has been pioneering during the past few years in preparing its pupils for a home on the land. This school strives to imprint deeply in the minds and hearts of children the philosophy of agrarianism. It presents facts and arguments. For the boys who express a desire to prepare themselves for a home on the land, courses are offered in agriculture and farm shop. The curriculum has been outlined by the Iowa State College authorities, has full approval, and is accredited by the Board of Secondary-School Relations. It is somewhat on the general lines of the Smith-Hughes courses in the Iowa public school system. It differs in that the Assumption High School seeks to prepare boys for *farming-for-a-living* (subsistence) first and holds up that type of homemaking agriculture as the ideal. The farm-shop work seeks to prepare them to be able to do the very things they will need in their future homes and on the farm. Practical projects of all types are carried through, most of them very interesting and useful.

A summary of the work offered to the boys:

Animal husbandry	Landscaping and floriculture
Crops and soils	Fruit growing
Vegetables — production and management	Bee culture — the most interesting of all subjects

Graduates from a rural high school should be ready and equipped to take care of the ordinary needs of building and repair that do not require highly specialized knowledge:

Woodwork	Plumbing
Toolwork for woodwork	Repair of farm machinery
Glasswork	Care of ignition systems
Concrete work	Furnaces
Metalwork	Electric wiring
Soldering	Ropework
Forging	Leatherwork

The courses offered to the girls are perhaps more interesting and attractive:

Related art	Buying
Clothing construction	Planning and serving school lunch
Clothing selection	
Care and repair	Child care and development
Crafts: (*a*) weaving; (*b*) knitting; (*c*) crocheting; (*d*) rug making, embroidery, drawn work, stitching, smocking	Home care of the sick
	Personal grooming
	Family relationship
	Home management
Planning and preparing food for the family	Home furnishing

Study and Work

Paying a visit to the arts and crafts room, any school day afternoon from 1 to 3:30 p.m., we shall find a class taught by a Sister of Mercy. We notice a girl making a new apron, while others, here and there, are refitting an old dress or coat. The girls wear uniforms while in school, and all the uniforms are made by the arts and crafts class. Mending or patching is the task another girl is performing. That is the work of a housewife and a very important work. Mending and patching is an art, and it can even be a science. At any rate, it is an economic and social necessity. A woman who is to conduct a home on the land should be an expert in it. In the meantime we perceive that a girl has just gone up to the Sister, who teaches the class, and is asking about a slight difficulty in the embroidery of pillowcases. There, again, two girls are working together at cross stitching a very attractive bedspread. You can buy a bedspread or bathroom adjuncts, but nothing replaces a tasty homemade guest towel or the like. Frills and fancy objects may be bought for parlor or dining rooms, but very few come up to handmade bits of decorative art in cloth, wood, or metal, produced in the home itself.

The Mother and the Home

A sense of taste is developed at the same time and an opportunity is given for self-expression. Part of the classwork is to teach the girls proper planning and the actual carrying out of projects within their own home. The mother in the home should know just what will be needed in the way of foodstuffs during the period of a year. And here enters in the proper family planning for food production and storage. The principle is this: Produce all you need for the family. Approximately five acres, with the addition of a cow and some pigs, can take care of a family of ten. The production of some wool and flax might be included. And, then of course, in the Assumption High School, the girls are taught the proper principles of dietetics, the planning of meals, the variety needed, etc. Above all, the emphasis is put where it should be, not on parties or society dinners, but on plain family meals.

The Home and the Community

A home on the land means children and a working husband. It means happiness of the highest type created from within the family circle and not sought for in bridge and clubs. Girls preparing for a home on the land, must learn to take part in community activities, they must know how to preside at meetings, how to keep club records, etc. All of this is a means and not an end in itself. However, proper family planning implies a keeping of family accounts, and so that, too, must be learned.

But we have forgotten that we are still in the arts and crafts room, and we come now to a most interesting part, the looms. The boys made most of the looms in the farm shop. The girls use them. Beautiful rugs and patterned pieces are turned out. Some of these have been exhibited at the Iowa State Fair and elsewhere, and have won prizes. Here is a large loom, all warped with wool yarn, and the girls working at it are personally acquainted with the sheep that produced the wool. It belongs to a 4-H Club boy whose family owns one of the homesteads.

The few years of experience at Granger with subjects in the school curriculum definitely related to the future life of those who remain on the land, have made it clear that such developments in education, in rural schools especially, are necessary for the economic, social, and spiritual enrichment of rural life. The currents of our social and economic life are flowing in the wrong directions. There is too much in education which leads to the white-collar job and the swivel-chair position. Too many people abandon the land and the advantages of an intelligent, independent, cultural country life. There is not enough vocational guidance in agriculture. One agricultural college, a few Smith-Hughes teachers in a few public high schools and a few 4-H leaders in each state, even though their work is magnificent in many of their projects, cannot adequately develop rural vocations, a generally sound agricultural science and practice, rural culture, and rural spiritual values. Too many schools in the country follow stereotyped, urban patterns; that is, they give the country people only another urban school.

Teacher-education institutions should make it a point to prepare rural teachers more specifically for their work. This means that the administrative heads and the faculties of such institutions engaged in preparing students for service in rural schools must become aware of the problems of rural life and their possible solutions. Both faculties and students must engage in direct observations and first-hand contacts with the problems of rural life. Teachers in the country schools should be acquainted with the social and economic problems of the community in which they work. They should understand the essentials of a satisfying rural life and the importance of education for a life on the land. Too many teachers who work in the country schools (*Country Schools* here includes the schools situated in the smaller towns and cities, and even many schools in the environs of the large cities) know nothing but the city way of life, its factories, its trade, its canned culture, and its mechanical preoccupations. Those who preach a philosophy of urbanism, mass production, and proletarianism in the classroom and outside of the classroom, cannot develop the interests, the capacities, the vital needs of those who should remain on the land and lead the way in the building of a better rural life.

The enrichment of the lives of rural people, the careful guidance of many of our boys and girls in scientific agricultural pursuits centered around the home on the land is a matter of vital importance. This is true whether we view it from the standpoint of the rural people themselves or from the standpoint of the nation as a whole. Urban leaders as well as the rural leaders in education must come to recognize this fact. If educators accept this challenge and become instrumental in raising the cultural, the spiritual, and economic standard of life on the land, the education in rural areas must be greatly improved. There must be special adaptations of educational services with the special needs of a rural population definitely in mind.

Chapter 16

COOPERATIVE GROUPING ON THE LAND

The signs are before us. The voices of the would-be dictators pour into our ears from radio and platform. The dictators are always the vocal ones. They have plans. They have formulas and panaceas. Sooner or later one will be so plausible and fair-seeming that the masses of the people, uneducated in economic action, blinded by their own hunger and distress, left leaderless and unguided for so long, will rise in a body and follow him into an American version of the never-never land. But let the people get one glimpse of hope, let them feel for the first time their own innate strength and power, and they will start to build for themselves. A great demonstration has come out of Nova Scotia, a demonstration which is a challenge to every man and woman who, by virtue of chance and circumstance, is in a position to assume leadership in the Little Dovers of America. — Bertram B. Fowler, *The Lord Helps Those.*

Mutual Self-Help

The story of the "Little Dovers," the cooperatives of Nova Scotia, is the educational achievement of a great university, St. Francis Xavier University. The faculty members of this university went out to help the poor in their grim struggle for the needs of body and soul. Here the educational leaders helped the poor to regain faith in themselves and inspired them through *mutual self-help* to gain economic independence based on social justice. This education was something more than the mere dissemination of the theories of dry textbooks. It outlined a *program.* It prepared the people for *action.* It was the economic course of *cooperation,* the course of a people who are *democratic,* a course that lies between the totalitarian wings of Communism and Fascism. Here vanished ownership and the control of the means of life were brought back to the people, through a cooperative movement that gave them a vital philosophy of economic life. The people of the various communities are now raising their standard of living, and the development of mind and personality rises to a higher plane intellectually and spiritually.

A happier day has dawned for Nova Scotia because its people and its educators have followed up the social teachings of two great Pontiffs, Leo XIII and Pius XI. Here social reconstruction is being preceded by a "profound renewal of the Christian spirit," men and women with mutual understanding are uniting in "associations of mutual help."

To the citizens of every nation the Church says: "Unite and combine for self-help"; "form *associations* of mutual help and service"; "where you are in the same trade or the same profession or the same industry combine into *vocational* groups"; "unite and combine into *occupational* groups for mutual help and service."

The Problem of Distribution

Economic life built on shifting sands brings a pitiable ruin of souls. Christian principles must go into the building of economic foundations. People must once more be drawn together and taught to think and act for themselves. They must study the whole question of *distribution*. In their own groups, the people must get a vision of what they can do by their own united strength and ability in correcting the evils of a system which has become stagnant and paralyzed with greed for profit.

Reason teaches us that human beings are so constituted in their very nature that they demand for their existence and perfection the help, association, and companionship of other human beings. God has created us that way. He has given us the social virtues of justice, charity, and the like, to help us. And He wills that we exercise those virtues by living, according to our nature, in societies of mutual help and service. The family is a society; and who will doubt that the very nature of man calls for such a form of social life? The state or civil government is a society; and mankind has always recognized that numerous families cannot live in close proximity without some form of civil society. The state, too, is a natural society, i.e., a demand of our human nature.

Relations of Family and State

These two societies, the family and the State are, of all merely human societies, the most natural and essential to mankind. But first and foremost in time and importance is the family, not because it is a society (all societies are merely means to an end) but because of the sacredness of its primary purpose; namely, the proper rearing of children, the propagation of the human race to the glory of God. It is to the family that God has entrusted, primarily and irrevocably, the sacred duty of caring for the proper physical, mental, moral, and religious development of the child. And from these grave, unchanging duties, arise proportionately sacred and inalienable rights, which all other societies must respect and safeguard. Families, then, band together to make up that other society called the State. They do so in answer to a natural need they have for such a civil society. But, it must be remembered that the State remains always a means to an end, whose sole right or reason for existence is to protect and serve the families and individuals who constitute it. Its purpose is to supplement the efforts of families and individuals, not to supplant them.

Authority and Human Liberty

The life blood of civil society is authority. Without it there is no function. Authority is the moral power residing in the State to direct the actions of its subjects toward a common good. Authority is conceded, ordinarily, in the form of constitutions or laws. But it is in the very nature of things that to concede authority is to lessen the personal liberty of the subjects. If I give the government authority to tell me what I am to raise on my farm, then I no longer have the liberty to make that decision myself, then I have sacrificed my personal liberty to some extent. There is nothing wrong in that, it is true, if I am certain that there is sufficient reason for my doing it. Humankind has always recognized the principle that there is liberty under law and protection and regulation for the common good. But the high dignity of the human being, created by God with intelligence, free will, and an eternal destiny, as well as the sublime and sacred office of the family with its incumbent duties, demand that both the individual and the family retain the greatest possible degree of personal freedom which the common good of mankind will allow. And in the right ordering of things, this will always be a large measure.

There should always be a large possibility of local autonomy for the work of private associations of mutual help and service. The situation described in the following passage, taken from the Encyclical, *Quadragesimo Anno,* is more clearly applicable to some European countries, such as to later Nazi Germany, where practically all private associations have been wiped out, leaving only the helpless individuals and the dictatorial state. But we quote it here to show the importance that should be placed upon these associations in any nation.

Things have come to such a pass that the highly developed social life which once flourished in a variety of prosperous institutions organically linked with each other, has been damaged and all but ruined, leaving thus virtually only individuals and the state. Social life lost its organic form.[1]

Smaller Associations of Help and Service

Private associations are not new. Mankind has always recognized their value. In their broad sense they range in variety from the simple temporary association, such as the old-time "barn raising," the "husking bee," or the "threshing run," to the highly organized and enduring cooperative associations and labor unions of modern times. In this country the great menace is not that the State is wiping out smaller associations, but that the giant corporations, which actually dominate the economic world, are making it impossible for small private associations of mutual help and service to exist. The following passage from the same Encyclical applies more closely to our American scene:

It is indeed true, as history clearly proves, that owing to the change in social conditions, much that was formerly done by small bodies can nowadays be accomplished only by large corporations. None the less, just as it is wrong to withdraw from the individual and commit to the community at large what private enterprise and industry can accomplish, so too it is an injustice, a grave evil, and a disturbance of right

---

[1] *Quadragesimo Anno,* N.C.W.C. Edition, 1931, pp. 26, 27.

order for a larger and higher organization to arrogate to itself functions which can be performed efficiently by smaller and lower bodies. This is a fundamental principle of social philosophy, unshaken and unchangeable, and it retains its full truth today. Of its very nature the true aim of all social activity should be to help individual members of the social body, but never to absorb or destroy them. . . . To this grave disorder which is leading society to ruin a remedy evidently must be applied as speedily as possible. But there cannot be question of any perfect cure, except well-ordered members of the social body come into being anew, namely, vocational groups, binding men together . . . according to the diverse functions which they exercise in society. For as nature induces those who dwell in close proximity to unite into municipalities, so those who practise the same trade or professions, economic or otherwise, combine into vocational groups. These groups . . . are considered by man to be, if not essential to civil society, at least its natural and spontaneous development.[2]

If farmers do not organize, then corporations will take over the field of agriculture, as in many parts of the country they are beginning to do, and farming will go on, but the independent, farm-owning farmer will disappear. American farmers will then become, at best, a peasantry, much lowered in the scale of human existence.

The Essential Traits of Private Associations

Summing up, therefore, the doctrine and the recommendations of the two great Pontiffs, with the American farmers in mind, we conclude that their associations must be "private," set up by the farmers themselves; they must aim at the "mutual help and service" of the members; they must be based upon the occupation or industry, "vocational groups" according to their respective "professions or trades," and finally, they must look forward to including farmers in a national affiliation of local groups so that the whole industry can be co-ordinated in all its parts for the common good of all farmers. If we do not have such groups, powerful corporations will continue to "arrogate to themselves functions which can be performed efficiently by smaller bodies." The smaller organizations of farmers must become strong by reason of unshaken

[2] *Ibid.*, p. 27.

loyalty and the bond of Christian charity. These associations must, on the other hand, be built upon such sound principles of social justice and Christian charity that they will of their very nature promote, effectively, harmony within agricultural groups and a happy co-ordination between agricultural and other organized vocational groups.

Benefiting by Experience of Others

With these broad essentials in mind, and having carefully considered the "principles of organization" cited above, we have turned to a study of existing organizations with the hope of finding such a type as would meet the above requirements and, at the same time, be adaptable to the "national character, practice, and experience" and to the "nature and aim and scope of present-day Americans." Such a type of association already exists. It has been tried by years of experience and found highly practical. Authorities comment favorably upon it as meeting, in an eminent degree, the requirements of democracy, social justice, and social charity. Cooperatives are operating with astounding success among the farmers and industrial people of at least twenty-six different nations — nations as diverse in size and temperaments as Finland and Italy, Ireland and Denmark, India and Australia. They are strong in Canada, and are multiplying in the United States. Economists, sociologists, moralists are manifesting a growing interest in them. The American Catholic bishops have strongly recommended them.

New Cooperative Technique in Rochdale — 1844

Ninety years ago twenty-eight weavers of Rochdale, England, set down on paper the principles of cooperation. These principles were to constitute a declaration of economic independence for the groups who would follow them. The Rochdale principles, first put into action in a tiny store on Toad Lane have become the foundation of the cooperative movement all over the world. This movement develops best in the Scandinavian countries and in Nova Scotia where the leaders are building on the solid foundations of education, represented for them in the Folk Schools in the northern countries of Europe and the extension and study-club work of St. Francis Xavier University in Nova Scotia. In these places cooperation is *more than a method of doing business.* It is a philosophy of action which permeates the communities, working drastic changes in their economic, social, political, and religious thinking.

In the more successful Rochdale cooperative movements the primary producer is considered equally as important as the consumer. The individual is always protected. As a producer, the producer cooperatives help him to secure a fair return on his labors. As a consumer, the consumer cooperatives protect him against the exploitation of monopolies. The memberships in both types of cooperatives often interlock. These cooperatives are not allowed to become too vast in memberships and operation. As a result the membership is intelligent and alert. High-powered publicity and commercial, promotional methods do not secure vitality in cooperative groups. This requisite vitality and intelligence in memberships cannot be secured without education, a continual, effective education, and the use of the best educational agencies and methods. Too many groups have used the empty forms of cooperation. They have never attained the Rochdale ideal of progress through increased knowledge and sound self-help.

St. Francis Xavier University Educates[3]

At St. Francis Xavier University, study and teaching build up cooperatives and cooperative communities. There is no high-powered advertising and drafting of memberships. The Rochdale principles and every detail of cooperation are studied, with a special regard for local problems. Usually the first cooperative enterprise in any community is a special plan to solve some special problem. There are such special problems in every community. In general they are the problems of credit, and the prices of goods, or a special line of goods, either from the side of the producer or the consumer or both.

Following is a short summary of some of the things that must be carefully taught and studied in any community that desires to achieve economic independence through cooperation.

---

[3] Cf. Appendix: Nova Scotia "Rochdale" Cooperatives.

Rochdale Principles of Cooperation

1. One vote for each member (regardless of the number of shares).
2. Not more than the prevailing low rate of interest on capital invested in the cooperative.
3. Surplus savings to be used for: the common social good of members or distributed as savings — returns to be made in proportion to purchases or patronage.

Added Principles Strongly Recommended

1. Adhere to *current price level* (avoiding cut-rate competition with private concerns).
2. All transactions are to be on *cash basis*.
3. *Federate* as soon as possible with approved neighboring cooperatives but maintain *local autonomy*.
4. Maintaining a *committee on education* for promoting proper understanding of cooperation.

Preliminary Measures to Insure Success

1. Before organizing let prospective cooperators meet weekly to study and discuss the history, the aims and the methods of cooperation until familiar with them.
2. Base study and all cooperative endeavor upon strict Rochdale principles.
3. Make the group sufficiently large for the purpose of the cooperative enterprise and give all of them sufficient training to make them cooperative-minded.
4. Appoint a preliminary committee to secure all available information on the details of organization and also to study qualifications of prospective members with view to making nominations for the board of directors, educational committee, and the like; and to give thought to a suitable manager.

First Organization Meeting

After above preliminary measures, the first organization meeting is called. This may be conducted thus:

1. Adoption of constitution and Rochdale principles.
2. Election of president, secretary, and treasurer.
3. Election of board of directors.

4. Election of committee on education.
5. Selection of business location, and the like.

Some Errors Which Lead to Failure

1. Violation or neglect of the above principles and preliminary measures, especially the three *Fundamental Rochdale Principles*.
2. Starting with too little capital.
3. Extending credit to members.
4. Employing incompetent manager.
5. Failure to have books audited regularly by an expert.
6. Disloyalty or distrust of members.
7. Engaging in price competition with private enterprises.
8. Neglecting educational work in cooperative principles and methods.

Important Points for Successful Cooperation

1. The capital with which the business is to be operated is subscribed by members of the association, each taking one or more shares.
2. The interest paid upon this capital stock is limited to a low rate of interest, say 4 per cent each year.
3. In the direction of the business each member stockholder has but one vote, even though he owns more than one share of the stock. And voting is only by persons, not by proxy.
4. The profits of the business are to be used:
    a) To form suitable reserves for the carrying on of the business;
    b) To pay the fixed interest on the capital stock;
    c) The balance is divided among the members as patronage dividends, that is, in proportion to the amount of their purchases.
5. The selling price of goods is substantially the same as that prevailing in the community where the cooperative is located.
6. Cash sales only are permitted.

Three points especially are to be noted in this plan. With reference to the above principles, they are:

5 and 2: The bulk of the profits are returned to the members in the form of patronage dividends. The capital stock is paid a fixed rate of interest and no more.

4. The savings of the cooperative enterprise are returned to the members, not in the form of diminished purchase prices for goods, but in the form of patronage dividends issued every six months.

3. The principle of one vote per member regardless of stockholdings makes this enterprise truly democratic. The big stockholder cannot control the policies of the society as happens in corporations.

Necessity of Education in Cooperation

No man attempts to do what he knows nothing about. Cooperation can progress no faster than the people can be trained to understand it and administer its business. In working out a different social method, there must be much study and planning. We must see what is wrong, realize what our aims are, and we must know the means that are necessary for reaching the goal. Since the principles of cooperation are opposed to privilege, there is double need of education. Naturally there has been some bungling in the past. Not a few farmers have been duped into joining up with "cooperatives" which were cooperatives in name only. Ignorance of *genuine* cooperation made such mistakes possible.

Are We Lazy?

A cooperative is a democratic organization. Now, in any democratic organization, even in a democratic state, people will get nowhere without study, and will accomplish very little without work guided by intelligent vision. In these days of distress, a "slacker" is one who, through vanity or indolence, refuses to think straight about the various problems concerning himself and other people. We try to soothe our consciences on the pretext that external influences, such as governments, climate, etc., are responsible, but deep in our hearts is the conviction that ignorance of our own forces is the actual cause. Education is power. If we are to throw off the evils of excessive paternalism on the part of governments, we must learn to solve our own economic problems independent of government regimentation. Government regimentation has opened the way to much graft and exploitation, excessive taxation and general loss of true liberty. To combat this we need many *educated, cooperative* communities.

What Do the Experts Say?

The leaders in the cooperative movement all admit that the chief reason for the slow progress of cooperation is the lack of education in the cooperative spirit and methods. They also say that the chief initial step toward real progress is education — education in the spirit and methods of cooperation. Education points out the reasons for failure in the past, and shows the sources of success for the future. The understanding and loyalty of the members of cooperative organizations depend much upon their appreciation of the principles and practices of cooperation. The necessity of education along cooperative lines is also brought home very strongly by the fact that where "high-pressure propaganda and salesmanship" have been used to accelerate the spread of cooperatives, such cooperatives nearly always have proved failures — simply because the members have not had sufficient time to educate themselves up to the true spirit of cooperation.

Cooperative Principles Are Democratic

Education in cooperation is an education in democratic principles. It is a powerful means of self-defense against totalitarian dictatorships like Fascism, Nazism, Communism. If the principles of cooperation were well understood by a greater number of Americans, our political affairs would be more efficiently handled. We could no longer be exploited with ease. We would know what we want, and know how to have those wants supplied. We would no longer need to appeal to others to fight the trusts for us. Education, and the economic power gained through the practice of cooperative principles, would enable us to realize what the true solution for concentration of wealth in the hands of a few really is, and would give us the power to do the decentralizing of that wealth ourselves. Cooperation will correct that undue emphasis on property which is so prevalent today. We are altogether too bourgeois, we are materialists in our whole outlook on life whether we admit it or not. The average parent who sends his boy to school wants him to get the sort of education that will best help him to acquire a fortune. Learning cooperative principles gives us a better sense of values, from the ground up.

Problems Concerned with Property

The cooperative movement is centered around private property. One cooperator well says that the whole movement is best expressed in the term "building a home." The idea of home, the very heart of the people, provides the spiritual base which is necessary to the permanence of any movement. The fact, therefore, that private property (its use and abuse) forms the core around which so many problems and debates are centered urges us to see to it that we are well grounded in the true principles of man's rights concerning private property, so that we may be properly prepared to stand our ground against the ignorant and the greedy who would attempt to run things their own way regardless of the individual's rights or the interest of the greater number.

Erroneous Theories on Property

Socialists, Communists, economic liberalists, finance-capitalists — all are the adherents of erroneous doctrines concerning man and property. All are doing their best to put their theories into practice, not just for themselves, but also for the rest of us who are living in the same commonwealth. Are we going to allow these false theories to get the upper hand? Only when we have the true principles in regard to property clearly in mind, and understand the weaknesses and the fallacious assumptions of the other systems, can we combat them intelligently.

Property and Individual Morality

What about promoters' profits, stock watering, tax evasion, dividends with the sky as the limit, employment of workers at less than an annual living family wage, dismissal of workers through the establishment of giant scale, inefficient, corporation technocracy? Can it be that we are ignoring social justice and social charity in such practices? And then when we plan for vocational grouping and for cooperatives as an approach to vocational grouping, we must remember that we must find ways of keeping two passions in restraint; namely, cupidity and greed. The growth and permanence of cooperation depend very largely on the unselfishness of cooperators. Reform must begin at home, in the heart of every cooperator. In a Christian cooperative men unite their economic efforts in order to achieve a degree of economic security necessary for well-ordered social and family existence.

Such economic-social grouping is of special importance to farmers.

Social justice and social charity forbid that any individual shall make unlimited profits. The good of all is most fully achieved when each is willing to subordinate his own advantage to the general welfare, willing to devote part of his time, strength, initiative, intelligence, and material possessions to the economic advancement of his neighbor, instead of expending everything that is in him and everything that he possesses upon the limitless acquisition of personal fortune. In the Encyclical, *Divini Redemptoris,* Pius XI teaches that: "It is of the very essence of social justice to demand of each individual all that is necessary for the *common good."*

The Christian cooperative stands out in sharp contradiction to the teachings of economic individualism, according to which each individual produces, purchases, sells, finances, and accumulates without reference to the needs of his neighbor. Christian cooperation is a positive ideal with a positive ethical content, even though it expresses itself in the handling of material goods. In the Christian life ethical relationships are *de facto* inseparable from man's supernatural destiny and his status as a member of the Mystical Body of Christ. Our participation in the Christ-life, through the indwelling of the Holy Spirit, implies a duty of mutual charity which can only receive its full expression, in the economic field, through many forms of genuine cooperation for the *common good,* and the curbing of self and private advantage.

As primarily ethical and religious in character, the Christian cooperative rejects any type of organization inspired by purely materialistic motives. The *common good* is not a maximum of material production. It is the sum total of those conditions of earthly living, whether in the local community, the nation, or the world at large, according to which each individual can most easily achieve his full temporal and spiritual development. The Christian cooperative is not proposed as a panacea for all conceivable economic ills, but it is proposed as a positive remedy for certain definite evils resulting from an individualistic economy. Members who join a cooperative with a purely materialistic, or exclusively utilitarian outlook injure the material welfare of the cooperative itself, for such membership opens the door to graft and racketeering, to fraudulent administration, to misrepresentation of consumers' goods and other flagrant abuses. Again to quote Pius XI in his *Quadragesimo Anno:*

> The union of hearts and minds through charity binding men together, is the main principle of stability in all institutions, no matter how perfect they may seem, which aim at establishing social peace and promoting mutual aid. In its absence, as repeated experience proves, the wisest regulations come to nothing. Then only will it be possible to unite all in harmonious striving for the common good, when all sections of society have the intimate conviction that they are members of a single family and children of the same Heavenly Father, and further, that they are one body in Christ and everyone members of another.[4]

While the Christian cooperative may in certain instances make use of a certain degree of communal ownership for utilitarian purposes, it is primarily an association of persons who retain the free exercise of their right to private property, although they willingly limit and combine this free exercise in the interests of the common good.

Cooperatives Stop the Growth of Proletarianism

Cooperatives provide an effective remedy against the further extension of proletarianism in assisting helpless individuals against ruthless large-scale enterprise. Without cooperatives we are at the mercy of the economically powerful, and there can be no resistance to the concentration of wealth, save through the hands of a centralized government. Christian cooperatives are schools of self-help, affording effective instruction in all the social virtues, natural and supernatural, in resourcefulness, enterprise, diligence, honesty, thoughtfulness for others, social charity, personal self-sacrifice, helpfulness, cooperative spirit; in short, the virtues that make social life possible and are the logical fruit of the Christian philosophy of life. Cooperatives provide a stable foundation for an active, local community life, and in giving social stability, provide a foundation for the organic functioning of society along the line of vocational groups. Organic structure in society must be founded upon homogeneous groups.

---

[4] *Quadragesimo Anno,* N.C.W.C. Edition, 1931, p. 44.

Cooperatives do not represent the complete process of organic reconstruction, but they form the building blocks for any general, organic structure of industry and agriculture. No far-reaching legislative changes are needed to begin the building of the foundational groups for cooperation.

The Rochdale cooperative is first of all an *organization of people,* and not, as in the case of the prevailing modern corporation, an *organization of capital.* The Rochdale cooperative when it receives a charter for incorporation sets out to render a banking, an industrial or commercial service at cost. It is a democratic organization in which each member has one vote and only one vote. In a cooperative, money is the servant of the people. Savings are distributed to members in proportion to their patronage, and this leads to a more equitable distribution of wealth among the many. The ordinary "American Company" or corporation on the other hand is an organization of capital which serves the public for profit. In this type of corporation votes multiply with shares of stock. Plutocracy, money in control of the few, rules such an organization. Capital receives all the profits. Money is the master. Profits are distributed among the stockholders in proportion to their holdings. Money always receives the benefits, and wealth is centered more and more in the possession of the few.

Anyone who makes an honest study of the history of "corporations of private privilege" learns that an effective regulation of them is needed in the interests of good government and a good society. One way to regulate the giants of private privilege is to use officers and courts. But a better way to bring *corporations of private privilege* into line with social justice and social charity is to build, soundly and intelligently, many *corporations of mutual service;* namely, the corporations of vocational groups and the corporations of local cooperatives.

Denmark: A Social Laboratory

For those who are to do this work in America, Denmark serves as a social laboratory. Denmark is today a land of small farms, and its farmers know how to build cooperatives. Not many years ago the Danish farmer worked under the same destructive agricultural forces that now prevail in the United States. The Danish farmer was enveloped by inefficient middlemen who exploited both producer and consumer. He produced and sold for an unknown world market. The products of Danish farms were marketed and processed by disinterested agencies of private profit. The hands of monopoly buyers whose power and control was closely united with the banks, railroads, and other commercial corporations set the producer and consumer prices on practically every food product.

Today almost every phase of agriculture in Denmark is in some way engaged in cooperation. In *Denmark: The Cooperative Way*, there is given the interesting story of the origins of cooperation among the Danish people.

During the winter of 1881–1882 a young man came to an inn in the western part of Jutland; from there he sent word to the surrounding farms that on a certain afternoon he would give instructions to anybody desiring it on the ways and means of making the best butter. Quite a number of farmers came. And the young man told them how great an advantage it would be if an association could be started, the aim of which should be to engage the services of an expert. This expert was to give instructions in homes on how to produce fine butter of a uniform quality; he would then receive at some center, conveniently situated for all, the butter which had been churned in the farm houses. There it should be weighed, classified and treated scientifically, welded, and packed in butter-barrels. This proposal aroused great interest, for the old ways and means of earning a living (the sale of corn, breeding, and fattening) had no longer been satisfactory, nor sufficient. A group of men arranged another meeting. At this meeting, the opinion of the majority was that it would be better to collect the milk than the butter. A young dairyman present warmly recommended this, and the greater part of those present approved of the plan to build a common dairy; each man joining in the enterprise was to have his share of the profit in proportion to the weight of the milk delivered by him.[5]

The idea was carried out and the plan became a reality. Today Danish butter from the Danish cooperative dairies is a well-known article on the world market. Denmark markets one third of the sum total of butter in the world market, and nine tenths of

---

[5] Howe, F. C., *Denmark: The Cooperative Way,* Copyright (New York: Coward-McCann, Inc., 1936), p. 81.

this butter reaches the markets through the farmers' own cooperative dairies.

When the experiment worked out successfully, the cooperatives began to improve the quality of the butter. They did this for business reasons. Good butter returned a higher price than poor butter. The quality of Danish butter has since been standardized. It bears a "hallmark" like sterling silver. It is known the world over for its excellence. It is well to bear in mind that it was the farmer himself who established the cooperative market. He not only established it, but continues to enforce it. The cooperative places a fine upon any farm member who does not live up to the standards.

Through the use of cooperatives, the continuation of the family as an economic unit, and the proper utilization of the land, the Danish people have become intelligent land owners and cooperative leaders. Fifty per cent of the farms are not larger than 30 acres, the majority being between 20 to 70 acres. About 93 per cent of the 204,000 farms are owned by the operators. In recent years extensive use is made of modern, "human scale," agricultural machinery. On most Danish farms the usual returns from livestock enterprises constitute 80 per cent of the gross income.

We should bear in mind that the Danish organizations have grown from the "bottom up," i.e., from the farmer to the organization, rather than from the organization to the farmer. No doubt, this has caused a certain amount of slowness in organization, but on the other hand it has created a genuine "working together." There is a strong element of mutual responsibility, and a complete absence of the undesirable, centralized type of cooperative control.

Growth and Structure of Danish Cooperatives

With the exception of the credit associations which came into being through legislation, Danish cooperatives have developed under no special law, either to encourage or restrict them. Under the status of incorporated associations these cooperative groups are bound to follow the Rochdale principles of cooperation while also the principles of the common law are applicable to them. In the cities, the consumers' societies and the workers' productive associations are slowly gaining headway. There are two types of cooperative associations in Denmark. First, there are the general educational societies organized to disseminate scientific and technical information. About 90 per cent of the farmers belong to these general agricultural societies. Second, there are the business societies consisting of the commodity sales association, cooperative stores, and purchasing societies, and lastly the cooperative credit unions. In 1933, the 6,860 Danish cooperatives listed a membership of half the total population. Each cooperative society is usually limited to a single specific function. A farmer may belong to an egg-collecting society, a bacon factory, or to a dairy. The executive committee of these various societies may be identical, but the business of each is kept separate. Societies of each type are usually federated in their own district and provincial associations, finally coming together in the Federation of Danish Cooperatives, whose executive body is the Central Cooperatives Committee. According to the secretary of the Central Cooperatives Committee, this plan of organization permits a greater decentralization than is exhibited by the cooperative movement in other countries.

Cooperation is extended as far back as possible into the production operations. Production and marketing are closely co-ordinated. Two production factors made possible an outstanding success in the cooperative packing plants: (1) the supply of hogs was regulated to keep plants operating at optimum capacity and (2) all the farmers made a special effort to produce the same uniform, high-quality bacon. The producers achieved such co-ordination that they were soon able to market a product without a peer in the markets of the world and they were ready to ship this uniform product regularly.

The Folk High Schools

Another factor of very special significance has been the leadership, understanding, and influence of educators. A Folk High School was established by Bishop Grundtvig in 1844, the same year in which the Rochdale Pioneers of England established their cooperative. The Danish Folk Schools now give instruction to 7,000 students annually, on subjects of general culture, on the practical and technical subjects of social grouping and cooperative organization, and on the various techniques of agriculture. In 22 of the 60 Danish Folk Schools four fifths of the curricular time is devoted to the giving of technical training in scientific agrarianism. Subjects of general culture are always given but much emphasis is also placed on the practical and technical subjects. In their book, *The Folk High Schools of Denmark,* the Folk High School teachers, Peter Manniche, Holger Begtrup, and Hans Lund, tell us they work with renewed courage because they feel that they have a good message to carry to their fellow countrymen, a message that the world, more than ever before, requires for the furtherance of its welfare. They are trying to help all young people in Denmark find happiness in their daily work and to have a spiritual understanding of active human life. It is the aim of the schools that their young people return to the farm, the craft, or trade from which they come, with an undaunted spirit and a brighter intelligence, with a better knowledge of religion and culture, a better knowledge of local history, local government, local geography, and the understanding of the natural sciences, and of sound agricultural techniques. The Folk Schools keep alive the spirit of cooperative association and are one of the real creative forces in the development of cooperative marketing and the establishment of the family unit, the farm home.

The excellent Danish philosophy of ownership is expressed in the line of a Folk School song composed by Bishop N. F. S. Grundtvig, the founder of the Grundtvigian movement in education:

> Far more of those metals so white and so red
> Find others by digging and selling,
> We Danes, though, can point to everyday's bread
> In even the lowliest dwelling —
> Can boast that in riches our progress is such
> That few have too little, still fewer too much.

The changes in agriculture and farm operations at the suggestion of cooperative groups, agricultural societies, and agricultural schools have been more marked in Denmark than in other countries. The cooperatives and the Folk Schools have given the Danes better farming, better business, and better living.

The Danish Folk High School system is being adopted in other countries. There are at present 32 in Norway, 52 in Sweden, and 6 in America. The citizens of northeastern Nova Scotia — priests, teachers, businessmen, miners and storekeepers, fishermen and farmers — are rebuilding a democratic society with this system of education and cooperative enterprise. Here education and cooperative enterprise are lifting people out of the depths of poverty, ignorance, and despair. Men and women are improving their worldly state by intelligent work with their fellows for the common well-being. These people are not waging a class war, and there is no hatred of the enemy in the personal sense. The battle is the battle of *Democracy* against impossible physical conditions and artificial systems and complications which deprive men of hope. It is a war waged on the victorious battleground of reason against the antisocial elements in man.

Chapter 17

ADVANTAGES AND TECHNIQUE OF COOPERATIVES

THERE are many reasons why there must be a rebuilding of a democracy in America. And the only sensible and peaceful way to rebuild it, is to follow the leadership of the Danes and the people of Nova Scotia. They have given an example of proven value which is worthy of imitation.

The two following diagrams indicate clearly what the economic reasons are for the establishment of cooperatives in the United States.

The Consumer and Distribution

Diagram 1 represents graphically the various agencies through which articles pass before they come into the hands of the consumer. It also represents an estimation of the amount of the purchase price per dollar paid by the consumer, which is received by each of these agencies.[1]

Diagram 2 represents the amount of the purchase price per dollar received by the farmers on the one hand, and the various middlemen between the farmer and the consumer on the other, in regard to the ten most commonly used articles of food. The tabulation includes: beef, pork, hens, eggs, wheat for bread, wheat for flour, milk, butter, cheese, and potatoes. By processors are meant meat packers, flour millers, bakers, butter makers, cheese makers, etc. By marketers are meant commission men, wholesalers, and retailers. These figures were obtained through a United States Government survey and were published in the *Consumers' Guide* for April 8, 1935.

---

[1] Based upon figures from Harris, E. P., *Cooperation: The Hope of the Consumer* (New York: Macmillan Co., 1918).

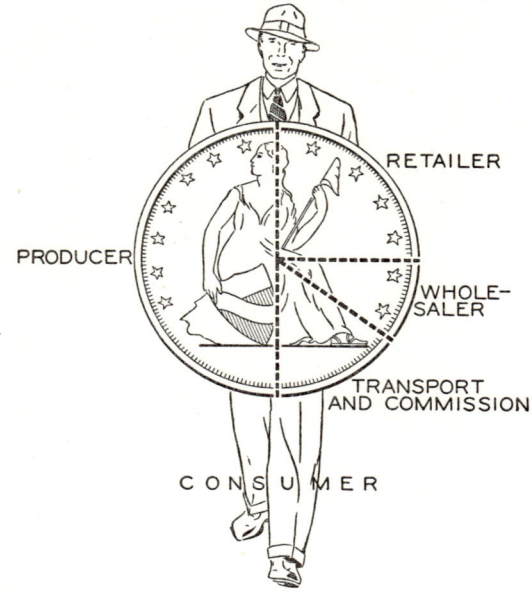

Diagram 1.

Loss to Producer on Farm

Each of these diagrams brings out the fact that the original producer receives less than one half of the final purchase price of goods, and in the case of the farmer of considerably less than one half of the purchase price of articles of food. In other words, the processing and marketing of articles, and in the case of some of these, the marketing alone, is responsible for more than one half of the price paid by the consumer for these articles.

In a recent book the author takes his readers on the regular trip of a crate of celery from Norfolk, Virginia, to New York City.[2] The producer in Norfolk sells the celery for 40 cents; commission man number one sells it for 60 cents; commission man number two for 75 cents; commission man number three for 90 cents; commission man number four for $1.05; commission man number five for $1.15; commission man number six sells it

---

[2] Heddon, W. P., *How Great Cities Are Fed*, p. 139.

Advantages and Technique of Cooperatives

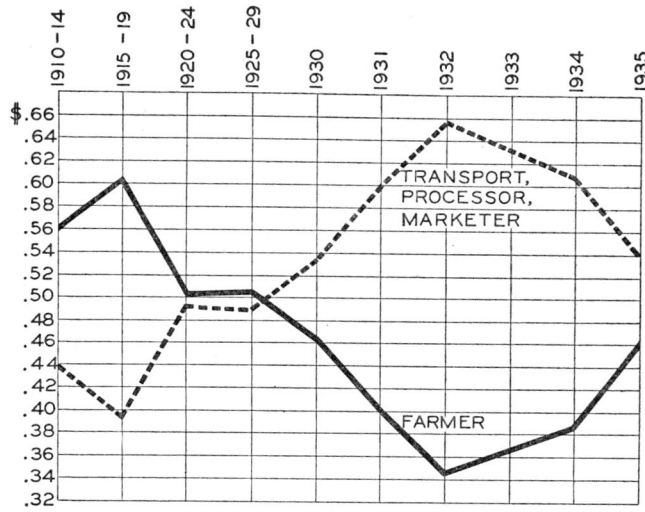

Diagram 2. Farmer's Portion of Consumer's Dollar.

to a grocery-store buyer for $1.25; the grocery-store buyer sells it to retail grocers for $1.35 and the grocers retail it to the consumer for $2.60. Only 15.4 per cent of the final selling price goes to the producer. Looked at in another way, the consumer pays six and a half times as much as the producer receives. In the supply of apples from the State of Washington to New York, the grower receives 23.6 per cent; the shipping organizations, 5.4 per cent; transportation, 16 per cent; wholesalers, 7.8 per cent; jobbers, 9.8 per cent; and retailers, 37.4 per cent of the consumer's dollar.

The processing and distribution agencies generally take more out of the consumer's dollar than all that the farmer gets for growing the product — sometimes more than twice as much.

Let us examine the prices for milk in one metropolitan area. The situation in this area may be taken as typical in the marketing and distribution of fluid milk. There are in this agricultural territory adjacent to this metropolitan area three thousand farmers who supply this fluid milk. These farmers have investments in three thousand herds of cows, three thousand farms, three thousand barns, cooling systems, etc., and they work long hours each day in the production of the fluid milk. Besides, although the milk companies run their trucks out to the farms, the farmers must pay for the cost of running the trucks, in the hauling of the milk from the farms to the company milk docks in the city. At this point the twelve companies delivering milk to the homes in the metropolitan area begin their work. When one studies the high-powered advertising connected with this part of the fluid milk process, one can scarcely avoid coming to the conclusion that milk, as it comes from the farm, is poison and that old "Bessie" is not such a fine source of good wholesome food as in the days of old. One wonders how the people in the country retain their health at all, and what will happen to them if they continue to drink their milk in the old way.

These advertisers do not tell us that most of their new processes in the care of fluid milk must enter in as a result of repeated handling and the time consumed in the delivery of it, to people in concentrated areas. In this particular urban area the milk is pasteurized, "radiated," "embalmed," etc., and then delivered to the homes.

The consumer's dollar in this city buys ten quarts of milk; thirty cents goes to the farmer for his part in production, and the major part, the remaining seventy cents, goes to the milk company for its high-sounding milk processes and its work of delivery to the homes, hotels, restaurants, etc. In buying their year's supply of milk the city consumers spend ten million dollars; three million dollars of this goes to the three thousand farmers as compensation for their major part in the production of milk for the city, and the remaining seven million dollars is retained by the twelve companies for their minor part in the processing and delivery of this milk within the city itself. From these figures it is clear that the consumer should know more, much more about the history of the little bottle of milk placed on his porch every morning. Why should the consumer pay such a high price for his bottle of milk when the farmer gets so little for it?

In this case three thousand farmers with their major investments and long hours of labor receive annually from the consumers three million dollars, and the twelve milk companies with their minor investments and their short hours of labor receive annually from the consumers seven million dollars. And yet it is not an easy task to get the consumers to consider this problem intelligently. Recently when this farmer group protested that they were not getting their just share of the consumer's dollar, the twelve companies and their metropolitan customers resorted to threats that involved some strange social and economic consequences, but the threats were enough to silence the just demands of the farmers. The companies threatened that they would take steps to develop a new milk shed several hundred miles beyond the metropolitan area and then ship in the supply of milk. The threat and the plan was hailed enthusiastically by the very city people who would have suffered most by the breakup of the local dairy farms and the loss of purchasing power in three thousand farm families. These city people already suffer in two ways; first, they pay too much for their milk, and secondly, since these neighboring farmers do not get an adequate and just share of the city's consumer dollars, they cannot buy the various goods and services which the businessmen of the city offer for sale, and the city continues in a state of business stagnation and depression.

The *Farmer* (February 25, 1939) points out that a 24-pint case of frozen raspberries was selling for $4.80. In the preceding summer the growers received an average price of $1.80 for such 24-pint cases. The actual cost of freezing and storing such a 24-pint case of raspberries for seven months is $1. The difference between $4.80 and $1.80 is $3. That leaves a profit of $2 a case for the man who freezes and stores the berries.

Saving for Producer and Consumer

If raspberry growers were organized in a cooperative association, they could sell in the picking season what the market demands, and the surplus could be frozen and stored by the association. The berries would still belong to the growers and any profit derived from the frozen berries would be pro-rated to the growers. It is evident here how a producers' cooperative in agreement with a consumers' cooperative could return $1 additional per case to the grower and save $1 per case for the consumer. The three objectives: (1) A greater return to the producer, (2) a better quality product, (3) at a saving to the consumer, could easily be worked out in the direct and local cooperative processing, marketing and buying of meats, vegetables, grains, fruits, etc. With efficient home-milling machines, canning apparatus, etc., available, the urban consumer should be buying the sacks of wheat and the bunches of vegetables directly from the farmer or from the farmer's own cooperative-marketing stores. Or small groups of families could do the canning and the milling in cooperative community projects. The farmer should do more than simply raise his product. He should himself, through his cooperative association direct the marketing and some of the steps in the processing of the farm product.

To express the real purpose and spirit of cooperation, we must get away from the parlance of ordinary business and commerce. Real cooperative elevators do not exist to buy grain from farmers in the commercial sense. Instead, in their function of handling grain from the farm they exist to market grain for farmers. Cooperative elevators use the commercial method of paying the market price of grain at the time of sale, but they depart from the commercial method in returning to patrons any profit, or saving, that is made. Perhaps it would be better if marketing cooperatives did not come into the ownership of the products of the farm at all, but simply marketed them for patrons and returned the proceeds minus the cost of operation.

Cooperative creameries, for example, are not in business merely to buy butterfat and make it into butter in a commercial way. Their purpose is to market the butterfat of farmers in the form of butter and return to them the full proceeds, minus operating costs and additions to reserves. This they do by making patronage refunds in addition to the first price, or by the pooling plan.

Likewise in consumer cooperatives, the purpose is not to "sell" goods to patrons, but to supply them with goods. In other words, a consumer cooperative buys goods for its members and patrons. Cooperation is not exemplified, therefore, in campaigns to "sell" goods to members and patrons, but in getting people to buy together through their own cooperative. When they understand this cooperative concept, the members of a consumer cooperative do not look upon the goods on the shelves as goods the cooperative has to "sell." Instead, they are goods bought for the members and patrons and kept on hand to supply them when they need such goods. This means that members have an obligation to go and get the goods that have been purchased for them, rather than go elsewhere and buy. When those who operate our cooperatives grasp these distinctions, they think in terms of service — the true purpose of cooperation. And when members and patrons grasp these distinctions, they have a greater sense of responsibility for and obligation to their cooperatives.

Inefficiencies in Distribution

Are the mass-production processors and marketers of food and other articles always exacting excessive profits? In many cases this is true, but we cannot say that it is true in general. The present system of distribution gives too little to the farmer and takes too much from the consumer because it is inefficient. And it is due in large measure to this inefficiency that the purchase price of goods is higher than it should be. For one thing there are too many agencies between the original producer and consumer. The way should be made straighter and more direct. Another factor of inefficiency is that expenses take place within the system which might easily be eliminated.

One of these expenses is unnecessary advertising, by producers, wholesalers, retailers, etc. One company advertises its merchandise and its competitors are forced in self-defense to do likewise. And ultimately it is the consumer who pays for this advertising in an increased purchase price. Again the purpose of a great deal of modern advertising is not to sell people what they need, but rather to create wants in them; to arouse desires for things which they really do not need. A somewhat similar expense is involved in the salaries paid to salesmen of the various competitor firms, an expense which under a really efficient system of distribution would be unnecessary.

Does America realize when it goes to market that 59 cents of its dollar goes simply for distribution costs? As more and more goods enter the labyrinth of mass production with its gamut of sorters, handlers, truckers, railroaders, auctioneers, commission merchants, etc., distribution becomes more inefficient and costly. In the multitude of transactions which are built up between the initial producer and the final consumer, our agricultural goods and manufactured goods shuttle back and forth across the country.

In their book, *Does Distribution Cost Too Much?* (Twentieth Century Fund, 1939), Paul W. Stewart and J. Frederic Dewhurst point out that a greater saving must be made through the simplification and the streamlining of the distributive process. Only a highly diversified agriculture producing much of the food supply for local cooperative markets and local cooperative processing units can eliminate the twists and turns of unnecessary transportation, the wasteful recirculation of goods, and their costly rush this way and that in the labyrinth of specialized commerce.

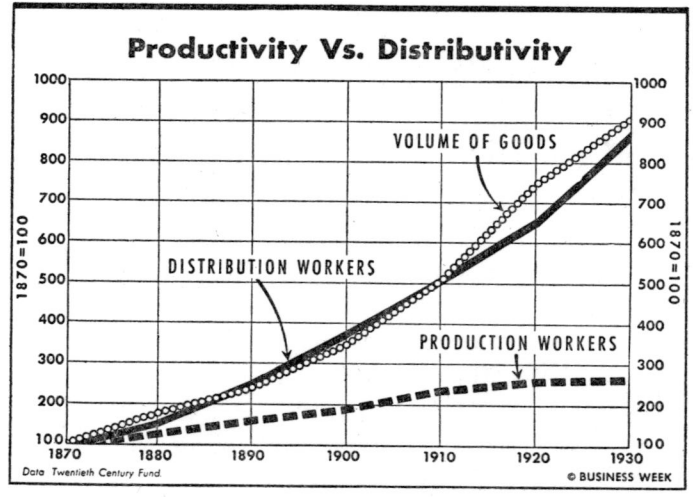

In their studies of distribution, Stewart and Dewhurst found that the multiple processing and transportation throughout the economic system results in a tremendous turnover of the *same* goods. For example, in the year 1929, $12,400,000,000 of agricultural products, $4,900,000,000 of mineral products, and $4,400,-000,000 of general imports originally entered into American channels of trade. The total value of these goods, then, in the hands of the initial producers was $21,700,000,000, but before these raw materials and goods reached ultimate consumers, they were turned over ten times with an aggregate sales along the line amounting to $218,599,000,000. The final economic value of the goods, or the price paid for them by the consumer was $65,632,-000,000. In this building up from an initial value of $21,700,-000,000 to a final price to the consumer of $65,632,000,000, *processing* and *manufacturing* added a cost of $22,400,000,000, *intermediary trade* added a cost of $7,100,000,000, retailers added a cost of $12,200,000,000. The goods went round and round and back and forth again and this required *transportation* which added a cost of $8,800,000,000.

Inefficiency also arises from the fact that there are too many wholesalers and too many retailers. And the cost of maintaining these duplicated agencies of distribution is ultimately charged up to the consumer in increased purchase prices.

Finally, there is the fact that each one of these agencies is looking out for its own profit — as great a profit as it can possibly get without detriment to its volume of business. And when savings are made by means of more efficient methods of distribution, these savings invariably accrue to the agency which makes them, not to the consumer.

Chain-Store Efficiencies

Now all these are undoubted factors of inefficiency in our system of distribution. But are they so essentially connected with any system of distribution that in practice it is impossible to eliminate them? The answer is "No," emphatically "No!" They have been eliminated in actual practice by a very potent factor in present-day distribution, the chain store.

Chain stores have made the path from producer to distributor much more direct by dealing immediately with the original producer or manufacturer and by setting up their own warehouses and supply houses in the cities where they operate retail stores. In this way they obtain the benefit of a double saving. Buying as they do for a great number of stores, their purchases are made in vast quantities and thus they secure the lower prices which quantity buying always commands. A second great saving results from the fact that their central warehouses and supply houses enable them to serve as their own wholesalers and commission men. In addition they have done away with all unnecessary advertising; contact men and traveling salesmen have no place in their system; and they have avoided all unnecessary duplication of their retail stores. As a result of this more efficient buying and distribution, chain stores are able to offer goods at considerably lower prices than the unorganized retailer. In some cases, part of this lower price is attributable to the fact that the chains have gone into the business of production also, operating their own packing houses, canning factories, and bakeries. As might be expected, an immense volume of business and great profits have been attracted to these chain stores. Thus for the year 1930 the Atlantic and Pacific Tea Co., carried on a business of $1,065,807,000 and earned a net profit of $30,742,000. During the same year the Kroger Grocery and Baking Co. had annual sales of $270,000,000 and profits estimated at more than $8,000,000. Similar figures might be given of other chain stores handling groceries, drugs, tobacco, bakery products, etc.

Evils of Chain Stores

But efficient as the chain store is in the system of distribution, it must be stated that it does not result in the common good. The chain store takes from the community where it is located and gives little in return. Its great profits are transferred outside the community where they are made to the locality where their principal owners are residing, and no return is made except that slight return in the form of wages to employees.

But the menace of the chain store is even greater. If ever the day comes when the small retail competition is completely destroyed and there remain in the field only chain stores, it would be very easy for these powerful chains to make agreements among themselves and charge consumers whatever prices they wish. In like manner they might set the wages of their employees at whatever figure they choose. And even now instances are on record of unfair business practices by chain stores — using short-weight measures, bribing city weights and measures officials, dictating prices to manufacturers, and when these latter refused to accept what they considered unfair prices, ruining them by underselling their products on the market at a loss to themselves. As with other large corporations the chain stores result in almost limitless power being placed at the disposal of their owners or chief stockholders, and there is always the danger that this tremendous power will be used to the detriment of the common good.

A Better System of Distribution: Local Rochdale Cooperatives

Distribution through Rochdale Cooperatives combines the efficiencies of the chain stores, and does not concentrate wealth and power in the hands of the few. And we might note in passing that Communism is far from being this type of distribution. For by taking away from the individual his natural right to own private property, Communism utterly destroys property. Under Communism, economic control of human affairs would be transferred from the hands of a group of capitalists where it now rests in this country, into the hands of the few men who actually run the government. The individual Russian of today does what Stalin and Stalin's associates in the Communist party decide that he is to do—or else he is evicted from his government-owned lodging and denied food at the government food stores.

Beginning a Cooperative Association

The very first step toward founding a cooperative association is to have or to organize a group of people who are bound together by some strong tie of friendship, common interest, common work, or common nationality. Such a group would be a study club, a farming community with the same general problems, the members of the same labor union, etc. Then once this group has been organized, they must be made "cooperative-minded." For a cooperative enterprise to succeed, its members must be unfailingly loyal. Cooperatives do effect savings for their members, but these savings are not to be brought about in some miraculous manner, but only as a result of careful planning and efficient business methods. And because of the difficulties and extraordinary expenses involved in getting started, these savings may not become evident during the first months of the cooperative's existence.

Let us now suppose that the proper group has been formed, enthusiasm for cooperation aroused, and a rather thorough study of the individual cooperative made. In general, at this point it would be best to begin with a buying club. A number of individuals could pool their orders for various articles of food, cattle or poultry feed, fertilizer, or some other product in which bulk buying would mean reduced cost. Information should previously have been obtained as to the possibility of buying these articles from existing cooperative organizations in the vicinity. If a cooperative grain elevator or other marketing or producing cooperative is already in operation in the town, this buying might be very easily done in connection with it, and then it could be used as a distribution center.

Such a buying club would demonstrate the advantages of cooperative action, would furnish valuable experience in cooperative buying, and would put to a practical test the real cooperative spirit of the group. And if the club proved to be successful, it could very easily develop into a full cooperative store.

The Rochdale Pioneers began their cooperative store by selling only four articles: flour, butter, sugar, and oatmeal. During the first few years of their enterprise they, moreover, had a very hazardous existence. Yet they had faith in their idea and built soundly. This faith and this sound building can be secured only by living up to the following conditions:

a) Members thoroughly educated to cooperation.

b) Strict adherence to the Rochdale principles.

c) Continual contact with other cooperative associations in the vicinity, and with sound cooperative enterprise throughout the country.

Cooperatives for Producers

The marketing cooperative is an association of producers or a group of farmers, who band together for the purpose of conducting whatever business is connected with the selling or marketing of their commodities, such as farm produce, dairy products, fruit, and so on. The marketing cooperative must be so founded and its organization so constructed that it will help the producers to sell or market their produce and carry on the other business activities connected with it, along sound and successful lines. It should help its members in two ways: first, to do business along better economic lines; second, to help toward intelligent production by obtaining and distributing information that will aid its members to fit their production and marketing according to the best possible prices and demands.

It should be noted here, that although the first and chief purpose of forming a cooperative of any kind apparently is to do better business, still there is another and, in its way, a far more important side to the question; and that is the educational and social value which the group of producers should and ought to receive from banding together for mutual support and success in a spirit of Christian good fellowship, a spirit that will call for sacrifice here and there, but will be rewarded both in a social and economic way.

How to Organize

In developing the subject let us treat the matter in a twofold way: first, the structure of the organization, that is, how to start a marketing cooperative, including type of organization and membership relations; second, operating practices, including financing, management, and selling.

There are various forms which a marketing cooperative may take in regard to structure, but most of them vary only in minor details; that is they must fit the locality, the number of members, the amount and kind of produce, and so on.

Now let us go about forming a marketing cooperative. Ten prosperous farmers around Grainville, for example, decide to begin a "trial" cooperative. Their main produce is cattle. They sort out some of the stock that is ready for market and ship it in common. No capital, that is, money, is subscribed and no contracts made between the members; their only agreement consists in the common shipment of the cattle. The market is watched for a few days; or they may appoint one of the more experienced members to do so, and then notify the rest of the members when he thinks the prospects are most favorable. At a good time, the stock is brought to the yards, sorted out carefully into carload lots as nearly uniform as possible. One or two of the members travel with the cattle to see that they are properly cared for. All the ten men "chip in" to pay the expenses of the men. After the shipment is sold, the returns are portioned out to the members — and all is over. There are no further obligations; the enterprise has served its purpose. Each man has received the benefit of marketing his stock in a uniform carload lot, which always is an advantage in marketing. He may have profited by the help of his nine neighbors in sorting and loading his stock. He has profited by the information on the favorableness or unfavorableness of the market; and he has profited by being saved much of the cost to the market. Lastly, it is noteworthy that commission men will always show special consideration to a shipment from a group of men over that of one individual; this shipment may lead to new and better contracts between the commission men and the group members.

Now let us say that the group of men whose experiment we have just described decide to form a real cooperative association, that is, a marketing cooperative. A meeting is called of all the farmers around Grainville. Fifty of them respond. The following will be the order of procedure, after the purpose of a marketing cooperative has been explained to those present:

1. The election of officers; president, vice-president, treasurer.
2. By-laws submitted and approved. A copy of by-laws may be obtained from a government agent or elsewhere, following the Rochdale Plan.
3. Capital consisting of shares subscribed by members. Note the Rochdale Plan.
4. Manager hired. Experienced man, reliable.
5. Legal charter of incorporation obtained from State or Federal Government. Consult local attorney.
6. Purchase of plant and equipment, etc., or construction site and plans decided upon. Cost estimated, and contract placed.
7. Manager takes charge, and business begins.

We shall devote a short paragraph to each of the above numbers which may need clarification.

1. First, a secretary may be added to this group; or, as in the case of a commercial corporation, the management consists of: four or five directors whose duty consists in watching the general procedure, and to whom all other minor officers must answer. Second, the so-called officers, whom we have indicated above — president, vice-president, and treasurer — have the duty to do the contact work and the specified duties of watching the market and securing all necessary information.

3. A copy of the Rochdale Plan should be studied. In general it consists in this: That the number of shares are restricted, so that no one individual or small group of individuals secure a majority control by investment. The second feature is that each member has but one vote no matter what number of shares he may have.

5. By obtaining a charter from the State or Federal Government, the association becomes by that very fact incorporated, no matter what plan is followed in founding it. Several worth-while advantages follow from being incorporated. The main one is that in case of failure, less damage will come to the members than if they were not incorporated, since they will be liable only to so much loss as their share in the corporation.

Here are some well-recognized principles for the individual and the incorporated cooperative. (Please note that a so-called "individual" or partnership cooperative is simply a cooperative which is not chartered by the government.) (*a*) The voting should be on the basis of members — each member having only one vote. (*b*) A limit is placed on the amount of stock; this being usually necessary to preserve the cooperative or "helpful" spirit of the cooperative organization. The cooperative must by all means be really democratic and mutually helpful to each and all of the members. (*c*) The dividend rate on the capital stock should be limited to the current low rate of interest. The net earnings in a cooperative, which come in the course of business operations, are returned to the members on the basis of volume of business done, rather than on the amount of capital each supplied. A cooperative should not be primarily a profit-making organization in this respect that it pays high rates of dividends to its members, because if it did, the members would look upon themselves as investors rather than cooperators. The principal return of a marketing cooperative is the service it gives, by which the producers try to control in varying degrees the processes involved in getting their produce marketed.

To summarize briefly; a cooperative may be formed without or with capital stock; that is, at least in the beginning. The principle features of the Rochdale Plan should be used since it has been proved the best; namely, each member shall have but one vote, and dividends are to be paid with reference to the patronage of the members rather than to the amount of shares they have taken. Fixed interest on shares should never be more than 4 per cent.

Membership in a Marketing Cooperative

The simple, individual cooperative, consisting of a number of members taken from a certain locality, may, for greater facility in marketing and financial gain, join with another or even a third such organization. The members of the cooperative must first of all appreciate the services of their organization and learn its principles and practices. To insure financing, insurance sales, and management, it is necessary that a steady and dependable volume of business, that is, amount of produce be assured. The business success of a cooperative depends entirely on the members. The prime reason is, of course, that the organization helps in marketing the farmers' commodities, and it is not a purely profit-making scheme as the general commercial corporation. Therefore only members should be dealt with. However, this raises the point whether others than members may be permitted to market, though the cooperative can decide this point when the question arises at one of the meetings. If a cooperative is to last through years of success let this be said as a warning! The cooperative exists first and foremost for the members, and consequently any foreign influence must be carefully watched.

The Marketing Contract

A marketing cooperative can best merchandise its products only by definite and well-adhered-to contracts with a commission man or a terminal market who look to it as a source of supply

Advantages and Technique of Cooperatives 289

that is more dependable than others which happen to be available. Besides this satisfactory supply, the customer will want a satisfactory volume. And, thirdly, this volume or amount must be on hand at the proper time. Therefore, to sum up briefly: The association must be ready to supply a volume of produce which is: first, high grade; second, sufficient to meet the demand; third, ready at the proper time.

As is clear from the foregoing, this entire setup calls for intelligence and fine cooperation on the part of all the members of the cooperative among themselves and with their representative officer or officers who maintain the contacts with the customer.

The contract between the customer and the cooperative should not be "ironclad," but should be made flexible so as to meet the changing conditions which the producers have to meet. (For greater clearness it should be explained that a contract may exist between the customer and the cooperative; and another between the cooperative taken as an association and the members.) The contract just spoken of above is that existing between the customer and the cooperative.

Since the success, and to a certain extent, the very existence of the marketing cooperative depends on the fulfillment of the marketing contracts on the part of all the members to the best of their ability, it is of the highest importance that all members, and not merely the officers and a few others, be fully informed regarding its operations, policy, and progress; its understanding with other cooperatives and business groups, and with the general public. All the members want to know minutely what is being done, and will support an organization only if they feel that it is being well managed, and is working for their interests and welfare. Therefore, it is suggested, that frequent meetings be held, to which all the members are invited, and at which everything that has been done is gone over. In addition to these meetings, information might be sent around to all members by mail if something of general interest occurs which is not sufficient for calling a meeting. In this way each and all the members will feel a personal interest in the organization. This point cannot be stressed too much; namely, that a cooperative will live and succeed only on the condition that all the members work in a mutually helpful spirit, a spirit of cooperation. This comes about only if everything is done to keep the members personally interested in and confident of their organization.

Financing and Marketing Credit

The money or capital that may be required for plant, equipment, and other needs connected with the business of the cooperative may be obtained in either of two ways, by shares or by suitable reserves from profits voted by members to be used for expansion.

Marketing credit means money borrowed by the association from a third party, as from a bank, to pay advance money to the producer members of the association upon the delivery of their goods. This need arises only when the association stores the commodities, and feeds them into the markets when circumstances are favorable. It would hardly arise in the case of a livestock shipping association or the like, where the cattle are sent immediately on to the markets. Great care should be taken by the association in the matter of securing credit. The matter cannot be entered into minutely here; it must be left to the discretion and prudence of the association to secure the best source of credit, the amount of funds needed, and the safety of the transaction. It is worthy of note that in case the association makes excessive advances on money (that is, borrowed money) to the members, it has a legal right to recover from them. So also if the association happens to go into bankruptcy or into the hands of a receiver, the receiver has the legal right to recover excess payments from the members.

Production Credit

Production credit has to do only with the producer. It means that the producer borrows money from a third party on the future sale of his produce through his association. This is legally possible. However, a creditor may object to this if he knows that the farmer will sell his goods only through an association and not privately. Shall the farmer inform his creditor about his intention? It were better if he did. Difficulty might arise if the farmer borrowed on his crop without informing the creditor that he is bound by contract to do business with his cooperative association. To get rid of this difficulty some states have enacted laws which require the recording and filing of farmer's contracts with cooperative associations so that any creditor may inform himself of the condition of his farmer friend to whom he intends to loan money.

Management and the Selling Program

The management of the cooperative is the most important feature of its life. The management of a cooperative differs somewhat from the ordinary business enterprise. An intelligent management is especially called for. In a broad sense the management means the control and direction of all the activities of the association: merchandising, market analysis — that is, getting information about the market and watching its rise and fall — membership relations, financing, office operations, bookkeeping, publicity, and other activities.

This means a policy of setting the price for products and regulating the sales. The board of directors and the manager should see to this duty.

The *price* demanded for commodities should be reasonable. We say this for two special reasons: First, a cooperative association cannot get such control of a product or of the market that it can dictate its own prices without looking to its supply and the demand for it; and even should this be the case it must not be excessive in its demands. No cooperative should even attempt this. Doing so, it will lose ground even on business lines; and it is going beyond the just and reasonable character of a cooperative, which is to obtain only just and fair prices for commodities. A cooperative such as is advocated here should not fight the grafter by becoming one itself. Second, the association cannot demand prices which are out of line with the current economic conditions. And thirdly, it will reap the largest good in the long run by adjusting its supply to the demand more or less as it is met, and not by overcrowding or "starving" the market.

In its *selling program* the association will do best by endeavoring to be of service to the customer, rather than by being at variance with him in holding out for higher prices, etc. Generally speaking, it must sell to market demand at market prices. Again, in the long run, this will be found best, as experience has taught many cooperative organizations in the past.

Other Selling Factors

Two further selling problems must be mentioned. First, dealers and manufacturers generally do not want to buy when the price is falling, believing that it will drop still lower. A program of selling could be worked out that would take advantage of short-time swings in the price by selling in answer to demand, which is generally strong during periods of rising prices, and by holding back sales during the fall of prices. Small cooperatives might get in touch with larger ones for information on this point.

Second, the grading of products should be standardized for best results. The rule to follow is to know the needs of customers so that proper provision can be made for them.

The aim which the cooperative should have before it always is: *the best possible service to the customer.*

Chapter 18

DEMOCRACY REVIVED ON LAND AND IN CITY

> A time there was, 'ere England's griefs began,
> When every rood of land maintained its man:
> For him light labor spread her wholesome store,
> Just gave what life required, but gave no more:
> His best companions, innocence and health:
> And his best riches, ignorance of wealth.
> — *Deserted Village,* Oliver Goldsmith

Goldsmith rightfully regretted the industrialization of England. With the advance of industrialization and urban concentration, humanity suffers more setbacks than gains, no matter what standards we apply.

In 1891 Leo XIII set forth the evils vividly in his Encyclical *Rerum Novarum:*

By degrees it has come to pass that workingmen have been given over, isolated and defenseless, to the callousness of employers and the greed of unrestrained competition. The evil has been increased by rapacious usury, which although more than once condemned by the Church, is nevertheless under a different form but with the same guilt, still practiced by avaricious and grasping men. . . . To this must be added the custom of working by contract, and the concentration of many branches of trade in the hands of a few individuals, so that a small number of very rich men have been able to lay upon the masses of the poor, a yoke little better than slavery itself.[1]

In 1931 Pius XI in his *Quadragesimo Anno,* "Forty Years After," repeats:

Nevertheless, the immense number of the propertyless wage earners

---
[1] *Rerum Novarum,* N.C.W.C. Edition, 1931, p. 146. Cf. Latin edition (America Press, 1931).

on the one hand, and the superabundant riches of the fortunate few on the other, is an unanswerable argument that the earthly goods so abundantly produced in this age of industrialism are far from rightly distributed and equitably shared among the various classes of men.[2]

Because of some widespread comforts, such as electricity and running water and the easy-credit automobile, the masses of the poor have believed themselves rich and the rich have refused to believe in the existence of poverty. Someone has called wealth, the lifeblood of the nation. There is truth in the statement. The comparison of the blood is very appropriate. In a healthy body the blood courses through the veins and is distributed proportionately according to the need of the individual organic units. If it becomes concentrated in an arm or a leg, it is harmful, and if it goes to the brain apoplexy occurs. If money or wealth be considered as the lifeblood of a nation, that same proportionate distribution should exist, not equal to each part, but properly distributed as to special works and need. The rush of the blood to a portion of the body is pleasing, indeed needed and helpful at times, but a congestion is most harmful, and a continued state of congestion proves fatal.

The unbridled race for profit has unduly concentrated wealth. The substitution of mammoth technocracy for human-scale technocracy has dislocated the balance of population. Continued migration from the land to the crowded city has caused deterioration in the countryside and in the cities. One half of the wealth produced in the country has been going to the city year after year in the form of rent, interest on debts, and by way of farm boys and farm girls reared and educated and sent into the cities with their inheritances. These concentrations of both wealth and population have been injurious to both the country and the city.

The evils can be remedied by what Leo XIII calls "the ownership of a few acres":

If work people can be encouraged to look forward to owning a few acres of land, the result will be that the vast gulf between vast wealth and deep poverty will be bridged over, and the two orders will be brought nearer together. Another consequence will be the greater

---

[2] *Quadragesimo Anno*, N.C.W.C. Edition, 1931, p. 21.

abundance of the fruits of the earth. Men always work harder and more readily when they work on that which is their own; nay, they learn to love the very soil which yields in response to the labor of their hands, not only food to eat, but an abundance of the good things for themselves and those that are dear to them. It is evident how such a spirit of willing labor would add to the produce of the earth and to the wealth of the community.[3]

There is no liberty possible where there is no widespread ownership of productive property. Reliance upon one's self, the sense of superiority and independence that comes directly from cooperating with nature in producing food, clothing, and shelter, have real values and implications. The best and easiest type of ownership of productive property is to "have a few acres of land."

However, it is very far from the minds of those who are sponsoring "forward on the land" movements to think that all present-day maladjustments could be rectified promptly by the adoption of the agrarian, distributist philosophy and its actual practice. Pliny gives us an interesting quotation from Cato: "The agricultural population produces the bravest men, the most valiant soldiers, and a class of citizens, the least given of all, to evil designs."

Nevertheless, the agrarians do not claim perfection for all agriculturists. It should not be the purpose of a leader in agrarianism to breathe antagonism toward the city, but rather to set forth the practical aims of a true philosophy, a philosophy that will save the cities and their industrialism from decay and final chaos. The cityward trend has been working and is working against the best interests of individuals, and families and our national life. It is not a natural move for any nation to abandon its land. While apparently improving some conditions of living, life in our congested cities has actually reached a lower material and spiritual standard. Millions of our people have lost that admirable American quality of self-reliance and initiative. They have become the easy prey of selfish greed under the guise of better wages and higher standards of spending. If agriculture is finally

---

[3] *Rerum Novarum*, N.C.W.C. Edition, 1931, p. 171; cf. Latin Edition (America Press, 1931).

completely commercialized, we know that we must have less and less farmers and more and more pauperized dependents in our cities — dependents who are ready kindling when revolutions threaten.

The First Law of Farming

In an article entitled "The First Law of Farming," Mr. Harris Dickson gives, in contrast to all this, a clear picture of that homemaking agriculture already repeatedly described in these pages when he related the story of Prairie Plantation in Mississippi. This farm has been owned and farmed by one family since 1816. Five generations ago the original owner wrote in a ledger his "Admonition to heirs and descendants":

> First Law — to wit: before anything else be done, every subsequent owner and every manager is required to produce a generous harvest of food for man and beast that cultivate the land. Hogs must fatten on corn, mules grow strong on oats and hay, and man be fed by all the kindly fruits of the earth and then — cotton.[4]

The real farm is always the livelihood farm — the farm of varied production where the annual harvests are gathered and stored away in the cribs and barns and cellars against the barren winter. In this farm there will be as many acres as will keep the family in comfortable circumstances. The number of acres will vary according to the location, the richness of the soil, the size of the family, and the plan of the family to engage in full-time farming or in part-time farming. The farm should not be so large that the family cannot know the fields intimately, nor so small that the family will fear want. The little fields will be well tilled and the little home will be well filled. Life will be happier there, than in a palace or on a six-hundred-acre farm.

The members of this family will work hard without becoming slaves to the earth. They will not be wage slaves, or peasants, but they will be free men, free women, and free children. There are some who will call it "peasantry," but life will be more free, more secure, more independent than life under heartbreaking land

---

[4] Dickson, Harris, "The First Law of Farming" in *Saturday Evening Post*, Sept. 1, 1934.

rents, land mortgages, land taxes, and high operation costs on the big farm. The big commercial farmer becomes a slave to the earth when he furnishes a living first of all to the railroad magnates, the truckers, the owners and operators of grain elevators, the board of trade, the mill hands, the wholesalers, the commission men, the traveling salesmen, the retailers, and the delivery boys. May the Lord bless all these good people! But why should the farmer think of them ahead of his own family? Why should he, finally, through his agricultural commercialism, drive his own sons and daughters to the canyons of the cities in search for jobs? Why should the farmer get his family supply of food through a system of specialized commercialism and inefficient distribution which gives the average American potato a useless trip of 741 miles, puts meat into an air-conditioned freight car for a ride of 944 miles, and provides dairy products with a round-trip ticket for 1,033 miles?[5] Has all this food travel any connection with well-baked potatoes, well-dressed meat, and dairy products rich in vitamins? Why should the farmer get his family supply of food through a system which taxes a loaf of bread 58 times, a can of peaches 32 times, a piece of meat 38 times, and a quart of milk at the rate of $1\frac{1}{2}$ cents per quart? Why should the farmer enter a food distribution system in which out of each $150 purchase of food, the tax gatherers take $30?[6]

Domestic Economy on the Farm Means Security

The city man is caught in the "service-and-tribute" system. The commercial farmer enters it freely and deliberately. This gives us the tragic conditions in American agriculture. Strange but true, the American farmer has used the trial-and-error method. Slowly, he learns that he must tear down his land factory and

---

[5] Publications of the Association of American Railroads.
[6] State Committee for Tax Information, Florida.
 The Nebraska Federation of County Taxpayers Leagues thus expresses the situation: "58 taxes on a loaf of bread, 45 taxes on sugar, 38 taxes on bacon, 32 taxes on peaches, $1\frac{1}{2}$ cent tax on every quart of milk, 154 taxes on a cake of soap, 6 cents tax on every package of cigarettes, 126 taxes on a pair of shoes, 148 taxes on a pair of overalls, 125 taxes on just an ordinary house dress. $231.72 a year hidden taxes charged against every man who draws $100.00 a month salary, if he spends the salary to live. People are slaving their very lives out to support a governmental structure that has become intolerably heavy." — Eighth Annual Report, Frank G. Arnold, President.

once more build up the homestead with its own food supplies and its own domestic economy. And when this is done the man on the land soon discovers that this domestic economy binds his family together more closely by means of the old bonds of mutual help and love. In this domestic economy there is work in which all the members of the family can cooperate. All are brought into closer relations with each other. A multiplicity of chores brings returns and even the children can help in the work with profit to their health and character. Out of the mutual family helpfulness grows understanding, love, and confidence — bonds which strengthen family unity and stability. Not only husband and wife are more closely united, but also parents and children. The homestead parents can easily become the natural confidants of their children in their difficulties and troubles. Wholesome family companionship becomes the training ground for character.

Family Economics Strengthens the Family Unit

The homestead rebuilds the human family, that oldest and most venerable institution on earth. The family is older than the Church. It is older than the State. It is the smallest organized group in which authority is vested and obedience required. Its charter comes straight from God Himself. The family is the unit of which both Church and State are composed, and without it, neither can, humanly speaking, endure. It is no exaggeration to say that both the Church and the State are dependent on the family for their success.

Birth statistics show conclusively that the farm family is the most important source of population growth. In view of the population declines in the cities, leaders everywhere are beginning to realize the necessity of strengthening rural life. Eighty per cent of the Catholics in the United States are in the cities. The small number of Catholics now living in rural districts will not be able to offset declines which are growing in the cities. No policy of the Church could be more sound and forward looking than that of building up vigorous country parishes. The homestead way of life and intelligent ownership and use of land contributes to the growth of Christian families blessed with a large number of children, and will enable the old rural parishes to prosper and establish the communities for the foundation of new parishes.

Benefits for Conjugal and Parental Society

Agricultural society is characterized by the strength, permanence, and union of the marriage bond, and the comparative rarity of its dissolution. This arises from the very nature of the farm, which requires the wife to be an active partner in the whole enterprise. The farm office and management is in the home, and not in some remote office building. The rural husband and wife share in the business management of their affairs. Little children are always welcome members of this homestead unit. They do not grow up in enforced idleness. Industrial society breaks the home with its birth control, its numerous divorces, its temporary unions, and its companionate marriages.

Wisely the Catholic bishops of the United States in their joint utterance of 1933 have said:

> One hope for relief in the universal misery of the present lies in the reversal of the policy which produced the factory and the factory system. This reversal without depriving men of the benefits of industrial progress, would reinstate them as independent home owners in rural communities. Such a change in the living conditions of millions of people would be a revolution, but some radical adjustment in restoring the balance between rural and urban population is imperative if our country is to survive and if our civilization is not to disappear.[7]

Spirituality, Sanctity, and Environment

For the success of the Church, that is, for the fulfillment of her purposes, it is absolutely necessary that human beings have the possibility at hand to achieve certain minimum intellectual, moral, spiritual, and material conditions of existence. A human being should have the opportunity of using and developing his God-given intelligence and will power. These spiritual faculties should not be dwarfed by external circumstances and should be free from undue influences yet guided by sound training and solid motives. There should be in society a sufficient amount of ennobling influences to make possible the realization that a human

---

[7] American Bishops, *Statement on the Present Crisis*, 1933, p. 42.

being is not a mere machine or a beast of burden. Opportunities for a full realization of man's spiritual qualities and eternal destiny should be present. And from a material viewpoint, the shelter should be such that it is consonant with man's qualities and the tradition of the surrounding world. His food should be not only sufficient for sustenance, but for a healthy existence. The Church that preaches the existence of an omnipotent all-perfect God and a Divine Providence "that arranges all things sweetly," must have a condition of existence for human beings that will not contradict her fundamental teachings. Certain minimum intellectual, moral, spiritual, and material conditions must exist. The minimum may change according to time and if less, we might as well admit that the Church cannot prosper.

Knowledge of Nature and Laws of Life Makes Mind Secure

When man is on the land he is near nature and takes a joy in beholding her marvelous work of producing the fruits by which man lives. For the man who plants, and waters, and watches things grow, nature unfolds her secrets and the great fundamental truths of life and death, toil and pain, time and eternity, and God take on a new and deeper meaning. The man's character develops, expands, and matures with the plants and animals he tends so carefully, until he partakes of that natural wisdom that is characteristic of the people throughout the world who live close to the soil. Thought and meditation to which the quiet, tranquil work on the land invites one, ripens judgments and broadens intellectual horizons, so that one is not left at the mercy of every radical opinion found in the news section, the editorial page, the cheap periodical, the tabloid, the broadcast, the movie, and the play. The man on the land is a man of serious thought and deep-seated convictions. Because he has such convictions, because truth, the principles and verities on which life is built, really mean something to him, he is usually a man with genuine strength of character. He is usually a good man, loyal to his home, his friends, his country, and his God. Life on the land is not artificial, mechanical, a matter of trade and commerce. It brings into human existence a closer alliance with the open field, the starry sky, the growing plants, and the animal world — an alliance which is good for the human mind. Intimate association with God's creative work and the self-sustaining power of an agrarian civilization are great foundation stones of right human existence. Morality, the obedience to God's revealed mandates in all their range, requires that the individual human being be endowed not only with God-given freedom of action, but also that he be helped by his surroundings in the fulfillment of God's will.

Anxieties in the Proletarian Mind

The mental worries of unemployment, the utter helplessness under governmental relief and charity, the complete dependence on an uncertain job, the pauperism, the unhealthy crowded city dwellings, the necessity of cash for the purchase of every little item of food are conditions and surroundings that lead only to dull resignation and radical conclusions. They bring on the revolts of the propertyless. There is no pride of achievement, no sense of responsibility. Such surroundings are not a good field for moral living and they are not a successful field for the Church in her work for the sanctification of souls. If the Church is forced to build and rely upon a civilization that more and more exemplifies the very antithesis of what she teaches, we can see how quickly irreparable spiritual losses are sustained. The materialistic philosophy of industrialism, of city life, of selfish, greedy competition, has been and is the real opponent of Christianity, much more than Communism as an economic theory. Extreme industrialized urbanism is an enemy more dangerous because it comes forth in sheep's clothing, whereas inwardly it is a ravenous wolf.

The farmer lives in a natural world. The city man lives in an injurious, artificial world. The farmer's thoughts are largely organic, biological, while the city man's thoughts are industrial, mechanical. The farmer thinks in terms of plants and animals, and the city man tends to think of wheels and machines, buying and selling. The movement away from the farm and to the city has not merely meant a change in the post-office address. A far-reaching change in one's philosophy of life is often involved in the move. Agriculture is based on life processes, and city occupations are based on manufacturing and commerce. This explains why we have today so many urban industrializers of agriculture. Lost in their trade and mechanics, they completely overlook the biological side of farming and consequently lead the farmer into many errors, in reference to his work and utilization of the land. Dr. O. E. Baker, famed economist in the Bureau of Agricultural Economics, says: "To the city child, milk is associated with a bottle, not with a cow; an apple comes from a box, not from a tree; and these earlier impressions influence, I believe, the ideas of later life."

We do not mean to infer that the city alone is guilty. Today the countryside is also infected to a very considerable degree with the commercial philosophy of life. The countryside has adopted an urban philosophy and has thereby brought failure to itself. Commercialism loudly proclaimed economic progress for its urban and rural followers, but it has led to loss of ownership, landless tenants, and industrial wage slavery. Commercialism aimed to fill all life with its glittering material pleasures, but it has brought forth untold suffering, want, and misery. Commercialism cried out for liberty with its false liberty leagues, property foreclosures and tax sales, and it created a nation of slaves; slaves to vice, slaves to greed, slaves to murderous competition. A veritable law of the jungle in the name of modernity and changed times! Commercialism held forth visions of wealth, comfort, educational opportunities. Instead, it brings forth poverty, slums, canned thinking, and loss of faith.

Urbanism, Commercialism, Proletarianism, and Spiritual Losses

In October, 1937, the *Homiletic and Pastoral Review* published figures giving the spiritual losses in a certain city parish, which contained 5,489 baptized Catholics. Of this number, 1,880 claimed to be Catholic, but they did not attend Mass or receive the sacraments. But worse even than this, there were 392 baptized Catholics who claimed they were Catholics no longer; 254 men and 138 women. In the parish there were 151 invalid marriages. These losses can be duplicated in other cities. The Church cannot hold its members and care for them if the surrounding world has a philosophy in many respects diametrically opposed to her own.

Firm Faith in the Countryside

Yet in all changes that come over communities, governments, and civilizations, we find that the rural group is consistently the last group to abandon its religion and traditional culture. As Macaulay styled it, they are faithful to "the ashes of their fathers and the temples of their gods." The word *pagan* comes from the Latin word *pagus,* "little village." The title "pagan" meant, in the early centuries of Christian era, an inhabitant of the countryside. The people of the countryside remained attached to the worship of their gods long after the cities had made religious worship a mere function of the State, and an empty formality. Hence the word for the worshiper in the open country and the worshiper of the gods became synonymous. In France, during the Revolution, while Paris enthroned a woman as goddess, the rural homes of France continued to be the sanctuaries of Christianity. The Ikons are still honored today in the humble dwellings of the Russian peasants. And long after our unbelieving cities will have completely abandoned Christ and the Commandments, the American rural dweller will bow in the simplicity of his heart in silent prayer to thank God for the bountiful gifts of mother earth.

Rebuilding America on the Land

As an illustration of what can be accomplished in rebuilding America on the land we may cite the example of Francis Hoess, a businessman of Hammond, Indiana. He began by erecting houses on farm land situated along a main highroad with a bus line and a high line for electricity. This building project is fifteen miles from the two industrial centers; Hammond and Gary. Each house and the one-acre plot of land that goes with it, costs $2,600. Each house is firmly built. It contains a large kitchen, a living room, two bedrooms, a small bathroom, and an unfinished attic in which other rooms can be built.

When the worker and his family enter into an agreement of purchase with Mr. Hoess they receive this "basic house," without paint or interior decoration, with a small furnace and wired for electricity, but without fixtures. Mr. Hoess does not build the "ideal house" or "dream house," beyond the reach of his clients, but he gives them the essentials for $2,600, a sum that can be paid by people in the factory-wage brackets. Painting, interior decoration, installation of fixtures, etc., are jobs that are done by the new owners themselves. The new owners find no difficulty in doing this work, because even when they are fully employed they work but forty hours a week in the factory. Their new homes solve their problems of leisure-time activity and each family actually appreciates its home more, because it represents not only a secure investment, but it is also something which they can and do incorporate their own planning and labor.

Ordinarily the buyers of these homes make a first payment of several hundred dollars, but some of the houses have been sold to men who did not have a cent for first payment. Normally the factory worker spends about a quarter of his income per month for rent, and hence the monthly payments on the new home; amortization, taxes, 6 per cent interest, etc., are worked out on this basis, with a reduction from month to month with every payment of amortization. If the buyer's wages are reduced, Mr. Hoess automatically reduces the charges on the house in exact proportion and if the buyer loses his job, payments on the house are suspended until new employment is found.

In the eyes of so-called "modern" bankers and the real-estate barons, surrounded with their mortgages, foreclosures, and frozen assets, of course all this is highly unorthodox, but experience proves that Mr. Hoess's methods are sound. People who know a house belongs to them, no matter what happens, take excellent care of it. And Mr. Hoess is right when he says that his money might as well be sitting in those houses as in a bank. Again when a baby is born to one of the families, Mr. Hoess often suspends payments for a short period. Mr. Hoess explains: "A worker can't pay for a baby and pay for a house at the same time, but if there is a baby, the family will care more about the house."

When the houses are paid for or the debt reduced to a certain point, Mr. Hoess is ready to build a garage or add a wing or make some other improvement, if the new owner has not already made such additions himself. But the total debt at any time is not allowed to exceed the original limit of $2,600.

Mr. Hoess does not wish to be called a philanthropist. He insists that he is building these houses in order to make money; and that he is making a good 6 per cent on his investment. Mr. Hoess may not realize it, but in reality, he is the best banker, the wisest real-estate man, and the most intelligent and effective social leader in his community. Mr. Hoess may insist that he is only a builder of homes, but in building these homes he gives his buyers the security of a productive home on the land. He makes it possible for them to become the responsible owners of a decent home for their children in a decent community. And with land to produce vegetables, small fruits, and feeds for some chickens and perhaps a cow, these families are removed from the proletarian helplessness which surrounds them when they reside in the shacks which crowd each other into the shadows of the mass-production smokestacks.

This country needs a Mr. Hoess in every community, men with wealth who will put their dollars to work in the constructive work of restoring home ownership and the restoration of family and community security through the land. Social leadership groups, private associations and government agencies as well, can make no better use of their funds than to use them according to Mr. Hoess's plan or some close adaptation of it.

The rebuilding of family units is not only a work for dollars and builders, but it is also a most important work for our schools. Education for productive home ownership is essential. Educators can rebuild family units on the land by providing an educational program that will adequately educate for a modern, cultured, happy life in a home on the land, and in leadership in small, well-co-ordinated communities. They can give the proper religious motivation; teach principles of ownership, security, liberty, responsibility; develop social grouping and leadership for economic needs; advocate social organization for health, recreational, and educational needs; provide technical training in soils, crops, and animals, in the employment and care of many small machines, family, human-scale machines, in the use of electricity, the processing and storage of food. Finally they can impart some knowledge of the work of building and repairing, as much as is needed for the proper management of a family farm.

Crop Diversification Contests

The local newspaper can contribute much in an educational way and help to break the stranglehold of commercial crops. In Memphis, Tennessee, *The Memphis Commercial Appeal* launched in 1934 a Plant-to-Prosper program, an annual newspaper contest with cash prizes for farmers who show the greatest farm and home improvements. This privately financed educational enterprise is breaking up the one-crop cotton system which bred the sharecropper, with his rags, his hunger, and his apathy, and which is remaking the lives of thousands of his class, as well as tenants and small owners, through a simple program which is pointed toward crop diversification, soil conservation, self-sufficiency in food and home improvement.

Even though only a few of the families win prizes, yet each farm family participating in the contest, wins better living conditions, a larger supply of food, more productive land, and more money than is earned on the cotton farm. In the year 1938, the contestants, 42,000 families in nine states, planted vegetables, soy beans, and feed crops on a total area of 600,000 acres that had for years been planted to cotton. They raised $10,000,000 worth of food that they never would have raised otherwise. Livestock increased about 10 per cent on the farms, and feed valued at $6,000,000 was harvested for the livestock. Some of the farm families even grew their own coffee. The total cash gains ran into the tens of millions. One hundred new farm homes were built, and $100,000 was spent for furniture and household repairs. Each farm participant has nearly doubled his cash income.

The brilliant results of these contests are attained at a private annual expense of only $50,000, a sum which is less than the National Agricultural Program spends in its confusion every twenty-four hours.

Medical officers in the region of the Plant-to-Prosper program say the returns in better health for the families are astounding. A varied diet has replaced the traditional deficiency diet of sowbelly and corn meal, which causes pellagra and other deficiency diseases. City merchants and bankers take an active part in the promotion of Plant-to-Prosper contests because the increased purchasing power, which is being built up in the farm families through intelligent land use and energetic planning, brings new prosperity to business enterprise. Some of the bankers in this region, when they make loans to rural families, insist that the Plant-to-Prosper methods be used on the farms which these families operate. After a year or two of farming by these new rules about one fourth of the contestants become owners of small farms.

The Land, Primarily for Home Building and Family Subsistence

The land, the most precious thing that any nation possesses in the way of natural gifts, must be distributed among many families and must be used as a lasting, solid, economic foundation. Land cannot make its proper and complete contribution to a nation's welfare when it is broken up into cotton belts, wheat belts, fruit belts, corn belts, and vegetable belts. Land makes its best contributions to a nation's welfare when its best acres are landscaped with many country homes, homes that are not tents and hovels and planters' hotels, but beautiful structures owned by families and equipped with more and more modern conveniences. Only then, can agriculture regain the place of primacy which it should hold in the life of a nation. In the restoration of this primacy of agriculture, through the development of correct land tenure and land use, sociology, economics, religion, all have a significant role to play. Economists must keep before us the agrarian type of family farm economy. The sociologist must give us the scientific principles for the preservation of family life as an economic institution in farm activity, develop rural social life, improve rural health, and provide for cultural advancement. Ministers of religion, besides taking an active interest in every phase of the agrarian program, must give us the philosophy and the theology, the principles and motives, natural and supernatural, for farm life and its desirability as a way of life guaranteed through continued existence and security of family-owned farms.

Successful Agriculture

Many farmers in Pennsylvania and others sparsely scattered throughout the nation have remained faithful to the agrarian plan of family subsistence and steadfastly have refused to be duped by the wild agricultural schemes of commercial-minded neighbors. The fact that these farmers are enjoying a greater security today than their specialized cash-crop neighbors is sufficient proof that self-providing, diversified agrarianism is a permanent, solid, safe form of agriculture. The practice of greater consumption at the point of production gives the family farm an economic efficiency that cannot be matched by the inefficient, costly, monopolistic business of centralized food processing with its remote production and distribution centers.

Economic Strength in Family Agriculture

There is a unique economic strength in "production-for-the-home" agriculture because it is a family enterprise. With finance-capitalism satisfied to build its tottering house on the efficient individual, and refusing to give proper recognition to the family in its system of artificial economics, the family-owned, self-providing farm remains as the only modern economy which preserves the family as the basic economic unit. Such a farm utilizes the services of all the adult and adolescent members of the family, with due regard for their divergent capacities. Children are welcome on such family farms, because at an early age there is much wholesome work that they can do with profit to the family and with profit to their own character and health, work being selected for them that is neither injurious to health nor calls for a curtailment of education. Through this preservation of the family economy and family life, the family farm gives us the rising birth rate needed to replenish our dying urban populations.

Liberty and Security in Family Agriculture

There is a permanent economic strength in this type of farming, because it gives us well-balanced, soil-conserving, character-building agriculture. There is a wise, democratic, Jeffersonian political economy in this type of farming, because it gives us a large class of responsible, property-owning citizens. Not mere stockholders and proletarians, but citizens who through their effective private ownership and personal control can still be free and independent in these days of fluctuating stocks, devaluated bonds, and uncertain jobs! Such farmers constitute a class of citizens who can lead a free, Christian, democratic life in all its fullness.

Human-Scale Technology in Family Agriculture

Modern agrarianism welcomes the development of rural electrification and all "human-scale" technology in the restoration of the economic and social primacy of family agriculture. Such technology will help the feminine partner in the agrarian home economy to do her great part in making the farm kitchen once more a place for scientific food processing and preservation. Such technology can remove the drudgery that caused farm kitchens to become like urban kitchens, mere storage closets for packers' products and canning companies' supplies.

Leadership and Union Must Preserve Fields for Families

But, unless we unite in a final stand for economic freedom through family-unit ownership and enterprise in a biodynamic land use, the joint-stock corporations, banks, insurance companies, and farming corporations will capitalize the land in the same way that they have capitalized everything else. In their hands the fields become factories, and the farm homes are converted into hovels where cheap labor may rest for the night, until cheaper labor is found. The joint-stock corporation, even as a landowner, will keep its factory concepts and use its factory methods. Home, family life, religion, culture, human rights, and liberties — all become matters of merely a remote secondary importance, if they retain any importance at all. The country field, transformed into the new corporation sweatshop, will be expected to turn out high dividend and stock profit for the privileged few in the same way that any automobile factory or steel plant is calculated to do. Slum and factory will then exist in both city and country, for the land itself will have become a factory for a few years, until these new commercial hunters and exploiters reduce it to a desert, impoverishing the farm workers and finally themselves. Under a commercialized "corporation" agriculture, life in the country will be turned into a proletarian life, life which, as we know it from conditions in the cities, will become more and more that of a slave.

APPENDICES

1. America's First School of Living
2. Milling at Home
3. A New Design for Living
4. St. Teresa's Village
5. Factual Outline of the Granger Homesteads
6. Nova Scotia "Rochdale" Cooperatives
7. Farm Tenancy Report Made to the President
8. Extracts from Farm Tenancy Committee Report — Iowa

1. AMERICA'S FIRST SCHOOL OF LIVING[1]

The period of re-settlement and community building now opens before us. Instead of encouraging the further building up of metropolitan areas, already overburdened, a rational policy demands a systematic urban re-settlement in Greenbelt Towns, with a minimum expenditure on the elaborate mechanical means of congestion, and a sane provision of opportunities for living. . . .
What are the new dominants in the opening biotechnic economy? They are not far to seek; the dwelling house and the school, with all their specialized communal aids, constitute the essential nucleus of the new community. — Lewis Mumford in *The Culture of Cities.*

Almost at the same time the vision in these words was uttered, the reality has come true. When Lewis Mumford was reading first proofs on his book the foundation stone of the new School of Living was being laid at Suffern, New York. At the time when Ralph Borsodi, the economist who created the School of Living, was watching the spring seeding of the grounds about his new school, the earliest reviewers in New York were reading Mumford's prophecy of the community of the future. When before have prophecy and fulfillment, ignorant of each other's scheme, run so closely parallel?

The biotechnical community of the future is here. A School of Living exists in the midst of a community of homes. It not only exists and is prepared to challenge the values of the industrial city; it is prepared to challenge them in the very shadow of the world's greatest metropolis.

The School of Living is less than an hour by motor car or bus from Times Square; nevertheless it is located in a purely rural setting, at the foot of the Ramapo Mountains and adjacent to the southwestern end of Interstate Park in Rockland County.

The School of Living occupies a large homestead site at the Bayard Lane community. Bayard Lane is a private and restricted

---
[1] This is an article by George Weller, Director-Secretary of the Homeland Foundation, published in *Free America,* July, 1938.

homestead association built on a nonprofit land plan and cooperative building formula. It has no governmental support of any kind; it is nonphilanthropic and self-liquidating. Most of the homesteaders commute daily to jobs in New York City. The homesteads surrounding the School of Living were financed by the Independence Foundation, Inc., a borrowing and lending institution devoted to furthering the homestead life in America, and making homes on the land available at the lowest possible cost to wage-earning families in the middle and lower income brackets.

Dedicated on Independence Day, 1938, to the "economic independence of the American people," the School of Living teaches the art of balanced and healthy living in which the home and the land are the two productive instruments. Neither exotic nor primitive in its ideals, the School gives instruction to adults who wish to begin following a modernized homestead way of life.

The Administration Building is a simple and beautiful structure. Its main floor has a large living room with fireplace, offices, a research library, and a highly modern kitchen adjacent to a part of the living room which is convertible into a dining hall. The second floor contains the bedroom quarters of the students, who may be residents at the School or not as they choose. The basement floor has another large meeting hall with simple whitewash finish, and a laundry room.

In the kitchen and laundry room tested analyses are made of various home processes: cooking, preserving, buying foods in bulk, and laundering and ironing with various pieces of modern electrical equipment. The purpose of these tests is to determine which foods consumed in the home are more economically processed therein than outside, and what home laundering costs (time, labor, and depreciation included), as compared with commercial laundry processes. This department is known as the Homemaking Division. Researches already undertaken and published by the Borsodis prove that the home is a more economical locale for nearly all the services now carried on outside.

The general curriculum of the School is separated into two parts — Principles of Living and Practices of Living. In the latter group is included, besides the Homemaking Division mentioned above, the Agricultural Division, which will teach the cultivation of the kitchen garden, the care of poultry and dairy animals and their maintenance on a labor-paying basis.

Because the School of Living is primarily not a day school but a research institution, its principal labor is the publication of a series of cost analyses of home processes. Bulletins already announced, at a price of 25 cents each, are those on "How to Economize on Laundry," "How to Economize on Bread, Cake, and Pastry," and "How to Economize on Flour and Cereals," and further bulletins are in preparation on: "How to Economize by Sewing at Home," "How to Economize on Home Painting," and "How to Economize on Milk and Cream."

The Craft Division, equipped to teach the establishment of the small decentralized woodworking and furniture factory (such as is already in action at the School and has made most of its beds, tables, and chairs), and the construction and operation of home looms and home weaving, are in this group.

The part of the curriculum called Principles of Living consists of a number of lecture courses on the philosophy of the family homestead way of living and its place in the national economic scheme. Instruction is also given in the meaning of history, and current events, and present crises, as a basis for the plotting of a creative, responsible, and independent life for the individual. While the burden of most of the instruction in this field falls upon Mr. Borsodi, open discussion is encouraged. On Sunday evenings there is held a general discussion by a guest speaker.

The Building Division is a unique feature of the School. It offers the first opportunity ever given to the builder of a home, the dwelling-consumer, to learn what honest home building is and what it should cost. The cost records of the homes built under the sponsorship of the Independence Foundation at Bayard Lane and at Van Houten Fields, the recently established independent homestead community at West Nyack, are available for study. It is from this division, it is hoped, that there will be graduated the families of the independent homestead communities of the future.

Because of the general terms employed in this description it may be imagined either that instruction tends to the abstract, or that a wide and distant relationship is maintained between teacher and the taught. The contrary is the case. Each division is in charge of a single person. The School itself is decentralized, small, but able to do accurately and well any factual analysis of the cost of modern living. Every subject is taught by doing, a plan that can better be carried out in a building corresponding in size to a modern home than in a giant edifice of laboratories. An excellent research library of economics is on hand, with a probably unequaled file of clippings of the cost of decentralized vs. centralized productive processes. Naturally the literature of consumer research is complete and up to date.

The paintings by George H. Macrum which decorate the walls of the School's living room record the American homestead as it was in the past. They portray homesteads from New England to New Mexico, from the Northwest to Virginia. The School itself is a monument to the working principle of decentralization in art, for most of its design has been carved out by a Rockland County craftsman.

The School of Living's curricular year is divided into four seasonal quarters: September 27 to December 17, January 2 to March 25, April 8 to June 24, and July 5 to September 20.

The standards of eligibility for matriculation depend rather on personal qualifications than previous learning. Adult students are favored, for this is intended to be a school of training for leadership and teaching.

An attempt more radical in its way than any other of the School's innovations is being made to adapt the schedule of courses to the peculiar needs of the students themselves. The theory which gave rise to the city night schools, i.e., that education should be made available at the time and place when working people are able to come and get it, has led a step further in the rural program of the School of Living.

Nor is it necessary for a person to register for an entire term and pay the sometimes excessive term fees that are required by many institutions. It is uniquely possible at the School of Living to attend individual lectures and ascertain whether one wishes to go on with the course offered. In this way a self-paying democratization of learning is achieved, similar to that of the old-fashioned lyceum.

It is probably exact to describe the School of Living as the first

America's First School of Living 317

American school of biotechnics. Its modernity is emphasized in the use of the most advanced electrical and mechanical equipment. If the School succeeds spiritually, it will not become a large and larger institution; it will rather spring up elsewhere and be imitated in other decentralized Schools of Living intimate in their dimensions. Already there are hopes that the other homestead communities of the Independence Foundation will find that they wish to have similar Schools of Living in their own communities. Whether they do so or not, one fact is clear: the biotechnical community, built around the home and the school, has set itself down beside megalopolis, and the newcomer is alive and kicking out in all directions.

2. MILLING AT HOME[1]
(A Homestead Research Study)

. . . Our ancestors, the pioneers who subdued the virgin forests and conquered the frontier, subsisted on a hardy diet of whole grains. They could scarcely have survived the hardships to which they were subjected if they had consistently eaten what the American public eats today, chiefly breadstuffs made from denatured and debased wheat and corn, totally different products from the pioneers' whole grain breadstuffs.

The factory-begotten products, white flour, bleached middlings, starchy corn meal, parched corn flakes and bran, are undesirable forms of very desirable foodstuffs. The public is not eating a superior foodstuff because factories have taken over the milling of wheat and corn. On the contrary, in developing the many different industries which use wheat, corn, and other cereals to produce foods of various kinds, the millers have succeeded in eliminating from them most of the tissue-building vitamins, mineral salts and colloids, including the salts of iron, phosphorus, sodium, potassium, silicon, calcium, fluorine, magnesium, manganese, and

---
[1] Excerpt from *A Manual for Milling at Home,* Homestead Bulletin, School of Living, Suffern, New York.

A long series of similar studies, each indicating a separate possibility of economizing, has been issued by the school, extending from economy on matters of health to economy in financing a home or buying land.

sulphur. These are sifted out, leaving behind the white starch cells and refined gluten of the interior part of the kernel.

Whole wheat is now a negligble part of the milling industry, yet it contains far more nutriment than the anemic but universally popular white flour. Whole wheat contains 10.6 per cent water, 12.2 per cent protein, 1.7 per cent fat, 73.7 per cent carbohydrates, 1.8 per cent mineral matter; white flour contains 12.0 per cent water, 11.4 per cent protein, 1.0 per cent fat, 75.1 per cent carbohydrates, and 0.5 per cent mineral matter. While the difference in protein (0.7 per cent) is of great importance, the difference in the mineral matter (72.2 per cent) which contains the most vital elements becomes enormous when you consider the fact that bread is still supposed to be the staff of life, eaten three times a day, every day of the year.

Patent flour, the highest grade of white flour, contains less than one half of one per cent mineral salts; the bran and germ of the wheat berry — those parts which are now ironically enough ground into feed for cattle and chickens — contain nearly ten times as much. Of phosphorus compounds alone, bran contains twelve times as much as patent flour.

What the Public Could Save Every Year By Home Milling

	Saving per Family	Saving for Entire Public
Flour	$14.94	$407,504,018.51
Breakfast Foods	5.66	154,560,137.09
Other Cereals	1.38	37,623,730.68
Total	$21.98	$599,687,886.28

White Bread Not the Staff of Life

White bread is no longer entitled to be called the staff of life. It is rich in heat units (starch) but lacking in tissue-building and energy-giving material. Nutritionists who recommend white bread (and doctors who have a kindly word for it) usually add the highly important reservation that vegetables or other rich sources of minerals must be added to the diet to offset the deficiency in bread.

Careful scientific experiments have proved beyond doubt that white bread is not suitable for human or animal consumption. When monkeys, chickens, guinea pigs, or mice have been fed on an exclusive diet of white bread, they have lost weight, become diseased, and died. Numerous instances are recorded of human beings literally starving to death on white bread — the most conspicuous example being the loss of 4,000 men forced to live on a white-flour diet while constructing 222 miles of track connecting Bolivia and Brazil.

Nor is Factory-Made Corn Meal

What is true of white flour and other bolted and sifted wheat products is true of factory-made corn meal, whose fibrous outer coats, oily germ, and flinty starchy parts have been mainly eliminated. The nutritive differences between the commercial product which comes out of the modern high-speed mill and the whole grain which can be ground at home are enormous. The whole kernel contains 10 per cent protein; refined corn meal, a fifth less — 8 per cent; the whole kernel has 4¾ per cent fat (a substance containing the "fat soluble A" which children require for growth and adults must have for good health), the refined kernel only about one fourth as much. Finally, the whole grain contains vitalizing mineral salts in the ratio of 15 parts to a 1000; in the factory product this has been reduced to 4 parts in a 1000.

"The near-corn for which man tries with little success to develop an appetite," said Alfred McCann, "will kill poultry, hogs and cows. Chickens fed on it will die in less than fifty days. Children fed on it to the exclusion of other offsetting foods will speedily develop pellagra. Children fed on it with insufficiency of milk and fruit so lose vitality and resistance to disease that they become lazy victims of any infection that passes along."

Consumption of White Bread and Refined Grains Has High Correlation with Many Ailments

White bread is not a normal foodstuff; it is an artificial food developed to fit the needs of the milling industry. Until recent times, the diet of bread-eating peoples consisted entirely of dark breads, and in many parts of the world white bread is still unknown.

In spite of the claims made by the milling industry for white flour, the fact remains that the introduction of large amounts of white bread and white-flour products into the dietary of civilized peoples has had a deleterious effect on their health. Many authorities believe that the alarming growth of constipation, cancer, and nervous disorders might be correlated with the widespread consumption of foods made from ultrarefined cereals. Far from providing adequate nutrition, white flour and breakfast foods are injurious to health in two particular ways: First, they are so meager in cellulose, mineral salts, colloids, and vitamins that they lower resistance to disease. Secondly, they are not entirely digestible, hence cause constipation; and constipation, medical science recognizes, usually prepares the stage for the appearance of more malignant and degenerative diseases.

Do You Want to Support the Milling Industry?

	Flour Industry	Cereal Industry
Number of Mills (1931)	2,412	111
Quantity Produced	$595,761,000	$135,676,000
Number of Wage Earners	22,840	7,018
Wages Per Week	$25.67	

The consuming public decides what industries it prefers to support. If you decide you prefer to modernize your home or to buy an automobile with the money you can save by home milling, you shift your support from the milling industry to the building or automobile industries.

(Source: *Statistical Abstracts of the United States*, 1933, pp. 631, 632.)

The products of the flour industry consisted of:

Wheat flour	115,364,000 bbl.
Rye flour	1,568,000 bbl.
Buckwheat flour	31,092,000 lb.
Corn meal and flour	8,889,000 bbl.
Other flour	16,514,000 lb.
Bran and middlings	4,826,000 tons
Feed, screenings	1,549,000 tons

The products of the cereal industry consisted of:

Breakfast foods (made from wheat, oats, corn, and other products)	$100,092,000
Prepared flour	31,992,000
Coffee substitutes	2,608,000
Others	984,000

(Figures from *Employment and Pay Rolls*, March, 1938, United States Department of Labor, Bureau of Labor Statistics, p. 16.)

Milling at Home

Doctors John H. Musser and George Morris Piersol, of the University of Pennsylvania, are specific in connecting the most common American ailment, constipation, with the irrational taste for white bread which the baking and milling industry has created in the public. "Dietetic errors," they say, "are among the most frequent general causes of constipation. These consist in food which is deficient in residue (bran) by reason of which the bowel is deprived of the mechanical and chemical stimuli necessary to promote proper intestinal activity." Their advice is to eat "whole wheat bread, whole rye bread, or pumpernickel — in preference to white bread." As far back as 1915, Doctor Horace Packard, of Boston University, listed the consumption of refined cereals among the suspected causes of cancer. Speaking before the Surgical and Gynecological Society of the American Institute of Homeopathy, he said:

The human family is underfed in mineral salts. A momentous fact is that the flour mills of the civilized world are sending out food material rich in heat units but pitifully meager in energizing and immunizing material. Since a critical examination of the habits of life of civilized cancer-plagued people in comparison with the habits of primitive cancer-free people shows that the main difference between them is a dietary poor in mineral salts among the cancer-free people, the most logical and rational course is to adopt this as a keynote to cancer treatment.

Research at the Liverpool School of Tropical Medicine proved that people who lived chiefly on bread made from wheat whose outer coats had been removed were subject to a form of peripheral neuritis. Dr. Benjamin Moore, Chief of the Biochemical Department of the same institution, definitely associated the popularity of white bread with the growth of nervous diseases.

Our nerves as a nation are much less stable than in the days prior to a white bread diet. All our work suggests that the growing tendency of the age to neurasthenia, "nerves," etc., is not unlikely due to removing from our diet those very elements of cereal food which nature has hidden in the husk of the grain, and which man, in his ignorance, discards.

Why Bleach Flour?

Not content with turning out flour robbed of most of its health-giving qualities, the millers have further cheapened their product by bleaching it by an electrochemical process. Flour as it comes from the mill is not white but slightly yellow, owing to the presence of a valuable yellow food substance, *carotene*. Flour turns white by the natural oxidizing process of the air if allowed to stand for several weeks or months. Millers, however, cannot afford to store flour for so long a time and hence an artificial mode of bleaching was invented. "What storage could not accomplish in 120 days, these bleaching processes miraculously do in one day!"

Bleaching not only destroys the carotene, a valuable source of Vitamin A (absence of which leads to retarded growth, poor appetite, and digestion) but leaves toxic deposits of nitrites in the flour.

The amount of carotene in flour is so minute that, offhand, its destruction by bleaching might be regarded as unimportant. But, as Dr. Monier Williams, of the British Ministry of Health points out, "bread forms a large part of the diet and the absolute amount of carotene which it can contribute is by no means negligible. . . . If the consumer takes the trouble to think about it at all, he will, I think, prefer that his flour shall retain its natural color and not be treated with a highly active oxidizing agent such as chlorine, which may have unknown effects on some unsuspected, but possibly important constituent of flour."

Not only is bleaching undesirable because of injury to health, but it permits inferior, spoiled, and discolored flour to be blended with small amounts of superior flour, and the resulting mediocre though uniform product may be sold off as grade A patent flour. This stratagem rewards the miller with from fifty cents to a dollar extra per barrel.

Switzerland, France, and Denmark have forbidden the bleaching of flour. In the United States bleaching is permitted, although the practice was attacked as long ago as 1906. Several states passed laws barring it, and so much controversy arose that the United States Public Health Service undertook an extensive study of the effects of bleaching. The gist of its findings, published in 1910, was that an amount of nitrates above the tolerance for safety was deposited in the flour, that this lessened the digestibility of the gluten of the flour, and that their ingestion should be decreased as much as possible.

Armed with this conclusive evidence, the Federal Government attempted to halt bleaching and actually won a victory over the milling industry in the Supreme Court. But, oddly enough, the Food and Drug Administration "read into the opinion of the Supreme Court an entirely antagonistic statement respecting injury to health . . . (and) the very law which the Supreme Court has said was enacted chiefly to protect the public has been turned into a measure to threaten public health and to defraud the purchasers of flour." Since the federal authorities were negligent, millers who at first refused to bleach were forced by competition to do so. The farthest the government would go in protecting the consumer was to require bleached flour to be so labeled if shipped in interstate commerce. . . .

What American People Could Gain by Milling at Home

Milling equipment such as the School of Living recommends can be purchased for $37. The mill can be used to make all your flour and breakfast foods, as well as to grind coarse feeds for cattle and poultry. This mill utilizes self-aligning burrs for the actual grinding, instead of the great, clumsy millstones which were used before the modern roller mill took over the production of flour and cereals.

With one of these mills, you become independent of the flour and breakfast food factory. If every American family baked and milled at home, the American people would save $599,687,886 annually. (See table on p. 318.) This vast sum could be diverted to the purchase of commodities which they cannot now afford.

The average family in the United States now consumes around 4.23 barrels of flour every year. Each mill put into operation in an American home would reduce the demand for factory-made flour and cereals by 4.23 barrels. About 30 million of these domestic mills would destroy the milling industry and the 27,805 persons now employed in flour and cereal mills would be released for other and more useful work.

If every family milled at home, it would do away with the incredible folly of concentrating huge armies of workers, salaried employees, and executives in the great cities where these large mills are now located; of shipping both the grain and its products back and forth across the continent; and of trying to support all these nonessential mills with superfluous million-dollar advertising campaigns to persuade you to eat more flour and cereals.

If every family milled at home, it would improve the status of the farmer, who then would produce for a local or regional market, with prices fixed by local consumption. Sacks of wheat and corn would be sold in all grocery stores instead of sacks of flour and cartons of cereals. The farmer would be in closer touch with the consumer, and a large number of nonessential middlemen would be eliminated. The net result would be higher and more equitable prices for the farmer without increasing the price to the consumer.

In addition, if the demand for devitalized white flour, ultrarefined corn meal, parched corn flakes, woody bran, and the like ended, not only would the nonessential mills disappear, but many of our patent-medicine factories would have to close. For a large part of the stock remedies in modern drugstores consist of patent medicines for the alleviation of constipation — laxatives, cathartic, and purgatives in liquid, powdered, and pill form. These products which are absolutely essential in this age of white flour and refined grains, become more or less nonessential if some of the principal dietetic causes of constipation are eliminated.

Manual for Grinding of Wheat and Corn Equipment

The School of Living recommends for home milling for the family in the income group to which this Bulletin is devoted, the following equipment:

A burr mill with a ¼-horsepower motor.

A hopper and stand with drawer, about 24 by 24 by 45 in., capable of holding 100 lb. of wheat, 100 lb. of corn.

A good hand mill, which can be purchased for as little as $2.50, is a practical substitute for the electrically operated mill if an investment of $37 is too large for the family.

The farmer who can also use a mill to grind feed for poultry

A New Design for Living

and livestock, should use a larger mill than the one recommended above.

3. A NEW DESIGN FOR LIVING[1]

Van Houten Fields is a restricted home community for families who wish to live in the country comfortably and economically while remaining within commuting distance of New York. It is organized upon a nonspeculative plan formulated by Ralph Borsodi, nationally known as an author, economist, and housing expert.

A Tested Plan for Home Ownership

Near Suffern, New York, about twelve miles from Van Houten Fields, a group of families established themselves in 1935 and 1936 to test the Borsodi plan. Speculative profits were eliminated from the cost of the land and the price was cut from one fifth to one third. Individually designed homes, built to endure, were constructed and financed on a basis fully acceptable to conservative banking institutions. Building costs were cut from 10 per cent to 15 per cent. Gardening, poultry keeping, and other opportunities for producing things at home resulted in sharp cuts in living costs. Families which in many cases could not afford even a down payment for suitable land became owners of homes and ceased pouring rent money into the landlord's bottomless pocket. The success of these homesteaders at the Suffern project, named by the homesteaders Bayard Lane, after Belinda Bayard, the pioneer woman settler of the tract, attracted national attention to the Borsodi plan.

Organizing Van Houten Fields

A committee from Nyack, New York, thereupon requested Mr. Borsodi, in view of the success at Bayard Lane, to assist in the launching of a similar independent association on a larger scale

---

[1] This is an explanation published by the Independence Foundation with reference to Van Houten Fields, West Nyack, New York. The communities at Bayard Lane Homesteads, Suffern, New York, and Ringwood Homesteads, Ringwood Manor, New Jersey, are being built up in the same manner under the leadership of the Independence Foundation, Inc. (1935), at Suffern, New York.

near Nyack, and to secure the support of the Independence Foundation, Inc., which had financed the Suffern home owners. The Van Houten Fields Association is a self-administering body of home owners. Under the plan adopted, no person or group of persons will secure any profits from the development of Van Houten Fields, while the certificate holders and mortgaging institutions backing the Foundation receive only interest on the actual amount loaned by them.

Van Houten Fields occupies the entire extent of a 106-acre farm which was tilled through the days of the American Revolution by the wealthy Dutch settler known in colonial records, as Thomas Van Houten, the first Justice of the Peace of Orangetown. The members of the association have adopted his name to do honor to the pioneer who built the first homestead upon the land where their families are establishing garden homes.

A Planned Residential Community

There are forty sites for small estates at Van Houten Fields. The land, which has been surveyed and tested for its gardening qualities, occupies a long sloping ridge overlooking the upper valley of the Hackensack River. An excellent county highway passes across the property. At the higher extremity a tract with a brook, now covered by woods and a deep ravine, forms a natural park. This tract has been set aside as a forest playground for the community. Down in the valley a spring-fed pond is available for swimming and other water sports. Here eight more acres of land are to be laid out in tennis courts, natural gardens, and playgrounds. The 100-year-old Van Houten homestead is to be rebuilt as a community center and meeting place and will be used to develop the cultural and social life of the community. A bridle path extending many miles crosses the property.

One- to Five-Acre Home Sites

The land is divided into home sites from one to five acres in size. These vary in cost according to location. Land in similar developments costs home buyers, if individually purchased, from three to five times as much as under the plan adopted for Van Houten Fields. This great economy is made possible through the purchase of an entire farm and the transfer of possession at cost and without profit directly to the home owners. In this way the inflated profits of ordinary subdivided land are avoided. The home owner, instead of the land speculator, secures full advantage of large-scale subdivision. The association, of which he is a member, and not a commercial developer, is the beneficiary of the community's growth.

Immediate Building Possible

But the home builder does not have to pay the full cost of his land immediately in order to build. He pays in monthly installments of from $4.65 to $7.68 per acre, which include taxes and the cost of the roads and community improvements. Many families now are doomed to pay rent forever because they are unable at any one time to save the total amount of money that is needed to purchase land before building upon it. At Van Houten Fields the home owner not only gets his land at cost, but can begin to build his home as soon as he chooses a site for it.

While original cost of the land, roads, and development is being paid off, title remains with the Independence Foundation, Inc., as trustee. After amortization, it passes to the homesteaders as a group.

Advantages of Home Ownership

The advantages of home ownership and the complete elimination of rent from the family budget are more clear than ever today as a result of the depression. To buy land and build now is to create a shield against the possibility of inflation. For a family to own a productive country home is to be anchored in a safe harbor when jobs are insecure.

Economy — and Beauty, Too

While the utmost economy in land development, financing, and building is being realized under the plan upon which Van Houten Fields has been founded, the plan makes it possible to furnish every family the most beautiful home that it can afford to pay for. The houses are not built "overnight" to last only long enough to be paid off; they are permanent masonry homes built to endure for generations. Most of them are of native field stone, others are of special masonry blocks; yet they cost but little more than ordinary frame houses. Homes built by the Foundation are neither "antique" nor "modernistic"; they are built in the best native American designs. Inside they are equipped with every modern convenience to make it possible for the family to live a happy and successful productive life in the country. The homes built in Suffern have both early American fireplaces and modern heating plants — the one essential for the social life of the family, the other for its health.

Building Plan

The homes at Van Houten Fields are being built on a unique construction contract by the Clarkstown Building Guild and other cooperative organizations of building craftsmen sponsored by the Independence Foundation. Thanks to a careful schedule of construction throughout the entire year and a system of economy sharing between house owner and workmen — with the speculative contractor eliminated — the original craftsmen at Suffern have been steadily employed from 1935 to the present without reduction in personnel despite the financial depression and the seasonal unemployment in the building trades. Moreover, working 52 weeks in the year, they have earned higher annual wages than any known local group of workmen and yet have passed the benefits of low-unit costs on labor directly to the house owner. Six members of the Ramapo Building Guild at Bayard Lane, due to their secure employment, have already built, or will do so this year, homes for their own families in various parts of Rockland County.

Financing Plan

The Independence Foundation is a nonprofit credit institution operating on a new building and loan plan organized to finance home owners at the lowest costs and interest rates that can be obtained.

The plan has been devised to meet the needs of home owners, and to eliminate unnecessary taxes, legal fees, and other high costs ordinarily involved in borrowing money. Notable features of the

A New Design for Living

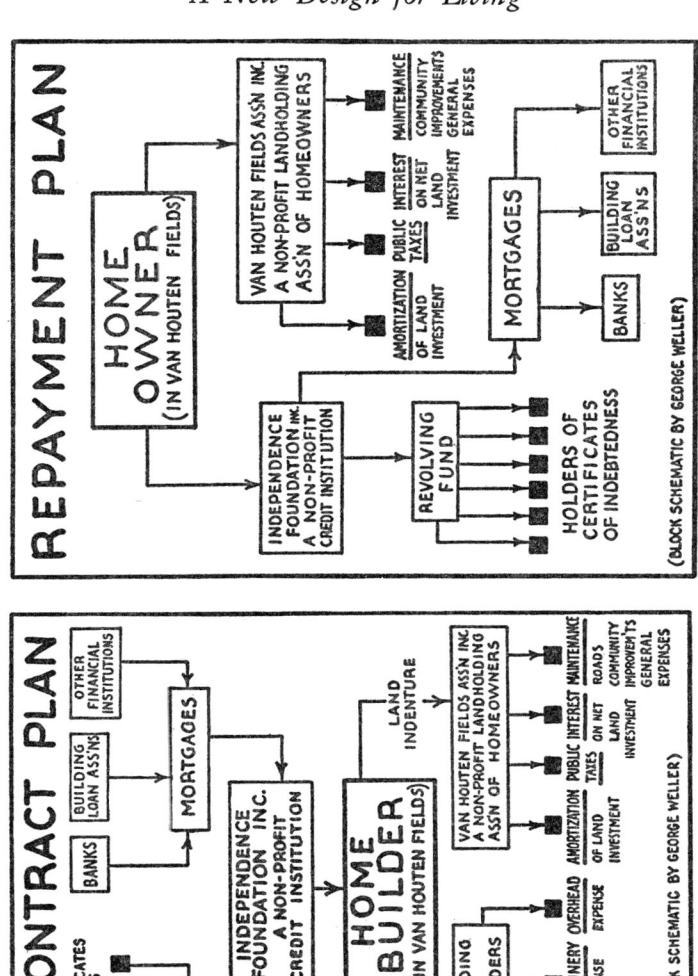

loan contract include a loan-value provision which makes it possible to borrow in an emergency on the paid-in equity without extra expense; a plan for financing the purchase of household equipment such as refrigerators and washing machines; a plan for paying fire- and life-insurance premiums as a part of the regular installments; a low-cost life-insurance plan which pays off the entire mortgage in the event of death of the insured; and a system for rebating savings on interest.

Security In a Productive Home

Since the average family can learn with modern equipment to make, build, or grow some of the things it uses, as has already been shown on the Suffern project, the plan of Van Houten Fields gives the families establishing their homes a similar opportunity to cut down their living expenses and raise their own standard of living by doing so. None of the plots at Van Houten Fields is laid out as a conventional 50-foot suburban site; each plot is large enough not only for beauty and comfort, but also for productive use.

The residents of Van Houten Fields therefore have another staff of security besides being their own landlords; they can if they will establish vegetable and flower gardens, keep poultry and plant fruit trees, and by bulk buying, home preserving, and canning achieve cash economies impossible in city or suburban homes. The plan does not invite city families to set up commercial farms; it merely gives them the chance to use a country home in the most profitable manner possible. No one is compelled to raise vegetables or poultry at Van Houten Fields, but the opportunity is offered for willing hands to lift the family standard of living and lessen its cash outlay. Tests of the soil made for the Association indicate that it is equal to the average farm land in Rockland County.

Each Family Is Independent

The purposes of the Association are limited to removing all speculative profits from landownership, finance, and construction, creating a restricted residential community, and protecting all the individual rights of each of the property owners. No fads or share-the-wealth ideas are included in its objects. Each family is independent on its own homestead, yet each enjoys advantages which heretofore have been available only to those who can afford to buy into an exclusive development.

Dedicated to Independence

The founders of Van Houten Fields consider it altogether appropriate that this second private, nonprofit association of home owners in Rockland County should be located in a countryside, sacred to the American Revolution. These homes and hearthsides are being established in the same woods and fields that sheltered the troops of George Washington when they won liberty for their own homes and freedom for the Republic.

4. ST. TERESA'S VILLAGE[1]
(A Cooperative Farm Community near Greenville, Alabama)

While traveling over a "parish" of 11,000 square miles in central Alabama, Father Arthur W. Terminiello came in contact with the pitiable plight of the sharecroppers. He determined to do something practical for them. The first step, which is part of the Rural Life Program of the diocese of Mobile presided over by Bishop Thomas J. Toolen, D.D., was to finance the purchase of 160 acres of land, and to lease an additional 340 acres, upon which to establish the village. The charter members of the little village are five families of sharecroppers.

Each family has a plot of ground for private cultivation and works the community acreage on shares. When money borrowed to start the project has been repaid, the land will be deeded to the residents. Each member has one vote in the administration of the affairs of St. Teresa's Village. A contract has been made with the municipal canning plant to handle the produce of the village.

The men, women, and children of the village readily catch the spirit of friendly cooperation. Putting his hand to a plow is nothing unusual for the village's founder, Father Terminiello, and he has turned many a furrow in starting the project. The joy of tilling their own land is now the happy lot of these poor share-

---
[1] Cf. *Action*, June, 1938, Vol. I, No. 3.

croppers. With almost loving care each man cultivates his tomatoes because they mean food, clothes, shoes, and implements for the village. Before, there was the miserable existence of virtual economic slavery, insufficient food and clothing, profitless cultivation of cotton on exploited land, a shack, and an impossible burden of debt.

When the land has been paid for, the village will be run on a strictly cooperative basis both as regards production and consumption. Until that time, both adults and children are being trained in the principles of cooperation so that they will be prepared for the time when they can take over entirely the management and government of the little community. Father Terminiello hopes, when sufficient funds are available, to found more such villages in order that the sharecroppers may in the future enjoy health, literacy, a reasonable degree of leisure, and ultimate economic freedom.

5. FACTUAL OUTLINE OF THE GRANGER HOMESTEADS

Legislative Origin:

Section 208, N.I.R.A., June 16, 1933, 73rd Congress.

First petition mailed to the Subsistence Homesteads Division, Department of the Interior, Washington, D. C., on December 15, 1933.

Approval of Project by the Secretary of the Interior, March 4, 1934.

Initial allotment $100,000 for fifty houses.

Local Corporation formed March 30, 1934. Local Corporation disbanded April 1, 1934.

Project Manager appointed for Austin, Minnesota, and Granger, Iowa, May 1, 1934.

An additional allotment of $25,000, July 15, 1934.

House designs completed by Division, August 10, 1934.

Bids for wells taken August 12, 1934.

New Project Manager for Granger appointed August 15, 1934.

Bids for houses taken on September 16, 1934.

Additional allotment of $50,000, October 17, 1934.

Factual Outline of the Granger Homesteads

Land purchased November 10, 1934.
Contracts for wells awarded February 10, 1935.
Contracts for houses awarded February 15, 1935.
Work on wells begun February 26, 1935.
Work by house contractors began March 4, 1935.
Resettlement Administration takes over Subsistence Homesteads Division, June 15, 1935.
Houses completed by contractor, J. E. Lovejoy, October 15, 1935.
Houses occupied December 15, 1935.

Acreage:

Total acres purchased by the government 223.93. The south portion of the Project contains 25 acres. The west side 50 acres. The north side 25 acres. The center triangle 114 acres.

The roads within the Project take up approximately 12 acres, with a total of 2.25 miles of roads.

The average acreage per Homestead is 4.02, making the average available ground for cultivation 3.50 acres. The largest acreage is 8.65 and the smallest is 2.32. The nearest Homestead to the village of Granger is 4 blocks from the city limits, the farthest is 1.25 miles.

Types of Houses:

There are 50 houses in the Project. Of these 5 are 4-room houses, 33 are 5-room houses, and 12 are 6-room houses.

The houses are wooden frame buildings of the ordinary Iowa type. The inside walls have plywood in place of plaster and the ceilings are of celotex.

There is a full basement under every house, tile walls, and cement floor.

The basement contains a hot-air furnace, a hot-water heater and tank, an automatic pressure tank connected with the electric well pump.

Rooms:

Equipped with hot- and cold-water faucets, sink, built-in cupboards.

Living Room: This is the largest room in each house and intended to serve as a living and dining room.

Bathroom: Fully equipped with built-in tub, lavatory, and stool.

In the 4- and 5-room houses the bathroom is located on the first floor. In the 6-room house it is on the second floor.

Bedrooms: The 4-room house contains two bedrooms. The 5-room house has three bedrooms, one downstairs and two upstairs. The 6-room house has four bedrooms, two downstairs and two upstairs. All bedrooms in every house have cross ventilation.

Outside the House:

An individual drilled well was part of each family unit. The deepest about 150 feet and the shallowest about 120 feet. An electric pump sunk in a cement pit and operated automatically furnishes the water to the pressure tank in each house.

There is a sewer pipe from the house to a septic tank which has a five-branch field disposal.

Outbuildings:

Homesteaders were given the choice of a combination garage and chicken coop or small barn. There are 12 barns and 38 garages. Many other small buildings have been added by the Homesteaders, since occupancy.

Electricity:

Each house is fully wired and the electricity is secured from the Des Moines and Central Iowa Inter-Urban Line with a 25 cycle. Each Homesteader has a contract with the electric company. The minimum rate is $2 a month.

Costs:

The average cost per Homestead is about $3,500, exclusive of the administrative overhead, which runs approximately, according to public reports, to $500 per house.

The period of payment will be according to present indications thirty years. The rate of interest 3 per cent, making the average monthly payment $14.75.

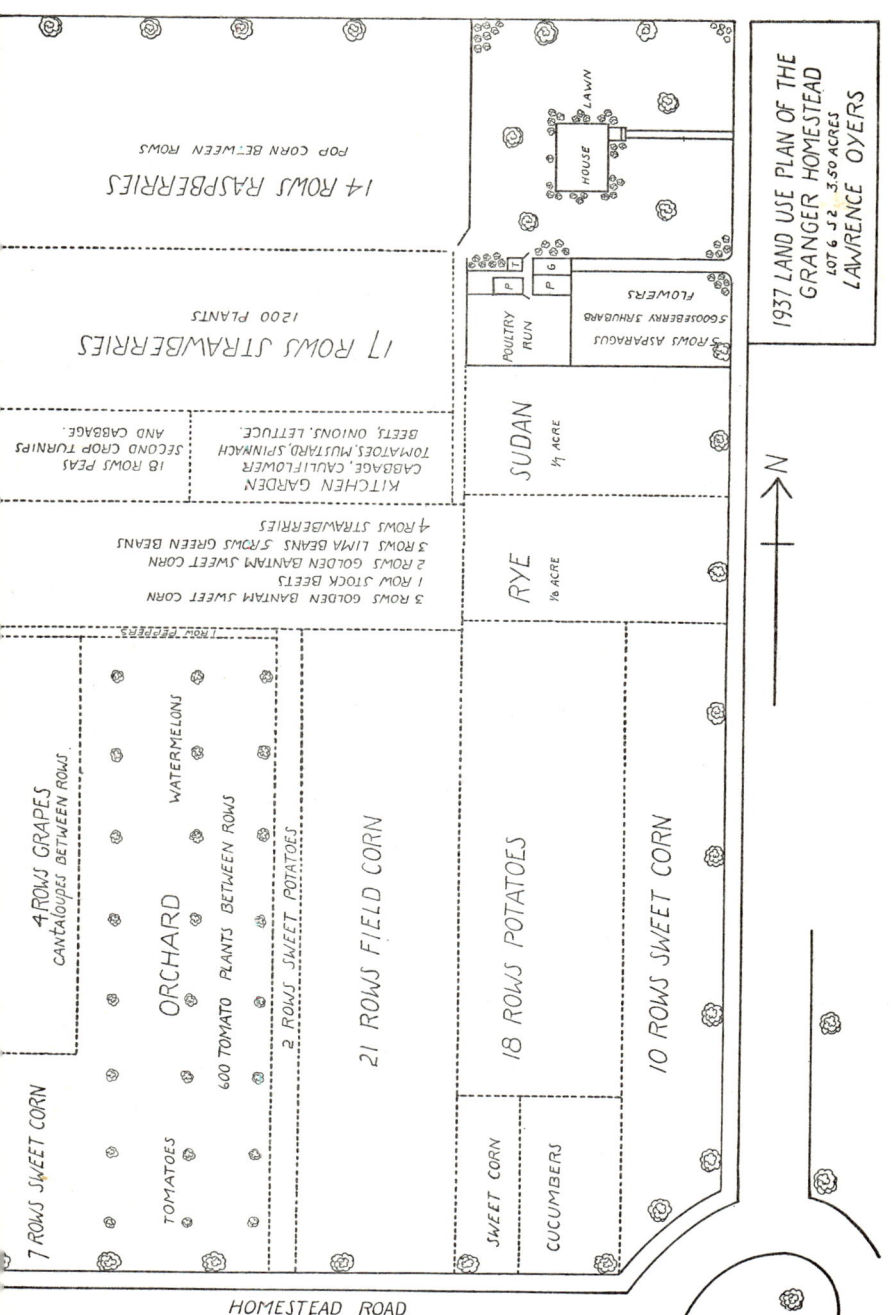

Taxes:

While the government holds title to the land and houses, no taxes are paid to local taxing bodies, but as soon as the titles will be transferred to the individual Homesteader, taxes will be paid.

Occupation of the Homesteaders:

Miners, 40; Store Clerks, 3; Railroad Men, 2; Carpenter, 1; Mechanic, 1; Barber, 1; Farmer, 1; Manager, 1.

Nationality of Homesteaders:

Italian, 18; Croatian, 11; other nationalities, 21.

Religion of Homesteaders:

Catholics, 33; Non-Catholics, 17.

This division of occupations, nationalities, and religion represents a cross section of the surrounding territory, especially in the mining camps.

The families were selected after application had been made and investigation conducted by the government officials.

Work and Income of Miners:

Average working days per year by miners in this vicinity approximately 150 days; leaving 150 days free and most of them in the summer months.

Wages:

The range of wages or cash income from industrial occupation range from $600 to $1,200 a year, average $800.

Subsistence:

A small acreage is only intended to furnish an additional means of employment of leisure days and additional side income. But it is not intended that the full family income be derived from the produce of the small acreage.

6. NOVA SCOTIA "ROCHDALE" COOPERATIVES
(St. Francis Xavier University Extension Program)

Origin

In 1928 St. Francis Xavier University decided to open an Extension Department for the promotion of adult education in Eastern

Nova Scotia. Dr. Coady, Professor of Education, was appointed head of the Department. He first made a survey of adult education in the United States. On his return in 1929 he was asked by the Dominion Department of Fisheries to organize the fishermen of Eastern Canada. The offer was accepted because it was in line with the program that had been tentatively drawn up for the Extension Department. In February, 1930, A. B. MacDonald, B.S.A., who was then Inspector of Schools, and who had wide training in the agricultural field, was added to the staff, after he made a study of University Extension work in Canadian Universities.

The actual work of the Department was started among the farmers and fishermen of Eastern Nova Scotia. In 1933 the Department began working in the coal and steel towns of Cape Breton. In that year a branch office was opened in Glace Bay, the center of the coal-mining area, and Mr. Alex S. MacIntyre, a former labor leader, was placed in charge. In 1934 two women were added to the staff to carry on adult education and promote handicrafts, etc., among the women. At the present time the staff consists of eight full-time members, not including the stenographers, and seven part-time field organizers. Besides these, the regular staff of the university, particularly the members of the education and social sciences, and scientific departments, assist from time to time. Local leaders, particularly the clergymen of all denominations, teachers, and the staffs of the various government agencies, assist very materially in the work of the Department.

Method

The promoters of this program emphasize particularly the diffusion of knowledge among the common people. The method of getting this knowledge to them had to be inexpensive and capable of being extended over a wide area. The technique decided on was the small study club with voluntary leaders who would act as contact people for the Department.

These study clubs usually meet once or twice a week during the fall and winter. Once a month the clubs of a given area meet to report progress and to discuss the larger issues arising in the small study groups. In addition regional conferences are held from time to time, and a large conference — the Rural and Industrial Conference — has developed, to which come leaders from all the local organizations.

After a brief experience it became apparent that it was necessary to train leaders for study groups. Accordingly the University has held for the past five years a four-week short course to which men and women are coming in ever-increasing numbers from all parts of the Maritime Provinces and a few more distant places.

In 1938 the Government of Prince Edward Island financed forty students for the course, and the Federal Department of Fisheries, Ottawa, 30 students from the fishing villages of Northern New Brunswick.

The Extension Department provides the groups with material for study. It publishes a bimonthly Bulletin which serves the double purpose of arousing the people to action and carrying organized material for continuous study of specific social problems. The Department also provides the groups with pamphlets, mimeographed material, small traveling libraries, and maintains a small open-shelf library. A grant from the Carnegie Corporation has enabled the Department to establish a library in the office of the Extension Department of Glace Bay. The Extension Department has also promoted the establishment of small regional libraries in other centers. The demand for these libraries is daily increasing.

Progress

It was believed from the beginning that study and thinking should issue in social action and economic betterment. This led the Department to promote cooperative enterprises in various fields of economic activity. During the past seven years 42 cooperative stores, 140 credit unions, or cooperative banking institutions, and 17 lobster canning factories, 10 fish processing plants, a great variety of marketing organizations, local cooperative industries and a large number of buying clubs have come into existence. The total volume of business done by these organizations runs into millions. The phenomenal success of these institutions has not only served as a stimulus to the people who own and operate them, but has made such an appeal to the country at large that the two neighboring provinces, New Brunswick and Prince Edward Island, and Newfoundland have passed laws enabling their people to carry on similar work in these provinces.

In 1934 the Commission of Government, Newfoundland, requested the University to send a man to carry out this program there. At present, five men who grew up in the St. Francis Xavier Movement are working in that colony. The Department has also been asked by the Dominion Government to direct the adult-education movement among the fishermen of New Brunswick and the Magdalen Islands.

During the past year 1,500 study clubs were active in Nova Scotia, 500 in New Brunswick, 390 in Prince Edward Island, and many others in Newfoundland. A conservative estimate would place the number of people in these clubs at 25,000.

A still greater number are indirectly connected with the movement through the financial institutions promoted by it. In Nova Scotia there are 25,000 people connected with the credit-union movement alone. The total assets are $650,000 and loans made up to date total one and three-quarter million dollars.

Indeed the movement has attracted the attention of people in many distant places. During the past summer, 200 people from 30 states of the Union and many others from practically every Province of Canada attended a three-day Institute held especially for them. These people afterwards made a five-day tour of Eastern Nova Scotia to see for themselves the practical achievements of the movement.

In other directions the movement has had favorable repercussions. Owing to the demand of the study clubs in Cape Breton, the Government of Nova Scotia passed a bill last winter enabling the county of Cape Breton to tax themselves for the establishment of a regional library. The Government has engaged a library specialist to make a survey of the library situation in the Province.

Among other intangible results of the movement may be mentioned the new hope, sense of responsibility and initiative it has inspired in the people. They have been aroused to take more interest in health, recreation, cooperative housing and other fields. It has brought forth labor leaders who exert a stimulating influence in the labor field and who counteract the ultraradical movements prevalent in this part of Canada. Since the 1,000,000 people of the Maritime Province have the same social and economic problems it is hoped that in a short time all the people of the Provinces will be mobilized for study and desirable social action.

The success of the past few years proves conclusively that the cooperative economic institutions promoted by the Department — credit unions, cooperative stores, lobster canneries, marketing organizations, producer cooperatives — can be established in every part of the Maritimes within a very few years. Through these institutions the people can work out for themselves a measure of immediate economic liberation, but they will also get through this work a new sense of responsibility and a stimulus for greater intellectual activity. Above all, through this movement the people of maritime Canada are forging instruments which in one decade, if the work goes forward with vigor, can again make them masters of their own economic destiny. They can again establish industries in the Maritime provinces which no interest can buy or bankrupt. When the people get a clear vision of the blueprint that is involved in this whole movement they will have a new pride in their own ability and a sense of realism that will have repercussions in the political and other spheres. This is a plan for tomorrow that works today, one which will give our people a chance to rise to their full civic stature.

High Praise from Vatican
A Letter of Pius XI to Most Rev. James Morrison, D.D., Bishop of Antigonish

The encyclical letters *Rerum Novarum* of the late Pope Leo XIII and the *Quadragesimo Anno* of the late Pope Pius XI are universally recognized as the most important pronouncements of modern times on the condition of labor and the need of social justice in human affairs. In his earnest and paternal solicitude for the social and economic welfare of humanity, Pope Pius XI gave a leadership that brought new courage to the struggling masses, while his continued warnings against the neopagan concept of life brought about an awakening to the necessity of Catholic social action and for the preservation of Christian civilizations. In this connection it is gratifying to note that Pius XI followed with deep and sympathetic interest the work that is being accomplished by

Nova Scotia "Rochdale" Cooperatives

St. Francis Xavier University of Antigonish. The following letter deserves to be widely known.

The Vatican,
March 8, 1938

Secretary of State
Of His Holiness

To His Excellency
The Most Rev. James Morrison,
Lord Bishop of Antigonish
Chancellor, St. Francis Xavier University.

My Lord Bishop:

The world today, which is hostile beyond measure to right living, brings many causes of grief to the Holy Father. Of late, however, something that is taking place in your country has come to his knowledge which has brought him great joy and which is an earnest of better things for the time to come.

I speak of your effort in the social sphere, which far and wide, is known by common designation as the Antigonish Movement. And since this redounds to the great glory of yourself and the teachers of St. Francis Xavier University, the Holy Father gladly adds, to the general expression of admiration and congratulation, his own tribute of praise.

Some there are who strive to escape from or overcome the serious crisis which the human race faces today without regard for, and even in contempt of, the Gospel. Reason, trained in the close investigation of events and results, can with certainty foretell whither those very unwise men are heading. For if the things that are eternal are cast aside in order that the things of this world may be secured, both, by a just retribution, are lost. The moral law controls and makes for the happiness and advancement of men. If God who watches over it is denied the rightful measure of religious observance, the law is shorn of its authority, and the minds of men are tossed hither and thither in a maelstrom of mad passion and slavery.

The teachers of your University follow a different plan. They are moved by such pity for men of slender means who toil to draw their daily bread from land and sea. They strive to help them better their lot in such a way that the full teaching of the encyclicals *Rerum Novarum* and *Quadragesimo Anno* may be put in practice. To this end, moved by brotherly love, they united, labor with the light of learning, the weight of counsel, efficiency in work, and wise leadership to bring due improvement to the lowly condition of the workers, as well in the civic and economic as in the religious sphere.

Not light is the task, indeed, but great the glory, the more especially because under favorable auspices many may be led to emulate your example.

May the work undertaken grow and flourish and, with unswerving purpose of mind and will, be carried on to complete fulfillment.

That you may the more carefully and earnestly proceed always with your undertaking, His Holiness considers it of the utmost importance that you constantly keep in mind the practical teachings of Christianity, whence the conduct of public life should draw its inspiration.

Foremost among these is this, that God, the Creator and Lord of all things, lets individuals possess property only on the condition that it serve to supply the needs of a decent and honorable life, and that, moreover, it redound to the common welfare. Wherefore, he lives a poor sort of life who lives for himself alone, and who, puffed up with his ill-gotten riches, scorns the poverty of his fellow men. Therefore, "He who has talent, let him take good care not to deny the benefit of it to others; he who has abundance, let him see to it that he does not become insensitive to the claims of mercy; he who has the knowledge and ability to do things as they should be done, let him particularly see to it that he share the use and benefit thereof with his neighbor."

Now, seeing that all good things are not regarded as of the same value, their inequality absolutely demands that those things that are of the least worth — and riches belongs to this class — should be subservient to the higher things, that is to say, to good health, the refining influence of the liberal arts, justice, beneficence, the adornments of virtue, knowledge, heavenly grace and glory.

If the correlation of things in the social order is thrown into confusion, if what is lowest in the scale is set highest, and, on the other hand, what is deserving of most honor is contemned, then there results a revolting accumulation of evils. And above all, this is to be kept in mind that social life has a sacredness all its own when imbued with the spirit of the Gospel and based on justice and charity. How praiseworthy, how beautiful it is that men endowed with strength of body and mind should dedicate themselves and their all to the betterment of the Christian people who, taken together, constitute a "royal priesthood" and possess a dignity that is surpassing.

Having given those exhortations, the Holy Father, with eyes uplifted to heaven, earnestly begs God to prosper your undertakings always. Moved with paternal solicitude, he bestows his Apostolic Benediction on the worthy Bishop of Antigonish, on the teachers of the University, and on the beloved workers for whom you are so profoundly concerned. Unto all of you he prays everlasting happiness and that real well-being, which in this life itself, is promised to the followers of the Gospel.

It has been a great pleasure for me to communicate this to you. With all respect, I express the wish that you may be always in perfect health, and beg leave to subscribe myself,

Yours most devotedly,
E. CARDINAL PACELLI

7. FARM TENANCY REPORT MADE TO THE PRESIDENT[1]

Part II — Recommendations for Action

The Committee's recommendations for Federal action include measures to facilitate farm-home ownership and to help existing owners keep their farms, measures for the rehabilitation of groups not now prepared to take over their own farms, certain suggestions for improving the condition of laborers, a program for aiding families stranded on submarginal land and taking such land out of cultivation, and proposals for the discouragement of speculation in farm lands. . . . The committee offers recommendations on facilitating farm-home ownership, but at the same time it is well aware of the limitations of this approach in solving the whole farm-tenancy problem. The value of the land and buildings now operated by tenants is about $11,000,000,000. The number of tenants has lately been increasing at the rate of 40,000 per year. To concentrate on facilitating ownership to the exclusion of other approaches would hardly be practical, at least until we can be reasonably sure that a good farmer on a good farm has a fair chance of holding onto his farm. In other words, while we need to create new opportunities for ownership, we need even more to create conditions which will make continued ownership possible. . . .

Land for Tenants

The Committee recommends a program of land purchase by the Federal Government and disposition of the land under long-term contracts of sale to operating farmers. It is recommended that the Secretary of Agriculture, through the proposed Farm Security Corporation, be authorized to acquire suitable farm land, subdivide or otherwise create from it the various types of holdings hereafter recommended, and provide for requisite improvements.

Contracts of sale should not be undertaken until after a trial lease period not to exceed 5 years. The trial period should be terminable as soon as the farmer demonstrates his integrity, industry,

---
[1] Report of the President's Committee: Prepared under the auspices of The National Resources Committee, February, 1937.

and capacity as a potential owner. At the termination of the trial period the Corporation should enter into a contract of sale under which the purchaser may pay up all the principal and obtain a deed any time after 20 years. At the minimum rate of repayment, a deed would be obtained at the end of 40 years.

Types of Holdings to Be Created

In general, the aim should be establishment of family-size farms. Families vary greatly, however, in their capacity for independent management. Farm sizes should be adjusted to these differences.

Certain economic disadvantages of the family-size farm can be, and should be, overcome through cooperative ownership of the more expensive types of farm machinery and breeding stock, and through cooperative buying, processing, and marketing. In some cases it may be found desirable for small holders to be cooperatively associated for the employment of technical supervision. The Farm Security Administration should be authorized to aid the formation of local cooperatives, either by technical assistance or by loans.

In some cases cooperative groups may well be aided to acquire land by purchase or long lease for subleasing to group members. The cooperative organization would serve the function of a non-profit-seeking landlord, working in the interest of its membership. Such an arrangement would relieve Federal agencies of much responsibility for management. It is recommended that such a policy be initiated also on an experimental scale.

While the majority of farms should be developed for full-time farming, a considerable number of small units for part-time farming should be created as subsistence homes for farm laborers and other rural workers who have outside employment.

Except where farms have to be subdivided or reclaimed, construction should be confined to repair and renovation, and carried out with due regard for the potential income of the family. . . .

Measures to Help Present Owners Avoid Losing Their Farms

Policies to convert tenants into landowners may prove futile if existing farm owners are permitted to lose their farms and become tenants or even migratory laborers. In recent years the Farm Credit Administration has been lenient in its policy of foreclosure and, through its refunding programs, has been of great assistance to farm owners. The debt conciliation policy of the Resettlement Administration has helped thousands of farmers, particularly those whose farms are mortgaged to private agencies. . . .

In the South a large proportion of farm families must go into debt for the means of sustenance, as well as for fertilizers and other requirements while making a crop. For these advances they rely on loans from merchants or landlords, for which they pay a combination of interest and "time" prices frequently equivalent to 30 per cent or more on the face of the loan. This system has perpetuated itself in part because the insistence of lenders on the production of cash crops has prevented the farmer from raising his food; and in part because the experience of the farmer himself and the nature of his equipment limit him largely to cash-crop production.

To this class of farmers we recommend that the proposed Farm Security Administration offer a system of rehabilitation loans associated with technical guidance. . . .

Program for Farm Laborers

The great majority of farm laborers, as we have noted, are only intermittently employed; their incomes are extremely low and uncertain; their places of residence continually changing; and their contacts with schools, churches, and other elements of community life variable and uncertain. Relatively little economic and social data concerning them have been collected, and in the short time available the Committee has not been able to secure the information necessary to an adequate consideration of farm-labor problems. A far greater degree of national attention should be focused on them.

Especially serious farm-labor problems are encountered in those areas where gangs of migratory laborers, a large proportion of whom migrate as families, are required for the arduous work of cultivating and harvesting such crops as sugar beets, berries, and market vegetables. These migrants should at least be provided with decent places to live during their short stays, and preferably should be supplied with more permanent habitations during the periods when they are not working in fields or orchards. . . .

Gradually, it is hoped, the new farm-purchase policy and the rehabilitation policy outlined previously will serve to re-establish many migrant families on the land as tenants or small owner-operators, and prevent others from becoming migrants. Such permanent attachment to the soil is desirable, particularly for many of those laborers whose employment is largely within a given community and does not require long-distance migration; even those laborers who cover long distances would be better off if definitely attached to the soil. Provision of small subsistence farms is recommended on either an ownership or a leasehold basis for some members of both classes of farm laborers. Such homesteads would materially increase the sense of security and stability of these families. . . .

Program for Farm Lands Submarginal for Present Uses

It has been noted that included among the classes of disadvantaged farmers are some 500,000 families living on land too poor to provide an adequate livelihood. They occupy holdings estimated in the aggregate at 95,000,000 to 100,000,000 acres. Their land is subject further deterioration under existing methods of utilization and their lot is continually growing worse.

The operators of this submarginal land are both owners and tenants. It has already been recommended that both be eligible for the farm-purchase program and the rehabilitation loans. It would require many years to aid all of these families in moving to good land or to other locations affording better opportunities. But in a large proportion of cases such an undertaking is a necessary objective. Merely to assume that the problem will ultimately cure itself when these families leave, unable longer to endure their deprivations, is a shortsighted and ultimately a costly attitude. When some families leave, others take their place — and the problem continues. The long-run costs of such a policy include lowered vitality, ignorance, and crime engendered by excessively low living standards among a class of our population characterized by high birth rates. In fact, in many such areas direct social costs for relief and various other subsidies amount in a comparatively short time to the entire price of the land.

Where such families are farm owners, removal to more favorable locations can be accomplished only by disposition of their present holdings. Everywhere there are tenants of owners willing to abandon their present holdings, some socially desirable uses need to be arranged for the land they leave behind. The land program of the present administration, under which some 9,300,000 acres of substandard farm land are being purchased and developed as forest, recreational areas, and wild-life refuges, is affording temporary relief employment with continued residence. In the Great Plains region low-standard arable farms have been converted into units sufficiently large to make possible a grazing economy or grazing combined with crops.

This program is an essential part of an adequate policy of land reform; continuance is therefore recommended on a scale which will retire from 2,000,000 to 5,000,000 acres a year at an average price of slightly more than $4 an acre. . . .

Discouragement of Land Speculation and Ownership By Nonfarmers

It has been pointed out that speculation has been one of the most potent forces retarding the ownership of land by farmers. The capital value of land tends to outrun upward trends in farm income. At times this condition has been aggravated by purchase of land by nonfarmers primarily for speculative purposes. Measures to avoid excessive overcapitalization and associated abnormal indebtedness resulting from widespread speculation are a necessary part of any fundamental attack on the evils of farm-land tenure.

The position of the Nation in this regard is in some respects safer than it was in 1918–20, for instance, by reason of the greater ability of the Federal Government to exert a restraining influence through the Farm Credit Administration and the Federal Reserve System. These agencies are well aware of the dangers, and are in a strong position to insist that appraisals and loan policies be kept well below advances in price levels and current farm incomes until the degree of permanence in such advances can be determined. In the light of past lessons it is probable that other important agencies lending on the security of farm land will also lean in the direction of greater caution. The influence of such agencies should be strengthened by an educational program among farmers as to the dangers of an unduly rapid increase of farm-land values.

Encouragement of extra payments on principal by farm purchasers in good years (similar to what was recommended previously for farms sold by the Federal Government), by leveling off the net income received by farm owners, would reduce fluctuations in land values caused by demand on their part for land.

As a further means of controlling speculation, it is recommended that the Federal Government at an early date insert a provision in the Federal income-tax law imposing a specific tax on capital gains from sales of land made within 3 years from the date of purchase. Due allowance should be made for improvements, including soil enrichment, beautification, reforestation, or other enhancement of value brought about by the owner. A capital-gains tax, taking a large percentage of the unearned net increment, would materially discourage buying land merely for the purpose of early resale, and would tend to keep land values on a level where farmers could better afford ownership. Special safeguards should prevent evasion through fictitious forms of ownership, and also prevent the tax working severe hardships in cases of unavoidable resale.

In order to discourage speculation and absentee ownership, it is also recommended that the Federal Farm Loan Act and the Emergency Farm Mortgage Act be amended so as to limit loans for the purchase of land to persons who are at the time, or shortly to become, personally engaged in the operation of the farm to be mortgaged.

Improvement of Lease Contracts and Landlord-Tenant Relationships

Although the Federal Government can do much to improve conditions of tenant farmers, some of the most fruitful fields of endeavor are under the jurisdiction of State agencies. Much can be done to better the terms and conditions of leasing. Through regulation and education tenant-operators can be given greater security of tenure and opportunity to develop and improve their farms and participate in community activities.

It is recommended, therefore, that the several states give consideration to legislation which might well include provisions such as the following: (*a*) Agricultural leases shall be written; (*b*) all improvements made by the tenant and capable of removal shall be removable by him at the termination of the lease; (*c*) the landlord shall compensate the tenant for specified unexhausted improvements which he does not remove at the time of quitting the holding, provided that for certain types of improvements the prior consent of the landlord be obtained; (*d*) the tenant shall compensate the landlord for any deterioration or damage due to factors over which the tenant has control, and the landlord shall be empowered to prevent continuance of serious wastage; (*e*) adequate records shall be kept of outlays for which either party will claim compensation; (*f*) agricultural leases shall be terminable by either party only after due notice given at least 6 months in advance; (*g*) after the first year payment shall be made for inconvenience or loss sustained by the other party by reason of termination of the lease without due cause; (*h*) the landlord's lien shall be limited during emergencies such as a serious crop failure or sudden fall of prices where rental payments are not based upon a sliding scale; (*i*) renting a farm on which the dwelling does not meet certain minimum housing and sanitary standards shall be a misdemeanor, though such requirements should be extremely moderate and limited to things primarily connected with health and sanitation, such as sanitary outside toilets, screens, tight roofs, and other reasonable stipulations; (*j*) landlord and tenant differences shall be settled by local boards of arbitration, composed of reasonable representatives of both landlords and tenants, whose decisions shall be subject to court review when considerable sums of money or problems of legal interpretation are involved.

Leasing provisions are strongly governed by custom and frequently fail to become adjusted to changing systems of farming and farm practices. It is, therefore, recommended that State agencies, particularly the agricultural extension service, cooperating with State and local representatives of the Farm Security Administration, inaugurate vigorous programs to inform landlords and tenants concerning methods of improving farm leases; and that State agricultural experiment stations adequately support research work to adapt leases to various type-of-farming areas. Research is also needed on the technical application of compensation clauses. For all of these purposes more funds are required; both State and Federal Governments should make early and liberal appropriations restricted specifically to work on improving tenant contracts. . . .

Differential Taxation of Farm Lands

One of the methods suggested for stimulating an increase in the number of family-size owner-operated farms is differential taxation favorable to such types of farms and farm ownership. Local studies have shown that, in addition to the objective mentioned, such a policy may be justified by the fact that in some tax jurisdictions there is a tendency to assess family-size farms at a higher rate than larger properties. Preferential tax treatment could be effected only after classification of property. In a good many states classification could be accomplished only by constitutional amendment.

During the past few years there has been agitation in various parts of the United States for a policy of complete or partial tax exemption of small homesteads. At least 7 states have already adopted the principle, and bills or resolutions on the subject were introduced in at least 30 states during the 1935 sessions of state legislatures. The policy of differential taxation of farm lands has been employed for many years in Australian Commonwealths.

The merits and demerits of such policies depend so largely on the particular provisions of the legislation and the special circumstances of the individual state that the Committee does not care to make a recommendation. Differential taxation in favor of small farm properties owned by their operators is an indirect method of attacking problems of tenancy and insufficient as a substitute for more direct measures.

Since uniform adoption by all the states at an early date is improbable, it cannot be urged as a nation-wide means of solving the problem of farm tenancy; but, in particular states, if associated with more positive measures of land reform, the steady pressure of differential taxation might exert an influence in favor of family-size farms operated by owners.

Safeguards of Civil Liberties

Within the past few years tenants, croppers, and farm laborers have organized to increase their bargaining power. Members of these organizations assert that they have been frequently denied the rights of peaceful assembly guaranteed them under the Constitution. They assert further that they have been subjected to physical violence and that some have been forced to flee for their lives.

We have not had opportunity to investigate these charges at first hand. But frequent press reports of violence in some areas where croppers or migratory laborers make up a considerable portion of the rural population indicate that such allegations cannot be ignored. A Federal commission, appointed to investigate conditions among migratory laborers in the Imperial Valley, found substantiating evidence of such practices.

The Committee strongly recommends that states guarantee to these groups and enforce the rights of peaceful assembly and of organization to achieve their legitimate objectives.

It also recommends repeal of State laws which make it a misdemeanor to quit a contract while in debt, since such laws abridge civil liberties of tenants and tend to nullify Federal antipeonage acts.

In making these recommendations, however, the Committee is not unaware that in many cases landlords and employers, as well as farm tenants, croppers, and laborers, have grievances. Among disadvantaged groups there are not a few individuals who have neither a responsible attitude in the fulfillment of their obligations nor any property that can be attached for nonfulfillment. For the protection of all interests, it is recommended that the committees of arbitration suggested be called upon to settle disputes and promote better relationships. . . .

Need for Education and Health Services

Ignorance, no less than poverty and instability, forces many tenant and other disadvantaged families into an inferior relationship to the community. Ignorance, as well as insecurity, is often responsible for failure to adopt enlightened methods of farm operation, particularly of self-help to improve the family's mode of life.

Education can go far toward enabling these poorer farm groups to apply family labor intelligently in improving home, school, and community by repairing, cleaning, and decorating rooms and buildings; repairing and making furniture and equipment; planting public grounds and home dooryards; properly selecting, preparing, and serving home-produced food.

It is strongly recommended that the rural educational systems of the various states be more definitely aimed at providing the kind of training needed by adult members of disadvantaged farm families as well as children. At the same time, the needs of the children should not be neglected. The elementary rural schools in many areas are such as to offer little opportunity to children of low-income families. Tax bases are inadequate; school terms are short; attendance legislation is not well enforced; teachers are poorly trained and even more poorly paid; too often methods of instruction are routine and ill calculated to equip the children to improve their environment.

This Committee prefers to leave to educational specialists the question as to the proper contribution of the Federal Government to a better equalization of educational advantages. A number of considerations appear to justify substantial Federal aid. The classes of farm families now below the margin of security are a principal source of the Nation's population, by reason of the high birth rates prevailing among them. The congregation in given areas of large numbers of such families frequently results in a collective poverty that is a primary obstacle to the provision, from local resources alone, of adequate educational advantages.

It has been noted that large numbers of farm families are severely handicapped by debilitating diseases, malnutrition, and general morbidity. Much so-called laziness and shiftlessness trace back to a low level of vitality and the resulting mental habits and attitudes. No fundamental attack on the problem of the disadvantaged classes of farmers would be complete without inclusion of measures to improve their general level of health. To a large extent this is a matter of education in improved dietary practices and personal hygiene, supplemented by more adequate medical service and more ample provision of clinics and public-health nursing. The grouping of counties into public-health districts appears to be a promising way of improving such services. It is urged that adequate funds be made available under the Social Security Act to take care of the health needs of rural communities, especially in areas of excessive tenancy.

Necessity for Action

Sturdy rural institutions beget self-reliance and independence of judgment. Sickly rural institutions beget dependency and incapacity to bear the responsibilities of citizenship. Over wide areas the vitality of American rural life is daily being sapped by systems of land tenure that waste human and natural resources alike. Security of tenure is essential to the development of better farm homes and better rural communities.

Vigorous and sustained action is required for restoring the impaired resources on whose conservation continuance of the democratic process in this country to no small extent depends.

The final emphasis of this report is consequently on the necessity for action; action to enable increasing numbers of farm families to enter into sound relationships with the land they till and the communities in which they live.

8. EXTRACTS FROM FARM TENANCY COMMITTEE REPORT — IOWA[1]
Part I — Present State of Affairs

... The welfare of the population in Iowa, as well as of the country as a whole, is closely connected with the welfare of the farmer. There is not a business, trade or profession in Iowa which does not suffer if the farmer suffers, or prosper if the farmer

---

[1] This report was drawn up for the Iowa State Planning Board. The chairman of the Committee was Mr. F. K. Hawley. Its value for the general reader consists in the fact that similar land tenure problems exist in every state.

prospers. In 1929 the total income from Iowa agriculture was estimated at 451 million dollars, as compared to only 194 million dollars derived from manufacturing, and 37 million dollars from banking, finance, and insurance. (*Iowa Studies in Business,* No. XIV, p. 20, State University of Iowa. The respective figures for 1934 are $298 million from agriculture, $123 million from manufacturing, and $24 million from banking, finance, and insurance.) If Iowa agriculture had obtained a share in the total Iowa income corresponding to its proportion of the Iowa population, the income from Iowa agriculture would have been around 650 million dollars. It is obvious that any sound and effective program designed to improve agricultural conditions in Iowa will ultimately benefit Iowa businessmen, laborers, and professionals as well. Every citizen in Iowa should be vitally interested in the prosperity of Iowa agriculture. It is, therefore, the interest of the entire citizenry of Iowa which this committee has at heart in submitting this report to the State Planning Board, the Governor, and the General Assembly of the State.

Nation-Wide Interest in the Farm Tenure Problem

Farm tenure problems have been discussed in recent years throughout the country. The growing interest in this question is reflected in the nation-wide attention given to the President's Committee on Farm Tenancy during the winter of 1936-37, in the tenant farm purchase and the rural rehabilitation program authorized by the Bankhead-Jones Farm Tenant Act passed by Congress in the summer of 1937, in the Landlord-Tenant Act passed by the Oklahoma legislature in 1937, and in the appointment of state committees on farm tenancy by the governors of two of the states, Arkansas and Iowa. These developments indicate that people feel an urgent need for improving certain farm tenure conditions through some form of legislative action. The serious land problems that are now confronting this country were experienced in older countries many decades ago, and many of these problems have been successfully met by legislative action and enlightened public opinion.

This committee is fully aware that not all tenure problems can be solved by legislation. Mutual cooperation, education, and the development of a sense of responsibility on the part of both landlord and tenant are essential. What legislation can do, however, is to provide a framework of certain minimum standards in tenure relationships which will facilitate a clearer understanding of the rights and responsibilities of the parties concerned, and will prevent certain practices distinctly detrimental to land and community. It is the duty of the people of Iowa to accomplish the development of such standards.

Seriousness of the Tenure Problem in Iowa

The proportion of farms operated by tenants has shown a steady increase, from only 24 per cent in 1880 to 50 per cent in 1935. A certain proportion of tenancy, possibly between one fourth and one third, is not undesirable as tenancy as a rung in the agricultural ladder toward ownership can fulfill an important function. If tenancy, however, approaches or even exceeds one half of all farms, serious problems arise. There was only one Iowa county in 1900 where half the farms were rented; in 1935, 57 counties had half or more of their farms operated by tenants. Considering the land area farmed under lease, the state average for 1937 was 58 per cent of all land in farms, varying between counties from 73 per cent in Emmet County to 34 per cent in Dubuque County. According to the "Summary of Findings" from the county hearings, a large number of people expect a continuing increase in tenancy unless effective action is taken to prevent it. It is estimated that between 4,000 and 7,000 owners are operating under the moratorium law which was enacted in 1933, brought about by overwhelming pressure of public opinion. Without the moratorium, many more farmers would have changed from owner-operators to tenants.

With respect to the total value of all farm real estate in Iowa in 1935, the equity of the farm operators was only 25 per cent. In other words, 75 per cent of the value of all farms belonged to landlords or mortgage holders. In Iowa the trend has been from a state of independent farm-home owners to a state of tenants and overburdened debtors.

In addition to the increase in tenancy and the drain on the farmer's equity in the land, the great insecurity of the renter's tenure adversely affects farm income, soil fertility, and community welfare. On January 1, 1935, the census revealed that 34 per cent or over one third of all tenants had been on their farms for less than 2 years when the census was taken. Such unstable conditions necessarily lead to severe soil exploitation, to neglect of farm improvements, to tremendous losses involved in frequent moving, and to reduced farm incomes of both tenant and landlord. In addition, rural institutions, particularly schools, churches, farm and cooperative organizations, and other social activities are suffering severely from unstable tenure conditions.

Causes of Tenancy

During all the public hearings held in every county of the state, the lack of adequate income from the operation of the farm has been held to be the first and most important cause of increasing tenancy and decreasing ownership among farm operators. Whether appearing as "Cost of Production," "Parity Prices" or "World's Market Plus Tariff," it was pretty generally agreed that, unless and until farm prices can be stabilized at a reasonable level, farm tenancy will continue to increase regardless of how low interest rates may be, or how easy it may be made to contract for the purchase of a farm. No tenure system can withstand the onslaught of extreme price fluctuations and the paralyzing effect of chronic price disparities between the things farmers sell and those they buy, a disadvantage under which agriculture has been laboring during many decades.

The following table should convince any fair-minded man of the truth of the foregoing:

	1900	1920	1930	1933	1935
Per cent of population on farms	35.0	30.0	24.6	25.3	25.0
Farmers' per cent of national income	20.5	14.9	9.0	7.8	10.5

Next to the chronic disparity of farm income, faults in our credit and taxation systems are blamed as major causes for the increase in tenancy. Eleven per cent of the total farm land in Iowa, or an acreage equivalent to eleven counties, was sold under foreclosures during the period of 1927 to 1934. This does not include the large number of voluntary transfers of deeds under hard financial pressure. The wholesale dispossession of farm families caused by factors entirely beyond their control has meant to most of these families the loss of the savings of a lifetime and the loss of hope for the future, in spite of the fact that the Iowa farmer is and has been a most efficient producer of foods and fibers.

The average tax burden on Iowa farm land increased from 56 cents per acre in 1914 to $1.40 in 1930; in terms of per cent of the land value the increase was from 0.45 per cent to 1 per cent during the same period. After 1930 the real-estate tax decreased to $0.89 per acre in 1934. Land values declined even more, so that the tax amounted to 1.12 per cent of the land value in 1934. In many localities, however, the tax burden upon the land is more than twice as heavy as the state average. This holds particularly true in certain drainage or consolidated school districts, or both, where the tax loads are sometimes almost confiscatory and are creating intolerable tenure conditions.

Besides these shortcomings in the price and taxation systems, many other causes have contributed to the increase in tenancy. Land speculation and investment in land by city people are frequently mentioned. Moreover, our present educational practices tend to stimulate, rather than counteract, the shift in the interests of rural youth from farm to city life. This growth of an urban philosophy of life, often associated with an exaggerated emphasis on money income and material comfort, leads many farmers to live beyond their means or to refuse to make even temporary sacrifices in their living standards for the sake of acquiring ownership of a farm.

Considerable emphasis is placed on the unsatisfactory tenancy system itself hampering the tenant in his ascent to ownership on the "agricultural ladder." It is pointed out that insecurity of tenants and high rents retard the accumulation of savings necessary to acquire equity in a farm.

Part II of the Farm Tenancy Committee is here given in outline. The Committee held that tenure conditions are affected by economic conditions throughout the country in general, and, by the agricultural situation in particular. The tenure problem, therefore, cannot be solved completely within a single state; nor can it be solved overnight. Here it is deemed advisable to indicate the main directions in which various Federal, state, and local policies should move in order to encourage the development of a sound and equitable tenure system in Iowa.

Regarding the Federal Government the policies recommended were: (1) stabilization of prices, (2) more adequate agricultural credit facilities, (3) Federal assistance in promoting farm home ownership; for the state (1) prevention of land speculation and of concentration of land holdings, (2) protection of the owner-operator's equity in years of crop failure and depression, (3) abolition of deficiency judgments, invalidation of waivers, of exemption rights, and limitation of the landlord's lien.

The measures suggested to improve the landlord-tenant relationship: (1) increasing the security of tenure on rented farms, (2) compensation for unexhausted improvements and for damages, (3) arbitration facilities to settle landlord-tenant difficulties.

The following general recommendations were made as deserving of serious consideration and careful study: (1) establishment of a state land commission, (2) revision of taxation system, (3) improvement of farm labor condition, (4) education for rural life appreciation, (5) promotion of better mutual understanding between city and farm people, (6) encouragement of cooperation, (7) enactment of a comprehensive land use and tenure chapter in the Iowa Code.

The specific recommendations were aimed in the first place at encouraging farm-home ownership. They were: (1) tax on capital gains from sales of land, (2) protection of farm operator's tenure in years of crop failure or depression, (3) revision of foreclosure procedure and abolition of deficiency judgments, (4) differential taxation of farm lands, (5) a joint resolution requesting Congress to expand materially the Tenant-Purchase Program of the Bankhead-Jones Farm Tenant Act, and to amend the act so as to prevent land transferred under it from entering the speculative land market by more nearly conforming to the recommendations of the President's Committee on Farm Tenancy.

It was further recommended that the National Government be requested to revise the Agricultural Adjustment Program to protect the interests of the tenant more adequately, to distribute the payments between landlord and tenant more equitably, and to furnish an incentive to better leasing practices.

Further specific recommendations were intended to improve the landlord-tenant relationship. They embraced: (1) Automatic continuation of year-to-year leases and minimum period of notice for termination, (2) compensation for unexhausted improvements, (3) compensation for damage, (4) arbitration provisions, (5) limiting the landlord's lien, (6) promotion of equitable lease forms.

SELECTED BIBLIOGRAPHY

Part I

Abrams, Charles, *Revolution in Land* (New York: Harper and Bros., 1939).
Adams, James T., *The Living Jefferson* (New York: Scribner's Sons, 1936).
Agar, Herbert, *The Land of the Free* (Boston: Houghton Mifflin Co., 1935).
——— *Pursuit of Happiness* (Boston: Houghton Mifflin Co., 1938).
——— *The People's Choice* (Boston: Houghton Mifflin Co., 1937).
——— and Tate, A., *Who Owns America* (Boston: Houghton Mifflin Co., 1936).
Baer, Urban, *Farmers of Tomorrow* (Sparta, Wis.: Monroe Publ. Company, 1939). (An excellent practical book.)
Baker, O. E., Borsodi, Ralph, and Wilson, M. L., *Agriculture in Modern Life* (New York: Harper and Bros., 1939).
Barnes, William C., *Story of the Range* (Washington: Government Printing Office, 1926).
Belloc, Hilaire, *Crisis of Civilization* (Boston: Houghton Mifflin Co., 1937).
——— *The Servile State* (Boston: Le Roy Phillips). (London: Constable Press, 1912.)
Berle, A. A., and Means, G. C., *The Modern Corporation and Private Property* (New York: Macmillan Co., 1933).
Borsodi, Ralph, *Flight from the City* (New York: Harper and Brothers, 1933).
——— *Prosperity and Security* (New York: Harper and Brothers, 1938).
Bowden, *Industrial History of United States* (New York: Adelphi, 1930).
Briefs, Goetz, *The Proletariat* (New York: McGraw-Hill Co., 1937).
Brunner and Lorge, *Rural Trends in Depression Years* (New York: Columbia University Press, 1937).
Campbell, Macy, *Rural Life at the Crossroads* (New York: Ginn, 1927).
Chesterton, G. K., *What I Saw in America* (New York: Dodd, Mead and Company, 1923). Sixth Printing.
Coady, Dr. M. M., *Masters of Their Own Destiny* (New York: Harper and Brothers, 1939). (The story of adult education and cooperatives in Nova Scotia.)
Cram, Ralph Adams, *The End of Democracy* (Boston: Marshall Co., 1937).
Cronin, Michael, *The Science of Ethics* (New York: Benziger Co., 1920).
Dawber, Mark A., *Rebuilding Rural America* (New York: Friendship Co., 1937).

Dempsey, Nell-Breuning, *Reorganization of Social Economy* (Milwaukee: Bruce Publ. Co., 1936).
Drucker, Peter, *The End of Economic Man* (New York: John Day Co., 1939).
English, Michael I., S.J., Wade, William L., S.J., *Rebuilding the Social Order* (St. Louis: John S. Swift Co., 1938).
Faulkner, Harold U., *American Economic History,* 3rd edition (New York: Harper and Brothers, 1935).
George, Henry, *Progress and Poverty* (New York: Doubleday Doran Co., 1937).
Gill, Eric, *Work and Property* (London: J. M. Dent, Ltd., 1937).
Gillette, John Morris, *Rural Sociology* (New York: Macmillan Co., 1936).
Haas, Francis J., *Man and Society* (New York: Century Press, 1930).
―――― *The Wages and Hours of American Labor* (New York: Paulist Press, 1937).
Hearst, James, *Country Men* (Muscatine, Iowa: Prairie Press, 1937).
Husslein, Joseph, S.J., *The Christian Social Manifesto* (Milwaukee: Bruce Publ. Co., 1931).
Jarrett, Bede, O.P., *S. Antonino and Medieval Economics* (St. Louis: Herder Co., 1914).
Jefferson, Thomas, *The Works of Thomas Jefferson,* collected by Paul Leicester Ford (New York: G. P. Putnam's Sons, 1905).
Jerrold, Douglas, *Georgian Adventure* (New York: Scribners, 1938).
Lord, Russell, *Behold Our Land* (Boston: Houghton Mifflin Co., 1938).
Michel, Virgil, O.S.B., *Christian Social Reconstruction* (Milwaukee: Bruce Publ. Co., 1937).
―――― *The Social Question Series* (Collegeville, Minn.: Liturgical Press, 1938).
Mumford, Lewis, *The Culture of the Cities* (New York: Harcourt Brace Co., 1938).
Phelan, G. B., *On the Governance of Rulers,* translation of St. Thomas, *De Regimine Principum* (Toronto, Can.: St. Michael's College, 1935).
Ross, Eva, *Survey of Sociology* (Milwaukee: Bruce Publ. Co., 1932).
Rowntree, Jennie I., Public Affairs Committee, "This Problem of Food," No. 33 (New York: Public Affairs Pamphlet, 1939).
Ryan, Msgr. John A., *A Better Economic Order* (New York: Harper and Brothers Co., 1935).
―――― *Distributive Justice* (New York: Macmillan Co., 1927).
Schmiedeler, Edgar, O.S.B., *A Better Rural Life* (New York: Wagner Press, 1938).
―――― *Introductory Study of the Family* (New York: Century Press, 1930).
―――― *Our Rural Proletariat* (New York: Paulist Press, 1938).
Smith, T. Lynn, *The Sociology of Rural Life* (New York: Harper and Brothers, 1940).
Steinbeck, John, *The Grapes of Wrath* (New York: Viking Press, 1939).

Selected Bibliography

Stewart, Paul W., and Dewhurst, J. Frederic, *Does Distribution Cost Too Much?* (New York: Twentieth Century Fund Inc., 1939).
Sullivan, Joseph, S.J., *Individual and Social Ethics* (Worcester, Mass.: Holy Cross College Press, 1929).
Tawney, R. H., *The Acquisitive Society* (New York: Harcourt Brace Co., 1920).
────── *Religion and the Rise of Capitalism* (New York: Harcourt Brace Co., 1926).
Taylor, *Rural Sociology* (New York: Harper and Brothers Co., 1933).
Thompson, *Population Problems* (New York: McGraw-Hill Co., 1930).
Vance, Rupert B., Public Affairs Committee, *Farmers Without Land*. No. 12 (New York: Public Affairs Pamphlet, 1937).
Waite, Warren C., and Cassady, Ralph, Jr., *The Consumer and The Economic Order* (New York: McGraw-Hill, 1939).
Woods, Ralph L., *America Reborn* (New York: Longmans, Green Co., 1939).

Part I — Journals

Baker, O. E., "Population Trends: The Rural People Survive," *Free America,* August, 1939.
Barr, Stringfellow, "The Art of Liberation," *Free America,* September, 1939.
Borsodi, Ralph, "Democracy, Plutocracy, Bureaucracy," *Free America,* August, 1939.
Bryant, Putney, Editorial Research Reports, *Government Aid to Farm Tenants,* Vol. II, No. 21 (Washington, D. C.: Government Press, December, 1936).
Cummings, Edward, "West Acres," *Christian Social Action,* North End Station, Box 74, Detroit, Mich., October, 1939.
Facts for Farmers, published by the Farm Research, Inc., Room 510, Peoples Life Insurance Building, Washington, D. C.
"Farm Employment, 1909 to 1938," *Monthly Labor Review,* June, 1939, Washington, D. C., p. 1241.
Farm Population and Rural Life Activities, a Review of Current Research, Bureau of Agricultural Economics, Washington, D. C.
Farmers Educational and Cooperative Union of America, *Publications* (varia), Jamestown, N. Dak.
Fogarty, James W., "Housing Projects Favor Birth Control," *America,* A Review of the Week, 53 Park Place, New York City. In which the author, a member of the Department of Welfare, New York City, points out that Federal slum-clearance projects are really "Birth-Control Houses."
Fortune, March, 1932, gives a masterly summary of the land situation, 135 East 42nd Street, New York City.
Gray, L. C., *Tenancy versus Ownership As a Problem in the Utilization of Farm Real Estate Annals,* Government Press, March, 1930.

Selected Bibliography

────── and others, *Farm Ownership and Tenancy*, U. S. Yearbook of Agriculture, Government Press, 1923.
"I Wonder Where We Can Go Now?," *Fortune*, New York, pp. 91–100, April, 1939.
"Is Distribution too Costly?," *Business Week*, New York, p. 25, July 29, 1939 (McGraw-Hill).
Jacobs, Harvey, "The Small Town Comes Back," *Free America*, July, 1939.
La Farge, John, "Minds Make Materialism," *America*, New York, July 29, 1939.
"Let 'Em Drink Grade A," in *Fortune*, November, 1939, New York, p. 83 ff.
Lippmann, Walter, "A Commentary on Liberty," *New York Herald Tribune*, July 15, 1936.
Memorandum on Population Redistribution Within the U. S. (Bul. 42), New York Social Science Research Council, 1938.
Money, Frank, "Do You Want to Buy a Farm?," *Free America*, August, 1939.
O'Neil, Patricia, "Good Things, Made Well," *Free America*, July, 1939.
Orton, Vrest, "Country Industry," *Free America*, August, 1939.
Pfeiffer, Ehrenfried, "Homesteading: Fertile or Futile?," *Free America*, July, 1939.
Taylor, Wheeler, and Kirkpatrick, Social Research Report, *Disadvantaged Classes in American Agriculture*. No. 8, Farm Security Administration and the Bureau of Agricultural Economics cooperating (Washington, D. C.: Government Press, 1938).
Temporary National Economic Committee, 1938–1939, *Investigations of Concentrations of Economic Power* (Washington: Government Printing Office, 1938, 1939).
Turner, H. A., *The Ownership of Tenant Farms in the United States*, Bulletin 1432, Department of Agriculture (Washington, D. C.: Government Press, 1926).
────── Department of Agriculture, *The Ownership of Tenant Farms of the North Central States*, Bulletin 1433 (Washington, D. C.: Government Press, 1926).
Webb, John N., *The Transient Unemployed*, Research Monograph No. 3, Works Progress Administration (Washington, D. C.: Government Press).
────── *The Migratory Casual Worker*, Research Monograph No. 7, Works Progress Administration (Washington, D. C.: Government Press, 1937).
Wilson, Charles Morrow, *America Becomes Animal-Minded* (New York: The Commonweal, July 21, 1939, 386 Fourth Ave.).
Woofter, T. J., *Landlord and Tenant on the Cotton Plantation*. Research Monograph No. 5 (Washington, D. C.: Government Press, 1936).
Works Progress Administration, *Studies of the Effects of Industrial Change*

Selected Bibliography 365

on *Labor Markets,* National Research Project, Works Progress Administration, Philadelphia.

Works Progress Administration, Division of Social Research:
1. *Farming Hazards in the Drought Area.*
2. *Changing Aspects in Rural Relief.*
3. *Rural Families on Relief.*

Part II

Baden-Powell of Gilwell, R.S.S., *Scouting for Boys* (London: WC 2, C. Arthur Pearson Tower House, Southampton St., Strand, 1938).
Belloc, Hilaire, *The Restoration of Property* (New York: Sheed and Ward Co., 1937).
Cather, Willa, *O Pioneers!* (Boston: Houghton Mifflin Co., 1913).
Centerville (New York: Scott, Foresman and Company, 1939). (Book Three in a group of four readers for grade schools. The Social Studies Series of readers.)
Chesterton, G. K., *The Outline of Sanity* (New York: Dodd, Mead & Co., 1927).
Chew, Arthur P., *The Response of Government to Agriculture* (Washington, D. C.: Government Press, 1937).
Cole, William E., and Crowe, Hugh Price, *Recent Trends in Rural Planning* (New York: Prentice-Hall, 1937).
Coogan, Gertrude M., *Money Creators* (Chicago: Sound Money Press, Inc., 120 W. Adams Street, 1935). (Also set of ten lessons and ten charts explaining the book.)
Davenport, Eugene, *The Farm* (New York: Macmillan Co., 1927).
Duggan, Raymond P., *A Federal Resettlement Project,* a monograph on the Granger Homesteads (Catholic University of America, Washington, D. C., 1937).
Fowler, Bertram B., *The Lord Helps Those* (New York: Vanguard, 1938).
Fritts, Frank, and Gwinn, Ralph W., *Fifth Avenue to Farm* (New York: Harper and Brothers, 1938).
Hill, George W., Smith, Ronald A., *Rural Relief Trends in Wisconsin From 1934 to 1937* (University of Wisconsin Press: Madison, Wis.).
Johnson, Charles S., Embree, Edwin R., and Alexander, W. W., *The Collapse of Cotton Tenancy* (The University of North Carolina Press, 1935).
Kains, M. G., *Five Acres* (New York: Greenberg Co., 1935).
Landis, Benson Y., and Haynes, George E., *Cotton Growing Communities.* Vols. I and II (New York: The Federal Council of Churches, 1934, 1935). Vol. I: Case studies of 9 rural communities and 10 plantations in Alabama; Vol. II: Case studies of 10 rural communities and 10 plantations in Arkansas.
Manifesto on Rural Life. National Catholic Rural Life Conference (Milwaukee: The Bruce Publ. Co., 1939).

Marsh, George P., *The Earth as Modified by Human Action* (New York: Scribner, Armstrong Co., 1874).
Mead, Elwood, *Helping Men Own Farms* (New York: Macmillan, 1920).
Nebraska: A Guide to the Cornhusker State, compiled and written by the Federal Writers' Project (New York: The Viking Press, 1939).
Penty, Arthur, *Means and Ends* (London: Faber and Faber Co., 1932).
Soddy, Frederick, *The Role of Money* (New York: Harcourt, Brace and Co., 1934).
——— *Wealth, Virtual Wealth and Debt* (New York: E. P. Dutton and Co., 1933).
Sorokin, Pitirim, and Zimmerman, C. C., *Systematic Source Book in Rural Sociology*, 3 vols. (University of Minnesota Press, 1930, 1931, 1932.)
Stewart, M. S., Public Affairs Committee, "Our Taxes and What They Buy," No. 28, revised (Public Affairs Pamphlets, 1939).
Terpenning, Walter A., *Village and Open Country Neighborhoods.* The Century Social Science Series (New York: Appleton-Century Co., 1931–32).
Thompson, Flora, *Lark Rise* (English Village Life) (New York: Oxford University Press, 1939).
Walker, Charles R., *Homesteaders — New Style* (New York: Survey Graphic, June, 1939).
Wallace, Henry A., *New Frontiers* (New York: Reynal & Hitchcock, 1934).
Whitney, Milton, *The Soil and Civilization* (New York: D. Van Nostrand Co., 1925).
Wilson, M. L., *Democracy Has Roots* (New York: Carrick & Evans, 1939).
Whyte, R. O., and Jacks, G. V., *Vanishing Lands* (New York: Doubleday Doran, 1939).

Part II — Journals

A Guide to the Literature of Rural Life, compiled by Benson Y. Landis, 4th Revised Edition, 1939, American Country Life Association, New York.
Bureau of Agricultural Economics, *Washington, Jefferson and Lincoln and Agriculture* (Washington, D. C.: U. S. Government Printing Office, November, 1937).
Coad, W. J., *Adding Millions to Nebraska Farm Income by the Omar Method* (Omaha: The Greater Nebraskan, July, 1939). Experiments at Omar Wonderland Farm point the way to practical, inexpensive, but scientific farm management.
Constitution and By-laws and various state publications of the Mutual Farmers' Educational and Cooperative Union of America. Nebraska Farmers' Union, Omaha, Nebr.
Consumers' Guide, Publication of the Agricultural Adjustment Administration, Washington, D. C.
Eaton, Jeanette, "Our Backward Farmers," *Forum,* September, 1939.

Selected Bibliography

Farm Management Service, *First Annual Report of Farm Bureau,* University of Illinois Press, 1931.

Hoffman, Paul G., "America Goes to Town," *The Saturday Evening Post,* April 29, 1939, Philadelphia, Pa. An article which gives the facts about city and country roads, the automobile, and the possibilities of modern productive homes on small acreages.

Hynes, Emerson, *The Cornstalk Philosopher* (Notre Dame, Ind.: Ave Maria, July 29, 1939), p. 129.

Journal of Agricultural Research (Washington: Bureau of Agricultural Economics).

National Catholic Rural Life Conference, *Catholic Rural Life Objectives.* (Series of Papers dealing with some of the Economic, Social, and Spiritual Interests of the American Farmer.) St. Paul, Minn.

National Planning and Rural Life (New York: American Country Life Association, 297 Fourth Ave., 1935).

National Resources Committee, *Consumer Incomes in the United States* (Washington, D. C.: U. S. Government Printing Office, 1938).

Report of the American Catholic Sociological Society, First Annual Convention, Dec., 1938, Second Annual Report, Dec., 1939.

Report of Committee on Population Problems to the National Resources Committee, *The Problems of a Changing Population in the United States* (Washington, D. C.: U. S. Government Printing Office, 1938).

Rural Electrification on the March, Rural Electrification Administration, Washington, D. C.

The Catholic Worker (Monthly), New York City, 115 Mott St. This magazine contains a page each month devoted to the Land.

The Future of the Great Plains, Washington: House of Representatives, Document No. 144, 75th Congress, 1st Session, 1937.

The People and the Land (New York: American Country Life Association, 1937).

U. S. Department of Commerce, *Part-Time Farming in the United States* (Washington, D. C.: U. S. Government Printing Office, 1937).

Works Progress Administration, Division of Social Research, *Part Time Farming in the Southeast* (Washington, D. C.: U. S. Government Printing Office, 1937).

Yearbook of Agriculture, 1936, 1937, *Soils and Men,* 1938; *Food and Life,* 1939; *Farmers in a Changing World,* 1940 (Washington, D. C.: U. S. Government Printing Office).

References to "Rural Life Objectives"

1st Series:
 Baker, O. E., *The Church and the Rural Youth.*
 Bishop, Howard, *Agrarianism: The Basis of the New Order.*
 Johnson, Geo., *The Professional Preparation of Teachers for Rural Schools.*

Kenkel, F. P., *The Ethical and Religious Background of Cooperation.*
LaFarge, John, S.J., *The Church and Rural Welfare.*
O'Hara, Most Rev. Edwin V., *A Spiritual and Material Mission to Rural America.*
Williams, Michael, *The Green Revolution.*

2nd Series:
Baker, O. E., *Will More or Fewer People Live on the Land.*
Christensen, Chris. L., *The Place of Youth in Agriculture and Rural Life.*
Crowley, Francis M., *Absentee Landlordism in a New Form.*
Michel, Virgil, O.S.B., *The Cooperative Movement and the Liturgical Movement.*
Miller, R. L., C.SS.R., *The "Quadragesimo Anno" and the Reconstruction of Agriculture.*

3rd Series:
Cram, Ralph Adams, *What Is a Free Man?*
Matt, A. J., *Economic and Social Justice for the Negro.*
Muench, Most Rev. A. J., *The Catholic Church and Rural Welfare.*
Sheen, F. J., *The Challenge to Our Democracy.*
Strittmatter, D., O.S.B., *Vocational Training for Colored Youth.*
Taylor, Carl L., *The Restoration of Rural Culture.*
Treacy, J. P., *Will Youth Be Served?*
Willmann, Dorothy J., *Reading in the Rural Home.*

Coop. Parish Activities Service, *Pamphlets* and Service (Effingham, Ill.).
Rural Life Bureau, N.C.W.C. *Pamphlets* (Washington, D. C.).
St. Francis Xavier University, Pamphlets (Antigonish, Nova Scotia: Canada Extension Bulletin).
School of Living, *Homestead Bulletins* (Suffern, N. Y., 1938–39).
The Catholic Rural Conference, Quarterly Bulletin (St. Paul, Minn.).
The National Forum, *Social Problems Visualized* (Chicago, Ill.).

References to "Catholic Rural Life Bulletin"

May, 1938
Muench, Most Rev. A. J., *Agrarianism in the Christian Social Order.*
Ostdiek, Joseph H., *The Rural School Program.*

August, 1938
Cook, Joseph A., *Quebec Meets Its Rural Problem.*
Michel, Virgil, O.S.B., *Christian Education for Rural Living.*
Ross, Eva J., *The "Middle Way" in Belgium.*
Treacy, John P., *Ruralizing Rural Education.*
Ward, Leo R., C.S.C., *The Land and Human Values.*

November, 1938
Connole, Roger J., *The Rural High School Program.*
Esser, Ignatius, O.S.B., *Significant Chapters in Benedictine History.*

Selected Bibliography

Hynes, Emerson, *The Dignity and Joy of Work*.
Nutting, Willis D., *The College and the Land*.
O'Hara, Most Rev. Edwin V., *The Catholic Rural Problem in America*.
February, 1939 (Vol. 2, No. 1)
  Deverall, Richard, *The Industrial and Rural Proletariate*.
  LaFarge, John, S.J., *Europe Reconquers Rural Life*.
  Nutting, Willis D., *Foundations of a Rural Christian Culture*.
  Reynolds, Pauline M., *"Lived Nobly and Well."*
May, 1939 (Vol. 2, No. 2)
  Hynes, Emerson, *Consider the Person*.
  LaFarge, John, S.J., *The Jacistes and 4-H*.
  Matt, Alphonse J., *The Family and Social Security*.
  Quinlan, Patrick T., *Rural Migrants on the March*.

New York Agrarian Publication, *Free America* (Monthly Magazine), (New York: 1938 numbers — References):
  Borsodi, Ralph, "An Excellent Series on Decentralization."
  Dresser, Peter Van, "Several Studies on the Technics of Decentralization."
  Fowler, Bertram B., "Series of Articles on Cooperatives."
  Ingerman, Charles, "Notes on a Changing Order."
  Michel, Virgil, O.S.B., "An Excellent Series on Property."
  Pfeiffer, Ehrenfried, "Series on Bio-Dynamics and Its Neglects."
  Spring, H. Powell, "Our Friend: The Earthworm."

Central-Blatt and Social Justice, Journal of the Central-Verein of America and the Central Bureau, St. Louis. (This monthly magazine contains many scholarly articles on Rural Problems.)

The Queen's Work Discussion Club Projects for Rural Groups, St. Louis:
  Cooperation and Cooperative Associations.
  Credit Unions.
  Education: Learning the Principles and Practices of Cooperation.
  Legislation.
  Private Property.
  The American Catholic Village.

Part III

Baer, Rev. Urban, *Farmers of Tomorrow* (Monroe Publishing Co.: Sparta, Wis., 1939).
Bergengren, R., *CUNA — Credit Union National Association*, Madison, Wis.: Raiffeissen House.
Bowen, E. R., *A Program for Economic Democracy* (New York: The Cooperative League of the U. S. A.).
Brownell, Baker, and Wright, Frank Lloyd, *Architecture and Modern Life* (New York: Harpers and Brothers, 1937).

Selected Bibliography

Carrel, Alexis, *Man, the Unknown* (New York: Harper and Brothers, 1935).
Chamberlain, W. H., *Collectivism; a False Utopia* (New York: Macmillan Co., 1935).
Chase, Stuart, *Rich Land, Poor Land* (New York: Whittlesey House, 1936).
Cowling, Ellis, *Cooperatives in America* (New York: Coward-McCann, 1938).
Cox, Joseph F., and Jackson, Lyman E., *Crop Management and Soil Conservation* (New York: John Wiley & Sons, 1937).
Daniels, John P., *Cooperation: an American Way* (New York: The Cooperative League of the United States, 167 West Twelfth Street, 1938).
Davies, Mrs. Noëlle, *Education for Life* (Williams & Norgate, Ltd., 1931).
Douglas, Paul, *Cooperation — a Middle Way for America* (New York: The Cooperative League, 1937).
Duryee, W. B., *A Living from the Land* (New York: McGraw-Hill, 1934).
Duthie, *4-H Club* (New York: Harper and Brothers).
Fowler, Bertram B., *Consumer Cooperation in the United States* (New York: Vanguard, 1936).
——— *The Lord Helps Those* (New York: Vanguard, 1938).
Gist and Halbert, *Urban Society* (New York: Crowell Co., 1933).
Goslin, Ryllis Alexander, *Cooperatives* (New York: Foreign Policy Association, 1937).
Greene, R. L., *The Chemistry of Health* (Indiana: Notre Dame University, 1928).
Hannam, H. H., *Co-operation — The Plan for Tomorrow Which Works Today* (Toronto: United Farmers of Ontario, 1938).
Hedden, W. P., *How Great Cities Are Fed* (New York: Heath & Co., 1929).
Howe, Frederic C., *Denmark — The Cooperative Way* (New York: Coward-McCann Co., 1936).
Jacks, G. V., and Whyte, R. O., *The Rape of the Earth* (London: Faber and Faber, 1939).
Jensen, Einar, *Danish Agriculture; Its Economic Development* (Copenhagen, Denmark: J. H. Schultz, 1937).
Kolb and Brunner, *Study of Rural Society, Its Organization and Changes* (Boston: Houghton Mifflin Co., 1935).
Lord, Russel, *To Hold This Soil* (Washington: Department of Agriculture, 1938).
Lymington, Lord, *Famine in England* (London: Whiterby, 1938).
Manniche, Peter, *Denmark: Social Laboratory*.
——— and Lund, Hans and Begtrup, Holger, *The Folk High Schools of Denmark* (London: Oxford University Press, 1936).
McWilliams, Carey, *Factories in the Field* (New York: Little, Brown Co., 1939).
Metlake, *Ketteler's Social Reform* (Philadelphia: The Dolphin Press).

Selected Bibliography

O'Hara, Most Rev. Edwin, *The Church and the Country Community* (New York: Macmillan Co., 1927).
Ormsbee, Thomas H., and Huntley, Richmond, *If You're Going to Live in the Country* (New York: Thomas Y. Crowell Co., 1937).
Pfeiffer, Ehrenfried, *Bio-Dynamic Farming and Gardening* (New York: Anthroposophic Press; London: Rudolf Steiner Publ. Co., 1938).
Root, A. I., *ABC and XYZ of Bee Culture* (Medina, Ohio: The A. I. Root Co., 1935).
Sanderson, D., Polson, R., *Rural Community Organization* (New York: J. Wiley & Sons, 1939).
Shadid, Michael A., *A Doctor for the People* (New York: Vanguard Press, 1939).
Sorokin, Pitirim, and Zimmerman, C. C., *Principles of Rural-Urban Sociology* (New York: Holt Co., 1929).
Stewart, M. S., Public Affairs Committee, "Saving Our Soil," No. 14 (New York: Public Affairs Pamphlet, 1937).
Warbasse, James Peter, *Cooperative Democracy* (New York: Harper and Brothers, 1923).
Wilcox, Walter B., *Planning a Subsistence Homestead* (Washington: Department of Agriculture, 1934).
Wise, *The Long Tomorrow* (New York: Appleton-Century Press, 1938).

Selected References for Chapters 12, 13, 14, and 15

Agricultural Techniques: Bulletins and Pamphlets issued by the Agricultural College of the state you live in. These are better than any present text we have.
Burkett, Stevens, Hill, *Agriculture for Beginners* (New York: Ginn and Co., 1914).
Faculty of Oklahoma Agricultural and Mechanical College, *First Problems in Agriculture* (New York: American Book Co., 1934).
Gardner, Bradford & Hooker, *Orcharding* (New York: McGraw-Hill, 1927). Excellent, gives the principles of growing, grafting, pruning, spraying, and common diseases of trees.
Grim, James Steward, *Introduction to Agriculture* (New York: Allyn and Bacon, 1935).
Grimes & Holton, *Modern Agriculture* (New York: Ginn and Co., 1931). Good chapter on livestock. Perhaps, best text in existence on the subject.
Pfeiffer, Ehrenfried, *Bio-Dynamic Farming and Gardening* (New York: Anthroposophic Press, 1938). The biological approach to farming, an excellent work on soil fertility, renewal, and preservation.
Storm and Davis, *How to Teach Agriculture* (Philadelphia: Lippincott, 1921). A book of method.
Craft Skills:
Brace and Mayne, *Farm-Shop Work* (New York: American Book Co., 1915).

Douglas and Roberts, *Instruction and Information Units for Hand Woodworking* (Wichita, Kans.: McCormick Mathers Co., 1936). Revised Edition. Very good in teaching the most elementary principles in the use and care of tools.

Hjorth, Herman, *Principles of Woodworking* (Milwaukee: Bruce Publ. Co., 1935).

McGee, R. A., and A. G. Brown, *Instructional Units in Wood Finishing* (Milwaukee: Bruce Publ. Co., 1929). Very good for advanced work and most useful as a reference book.

Newkirk and Stoddard, *The General Shop* (Peoria, Ill.: The Manual Arts Press, 1929).

Roehl, L. M., *Farmer's Shop Book* (Milwaukee: Bruce Publ. Co., 1936). Good as textbook or reference. Has some very good practical plans for blueprints.

Sharp and Sharp, *Principles of Farm Mechanics* (New York: John Wiley and Sons, 1930). Excellent as textbook, covers both wood- and metalworking.

Smith, Robert, *Agricultural Mechanics* (New York: Lippincott, 1933). Fair, good chapter on forging and metalwork.

The Home Craftsman (The Home Workshop Magazine), Monthly, General Publishing Company.

The Operation, Care and Repair of Farm Machinery (Moline, Ill.: John Deere Company), 10th edition.

Woodin, J. C., *Home Mechanics for Girls* (Wichita, Kans.: McCormick Mathers Co.).

Government Publications:

Organizing a Farmers' Cooperative (Washington, D. C.: Farm Credit Administration, 1939). Circular No. C–108.

Statistics of Farmers' Marketing and Purchasing Cooperatives, for the 1937–38 Marketing Season (Washington, D. C.: Farm Credit Administration, 1939).

Archbishops and Bishops of Canada, *Joint Pastoral Letter on the Rural Problem in Relation to the Social Doctrine of the Church* (Quebec, 1937).

Baker, O. E., *The Outlook for Rural Youth* (Washington: Department of Agriculture), Revised, 1937.

The Cooperative League, *Consumer Cooperation,* Monthly, New York.

Course of Study on Consumers' Cooperation (St. Paul, Minn.: State Department of Education, 1939, prepared for teachers of consumers' cooperation.

International Harvester Co., *Diversified Farming is Safe Farming,* Chicago.

―――― *Farm Prosperity Guaranteed,* Chicago, 1922.

―――― *Make the Soil Productive,* Chicago, 1931.

Leo XIII and Pius XI, *Four Great Encyclicals* (New York: Paulist Press, 1931).

Selected Bibliography 373

Louisiana State University, *Rural Sociology*, Quarterly Journal.
National Research Project, *Changes in Technology in Crop Productions* (Philadelphia: Works Progress Administration).
National Resources Board, *Report* (Washington, D. C.: U. S. Government Printing Office, 1934).
────── *Technological Trends and National Policy* (Washington, D. C.: U. S. Government Printing Office, 1937).
Prize Winning Designs in the Productive Home Architectural Competition (New York: *Free America*, 112 East 19th St., May, 1939).
St. Francis Xavier University, *The Extension Bulletin* (Newspaper). Antigonish, N. S.
U. S. Department of Agriculture, *Geological Survey Maps* (Washington, D. C.: U. S. Government Printing Office).
────── *Report of Inquiry on Cooperative Enterprise in Europe* (Washington, D. C.: U. S. Printing Office, 1937).
────── *Base Book of Iowa* (Agricultural Economic Facts).

Barr, Stringfellow, "The Training of a Free Mind," *Free America*, October, 1939, p. 3.
Carey, Graham, "Sufficiency, Security and Freedom," *Free America*, February, 1939.
Davidson, Donald, "On Being in Hock to the North," *Free America*, May, 1939.
Estey, Hayden, "Rails Over Dixie," *Free America*, April, 1939.
Fowler, Bertram B., "Program for Action," *Free America*, May, 1939.
Haile, Thomas H., "On the Nature of Agrarianism," *Free America*, October, 1939, p. 12.
Howe, Frederic C., "Land for the Free," *Free America*, February, 1939.
Hynes, Emerson, "World of Tomorrow," *Free America*, April, 1939.
Lubell, S. and Pollard, A., "Pine-Free Bankers" in *American Forests*, Dec., 1939 (Washington, D. C.: 919 — 17 St., N.W.). Cf. also *Reader's Digest*, December, 1939.
Russel Sage Foundation, "Subsistence Homesteads: A Bibliography," *Free America*, October, 1939, p. 18.
Special Supplement, "Five Prize-Winning Designs in the Productive Home Architectural Competition," *Free America*, May, 1939.
Van Dresser, Peter, "The Productive Home," *Free America*, February, 1939.
────── "An Agrarian Looks at Planning," *Free America*, April, 1939.
────── "The Technics of Decentralization," *Free America*, May, 1939.
────── "Portrait of a Productive Home," *Free America*, October, 1939, p. 8.
Woods, Ralph, "The New Deal and Decentralization," *Free America*, April, 1939.

Care of Food in the Home, U. S. Department of Agriculture, B. 1374.
Convenient Kitchens, U. S. Department of Agriculture, B. 1513.

Farmhouse Plans, U. S. Department of Agriculture, B. 1738.
Home Canning of Fruits, Vegetables, and Meats, U. S. Department of Agriculture, B. 1762.
Home Production of the Family's Food Supply, Agricultural Experimental Station, Michigan State College of Agriculture and Applied Science.
Home Storage of Vegetables, U. S. Department of Agriculture, B. 879.
Iowa State Planning Board, *Progress Report.*
———— *Report of Committee on Farm Tenancy.*
———— *Second Report.*
———— *The Forgotten House.*
———— *Water Use and Conservation in Iowa,* Vol. II.
Mechanical Equipment for the Home, Federal Housing Authority, B. 6.
Planning the Farmstead, U. S. Department of Agriculture, B. 1132.
Planning a Subsistence Homestead, U. S. Department of Agriculture, B. 1733.
Soil Erosion in Iowa, Iowa Agricultural Experiment Station, U. S. Department of Agriculture, Special Report No. 1, 1936.
Soils of Iowa, Iowa Agricultural Experiment Station, U. S. Department of Agriculture, Special Report No. 3.
Journals:
"Agricultural Education in Quebec," by Boulet, August, Ph.D., *The Catholic Rural Life Bulletin,* August, 1939.
"Basic House" (New York: McGraw-Hill), *Business Week,* July 22, 1939.
Borsodi, Ralph, and Rockwell, F. F., *A Book containing the Fifty-five Winning Designs for Productive Homes* in the Productive Home Architectural Competition of 1939, Whittlesey House Garden Series (New York: McGraw-Hill).
Brown, M. L. (Comment by eight American auditors), *A Budget Message from Eagle Bridge* (New York: Survey Graphic), July, 1939, p. 436.
"Co-ops and Rural Survival," by George Boyle, *Columbia,* September, 1939.
Cronin, John F., S.S., "Distribution," *The Sign,* October, 1939.
Detzer, Karl, "Farmer Ford Raises a Crop," *Reader's Digest,* October, 1939.
De Voto, Bernard, *The Paring Knife at the Crossroads* (New York: Harper's Magazine), April, 1939.
———— *Unrest in the Kitchen* (New York: Harper's Magazine), July, 1939.
Eaton, Allen H., *Handicrafts of the Southern Highlands* (New York: Russel Sage Foundation, 1937).
"Factors in Re-making the Local Community," editorial in the *Maritime Cooperator,* a paper for farmers, fishermen, and laborers, published by the Extension Department of St. Francis Xavier University, August, 1939.
Fifty Women Talk It Out (Washington: Consumers' Guide, June, 1939), U. S. Department of Agriculture.
Hallsted, A. L., and Mathews, O. R., *Soil Moisture and Winter Wheat, with Suggestions on Abandonment,* Kansas Agricultural Experiment Station, Bulletin 273, 1936.

Selected Bibliography

Hatch, J. W., and Lathrop, F. W., *Discovering Occupational Opportunities for Young Men in Farming* (Washington: Studies in Agricultural Education, Monograph 20, United States Department of the Interior, Office of Education).

Kent, George, "Plant-to-Prosper Sweeps Nine States," *The Country Home Magazine*, June, 1939 (The Crowell Publ. Co., 250 Park Ave., New York City). Cf. also *Reader's Digest*, June, 1939. This article gives the details of a campaign launched by the *Memphis Commercial Appeal*, a Tennessee newspaper. Since its beginning in 1934, this program has been the salvation of the 200,000 poor farming people who have followed it.

La Farge, John, S.J., *Discipline Not Arms Forms Our Strongest Defense* (New York: America), June 24, 1939.

Magee, H. W., "Half an Acre and Independence," *Popular Mechanics*, Vol. 64, September, 1935, pp. 392, 393.

McGuire, Paul, "The Method of Catholic Action," in *Columbia*, January, 1939.

——— "Apostolate of the Workers," in *Columbia*, January, 1938.

——— "New Youth for a New World," in *Columbia*, June, 1938.

——— "Kaleidoscope With Cross," in *Columbia*, September, 1938.

Melvin, Bruce L., *Rural Youth on Relief* (Washington: Works Progress Administration, 1937).

Nutting, Willis D., *The Road Back to Freedom* (Notre Dame, Ind.: The Ave Maria, February, 1939).

Patten, Marjorie, *The Arts Workshop of Rural America* (New York: Columbia University Press, 1937).

Pickett, C. E., "Social Significance of the Subsistence Homestead Movement," *Journal of Home Economics*, Vol. 26, October, 1934, pp. 477-479.

Ratcliff, J. D., "Bread de Luxe," in *Reader's Digest*, December, 1939, p. 102.

Robbins, H., *The Secret Battle* (London: The Tablet, 39 Paternoster Row, June 24, 1939).

Smith, C. B., *The Treasures of Youth* (Wellesley, Mass.: 4-H Horizons, National 4-H Magazine, July, 1939).

Social-Economics Service, College of Ste-Anne-de-la-Pocatiere. Books, Pamphlets, Bulletins, Periodicals, published by the Superior School of Agriculture of Ste-Anne-de-la-Pocatiere. (A Catholic Agricultural School in Canada — Courses lead to the Degree of Bachelor in Agricultural Sciences.)

Subsistence Homestead Projects; aiming to provide not merely a living, but a life worth living, *American City*, February, 1934, p. 75.

Taylor, Elliot, "The Productive Country Home," *Dynamic America*, September, 1939.

Thompson, Dorothy, "A Social Inventor," *St. Louis Post-Dispatch*, May 13, 1939, page 5A. An account of the plan followed by Mr. Francis Hoess of Hammond, Ind., in building "basic houses" situated on one acre of ground, and the final completion, payment, and development plan for the ownership of productive homes by workers and their families.

Van Vlissingen, Arthur, "A Home and an Acre — $2,600," *Reader's Digest*, October, 1939.

von Wald, Hans, *Unemployment* (Villanova: The Christian Front, June, 1939), Now, Christian Social Action, Box 74, North End Station, Detroit, Mich.

"Westphalia: Pattern and Promise," by Hayne, Donald, *The Catholic Rural Life Bulletin*, August, 1939.

Wilcox, W. W., *Planning a Subsistence Homestead*, U. S. Department of Agriculture, Farmers' Bulletin No. 1733, 1934.

Williams, B. O., "Mechanization of Agriculture and the South," *Rural Sociology*, September, 1939.

Wilson, M. L., "A New Land-Use Program: the Place of Subsistence Homesteads," *Journal of Land and Public Utility Economics*, Vol. 10, February, 1934, pp. 1–12.

Film:

Three-reel film, *The Lord Helps Those — Who Help Each Other* (New York: Harmon Foundation and the Cooperative League of the United States, 167 West Twelfth St., 1938).

Bibliographies and Compilations

A Guide to the Literature of Rural Life, compiled by Benson Y. Landis, Fourth Revised Edition, 1939, American Country Life Association, 297 Fourth Ave., New York City.

Agricultural Economics Literature (Washington: Bureau of Agricultural Economics).

Agricultural Labor in the United States, 1915–1935 and *Agricultural Labor in the United States, 1936–1937*, compiled by Ester M. Colvin, Josiah C. Folsom and Mary G. Lacy (Washington: Bureau of Agricultural Economics).

Bibliography of the Literature of Rural Life, Bureau of Education, Archdiocese of St. Paul, St. Paul, Minn.

Bibliography on Land Utilization, 1918–1936, compiled by Louise O. Bercaw and Annie M. Hannay (Washington: Bureau of Agricultural Economics, Publication No. 284).

Documentation for the European Conference on Rural Life, 1939, International Institute of Agriculture, National Monographs prepared by Governments, Rome, Villa Umberto I.

Farm Population and Rural Life Activities, a quarterly review of current research (Washington: Bureau of Agricultural Economics).

Farm Tenancy in the United States (selected list of references), compiled by Louise O. Bercaw and Mary G. Lacy (Washington: Bureau of Agricultural Economics, Publication No. 70).

International Bibliography of Agricultural Economics (English, French, German), Rome, Villa Umberto I.

Selected Bibliography

Part-Time Farming in the United States (selected list of references), compiled by Helen E. Hennefrund and Mary G. Lacy (Washington: Bureau of Agricultural Economics, Agricultural Economic Bibliography No. 77).
"Supplementary Reading in Decentralization of Population, Land Ownership, Government and Industrial Independence as a Program Leading to Economic Independence" (New York: *Free America,* 112 East 19th St., The Homeland Foundation).
The Filmstrip Library of the United States Department of Agriculture, Dewey and Dewey Laboratory, 632–56th St., Kenosha, Wis.
The Filmstrip Library of the United States Rural Electrification Administration, Dewey and Dewey, Kenosha, Wis.

Periodicals of Special Interest

Agricultural Situation (Monthly), Superintendent of Documents, Washington, D. C.
Consumers' Guide, Washington: Department of Agriculture, Agricultural Adjustment Administration.
Consumers' Union Buying Guide, Consumers' Union, 55 Vandam St., New York City.
Consumers' Union Reports, Consumers' Union of the U. S., Inc., 17 Union Square, West, New York City.
Crops and Markets (Monthly), Superintendent of Documents, Washington, D. C.
Experiment Station Record (Monthly), Superintendent of Documents, Washington, D. C.
Extension Service Annual Report, *Meeting the Challenge of Agriculture,* 1936; *Serving Farm People on Many Fronts,* 1937, Superintendent of Documents, Washington, D. C.
Extension Service Review (Monthly), Superintendent of Documents, Washington, D. C.
Journal of Agricultural Research (Monthly), Superintendent of Documents, Washington, D. C.
Les Publicationes Jacistes, J. A. C., 14, rue d'Assas, Paris, J. A. C. F., 31, rue de Tournon, Paris.
Madison Cooper's Gardening Magazine (Monthly), Calcium, N. Y.
Nebraska Union Farmer, 39th and Leavenworth, Omaha, Nebr.
Rural America, American Country Life Association, 297 Fourth Ave., New York City.
Rural Electrification News (Monthly), Superintendent of Documents, Rural Electrification Administration, Washington.
Rural Relief and Recovery, Works Progress Administration, Social Problems, No. 3, Government Press, Washington, D. C., 1939.
Soil Conservation (Monthly), Superintendent of Documents, Washington, D. C.
The Cooperative Consumer, Consumers' Cooperative Association, North Kansas City, Mo.

The Review of Politics, University of Notre Dame, Ind. (Vol. 1, p. 155, *Ownership and the Human Person,* Virgil Michel, O.S.B.)
Three Acres and Security (Quarterly), Elgin, Ill.

Bulletins:

How to Economize by Sewing at Home, Suffern, N. Y., School of Living, 1939.
How to Economize in Building Your Home, Suffern, N. Y., School of Living, 1939.
How to Economize in Buying Land for Your Home, Suffern, N. Y., School of Living, 1939.
How to Economize on Bread, Cake and Pastry, Suffern, N. Y., School of Living, 1938.
How to Economize on Buying and Storing Food, Suffern, N. Y., School of Living, 1939.
How to Economize on Flour and Breakfast Foods, Suffern, N. Y., School of Living, 1939.
How to Economize on Fruit, Suffern, N. Y., School of Living, 1939.
How to Economize on Vegetables, Suffern, N. Y., School of Living, 1939.

The City: America's First Decentralist Film. — A documentary film done from an outline by Pare Lorentz, with photography by Ralph A. Steiner and Willard Van Dyke, running commentary written by Lewis Mumford and music by Aaron Copland. Prepared by the American Institute of Planners, funded by the Carnegie Corporation of America, released by Civic Films, Inc.

INDEX

Absentee landlords, 81
Absentee ownership of land (graph), 83
Acreage, extent of in the U. S., 193; small, 10; small, raises purchasing power, 179
Advertising, expense of, 279
Aged, the, 65
Agrarian, mentality and life, 300
Agrarian movement, false notions of, 182 ff.
Agrarian schools, 114
Agrarianism, and independence, 295; cultural values, 135; progress through homemaking, 137
Agricultural Adjustment Program, 358
Agricultural College, Ames, Iowa, assistance given Granger homesteaders, 176
Agricultural Economics, Bureau of, 195
Agricultural extension service, 350
Agricultural fallacies, 213
Agricultural Situation, Bureau of Agricultural Economics, 195
Agricultural Statistics, 1938, 133 ff.; Department of Agriculture, 198, 199
Agricultural vocation, 240; danger of losing, 241
Agriculture, and industry, 158; biological science, a, 204 ff.; Franklin on, 72; in America (graph), 78; Iowa, lack of proportionate share of income, 354; opposed to mechanics, 204; organic factors in, 219; supplementing industry in Granger incomes, 177, 178; technical knowledge, 243
Air, source of nitrogen, 216
Air depletion, none, 211
Alfalfa, plant foods, 207
American agriculture, biologically unsound, 220
American birthright, dangers to, 8
American Bishops, *Statement on the Present Crisis*, 299
American Journal of Agronomy, 1939, "Moisture-Conservation Tests," 208 ff.
Antigonish, Rural and Industrial Conference, 338
Antigonish Movement, 341
Apartments, conditions resulting from, 60
Architects, and the home, 203

Architecture, and home, 203
Arkansas, committee on farm tenancy, 354
Arts and Crafts, 168
Association of Help and Service, 256 ff.
Assumption High School, Granger, Iowa, 250
Australian Commonwealths, differential taxation in, 350

Bacterial content of compost heaps, 218
Bankhead-Jones Farm Tenant Act, 354
Bargaining, collective, 39 ff.
Bayard Lane Community, 313
Bayard Lane Homesteads, 325
Biodynamic farming, 217 ff., 220 ff.
Biodynamics, 217
Biological factors, 203; in farming, 214
Biological science, neglect of, 192
Biotechnics, First American School of, 317
Birth control, 64
"Birth-control houses," 110
Birth rate, decline (chart), 67; falling, 64 ff.; urban deficits (chart), 68; urban deficits, rural surplus, 67 ff.
Bleaching of flour, effects of, 322
Borsodi, Ralph, 201, 202; and colleagues, work of, research studies, 190; authority on housing, 325; economist, 313
Bread, high cost of, 194
Building Division of the School of Living, 315
Bulletins prepared by the School of Living, 315
Bureau of Agricultural Economics, index numbers, parity charts, 195
Burr Acres, Productive Home Community, 303 ff.
Buying power of farm products, inadequate, 195

Cape Breton, 337
Carnegie Corporation, 338
Carotene, source of Vitamin A, 322
"Catholic Action in Rural Districts," Francis J. McGoey, 138
Central Cooperative Committee, Denmark, 270

Index

Centralization: people, factories, ownership, control, 15 ff.
Centralizations, 22 ff.
Cereal industry, costs in, 320
Chain store, efficiencies and evils, 281 ff.
Chemical fertilizers, 213
Christian people, betterment of, 342
Christian piety, 240
Christianity, in the country home, 303; practical teachings of, 342
Church, material conditions necessary for success, 299 f.; spiritual losses in city parish, 302; vs. Proletarian Mind, 301
Cities, antiquated, 111; congestion in, 111; decentralized, 112; growth of, 16; perfect, 13; wrong attitudes toward rural areas, 104
Civil liberties, 351
Civil rights, follow loss of property rights, 19
Civilization, benefits of, 56
Clarkstown Building Guild, 328
Clubs, 4-H, 228 ff.
Coady, M. M., 337
Collective bargaining, 39 ff.
Collectivism, technique of, 24
Colonization, practical, 147
Commercial farmer and the gardener, production compared, 198
Commercialism, 137; false ideals, 302
Commercialized farming, evils of, 297
Committees of arbitration between tenants and landlords, recommended, 351
Community, group, 113
Community activities, 251
Compost, 217 ff.
Compost yard, 217
Concentrations, 22 ff.; in specific industries, 21 ff.
Consumer dollar, farmer's portion of (graph), 275
Consumption, collapse of, 7; of food, 135 ff.
Consumption goods, 30
Consumption point, 200
Control, economic, 17
Cooperation, objectives in, 278; vs. Communism, 283
Cooperative, how to organize producers, 285 ff.
Cooperative banking institutions in Nova Scotia, 338
Cooperative Buying Club, 284
Cooperative canning factories in Nova Scotia, 338
Cooperative consumer stores in Nova Scotia, 338
Cooperative Farm Community, St. Teresa's Village, 331
Cooperative fish processing plants in Nova Scotia, 338
Cooperative Grouping on the Land, 253 ff.
Cooperative industries in Nova Scotia, 338
Cooperative marketing associations in Nova Scotia, 338
Cooperative marketing of farm products, 276 ff.; advantages, 276 ff.
Cooperative membership in a Marketing Cooperative, 288
Cooperative Parish Activities Service, Effingham, Illinois, 226
Cooperative producers, financing and marketing credit, 290; marketing contract, 289; meetings, 289
Cooperatives, 253 ff., 258; advantages and technique of, 273 ff.; and common good, 265 f.; and private property, 263 ff.; beginning a cooperative association, 283 f.; Democratic principles, 263; Denmark, 267 ff.; education for, at St. Francis Xavier University, 259 ff.; for producers, 284 ff.; grading of products, 292; in Nova Scotia, 335 ff.; management and selling program, 291 f.; planning for, 260 ff.; producers, production credit, 290 f.; Rochdale Technique, 258 ff.; vs. corporations, 267; vs. proletarianism, 266
Corporation, growth, 25; agriculture, evils of, 309 f.; competition, 26
Corporation farming, danger of, 92; evil effects, 93; public menace, a, 74; Supreme Court of Kansas on, 74
"Corporationism," 17 f.; disturbs democratic foundations, 26
Cotton belt, 103
County agents, in education, 168
Courses, in domestic science, 168; in farm-shop work, 168
Craft Division of the School of Living, 315
Credit, 167; need of improvement in credit facilities for rural people, 148
Credit unions in Nova Scotia, 338
Crop cycles, charts, 169
Crop Diversification Contests, 306
Crop rotation, 216
Crops, depend on plant foods and soil moisture, 211; mass-produced, home-produced, difference between, 107; variation of, 167

Cultivation, mass scale, 126; of land, destructive, 215
Curriculum for *Rural Schools*, 245 ff.
Curriculum of School of Living, 314

Dairying, evils of commercialized distribution, 276 ff.
Danish Folk High School System, 272
Darwin, Charles, study of the earthworm, 218
Decentralization, and electric power, 157; in government, in population, in production, 202
Democracy, restoration of, 30
Denmark, cooperatives in, 267 ff.
Department of Agriculture, 169; *Agricultural Statistics, 1938,* 198, 199; losses through forms of erosion, 214
Depletion of soils, relation to pauperization of farmers, human erosion, 215
Depressions, recurring, 192
Dictatorship, economic, 18; of business, 37
Dictatorships, causes, 19
Diet, poor in mineral salts, 321
Diet standards, scientific, charts, 169
Dietetic errors, 321
Diets and nerves, 321 ff.
Differential taxation, indirect method of attacking tenancy, 350
Disadvantaged classes of farmers, member of, conditions of, 346
Distribution, costs of, 201, 273 ff.; inefficiencies in, 279; of wealth, La Follette on, 46; problem of, 254
Division of labor, effects, 5
Domestic economy, 190; advantages of, 193; on the land, 297 f.
Domestic science, courses in, 168
Dominion Department of Fisheries, 337
Dornach, Switzerland, Agricultural Research Laboratories, 217
Droughts, 214
Dust, prevents moisture, 210
Dust bowl, 221
Dust storms, 214

Earthworm, relation to farm, 218
Earthworms, numerous in soils rich in humus, 211
Economic determinism, fallacy of, 113
Economic dictatorship, 18
Economy, domestic, 190, 297; industrial, blindly substituted for domestic economy, 199

Educating for productive homes, 305
Education for a home on the land, 238 f.; for homesteading, 114; for homesteads, 118; for rural life, 233 ff., 248 ff.; for rural living, 168; in rural schools, 352; of rural communities, 148; of rural youth, 233 ff.; teaching self-help, 152
Educational advantages, necessity of equalization of, 352
Efficiency, 200
Electricity, in the home, in the small factory, 107
Elements in soils, plant foods, 205 ff.
Emergency Farm Mortgage Act, 348
Environment, the home, 11
Equality, 154
Equities in farm real estate, 1930 (chart), 79
Erosion, 84, 214 ff.; in various forms affects 59 per cent of our countryside, 215; result of agricultural mining, 215
Extension program, St. Francis Xavier University, 335 ff.

Factories and transportation, effect on labor, 5
Factory, 201
Factory farming, greater evil than tenancy, 93
Factory farms, 73; statistics on, 77
Factory system, 4; effect on home occupations, 6
Families, of Granger project, 175
Family, 50 ff.; activities and duties of, 52; American, 101; and State, 255; dependence of, 57; foundation of the State, 71; fundamental society, 288; in city life, 65; natural unit of economic life, 61; natural unit of social life, 61; needs of, 200; on small farm, 75; production for (graph), 81; rural, 73 ff.; rural, unit of society, 112; unit, a, dependence of State on, "mother cell of society," 50; urban, 50 ff.
Family agriculture, and Christian democracy, 308 f.; economic strength of, 308 f.
Family budgeting, 251
Family-centered production, economic, social, cultural, ethical significance of, 12
Family farms, in countries of Northern Europe, 71
Family rehabilitation, St. Francis community, 141 ff.
Family-size farms, tendency to tax at a

382 Index

higher rate than larger properties, 350; type of holdings to be created, 344
Family unit, operation of farms, 220
Family unity on the land, 299
Farm, correlation on, 212; integration on, 212; place of the earthworm on, 218; production on, 106 f.; self-contained organism, 217; small acreage, 108; small family, 75
Farm Credit Administration, 160, 345, 347
Farm enterprise, contribution to family income, 162
Farm families, 357 ff.; principal source of nation's population, 352
Farm laborers, program for, 345
Farm lands, differential taxation, 350
Farm producer, share of market price, 274 ff.
Farm-purchase policy, 346
Farm real estate, equities in (chart), 79
Farm Security Administration, 344; rehabilitation loans, technical guidance, 345
Farm Security Corporation, 343
Farm-shop training, 246 ff.
Farm-shop work, courses in, 168
"Farm Talk Forums" of Northern Europe, 226
Farm Tenancy Committee, 85; Iowa, policies recommended for Federal Government, 358; report of, Iowa, 353
Farm Tenancy Report, President's Committee, National Resources Committee, 343; recommendations for states in, 349
Farm Tenure Problem, nation-wide interest in, 354
Farmers, returning to the "homestead" way, 116
Farming, full-time, 115; part-time, 63, 115, 149 ff.
Farming operations, depletion of plant foods in, 207
Farms, collectivized, 93; family-size, 344; loss of, 81; mechanization of, 131 f.; mortgaging of, 76; surrender of title deeds to, 76
Farms, migration from, 66
Fatherhood, wage earning, 55
Federal Antipeonage Acts, tendency to nullify, 351
Federal Farm Loan Act, 348
Federal Government, introduced into private affairs, 174; policies recommended for, 358
Federal Housing Commission, 160

Federal Subsistence Homesteads Corporation, 172
Federation of Danish Cooperatives, 270
Fermentation of organic substances, 217
Fertile soil, small portions plant foods (graph), 206
Fertilizers, chemical, 213; of commercial chemistry, 219
First American School of Biotechnics, 317
Floods, 214
Folk High Schools, Denmark, 270 ff.
Food, consumption of, 135; computation of consumption, 196
Food and Drug Administration, 323
Food production, at Granger, 176 ff.
Food supplies, subsistence, 130
Foods, chemical subversion, 197 ff.
Foreclosure for debt, 125
Foreclosures, extent of, 356
Founders of America, vision of, 71 f.
4-H clubs, 228 ff.
Free government, objectives of, 20
Freedom, 20; struggle for, 7

Garden crops, 169 ff.
Garden plots, 158 ff.
Gardener and commercial farmer, production compared, 198
"General Farms, Inc.," 75
Giant enterprises, their inefficiencies, 24
Glace Bay, 337
Government, attitude on rural projects, 148
Government supervision, Granger project, 173
Granger, financial success, 182; Iowa, Assumption High School, 248 ff.; laboratory of sociology and economics, 175
Granger cooperatives, 181
Granger families, social gains, 175
Granger homestead development, 160
Granger Homestead Project, 166; Granger, Iowa, 171 ff.
Granger homesteaders, income of, 335; nationality of, 335; occupation of, 335; religion of, 335; subsistence of, 335; wages of, 335; work of, 335
Granger homesteads, acreage, types of houses, rooms, outbuildings, electricity, costs, 333; factual outline, 332; legislative origin, 332; taxes, 335
Granger houses, 174
Granger incomes, 1936, 1937, 1938 (charts), 178
Granger plan, 172 ff.

Index 383

Granger production, varieties in, 175
Granger success, 175
Grazing economy, 347
Great Plains, region of low-standard arable farms, 347
Greenville, Alabama, St. Teresa's Village, 331
Grundtvig, Bishop, 270
Grundtvigian movement in education, 271
Gullying, area affected, 214; causes, results, 215

Herbs, medicinal, used in controlled fermentation, 217
Home, and machine, 202; as a school, 241; center of life, 62; food costs, 193; moral atmosphere in, 240; on the land, 99 ff., 105; productive, 204; reconstruction of, 62; worth-while legacy, 60, 61
Home advisers, reports of success in garden crops, 170
Home demonstration agents, for education, 168
Home economy, 201
Home equipment for production, 190
Home financing plan, of Independence Foundation, 328 ff.
Home gardens, 199
Home machines, 202
Home ownership, lack of, 57; percentage of, 163; production for, 129 ff.
Homemaking and agriculture, 249
Homes, bankrupt, 46; familial divergence, 61; familial solidarity, 61; in city, 64; productive, 109; reduced to flats, 199; results of Granger project, 176
Homestead, 75, 104 f.; definition of, 121 ff.; education for, 114, 118; false, conceptions, 119; Granger project, 171 ff.; overcoming of relief problem, 185; position of mother in, 250; production on the, 109; requires operator as owner, 117; tax-exempt, 127 f.; taxation on, 122; urban, 122; vital economic institution, 105
Homestead Bulletins, School of Living, 190
Homestead farming, "First Law of," 296
Homesteader, definition of, 117
Homesteading, details in the program, 153; problems in, 115 ff.; requires high intelligence, 118; success of Family Subsistence Agrarian Plan in Pennsylvania, 308; to replace tenancy and absentee landlordism, 119

Homesteads, children on, 181 ff.; exemption from taxation, 350; food production on, 112; increase stability of families, 346; loans for, 114; movement toward, 139 ff.; what is needed for success of, 151 ff.
Houses, of Granger project, 174
Housing, low cost of, 111
Housing programs, 109
Housing units, shortage of, 58
Humus, 205 ff.; mistreatment of, 208; restoration of, 217 ff.
Humus maker, the earthworm, 218

Income, family, 162; industrial, 161
Incomes, distribution of (graph), 47
Identity, 154
Independence, in a productive home, 330
Independence Foundation, home financing plan, 328 ff.
Independence Foundation, Inc., 314, 325 ff.
Independence Foundation homes, 328
Industrial wage earning and part-time farming, combination of, 12
Industrialism, 164; effect of, 54 ff.; exploiting land and families, 102; liberalistic, 4
Industry and agriculture, supplementing each other, 158
Iowa, committee on farm tenancy, 354; report of Farm Tenancy Committee, 353
Iowa farms, tax burdens on, 357
Iowa State Planning Board, 353
Iowa Tenancy Committee, on relation of size of farms and rate of tenancy, 77
Intermediate farming schools, 243
International Harvester Co., publication of, 205, 206

J. A. C., *Jeunesse Agricole Chretienne,* 243

King City, St. Francis Community, 140 ff.
King City families, letters of, 141

Labor, Adam Smith on, 42; status of, 33
Laboratories, of Agricultural Research, Dornach, Switzerland, 217
Land, abandonment of, 16; attractively situated, 193; basis of physical life, 189; capital value, tends to outrun upward trends in farm income, 347; concentration of, 73; for settlement, 5; foundation of the family, 71; health of, 217; home on the, 99 ff.; homestead dis-

tribution of, 74 ff.; increasing tax burden, 89; intelligent technology on, 189 ff.; primarily for home building and family subsistence, 307; proletariat on, 76 ff.; proper attitude toward, 62; re-settlement on, 138 ff.; safe in hands of small owners, 104; speculators in, 85; tax loads on, 88; training for land-ownership on, 222 ff.; unearned increment in, exploitation of, 87; wasted, exploited, 115
Land settlement, community basis, 145
Land speculation, ownership by nonfarmers, 347
Land taxation methods, 122 ff.
Land tenure system, 353
Landlord-Tenant Act, Oklahoma, 354
Landlord-tenant relationship, 90; improvement of, 348
Landlords, absentee, 81
Landownership, 135, 294 f.; determining factor in human well-being, 10; in Denmark, 269; in Nebraska, 79
Leaders, 154; attend 4-week short courses, 338; for local organizations, 338
Leadership, and the clergy, 225; proper choice of plans and organization for training leaders, 224; training for, on land, 22 ff.
Leasehold basis for subsistence farms, 346
Legumes, fixation in the soil, 216; to restore depleted acres, 216
Liberties, defense of, 20
Liberty, cooperative way, 255; ownership, guarantee of, 53
Libraries, regional, supply of material for study clubs, 338
Life, modes of, 10
Lime, 205 ff.
Livelihood, elements of, 57
Livelihood farm, first law of, 296
Livestock, 213
Living, new design for, 325
Loan Contract Plan, Independence Foundation, 329
Local organizations, leaders for, 338

MacDonald, A. B., 337
MacIntyre, Alex S., 337
Machines, 10
Magdalen Islands, 339
Man, responsibility of, 54
Management, effect on people, 41
Manufacturing, functioning periodically in the country districts, 158

Manure, value of, 216
Maritime Provinces, 338
Mass, production, 196; conditions of, 103; cost of, 279 ff.; inefficiencies of, 192; on farms, 131
McCann, Alfred, 319
McGoey, Rev. Francis J. (quoted), 147; builder of St. Francis community, 138
McGoey's plan, details and accomplishments, St. Francis Community, 138 ff.
Mechanics, not sound in agriculture, 204
Mechanization, of farms, 131 ff.
Medicinal herbs, used in controlled fermentation, 217
Men, created equal, inalienable rights, 154
Migrants, among farm laborers, 345
Migration, from farms, 66; from land to city, 294
Milling, at home, 317 ff.; at home, gains in, 323 ff.; equipment for the home, cost of, 323; industry, costs in, 320
Mining camps, condition in company-owned, 171
Missouri State University, Agricultural Experiment Station, *Soil Fertility Losses,* 205
Moisture, in humus, 212; losses of, 210 ff.; storage in soil through covering, 208; storage of, 209
Money, 167; emphasis on, in urban philosophy, 357; influence of, 46
Moore, Benjamin, Dr., 321
Morality, and property, 264; economic, 113.
Moratorium law, 355
Morrison, James, Most Rev., Bishop of Antigonish, 340
Mother, children lack guidance of, 59, 60
Musser, John H., Dr., 320

National income, 356
National Recovery Act, Section 208, 172
National Resources Committee, report on Farm Tenancy, 343
Nature, a storehouse, 167
Nebraska Agricultural Experiment Station, "Moisture-Conservation Tests," 208 ff.
Nebraska Federation of County Taxpayers League, 297
Nebraska State University, Agricultural Experiment Station, "Moisture-Conservation Tests," 208 ff.
Newspapers and education for productivity, 306

Index

Nitrates, commercial, injurious effects of, 220
Nitrogen, 205 ff.
Nitrogen fixation, legumes, 216
Nodules, on roots of legumes, 216
Nova Scotia, 337; Cooperatives, Self-Help, 253 f.
Nutrition, and factory foods, 197 ff.; lack of, in tenant homes, 356
Nutritional values, losses in, 198

Oklahoma, Landlord-Tenant Act, 354; tax exemption for homesteads, 127
Organic substances, fermentation of, 217
Organizations of farmers, denied rights of peaceful assembly, 351
Ownership, and effective control, in land, loss of, 10 ff.; fall in (graph), 78; natural to man, 240; of farm homes, 90; of land, relation to value of farm buildings, 80

Packard, Horace, Dr., 321
Part-time farmers, living and social conditions, 163
Part-time farming, 63, 149 ff., 344; and industrial families, 116; extent of, 155 ff.; government survey, 155; objections answered, 164 ff.; proposals pertaining to, 159; resettlement, 167 f.
Part-time farms, percentage of total, 156 ff.
Patent medicine, 324
Pellagra, 86
Pennsylvania, success of agrarian plan, 308
People, becoming masters of their own economic destiny, 340
Per-capita consumption of foods, 1889, 1932, etc., decrease in, 196, 197
Phosphoric acid, 205 ff.
Piersol, George Morris, Dr., 320
Plant food, elements in soils, 205 ff.
Plant foods, estimated pounds per acre in top six inches of soil, 205; methods of becoming available, 206 ff.; removal by crops, 205 ff.
Plant preparations, insertion of, into compost heaps, 217
Plant-to-Prosper Program, 306 f.
Pleasure, commercialized, 61
Poor, must be taught planning, sense of values, self-help, 154
Population, 352; age of (chart), 68 ff.; growth and farm family, 298 f.; of U. S., largely urban, 65
Potash, 205 ff.

Prairie Plantation, Mississippi, 296
Present Crisis, Statement on, American Bishops, 299
Price spreads, 1913–1937, 196
Prince Edward Island, 338
Production, centers of, 34; distribution of, 32; for exchange, 129; for family use (graph), 81; for home use, relation to ownership, 81; for use at home, 129; high cost of, 134; home and factory, comparative studies, 190; in the home, efficient, 189
"Production-for-the-home" agriculture, 308
Production goods, not widely distributed, 32
Production point, 200
Productive home, restoration of, education for, 237 ff.
Productive homes, 109
Productivity of homes, of Granger Project, 176 ff.
Productivity vs. Distributivity (graph), Twentieth Century Fund, 281
Profits, limitation of, 265
Proletaire, conditions for, 45
Proletarian attitudes, 301 f.
Proletarianism, effects of, 28 ff.; in the fields, 73 ff.
Proletarians, 28 ff.
Proletariat, rural, 86; status of, 29 f.; system regarding, 35 ff.
Property, and individual morality, erroneous theories on, 264 f.; for production, 31; goods that produce, 30; goods to be consumed, 30; ownership of, 53; productive, 86; rights and social duties, divorce of, 17; small holdings, 43 ff.

Rain cycle, 211; drop, action of, on surfaces, 210
Ramapo Building Guild, 328
Rebuilding communities, required arrangement of educational program, 168
Refrigerator, domestic, relation to ice industry, 201
Rehabilitation loans, 345
Rent contracts, long-range planning in, 85
Renters, transients, on farms, 87
Repayment Plan, Independence Foundation, 329
Report of Farm Tenancy Committee, Iowa, 353
Research, School of Living, Suffern, New York, 200
Resettlement, part-time farming, 167

Resettlement Administration, 160; debt conciliation policy, 345
Retail, costs of, 196
Ringwood Homesteads, 325
Rochdale local cooperatives, 283 f.
Rochdale Plan, 287
Rotation of crops, 216
Rural and Industrial Conference, Antigonish, 338
Rural boy, training of, 243
Rural children, not equipped to improve their environment, 352
Rural education, 242; following stereotyped, urban patterns, 251; in dietary practices and personal hygiene, 353
Rural environment, 242
Rural high school, a curriculum, 244 f.; curriculum for life on the land, 246 ff.
Rural homemaking courses for girls, 248
Rural homes, to be furnished with conveniences, 241
Rural life, 182 ff.; firsthand contacts with, 252 training for, 248 ff.
Rural living, 193
Rural parents and commercialism, 236
Rural priest, work for rural welfare, 243 ff.
Rural priests, guides of community activities, 227 f.
Rural problem, a city problem, 108; *in relation to the social doctrine of the Church*, joint Pastoral letter, Archbishops and Bishops of Canada, 240 ff.
Rural school, rural atmosphere in, 241; teachers in, 225; their neglect of farm problems and farm living, 123; training for rural life, 226 f.
Rural slums, 85
Rural sodalities, 225
Rural teachers, 244; courses and publications for, 225
Rural training for boys, summary, 249; for girls, summary, 249
Rural Youth, 234 ff.; interests of, shifted to the city by educational practices, 357

St. Francis Xavier Movement, 339
St. Francis Xavier University, Antigonish, Nova Scotia, 226; education for cooperatives, 259 ff.; extension program, 335 ff.; Nova Scotia, 253
St. Teresa's Village, Greenville, Alabama, 331
School, new type, agrarian, homestead school for new living, 114
School of Living, *Homestead Bulletins*, 190; bulletins prepared by, 315; Suffern, New York, 190, 194, 313
Schools, rural, 122
Security, in a productive home, 330
Self-sufficiency, 12
Serfdom, industrial, agricultural, 46
Sheet erosion, area affected, 214
Skim milk, fed to young livestock, 207
Slavery, economic, 41
Slum clearance, 72, 110
Slums, rural, 85
Smith-Hughes courses, 249
Social activities, organic concept, 224
Social leaderships, qualities of, 223
Social philosophy, fundamental principle of, 174
Social problems, continuous study of, 338
Social sciences, 192
Social Security Act, 353
Society, classes of, 18
Soil, and industry, 149 ff.; biology of, 219; elements exhausted, 197; fertility increased, 205; injurious substances in, 220; not a mine, not a machine, 102 ff.; organisms in, 219; raw materials in, 211; structure of, 205 ff.; sustains life, 205
Soil bacteria, 208, 211
Soil biology, 217 ff., 220
Soil-building, humus, making of, 217
Soil erosion, 84; extent of, in U. S., 214
Soil mining, 208
"Soil mining," soil robbery, 84
Soil problems, relation to social problems, 215
Soil treatment, 209
Soil washing and soil blowing, losses involved, 214
Soils, elements in, 205; rebuilding of, 216
South, tenancy situation in, 345
Stability of families, increased by homesteads, 346
Standards of living, true, false, 48
State Agricultural Colleges, 169
State agricultural experiment stations, 350
State and family, 255
Structure of soils, decrease in nitrogen and humus content, 205 ff.
Study-club method, 337
Study clubs, material for study of social problems, 338; number in Eastern Canada, results of, 339; regional libraries for, 338
Submarginal lands, 346

Index

Subsistence, economy in, 160; farming, 130 f.; garden program, 168
Subsistence farms, leasehold basis for, 346
Subsistence Garden Record, Iowa, 1938, 199
Subsistence Homesteads, 150
Success, new life values, 9
Supplies by trade, an inferior method, 12
Survey of part-time farms, size of household, sources of income, 161 ff.

Tax burdens, on Iowa farms, 357
Tax-exempt status for homesteads, 122
Taxation, excessive, 297; of land, 121; on farm lands, 350
Taxes, delinquencies, 123; on land, 88 ff.; on lands, 128
Teachers, training of, for rural schools, 252
Technological improvements, 150
Technological mistakes in agriculture, 213
Technologies, life processes, 212 ff.; overlooked by mechanics, 220
Technology, in the breeding of livestock, 213; on the land, 189 ff.; what constitutes, 191
Tenancy, 343, becomes ownership, 91; causes of, 356; effects on land, buildings, 85 ff.; problem of, 82; rates of increase, 82; relation to commercialism, 80; relation to institutions of the community, 84; rise in (graph), 78
Tenancy situation in the South, 345
Tenant, living condition, 101
Tenant contracts, necessity of improvement of, 350
Tenant-landlord relationships, improvement of, 348
Tenants, commercial, 81; effect on democracy, 84; effect on society, 84; Federal and state assistance, 85; homelessness of, 94; need for education and health services, 352; social participation of, 86
Tenure, insecurity of, 125; means of making secure, 90
Tenure improvements, 90 ff.
Tenure period, of land, relation to school, church, etc., 87
Tenure problems in Iowa, seriousness of, 355
Terminiello, Rev. Arthur W., 331
Toolen, Most Rev. Thomas J., 331
Town and country, need of proper balance between, 11

Tractor farming, 214
Tractors, 212; number of, cost of, 132
Trade, 13
Training, for rural life, 248 ff.; for leadership on the land, 222 ff.
Twentieth Century Fund, productivity vs. distributivity (graph), 281

Unemployment, 189
United Farms, Inc., evil effects of, 92
United States Public Health Service, 322
Urban homesteads, 122
Urban milieu, composed of quasi-societies, inorganic, 62
Urbanism and commercialism, 239 ff.; and dependency, 295 f.
Urbanization, rise of social and economic problems, 6
U. S. Department of the Interior, 172

Van Houten, Thomas, 326
Van Houten Fields, 325 ff.; building costs at, 327; community, 315
Vegetables, 169; raising of, 198
Vitalism, 113
Vocational grouping, 257 f.
Vocational guidance in rural schools, 251

Wage slavery, breaking up of, 10
Wages, and costs of essential necessities, 57; effect on character, 40; effects of, 41
Water, and plant food, 212; carrier of plant foods, 211; in the soil, 210; value of, in crop production, 208
Water conservation and humus, 208
Wealth, distribution of, 293 f.; its concentration, 46
Wheat, and corn grinding equipment, costs of, 324; comparative cost, 193 ff.
Wheat farming corporation, 74
"White Spot," no relation to land and farms, 89
Williams, Monier, Dr., 322
Wind erosion, area affected, 214; causes, results, 215
Women in the factory, 4
Worker, industrial, 55 ff.
Workers, mechanized, 58 ff.

Yields per acre, decreasing in United States, 133 ff.
Youth, movement to city, 212
Youth programs, 224, 225
Youth, rural, 234 ff.